DISCARDED

DI063965

This volume presents the first overall analysis, both theoretical and empirical, of the Asian Financial Crisis. It draws out the general lessons of an event whose potential long-term effects have been likened to the Crash of 1929.

Part One presents a factual and analytic overview of what happened: the role of 'vulnerability'; the interconnection between currency crises and financial crises; and why crisis turned into collapse.

Part Two considers more detailed issues, including: how the inflation of non-traded goods prices created vulnerability, welfare-reducing capital inflow owing to under-regulated financial markets; and the onset of speculative attacks.

Part Three assesses the many aspects of contagion, including both the channels through which it occurs and the role of geographical proximity.

Chapter 12 addresses policy issues. Joseph Stiglitz argues that there is much that can be done to reduce the frequency of crises, and to mitigate the severity of crises when they happen, and there is a comprehensive review of reform proposals. The volume finishes (Chapter 13) with a Round Table discussion of policy issues.

Pierre-Richard Agénor is Lead Economist and Director of the Macroeconomic and Financial Management Program of the World Bank Institute. He has written extensively on stabilisation and adjustment issues in developing countries. He is the co-author of *Development Macroeconomics* (Princeton University Press).

Marcus Miller is Professor of Economics and Associate Director of the Centre for the Study of Globalisation and Regionalisation at the University of Warwick. His previous books include *Exchange Rate Targets* and *Currency Bands* (Cambridge University Press, 1994), co-edited with Paul Krugman.

David Vines is Fellow in Economics at Balliol College, Oxford. He is the General Editor of the Research Programme on Global Economic Institutions of the British Economic and Social Research Council, and is also a Adjunct Professor of Economics at the Australian National University.

Axel Weber is Professor of Economics at the Johann Wolfgang Goethe-University in Frankfurt/Main, and Director of the Centre for Financial Studies.

The Asian Financial Crisis

Causes, Contagion and Consequences

The Asian Financial Crisis

Causes, Contagion and Consequences

edited by

Pierre-Richard Agénor, Marcus Miller
David Vines and Axel Weber

CAMBRIDGE
UNIVERSITY PRESS

PUBLISHED BY THE PRESS SYNDICATE OF THE UNIVERSITY OF CAMBRIDGE
The Pitt Building, Trumpington Street, Cambridge CB2 1RP, United Kingdom

CAMBRIDGE UNIVERSITY PRESS
The Edinburgh Building, Cambridge CB2 2RU, UK   http://www.cup.cam.ac.uk
40 West 20th Street, New York, NY 10011-4211, USA   http://www.cup.org
10 Stamford Road, Oakleigh, Melbourne 3166, Australia

© Pierre-Richard Agénor, Marcus Miller, David Vines and Axel Weber 1999

This book is in copyright. Subject to statutory exception and to the provisions
of relevant collective licensing agreements, no reproduction of any part may
take place without the written permission of Cambridge University Press.

First published 1999

Printed in the United Kingdom at the University Press, Cambridge

Typeset in Times New Roman 10/12 pt in QuarkXPress™   [SE]

A catalogue record for this book is available from the British Library

ISBN 0 521 77080 7 hardback
ISBN 0 521 00000 0 paperback

Global Economic Institutions

General Editor
David Vines
Balliol College, Oxford

The Global Economic Institutions (GEI) is a series of sixteen linked research programmes funded by the Economic and Social Research Council of Great Britain. The programme focuses on how existing global economic institutions and regimes operate, how they might be improved and whether new institutions are needed. Its principal findings are being presented in a sequence of five volumes, published as the series *Global Economic Institutions*. The topics covered by the five volumes include the Asian financial crisis and the role of the International Monetary Fund; the future of the World Bank; Europe, Asia and regionalism; the international trade regime and the WTO; and the reform of global economic institutions. Together the volumes will represent a major contribution to contemporary debates among economists, political scientists, politicians, business leaders and others with a shared interest in the growth and development of the global economy. Website: http://www.cepr.org/gei/gei.htm

World Bank Institute

The World Bank Institute (WBI) provides training and other learning activities that support the World Bank's mission to reduce poverty and improve living standards in the developing world. WBI's programmes help build the capacity of World Bank borrowers, staff and other partners in the skills and knowledge that are critical to economic and social development.

For over forty years the WBI has been the Bank's key instrument for delivering learning programmes on the full range of development issues to bank clients. The Institute's mission is to help build the capacity of clients in their development efforts through learning programmes. It offers its programmes to governments, non-governmental organisations and other stakeholders in topics related to economic and social development. The Institute delivers its interactive learning programmes using a broad range of face-to-face and distance education modalities, including seminars, workshops, conferences and a variety of print, broadcast and multimedia products.

Centre for Economic Policy Research

The Centre for Economic Policy Research is a network of over 450 Research Fellows, based primarily in European universities. The Centre coordinates its Fellows' research activities and communicates their results to the public and private sectors. CEPR is an entrepreneur, developing research initiatives with the producers, consumers and sponsors of research. Established in 1983, CEPR is a European economics research organisation with uniquely wide-ranging scope and activities.

CEPR is a registered educational charity. Institutional (core) finance for the Centre is provided by major grants from the Economic and Social Research Council, under which an ESRC Resource Centre operates within CEPR; the Esmée Fairbairn Charitable Trust and the Bank of England. The Centre is also supported by the European Central Bank; the Bank for International Settlements; 22 national central banks and 43 companies. None of these organisations gives prior review to the Centre's publications, nor do they necessarily endorse the views expressed therein.

The Centre is pluralist and non-partisan, bringing economic research to bear on the analysis of medium- and long-run policy questions. CEPR research may include views on policy, but the Executive Committee of the Centre does not give prior review to its publications, and the Centre takes no institutional policy positions. The opinions expressed in this book are those of the authors and not those of the Centre for Economic Policy Research.

Executive Committee

Co-Chairmen Guillermo de la Dehesa
  Anthony Loehnis

Jan Krysztof Bielecki	Denis Gromb	Mario Sarcinelli
Diane Coyle	Philippe Lagayette	Kermit Schoenholtz
Quentin Davies	Peter Middleton	Philippe Weil
Bernard Dewe Mathews	Bridget Rosewell	

Officers

President	Richard Portes
Chief Executive Officer	Stephen Yeo
Research Director	Mathias Dewatripont

Centre for Economic Policy Research
90–98 Goswell Road
London, EC1V 7RR
UK
Tel: (44 20 7878) 2900   Fax: (44 20 7878) 2999
Email: cepr@cepr.org   Website: http://www.cepr.org

March 1999

Contents

Part Three: Contagion

Part Four: Policy Responses

Figures

Tables

Preface

The Asian financial crisis hit the most rapidly growing and successful economies in the world, plunging them into deep crisis, with effects that will be felt for years to come; and it has, of course, generated an enormous policy debate. But little has been published in academic form. This book is intended to help fill the gap with a carefully selected set of papers covering the causes and consequences of the crisis, and possible cures.

Most of the contributions were commissioned for two key conferences on the Asian crisis held in England in May and July 1998. These meetings, at London and Warwick Universities, respectively, were collaboratively organised by the Centre for Economic Policy Research (CEPR), the World Bank Institute (WBI), the ESRC's Global Economic Institutions (GEI) Programme, the Centre for the study of Globalisation and Regionalisation of Warwick University (CSGR), and the Department of Economics at Warwick University (financed by ESRC project no. L120251024, 'A Bankruptcy Code for Sovereign Borrowers'). Additional financial support was also provided by Credit Suisse First Boston (CSFB). The meetings brought together a lively group of authors, discussants, and others from Europe, the USA and elsewhere, including members of the IMF and the World Bank, as well as academics and market participants. These meetings grew, in part, out of two earlier gatherings held in Cambridge and London in July 1997, and in London in February 1998, organised by CEPR, and funded by the UK Foreign and Commonwealth Office, HM Treasury, the Bank of England and the GEI Programme of the ESRC.

In addition to the papers commissioned for the conferences, related contributions by two of the participants have been included, chapters 3 and 12 by Michael Dooley and Joseph Stiglitz, respectively. The editors believe that these add substantially to the unity of the volume.

This is the second of a series of publications stemming from the Global Economic Institutions Programme of the UK Economic and Social Research Council. The first book, *Europe, East Asia and APEC: a Shared*

Global Agenda, was published in April 1998 in collaboration with the Australia–Japan Research Centre. Two more volumes, one on the future of the World Bank, and the other on Subsidiarity in the Global Economy are in the final stages of preparation, and there are plans for another on the overall future of global economic institutions.

Pierre-Richard Agénor
Marcus Miller
David Vines
Axel Weber

March 1999

Conference Participants

Financial Crises: Contagion and Market Volatility, London, 8–9 May 1998

Pierre-Richard Agénor, *World Bank*
Joshua Aizenman, *Dartmouth College, Hanover*
Sumru Altug, *Koç University and CEPR*
Zsofia Arvai, *National Bank of Hungary*
David Begg, *Birkbeck College, London, and CEPR*
Amar Bhattacharya, *World Bank*
Peter Brandner, *Österreichische Nationalbank*
Stijn Claessens, *World Bank*
Jenny Corbett, *Nissan Institute of Japanese Studies, Oxford, and CEPR*
Giancarlo Corsetti, *Yale University and Università di Roma Tre*
Ishac Diwan, *World Bank*
Michael Dooley, *University of California, Santa Cruz*
Rebecca Emerson, *Barclays Capital*
Andreas Fischer, *Schweizerische Nationalbank and CEPR*
Gabriele Galati, *Bank for International Settlements, Basle*
Reuven Glick, *Federal Reserve Bank of San Francisco*
Bernard Hoekman, *World Bank and CEPR*
Manmohan Kumar, *Credit Suisse First Boston*
Martin Lettau, *Humboldt Universität zu Berlin and CEPR*
Pongsak Luangaram, *University of Bristol*
Ian Marsh, *University of Strathclyde and CEPR*
Paul Masson, *International Monetary Fund*
Marcus Miller, *University of Warwick and CEPR*
Uma Moorthy, *Birkbeck College, London*
Paul O'Connell, *Emerging Markets Finance LLC*
Andrew Ockenden, *Bank of England*
Jacques Olivier, *HEC School of Management, Jouy-en-Josas, and CEPR*
Sule Ozler, *Koç University and University of California, Los Angeles*

Laura Papi, *Deutsche Morgan Grenfell*
Paolo Pesenti, *Princeton University*
Richard Portes, *London Business School and CEPR*
Mahmood Pradhan, *Tudor Proprietary Trading, LLC*
Frank Ren, *Barclays Capital*
Hélène Rey, *London School of Economics*
Jim Rollo, *Foreign and Commonwealth Office*
Mark Salmon, *City University Business School and CEPR*
Hyun Song Shin, *Nuffield College, Oxford, and CEPR*
Anne Sibert, *Birkbeck College, London, and CEPR*
Javier Suárez, *CEMFI, Madrid, and CEPR*
Mark P. Taylor, *University College, Oxford, and CEPR*
Bart Turtelboom, *Deutsche Morgan Grenfell*
Harald Uhlig, *CentER, Tilburg University, and CEPR*
David Vines, *Balliol College, Australian National University and CEPR*
Paolo Vitale, *London School of Economics*
Axel A. Weber, *Universität Frankfurt and CEPR*
Holger Wolf, *New York University and Georgetown University*

World Capital Markets and Financial Crises, Warwick University, 24–25 July 1998

Vinod Aggarwal, *University of California, Berkeley*
Philippe Aghion, *University College London, EBRD and CEPR*
David Aikman, *University of Warwick*
Joshua Aizenman, *Dartmouth College, Hanover*
David Baker, *Commonwealth Secretariat*
Nils Bjorksten, *OECD*
Christopher J. Bliss, *Nuffield College, Oxford*
Juntip Boonprakaikawe, *University of Warwick*
Luca Bossi, *University of Warwick*
Willem H. Buiter, *University of Cambridge and CEPR*
Olli Castrén, *Bank of Finland*
Jagjit Chadha, *University of Southampton*
Kevin Chang, *University of Southern California and CSFB*
Jorge A. Chan-Lau, *International Monetary Fund*
Zhaohui Chen, *International Monetary Fund*
Luisa Corrado, *University of Warwick*
Giancarlo Corsetti, *Università di Roma Tre*
David Diaz, *University of Warwick*

John Driffill, *University of Southampton and CEPR*
Maurice Ewing, *Hong Kong University of Science and Technology*
Gianluca Femminis, *Università Cattolica del Sacro Cuore, Milano, and CEPR*
Miguel Frasquilho, *Banco Espirito Santo, Lisboa*
Juan Garcia, *University of Warwick*
Jesus Gonzales-Garcia, *University of Warwick*
Charles A. Goodhart, *London School of Economics*
Philipp Hartmann, *European Central Bank and CEPR*
Simon Hayley, *HM Treasury*
Berthold Herrendorf, *University of Warwick and CEPR*
Madhu Kalia, *University of Warwick*
Kenneth Kletzer, *University of California, Santa Cruz*
Manmohan Kumar, *CSFB*
Eric Le Borgne, *University of Warwick*
In-Ho Lee, *University of Southampton*
Pongsak Luangaram, *University of Bristol*
Silvia Marchesi, *University of Warwick*
Marcus Miller, *University of Warwick and CEPR*
Gayle Milnes, *University of Warwick*
Alessandro Missale, *IGIER, Università degli studi di Brescia and Bank of England*
Paul Mizen, *University of Nottingham and Bank of England*
Uma Moorthy, *Birkbeck College, London*
Mats Nyman, *Svenska Handelsbanken*
William Perraudin, *Birkbeck College, London, and CEPR*
Richard Portes, *London Business School and CEPR*
Neil Rankin, *University of Warwick and CEPR*
Albrecht Ritschl, *Universitat Pompeu Fabra, Barcelona, and CEPR*
Jim Rollo, *Foreign and Commonwealth Office*
Philip Schellekens, *London School of Economics*
Hyun Song Shin, *Nuffield College, Oxford, and CEPR*
Michael Stephenson, *Financial Services Authority, Bank of England*
Jonathan P. Thomas, *University of Warwick*
Theodore To, *University of Warwick*
Phillip Turner, *Bank for International Settlements*
David Vines, *Balliol College, Oxford, Australian National University, and CEPR*
John Whalley, *University of Warwick*
Lei Zhang, *University of Warwick*

Acknowledgements

The editors and publisher acknowledge with thanks permission from the following to reproduce copyright material.

Goldman-Sachs, for data in figures 1.5, 1.12, 1.15 and 1.16.

JP Morgan, for data in figure 1.13.

University of Chicago Press, for data in figure 1.14.

Bloomberg, for data in figures 6.1 and 8.3.

Reuters, for data in figure 8.1.

Salomon Brothers, for data in figure 8.1.

Journal of Finance, for data in table 6.1, from R. La Porta, F. Lopez de Silanes, A. Shleifer and R.W. Vishny, 'Determinants of External Finance' (1997).

Journal of Political Economy, for data in table 6.1, from R. La Porta, F. Lopez de Silanes, A. Shleifer and R.W. Vishny, 'Law and Finance' (1998).

List of abbreviations and acronyms

ADB	Asian Development Bank
ASEAN	Association of South-East Asian Nations
BI	Bank Indonesia
BIBF	Bangkok International Banking Facility
BIS	Bank for International Settlement
BOT	Bank of Thailand
CAR	capital/asset ratio
CD	certificate of deposit
CEE	Central and Eastern Europe
CSFB	Credit Suisse First Boston
COMECON	Council for Mutual Economic Aid (FSU)
CPI	Consumer Price Index
DC	developing country
EEF	Exchange Equalisation Fund
EMS	European Monetary System (EC)
ERM	Exchange Rate Mechanism (EC)
EPF	Employees' Provident Fund
EU	European Union
FDI	foreign direct investment
FIRREA	Financial Institutions Reform, Recovery and Enforcement Act (1989)
G-7	Group of Seven
G-10	Group of Ten
G-22	Group of Twenty-Two
GDP	gross domestic product
GEI	global economic institution
IAS	International Accounting Standard
IBC	International Bondholders' Corporation
ICOR	incremental capital output ratio
IFI	international financial institution

IMF	International Monetary Fund
LIBOR	London Interbank Offer Rate
LOLR	lender-of-last-resort
MAR	market average rate
MSB	Monetary Stabilisation Bond
NAFTA	North American Free Trade Agreement
NBFI	Non-bank Financial Institution
NIE	newly industrialised economy
NPL	non-performing loan
NPV	net present value
OMO	open-market operation
OPEC	Organisation of Petroleum-Exporting Countries
OTC	over-the-counter
PPP	purchasing power parity
S&L	Savings and Loan
SRF	supplemental reserve facility
SRR	statutory reserve requirement
TFP	total factor productivity
UIP	uncovered interest parity
VaR	value-at-risk
WBI	World Bank Institute

Introduction

PIERRE-RICHARD AGÉNOR, MARCUS MILLER,
DAVID VINES AND AXEL A. WEBER

In countries hit by the Asian financial crisis there stalked dark shadows whose like had not been seen since the Great Depression: one after another, banks and currencies collapsed and confident growth ceded to fierce contraction. The waiting world watched in shocked surprise, and wondered: Why did the crisis happen? Why did it spread like wildfire from country to country in the second half of 1997? Why were its effects so serious? What can be done to aid recovery?

These are important questions, both for the world's citizens and for economic analysis. This volume brings together studies by a number of distinguished scholars and policy-makers who try to answer them.[1] The authors seek to clarify:

(1) the role of 'vulnerability' in what happened

(2) the interconnection between currency crisis and financial crisis, and how they combined to cause collapse

(3) what the mechanisms of contagion were

(4) what needs to be done, subsequent to this collapse.

The book is divided into four parts.

Part One begins with four wide-ranging chapters that, taken together, provide a systematic overview. In chapter 1 Alba, Bhattacharya, Claessens, Ghosh and Hernandez mobilise the research resources of the World Bank to provide a detailed empirical account of the crisis. In interpreting what happened, they make two major points. First, they show how events in East Asia have thrown up challenges for macroeconomic management in a financially integrated world. Second, they demonstrate the importance of avoiding risky financial structures. This first chapter documents how the build-up of financial vulnerabilities in East Asia was associated with reinforcing dynamics between capital flows, macro policies, and weak financial and corporate sector institutions. The authors argue that inappropriate macroeconomic policy responses to large capital inflows, weaknesses in domestic financial intermediation and poor corporate governance all interacted with and exacerbated the risks associated with large inflows. Lack of due diligence by international investors greatly facilitated this build-up of vulnerability.

In chapter 2, Corbett and Vines present an analytical framework which is highly complementary to the more empirical approach of chapter 1. They argue that the crisis turned into something so serious (what they call 'collapse') because of the interconnections between financial crises and currency crises. In the wake of the liberalisation of the late 1980s and early 1990s there was a wave of very substantial borrowing, encouraged by the widespread perception that financial systems would be bailed out in the event of difficulty. Given quasi-fixed exchange rates, this borrowing was done in foreign currency and unhedged. Once a shock caused the domestic currency to depreciate significantly, the increase in the domestic-currency value of foreign debt provoked financial crisis. There were fears that the bail-out payments, triggered by this financial crisis, would lead to sovereign insolvency. This then fed back into the currency crisis, triggering further collapse.[2]

Corbett and Vines criticise the application of 'orthodox' macroeconomic policies, and argue that there were alternatives which could have been implemented. Any preventive measures undertaken will require changes to the architecture of the international monetary system, particularly when there is a threatened or actual sovereign insolvency. In their discussion of this issue, the authors anticipate chapters in part four of the book.

The second two chapters in part one concentrate on moral hazard and financial crisis. Chapter 3, by Michael Dooley, is a prescient piece originating in 1993, reprinted here in revised form. Dooley argued that the large capital flows into emerging markets reflected investors' confidence *not* in economic performance of the recipient economies but in the ability of their governments to guarantee abnormal rates of return (at governmental expense) for a limited but predictable period of time. He suggested that Asian governments had essentially promised to pay out on such guarantees: and that investors would set up enough projects with negative expected returns to walk away with the state's capacity to pay out rewards. When that happened, there would be a crisis. Others have taken a similar view. In chapter 4, Corsetti, Pesenti and Roubini analyse the crisis as a one of moral hazard driven by excessive insurance (as does Krugman, 1998). Chapter 4 also provides econometric tests, and discussion of the policy issues which the crisis raised.

Part Two of the book contains three theoretical chapters on other aspects of the crisis. Aghion, Bacchetta and Banerjee in chapter 5 provide an account of the boom-and-bust feature of rapid investment in economies which undergo opening and liberalisation as in Thailand,[3] for example. Their analysis focuses on the role of non-traded goods prices. With low non-traded goods prices, the profit rate is high, generating an investment boom. For a while, increases in investment lead to increases in supply which can go hand-in-hand, sequentially, with increases in collateral and so enable further increases in investment. But eventually rises in non-traded-goods prices squeeze profitability and cause a reverse, leading to a slump.[4]

Chapter 6, by Agénor and Aizenman, emphasises the important point (implicit in Dooley's analysis) that capital inflows may be welfare-reducing in a second-best world where the financial sector is liberalised but under-regulated: and it investigates what then happens if this inflow is reversed. The chapter considers an emerging market economy where producers demand credit to finance risky investment. Financial intermediation is costly – banks should spend real resources in order to verify the investment outcome, and to force producers to service a fraction of the realised output. Banks enjoy market power, setting the lending interest rate high enough to generate expected profits which are a mark-up above depositor's interest rate. The chapter characterises the equilibrium financial spread, and identifies the welfare effects of financial integration. It shows that financial openness may be welfare-reducing if the foreign interest rate facing the economy is more volatile than the volatility under financial autarky. With upward-sloping domestic supply of funds and heterogeneous projects, opening the economy to unrestricted inflows of capital would magnify the welfare costs of existing distortions (such as congestion externalities), and might reduce welfare. In autarky, the welfare cost of the distortion is contained by the limited pool of domestic saving. However, in a financially open economy, such a distortion is magnified by the inflow of foreign capital.

Morris and Shin in chapter 7 present a subtle and important analysis of the onset of crisis. They are critical of 'sunspot' theories of multiple equilibria. In such theories, 'strategic complementarity' between speculators[5] means that, for a wide range of fundamentals, there exist multiple equilibria: either all sell, or no one sells, and these strategies are effectively coordinated by common knowledge. Morris and Shin argue that there is no good account in such theories of why and when flips from one equilibrium to the other happen. By contrast, they show in their chapter that, when common knowledge is lacking, speculators (who are aware that the authorities are progressively less willing to support the currency as fundamentals deteriorate) can forecast the behaviour of others and so determine a *unique* level of fundamentals at which the resistance of the authorities will be overwhelmed. The onset of a currency crisis happens when fundamentals evolve to the breakpoint.

Part Three presents three important chapters on contagion. Masson defines contagion in chapter 8 as a phenomenon where (1) an economy has the potential for both good and bad equilibria, and (2) an external event – a crisis elsewhere – triggers a move from the first equilibrium to the second. In the light of this definition, Masson investigates the conditions for multiple equilibria and analyses, theoretically and empirically, how events in one Asian country could have helped to push others from one equilibrium to another. A nice new feature of the model is that although contagion still triggers a crisis through its capital account effects, these can be traced back to a mechanism which works through trade channels. Bilateral trade weights thus matter for the strength of the contagion effects between the emerging market economies. The 'contagion-through-trade' story also provides the basis for the empirical work of Glick and Rose. Their chapter 9 investigates the relevance of economic interdependence in the Asian currency crisis and confirms empirically that currency crises do particularly affect those clusters of countries which are closely tied together by international trade. Diwan and Hoekman in chapter 10 push this argument further by examining empirically how export expansion by one country can spoil export opportunities for others. In doing so, they highlight the collective-action problem implicit in the simultaneous expansion of exports by a large number of countries, and they suggest that the Asian crisis can in part be explained as a 'fallacy of competition'. But this chapter also considers empirically whether overall economic expansion by certain key countries – China and Japan – could nevertheless be advantageous for the exports of other countries (as would be the case if the expansion in the key country caused an increase in the demand for the exports of other countries which more than dominated the increased competition).

Part Four of the book considers policy toward crisis resolution. Battacharya and Miller in chapter 11 outline three key aspects of the Asian financial crisis (bank runs, bubbles and sharks) and six key proposals recently made to avoid future crisis by redesigning world financial institutions. For their own part, they emphasise the unsustainability of continuous creditor bail-outs as a solution, and focus on the need for *bail-ins* – i.e. protection of debtors. Their own proposals for crisis prevention and resolution include, in particular, a key role for bankruptcy law and standstill mechanisms: the former affords legal protection to debtors while the latter, by allowing the temporary suspension of debt payments, could help to stop the decline in a currency and buy time to put in place credible adjustment and organise creditor–debtor negotiations.[6] In chapter 12, Joseph Stiglitz challenges the intellectual adequacy of *laissez-faire* as a response to increasingly frequent and severe financial crises. He warns that the fundamental theorems of welfare economics, which assert that competive equilibria are Pareto-efficient, provide no guide with respect to the question of whether financial markets, which are essentially concerned with information, are efficient: and he notes that national governments play a key regulatory role in the functioning of succesful financial markets. On the basis that the integration of the private sector has far outpaced the development of complementary international institutions, Stiglitz advocates 'reforms to the international economic architecture that can bring the advantages of globalisation, including global capital markets, while mitigating their risks'.

The volume concludes with a Round Table discussion of policy issues between Richard Portes, Charles Goodhart and Phillip Turner (chapter 13). Portes focuses on moral hazard, arguing that it is necessary, both on equity and efficiency grounds, that international lenders who do not take due care – and he would include in this category many of the international banks who lent to Asia before the crisis – should bear some of the costs of crisis resolution. In response to Portes' challenge, Phillip Turner describes the regulatory changes necessary. Charles Goodhart draws on the history of the nineteenth century to argue that countries which get into crisis need either to return quickly to their previous exchange rates or to default. What is so serious about the East Asian crisis, he argues, is the existence of a large volume of foreign currency debt along with heavily depreciated domestic currencies, the overhang of which is very difficult either to service or resolve.

The G-7 meeting in Cologne (June 1999) (like the preparatory one in Frankfurt in February) was concerned with the reform and new design of the international financial architecture. Many of the arguments in favour of this initiative come from the vulnerability of international financial markets shown by events during the Asian currency crisis. The book is therefore not only an account of the extraordinary events in Asia during 1997–8, it is also a key for understanding the current international policy debate.

NOTES

1. There has been much policy-related discussion about the Asian crisis but little of it has yet appeared in academic pieces. As yet the only volumes we know of are Macleod and Garnaut (1998); Kahler (1998) and Montes (1998).
2. Interestingly, this framework shares something with that presented by Soros in chapter 8 of his book *The Crisis of Global Capitalism* (1998). Chang and Velasco (1997) provide a formal model which shares a number of the features emphasised by Corbett and Vines. Eichengreen (1999) also presents proposals for the reform of the global financial architecture which are motivated by an analysis which is in many ways similar.

3. See in particular Peter Warr's 'Thailand', chapter 3 in MacLeod and Garnaut (1998).
4. An alternative explanation of the boom and the subsequent bust is provided by Edison, Luangaram and Miller (1998), in a model involving land as collateral.
5. This arises because the expected profitability to one speculator from selling depends positively on the number of other speculators who are also selling.
6. The chapter includes a proposal due to Joseph Stiglitz for a 'Chapter 11'-type of procedure which would give debtors quasi-autonomatic protection against extreme fluctuation of exchange rates. Stiglitz's argument can be read in conjunction with the discussion of sovereign insolvency by Corbett and Vines in chapter 2.

REFERENCES

Chang, R. and A. Velasco (1997). 'Financial Fragility and the Exchange Rate Regime', Federal Reserve Bank of Atlanta, *Working Paper* **97-16**

Edison, H., P. Luangaram and M. Miller (1998). 'Asset Bubbles, Domino Effects and "Life Boats": Elements of the East Asian Crisis', Warwick University, mimeo.

Eichengreen, B. (1999). *Towards a New International Financial Architecture: A Practical Post Asia Agenda*, Washington, DC: Brookings Institution

Kahler, D. (1998). *Capital Flows and Financial Crises*, Manchester: Manchester University Press

Krugman, P. (1998) 'Whatever Happened to Asia', http://web.mit.edu/krugman/www/DISINTER.html

MacLeod, R. and R. Garnaut (eds.) (1998). East Asia in Crisis, London: Routledge.

Montes, M. F. (1998). *The Currency Crisis in South East Asia*, Singapore: South East Asian Studies

Soros, G. (1998). *The Crisis of Global Capitalism: Open Society Endangered*, London: Little Brown

Warr, P. (1998). 'Thailand', chapter 3 in MacLeod and Garnaut (1998), *East Asia Crisis*, London: Routledge

Part One

General Accounts

1 The role of macroeconomic and financial sector linkages in East Asia's financial crisis

PEDRO ALBA, AMAR BHATTACHARYA, STIJN CLAESSENS,
SWATI GHOSH AND LEONARDO HERNANDEZ

1 Introduction

Private capital flows to developing countries increased sixfold over the years 1990 to 1996. These large inflows were not simply an independent and isolated macroeconomic shock but rather the manifestation of structural changes in the world economic environment and in developing countries themselves. The structural changes resulted in the transition by many countries from near financial autarky to fairly close integration with world capital markets. The capital inflow phenomenon, and the associated need to intermediate efficiently large amounts of foreign capital and address potential macroeconomic overheating, were the direct products of the transition between these polar financial integration regimes.

Countries in East Asia were at the forefront of the worldwide movement toward increased financial integration (see World Bank, 1997) and are good examples of both the benefits, and the risks, of integration. East Asian countries fared quite well during the initial stages of this integration process, especially in comparison with many developing countries outside the region. Indeed, in many ways lessons to be applied elsewhere regarding the appropriate adjustment to large capital inflows have been drawn from the experiences of East Asia (for example, Corbo and Hernandez, 1996). Countries in the region also weathered the storm associated with the Mexican currency crisis of December 1994 in relatively good form, suggesting that the policies they adopted to manage inflows also proved effective in rendering them relatively less vulnerable to a financial shock that created serious disruptions elsewhere. Nonetheless, the summer of 1997 and events since have made clear that this view could no longer be sustained. The crisis that struck Thailand, and the rapidity with which it spread to other countries in East Asia, made clear that all was not well and that the management of capital flows had not been without risks. In the new, more integrated environment, private capital could potentially flow

9

out as well as in, with asymmetric effects on the domestic economy of the recipient countries.

There are many explanations and typologies that have been put forward to explain the onset of this financial crisis (Corsetti, Pesenti and Roubini, 1998; Feldstein, 1998; IMF, 1997; Krugman, 1998, Radelet and Sachs, 1998a, 1998b; Sachs, Tornell and Velasco, 1996; and chapters 2–4 in this volume, among others). These papers provide typologies of different types of financial crises that may be applicable to East Asia, and try to differentiate between them. In this chapter, we take a different focus, and analyse the vulnerability of the countries most affected by the crisis, and the proximate causes of the build-up of these vulnerabilities during the 1990s. Hence, we do not try to differentiate between the various types of financial crises, to identify the triggers of the crisis, or to explain its subsequent evolution. We also do not discuss the international aspects of the crisis, in particular the role played by the lack of due diligence by foreign borrowers and investor herding, but rather focus on the domestic aspects.[1] Finally, we also do not address whether the macroeconomic policies pursued and other weaknesses represented fundamental flaws and made a financial crisis inevitable, or whether there was a financial panic in all or any particular country. While we believe that panic played a role, we also believe that the build-up of vulnerability was very large and allowed the crisis to take hold.

Our basic assertion is that the build-up of financial vulnerabilities in East Asia was associated with reinforcing dynamics between capital flows, macro policies and weak financial and corporate sector institutions. In its basic element, similar to the Chilean crisis of the early 1980s, the growing vulnerability can be attributed to the private investment boom and surge in capital inflows, in turn based on the region's success – particularly its strong economic fundamentals and structural reforms of the 1980s. But the pace and pattern of investment in the mid-1990s, and the way in which it was financed, made some countries vulnerable to a loss of investor confidence and a reversal in capital flows. This growing vulnerability was the result of private sector decisions rather than public sector deficits. These private sector activities took place, however, in the context of government policies that did not do enough to discourage excessive risk-taking, while providing too little regulatory control and insufficient transparency to allow markets to recognise and correct these problems. At the root of the problem were weak and poorly supervised financial sectors against the backdrop of large capital inflows. Equally, inadequate corporate governance and lack of transparency masked the poor quality and riskiness of investments. In addition, although macroeconomic policies were generally sound, pegged exchange rate regimes and implicit guarantees tilted incentives toward excessive short-term borrowing and capital inflows.

Table 1.1 *Magnitude and composition of capital inflows, 1985–1996 (per cent of GDP)*

	LAC[a]			ASEAN–4[b]		
	1985–8	1989–92	1993–6	1985–8	1989–92	1993–6
Net long-term capital flows	1.3	1.7	4.3	2.0	4.8	6.9
– Net official flows	0.5	0.3	0.0	1.2	1.3	0.4
– Net private flows	0.8	1.4	4.4	0.8	3.5	6.6
Bank/trade lending	0.3	0.0	0.5	– 0.3	0.9	0.8
Portfolio bond	– 0.2	0.2	1.2	0.2	– 0.1	1.4
FDI	0.7	0.9	1.6	0.9	2.3	2.4
Portfolio equity	0.0	0.3	1.1	– 0.1	0.4	2.0
IMF credit	0.0	0.0	0.1	0.1	– 0.1	0.0
Other private flows	– 0.7	0.7	– 1.0	0.3	2.0	– 0.1
of which: short-term debt	– 0.1	0.7	0.6	0.1	2.0	2.3

Notes: [a] LAC = Latin American countries.
     [b] ASEAN 4 = Indonesia, Malaysia, Philippines and Thailand.
Source: World Bank data.

The chapter starts in section 2 with a short overview of capital flows and macroeconomic developments in the region prior to the crisis. Section 3 explains a simple analytical framework of the macro-financial linkages and how they can exacerbate vulnerabilities, then goes on to describe the manifestations of vulnerability in East Asia, those that concern the economy as a whole and the financial sector in particular. These two sections set the stage for a more detailed discussion in the remainder of the chapter on the macroeconomic policies and financial and corporate factors that led to the build-up of the vulnerabilities. Sections 4 and 5 review in detail the macroeconomic policies and financial and corporate policies and institutional weaknesses, respectively.

2 Overview of capital flows and economic developments in East Asia

East Asia led the developing world in the resurgence of private capital flows in the late 1980s. It quickly emerged as the most important destination for private capital flows as its share of total capital flows to developing countries increased from 12 per cent in the early 1980s to 43 per cent during the 1990s. During this period, the composition of flows to East Asian countries also changed (table 1.1). In the second half of the 1980s, commercial bank

Table 1.2   *Investment, savings and capital flows, 1985–1996 (per cent of GDP)*

	LAC[a]			ASEAN-4[b]		
	1985–8	1989–92	1993–6	1985–8	1989–92	1993–6
Investment	20.5	20.6	20.1	25.7	32.6	35.0
National savings	20.6	19.6	17.6	23.9	28.6	30.3
– Private	16.5	16.2	15.1	13.2	20.0	20.4
– Public	4.1	3.3	2.5			
Current account deficit	1.0	1.1	2.4	1.1	3.8	4.6
Total capital inflows	0.7	2.4	3.5	2.2	6.7	6.8
Reserve accumulation	– 0.3	1.3	1.0	1.0	2.9	2.2

Notes: [a] LAC = Latin American countries.
[b] ASEAN 4 = Indonesia, Malaysia, Philippines and Thailand.
Source: World Bank data.

lending was replaced by FDI. In the 1990s, portfolio flows (both bond and equity) expanded rapidly as did short-term borrowing – portfolio flows amounted to 3.4 per cent of GDP during 1993–6, while short-term borrowing an additional 2.3 per cent of GDP. Whereas the dominant role of FDI distinguished East Asia from Latin America in the late 1980s and early 1990s, in the more recent period borrowing was skewed more towards short-term flows than was the case for Latin America.

Another important characteristic of private capital flows to East Asia was that, unlike Latin America, it was preceded rather than followed by a surge in investment (table 1.2). In the second half of the 1980s and the early 1990s, the bulk of the increase in investment was financed by a corresponding increase in national savings. During the more recent period, however, a higher fraction of the increase in investment was financed abroad. Nevertheless, the magnitude of private capital flows was much higher than the amount of foreign savings absorbed, leading to substantial reserve accumulation. There was considerable variation, however, at the individual country level: Malaysia and Thailand received the largest magnitude of capital inflows, cumulative in excess of 30 per cent of GDP; the Philippines also received substantial inflows during 1993–6; but Korea did not receive more than 15 per cent of GDP. In contrast, in Latin America there has not been an investment boom – the investment ratio has remained constant since the mid-1980s – but a decrease in savings, although again important differences among countries exists.

During the inflow periods, macroeconomic policies in most East Asian countries shared three broad elements in common:

- First, many adopted an exchange rate regime oriented toward enhanced competitiveness – i.e. the achievement of a real exchange rate target to complement the outward orientation embodied in structural policies. This policy was implemented through step devaluations in several countries in the region during the mid-1980s, followed in some countries by continuous depreciation, in some cases more than offsetting the differential between domestic and foreign inflation. In East Asia, therefore, unlike in many countries of Latin America, nominal exchange rate management during the capital inflow episode was not primarily devoted to the establishment of a nominal anchor. This exchange rate policy indeed seems to have been relatively successful in avoiding currency overvaluation from the mid-1980s to the mid-1990s.

- Second was the adoption of a tight medium-term stance for fiscal policy. Overall public sector budgets in the region, which had exhibited deficits not out of line with those of other middle-income developing countries at that time, moved steadily into surplus after the mid-1980s. By the late 1980s, several countries in the region had achieved sizable fiscal surpluses.[2] As the economies of these countries grew and the tight fiscal stance restrained (and at times reversed) the growth of public sector debt, public sector debt/GDP ratios fell throughout the region. As a result, by the mid-1990s several countries in East Asia had achieved ratios of debt/GDP substantially below those of many industrial countries. This fiscal stance also promoted the depreciation of the real exchange rate, and helped prevent the emergence of exchange rate misalignment.

- Third, especially once the sizable fiscal surpluses were achieved in the early 1990s, countries began to rely more on monetary policy to prevent overheating. Countries placed heavy reliance on monetary policy as a short-run stabilisation instrument, varying the intensity of sterilised intervention in the foreign exchange market in accordance with domestic macroeconomic needs. On the structural side, the economies of East Asia continued in the 1990s the process of liberalisation that had begun in the mid-1980s. Trade liberalisation, capital account liberalisation and especially financial sector liberalisation all proceeded during the inflow period.

This mix of structural and macroeconomic policies proved attractive to foreign capital and, in combination with tight fiscal policy, was largely successful in preventing macroeconomic over-heating, at least early in the inflow period. The World Bank (1997) found that countries that relied more on fiscal policy to prevent over-heating during the capital-inflow period were also more successful in avoiding excessive real exchange rate appreciation and achieved a mix of aggregate demand oriented toward investment rather than consumption. This link can be interpreted naturally as the outcome of the policy mix undertaken. Since the effects of tight money tend to fall disproportionately on investment, an outward-oriented strategy in which tight fiscal policy supports a depreciated real exchange rate exerts a systematic effect on the composition of aggregate demand favouring investment over consumption. During this period, East Asian countries saw sharp increases in their investment rates (figure 1.1). For example, in Indonesia investment/GDP rose from an average 25 per cent during 1985–9, to 32 per cent during 1990–6, while in Korea the investment rates rose from an average of 30 per cent to 37 per cent during the same period. Malaysia and Thailand saw even larger increases – from 26 per cent to 40 per cent, and from 30 per cent to 42 per cent of GDP, respectively.

By 1994–6, however, the acceleration in the growth of domestic demand, that was accompanied by an increase in net capital inflows, led to the emergence of demand pressures in all the four countries that were hardest hit by the crisis – Indonesia, Korea, Malaysia and Thailand. In all four countries the acceleration in the growth of domestic demand reflected both the pick-up in the growth of investment and to a lesser degree in consumption, although the relative mix differed across countries. But, in all four countries, with the sharp pick-up in the contribution of domestic demand, the contribution of the external sector to GDP growth turned negative during the period.

3   The build-up in vulnerability: a simple analytical framework

The growing vulnerability of East Asia was rooted in the private investment boom beginning in the late 1980s just described, but two factors amplified these trends and the build-up of demand pressures:

- First, the process of external financial integration, and the surge in private capital inflows that accompanied it, worked as an additional force to reinforce the upswing in the domestic business cycle. The increase in private capital inflows, which in the case of East Asian countries was motivated mainly for investment purposes, provided the additional liquidity that allowed banks and non-bank financial intermediaries to increase lending, despite efforts to sterilise inflows. Capital flows also contributed to increases in asset prices. Furthermore, the policy response to the surge in inflows, which increasingly relied on tight monetary policy and heavy sterilisation, provided further impetus to these flows, added to the process and aggravated the fragility in the corporate (and therefore) banking sector through sustained high interest rates.

Figure 1.1   *Macroeconomic developments in Asia, 1980–1996*

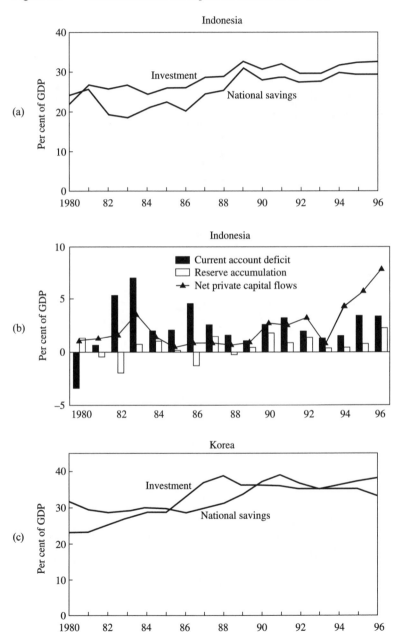

Source: World Bank data.

Figure 1.1   (*cont.*)

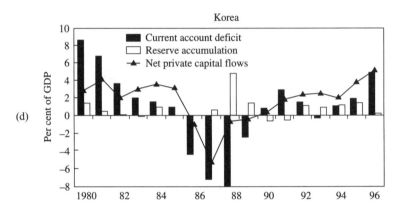

(d)

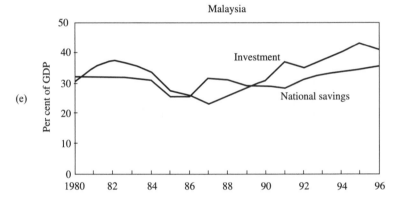

(e)

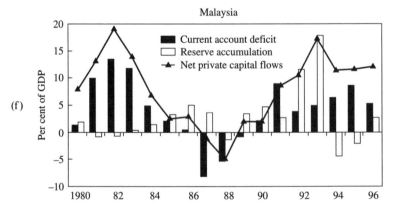

(f)

Source: World Bank data.

Figure 1.1   (*cont.*)

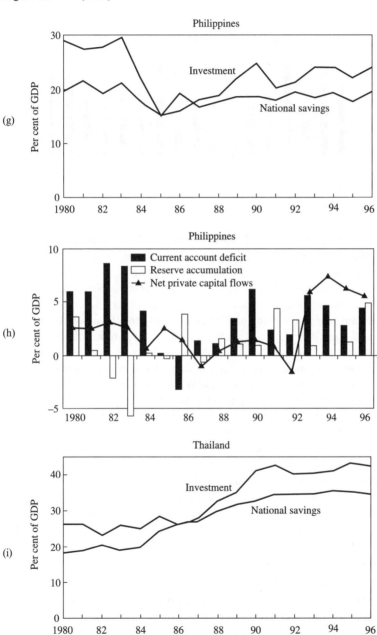

Source: World Bank data.

Figure 1.1   (*cont.*)

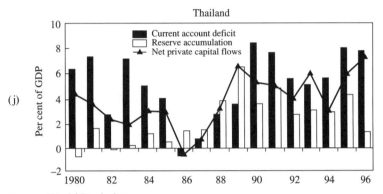

(j)

Source: World Bank data.

- Second, the high degree of segmentation of financial markets, and the growing importance of banks and non-bank financial intermediaries, allowed agents who could not directly borrow abroad to finance investments and increased expenditures through domestic borrowing. Indeed, banks dominate the financial systems in East Asia and credit plays an important role as the transmission channel of monetary policy. Except in Malaysia, equity and bond markets play a minor role in financing new investment and firms depend heavily on bank credit. Securities outstanding represent a much smaller share of financial intermediation than in the USA and other industrial countries (World Bank, 1997). In Malaysia, the capitalisation of the equity market is very large, but accounting conventions account for some of the market size. Table 1.3 illustrates the importance of the credit channel in East Asia through correlation coefficients between changes in economic activity and changes in credit and money during 1990–6. In all four Asian countries (except, perhaps, Korea) the correlation coefficients suggest that credit plays a more important role than money, although the lag structure varies between countries. Credit also seems to play a more important role in East Asian than in industrial countries in the sense in the latter that credit and money are broadly of equal importance. The credit channel thus played an important role in exacerbating the booms in asset prices, consumption and investment in East Asia.

Figure 1.2 illustrates the several self-reinforcing channels at work, and how the combination of weak initial conditions – in particular, concerning the quality of the intermediation process in the recipient countries – and macro policies can lead to a rapid build-up of macro financial fragility. For instance, the inflows that initially occur because of the economic reforms – and improved prospects – can lead to a lending boom which, in turn, can

Table 1.3   *The credit channel in East Asia: correlation^a between output and money, and output and credit^b*

	Money^c		Credit^c	
	Contemporaneous	Lagged One Quarter	Contemporaneous	Lagged One Quarter
Canada	−0.075	0.222	0.359	0.248
Germany	−0.012	0.360	0.159	0.333
USA	−0.036	0.205	−0.107	0.206
Indonesia^d	0.156	0.054	0.400	0.168
Korea	−0.117	0.143	0.12	0.088
Malaysia	−0.039	−0.130	0.277	0.011
Thailand^d	0.112	0.356	0.374	0.455

Notes: ^{a} Simple correlation coefficients of quarterly first differences during 1990–6.
^{b} Variables are in real terms and have been seasonally adjusted.
^{c} Credit includes both banks and non-bank financial institutions, except for Indonesia where it only comprises banks; money is M1.
^{d} The output variable is industrial production, except for Indonesia which refers to GDP, and Thailand which refers to electricity consumption (a proxy for output).
Source: Data are from IMF: International Financial Statistics, and country sources.

Figure 1.2   *Self-reinforcing dynamics resulting in increased vulnerability*

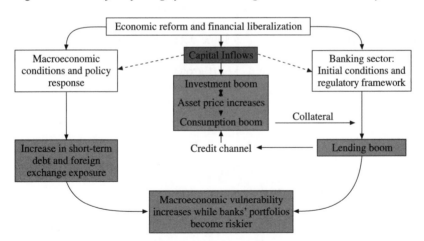

finance a real-estate boom and asset prices increases. If these assets are used as collateral for additional loans, then this will reinforce the increase in asset prices. The greater availability of credit will also accelerate economic activity, validating and reinforcing the expectations about the recipient country. The latter can lead to a surge in consumption, as agents believe that their permanent income and wealth has increased. In sum, the initial surge in inflows can put in motion a process in which the economy starts growing faster while economic agents – firms and households – increase their leverage. However, if the investment that is being financed is *ex post* of poor quality, then the process will prove to be unsustainable and a downward correction in asset prices will occur. The latter depends on the quality of the banking system – which depends in part on the supervisory and regulatory framework – and management in the corporate sector.

3.1 Dimensions of vulnerability

These self-reinforcing dynamics led to three key weaknesses in East Asia:

(1) increased banking sector fragility associated with lending and asset booms and rising exposure to risky sectors

(2) high leverage both economywide and in many individual firms

(3) currency and maturity mismatches that left some economies highly vulnerable to reversals in capital flows.

There were, therefore, two dimensions to this growing vulnerability. First, growing contingent liabilities that were not adequately recognised before the crisis. Second, increased risks of an external liquidity crunch primarily because a large build-up of external short-term debt, much of which was unhedged. In addition, there was some deterioration in economic fundamentals during 1995–6, in particular, widening current account deficits and slowdowns in productivity and export growth, although this started from strong initial conditions. Nonetheless, these trends may have led to growing perceptions among investors about a misalignment of exchange rates, in particular in Thailand, where the export slowdown in 1996 was very sharp and protracted.

3.2 Increasing banking fragility

Financial liberalisation, through decreasing reserve requirements, resulting increases in financial savings and surges in foreign capital inflows, led throughout East Asia to increases in monetary aggregates. In turn increased liquidity and monetisation resulted in a generalised surge in bank and non-bank financial institution (NBFI) lending, although the amplitude and duration of these cycles, as well as their apparent relationship with

Figure 1.3   *Lending booms in East Asia, 1989–1996*

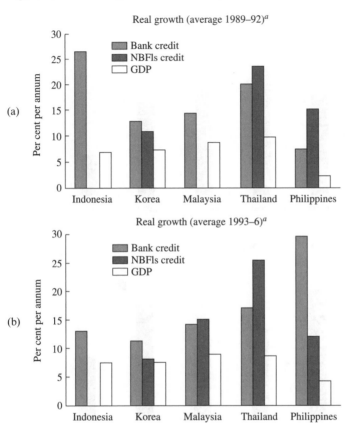

Note: [a] Rates of growth are calculated on an annual basis and in real terms.
Source: IMF, *International Financial Statistics.*

financial liberalisation and the surge in capital inflows, varied from country to country. For example, in Malaysia, the Philippines and Thailand, bank and non-bank credit to the private sector began growing at higher rates and on a sustained basis following the surge in capital inflows. In Korea and Indonesia, in contrast, the growth in bank and non-bank credit to the private sector was lower during the inflow period than in the years prior to the surge in foreign capital. Most important, however, is that the high growth in credit – in many cases several times the growth in GDP – strained banks in their capacity to properly screen and assess risk of borrowers and projects (figure 1.3).

Figure 1.4   *Profitability and efficiency in East Asian banking, 1991 and 1995*

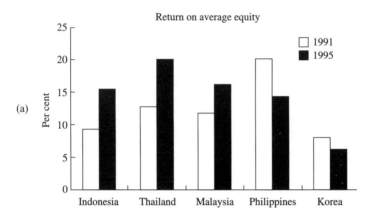

(a)

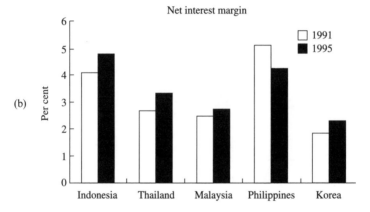

(b)

Source: Goldman-Sachs, *Banking Research* (September 1997).

However, the rising fragility was not detected during the lending booms as the growth in banks' loan portfolios was accompanied by rising measured profits. Figure 1.4 shows that in countries in which credit growth was high – except the Philippines – there was an increase in the profitability of the banking sector, consistently across all indicators. Conversely, in countries where the lending boom was smaller – in absolute terms or proportional to GDP – profitability tended to show a small increase, or even a decrease depending on the profitability indicator used.

As a result of the lending booms, banks and NBFIs became more vulnerable to economic shocks over this period. This occurred for two main reasons: by lending excessively to sectors or firms whose debt service

Figure 1.5   *Banks' exposure to risky assets, 1991–1995*

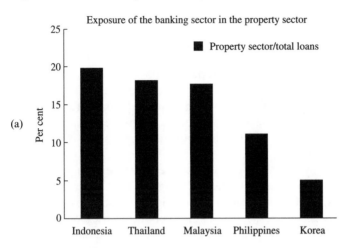

(a)

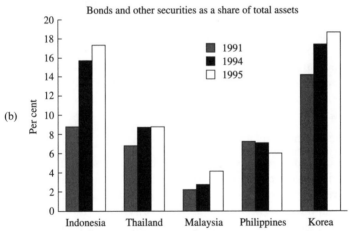

(b)

Source: Goldman-Sachs, *Banking Research* (September 1997).

capacity was particularly susceptible to shocks; and by reducing their own capacity to absorb negative shocks, especially by exacerbating currency and maturity mismatches and by under-provisioning for future potential losses.

3.2.1 Increased exposure to risky sectors

Real-estate lending was high and the banking sector exposure to real-estate was greater in countries where the growth of credit was larger than proportional to GDP growth (figure 1.5). It should be noted that data on real-estate lending are not comparable across countries and in several countries probably under-estimate the exposure of the banking system to the real-estate sector (as loans to developers are not classified as lending for real-estate). But, there were significant differences among countries. Korean banks did not have large property exposure; Korean banks did, however, increase the share of bonds and other securities in their portfolios to almost 20 per cent (in addition, Korean banks extended large amounts of guarantees on securities issued by corporates). Except for the Philippines, countries increased their exposure to bonds and other securities (see figure 1.5).

Both real-estate market and securities markets have been very volatile in East Asia. real-estate price fluctuations during the 1990s were the highest in Philippines and Malaysia, with ratio of highest to lowest prices since inflows started of 3 and 2, respectively. Still, in both countries, vacancy rates in 1996 were relatively low at around 2 per cent (and the banking sector exposure to real estate appeared to be low in the Philippines). In Thailand and Indonesia, the variability of real-estate prices was lower, with high to low ratios of 1.25 and 1.32, respectively. In both countries, vacancy rates in 1996 were relatively high at around 14 per cent and increasing. The space under construction in Southeast Asia at the end of 1996 already suggested a significant oversupply of real-estate during 1997–9, especially in Thailand (figure 1.6).

3.2.2 Increased foreign exchange exposure

Especially in Thailand, Malaysia and the Philippines, there was a significant increase in foreign exchange exposures of banks since the late 1980s (figure 1.7). Also, for Korea, Thailand and the Philippines, there was a very rapid increase in the stock of foreign liabilities of NBFIs. In Indonesia, the increase of foreign exchange exposure of banks was significant up to 1994, and was followed by a small decrease, but the overall exposure was small. Commercial banks in Korea did not show any increase in foreign exchange exposure during this period, but merchant banks in Korea did increase their foreign exchange exposures significantly.

3.3 Corporate sector vulnerabilities

Despite differences between countries, the financial structures of many firms in the four countries most affected by the crisis were very fragile by end-1996. Corporates in these four countries grew very rapidly during the

Figure 1.6   *Real estate office supply and vacancy rates, 1988–1999*

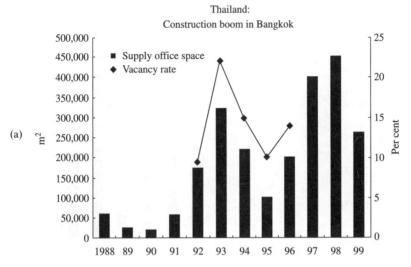

(a)

Note: 1997–9 comprises office space under construction.

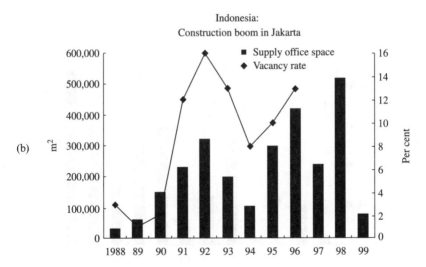

(b)

Note: 1997–9 comprises office space under construction.

1990s which, combined with declining profitability, led to a very large increase in external financing needs. Since firms in all four countries are very dependent on banks for external financing and equity markets are relatively under-developed, the asset expansion resulted in severely unbalanced liability structures. The vulnerabilities in corporate financial

Figure 1.6   (*cont.*)

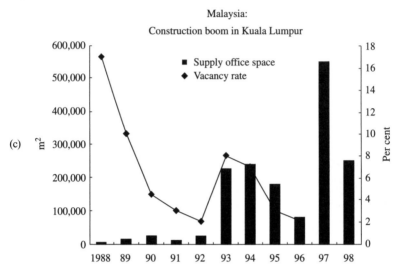

Malaysia:
Construction boom in Kuala Lumpur

(c)

Note: 1997–8 comprises office space under construction.

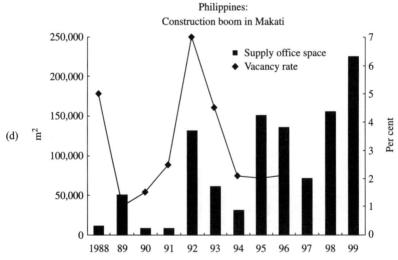

Philippines:
Construction boom in Makati

(d)

Note: 1997–9 comprises office space under construction.

Source: Jones Lang Wootton, *Asia Pacific Property Digest* (January 1997).

Figure 1.7 *Foreign exchange exposures in the banking system, 1986–1996*
(Ratio, per cent, of foreign exchange liabilities to foreign
exchange assets)

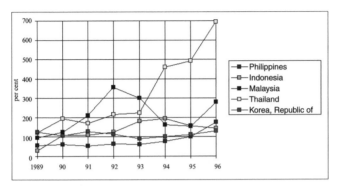

structures in the region built up quickly during the 1990s, and were evident before the onset of the crisis in mid-1997. Four key variables (table 1.4) illustrate this build-up of vulnerabilities:

- *Rapid increase in fixed assets*   Firms expanded at an unprecedented rate in these countries during the years preceding the crisis. Fixed assets measured in US dollars expanded on average during 1994–6 at 36 per cent in Indonesia, 30 per cent in Thailand, 22 per cent in Malaysia; and 20 per cent in Korea (1994–5), compared to 1 per cent–5 per cent in industrial countries (Pomerleano, 1998).

- *Increasing leverage*   Much of these new assets were financed through bank debt and East Asian firms tend to have high debt/equity ratios, while in Malaysia and Thailand, leverage increased during this period. Except in Malaysia, new equity was not widely used since stock markets are relatively underdeveloped and/or owners did not wish to dilute their control. In addition, internal financing was constrained by weakening corporate performance. According to Claessens, Djankov and Lang (1998), while generally higher than in industrial countries, real returns on total assets in local currency terms declined in Indonesia, Korea, Malaysia and Thailand between 1991–3 and 1996.

- *Declining interest coverage*   As a result of declining performance and rising debt, the ability of firms to meet debt service payments deteriorated substantially during the period. By end-1996, the median firm's interest coverage in Thailand and Korea was below investment-grade standards – that is, below that of the median Standard and Poors (S&P) single B firm in the USA during 1994–6 (figure 1.8).

Table 1.4   *Increasing corporate vulnerability in East Asia, 1991–1996*

		1991–3[a]	1994	1995	1996
Indonesia	Growth in fixed assets (%)	22	37	36	35
	Debt/Equity ratio	1.8	1.8	1.8	1.8
	Short-term/Total debt (%)	56	58	58	57
	Interest coverage	Na	2.2	3.1	2.4
Korea	Growth in fixed assets (%)	11	15	24	—
	Debt/Equity ratio	3.2	3.3	3.4	3.2
	Short-term/Total debt (%)	54	59	60	59
	Interest coverage	1.4	1.9	1.8	1.1
Malaysia	Growth in fixed assets (%)	15	21	18	26
	Debt/Equity ratio	0.6	0.7	0.8	0.9
	Short-term/Total debt (%)	73	73	72	70
	Interest coverage	9.4	11.7	9.6	6.7
Thailand	Growth in fixed assets (%)	25	47	27	17
	Debt/Equity ratio	1.5	1.6	1.7	1.9
	Short-term/Total debt (%)	71	72	67	67
	Interest coverage	4.4	3.8	2.5	1.9

Note: [a] The 1991–3 data for fixed assets refers to 1993.
Sources: Data on growth of fixed assets and interest coverage (EBITDA/interest payments) are from Pomerleano (1998). Data on leverage and composition of debt are from Claessens, Djankov and Lang (1998).

• *Large share of short-term debt*   Short-term debt represented a large share of total debt of East Asian firms relative to industrial country standards.

Thus, by end-1996, East Asian firms were highly susceptible to liquidity and interest rate shocks. As a result of high leverage, small shocks to interest rates or operational cash flow greatly affected the ability of these corporations to service their debts. In Thailand, for example, as a result of the crisis 114 firms out of a sample of 300 listed on the Stock Exchange of Thailand (SET), could not service interest from their earnings before interest and taxes at end-1997, up from 18 in 1994. Interest expenses could thus not be fully covered in 1997 from operating income and had to be rolled-over and financed from new loans, non-operating income or asset sales. The need to roll over interest obligations would exacerbate the already high liquidity risk implied by the high share of short-term debt. With high leverage, the increase in interest rates and decline in profitability led to a large number of firms running into debt servicing and liquidity problems, which in turn negatively affected output.

The combination of rapid fixed asset growth and declining real profitability is a micro manifestation of the parallel investment boom and slowdowns in productivity growth. The resulting widening of the current account

Figure 1.8   Increasing liquidity risks in corporate Asia, end-1996

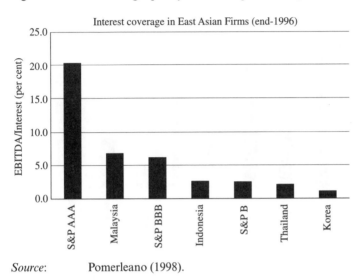

Interest coverage in East Asian Firms (end-1996)

Source: Pomerleano (1998).

deficits need not have been unsustainable as some countries in the past have sustained high current account deficits over a long period of time. But the current account deficits were progressively reflecting investments that were of uncertain quality. Whereas in the late 1980s, the surge in investment was directed primarily towards tradeables (and, in particular, exports) there was a large shift in the mid-1990s towards non-traded activities, particularly in Thailand and Indonesia. This shift was associated with lower overall productivity, although levels of productivity remained high relative to other regions (Sarel, 1997). The drop in productivity was in part caused by the exceptionally high rates of investment, but probably also occurred because many large investments were not subject to market discipline and supported by explicit or implicit guarantees or financing. In Korea, where most investments remained largely geared towards the tradeable sector, excessive expansion occurred in some sectors – for example, automobiles and steel.

3.4 Maturity mismatches and liquidity risk

Vulnerability also emerged in maturity mismatches, especially on the external financing side. With the exception of Indonesia, levels of external debt prior to the crisis were low in East Asia by international standards (figure

Figure 1.9   *External debt indicators, 1996*

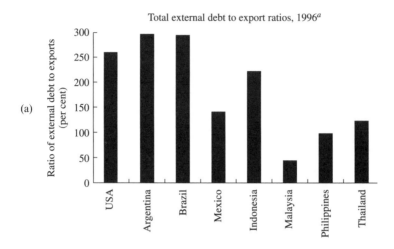

Total external debt to export ratios, 1996[a]

(a)

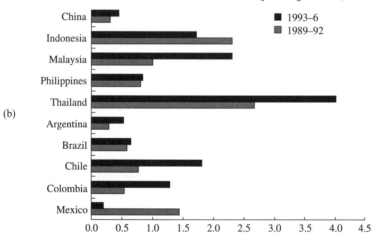

Short-term debt flows, 1989–92 and 1993–6 (percentage of GDP)[b]

(b)

Notes: [a] Debt Reporting System. Institutional Investors.
[b] IMF, World Economic Outlook, data base.

1.9). The accumulation of short-term external liabilities over the 1993–6 period, however, was rapid and most of this borrowing went unhedged (figure 1.9). Short-term foreign liabilities of banks grew extremely rapidly in Thailand, the Philippines, Korea and Malaysia. While short-term foreign liabilities of Indonesian banks did not increase rapidly, that of corporates

Figure 1.10   *Short-term debt, June 1997, per cent of total revenues*

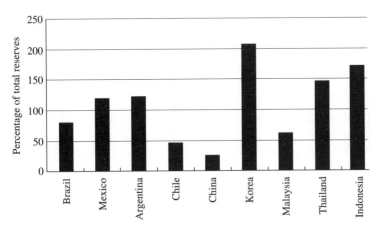

Sources: BIS; IMF, *International Financial Statistics*.

did. The crisis itself revealed that short-term borrowings were even higher than these figures suggest as many non-bank liabilities and much borrowing escaped national and BIS coverage.

The most telling indicator of vulnerability was the ratio of short-term external debt to external reserves prior to the crisis (figure 1.10). It shows that short-term debt exceeded external reserves by a large margin for Korea, Thailand and Indonesia in June 1997, exceeding that for many other developing countries. This high ratio of short-term obligations to liquid foreign exchange assets made these countries much more vulnerable to a potential run on their currencies in the face of a loss of investor confidence. See also Sachs, Tornell and Velasco (1996), Radelet and Sachs (1998b).

4 Contribution of macroeconomic policies to the build-up of vulnerability

As discussed, the large inflows of capital that the East Asian countries witnessed during 1990–6, were a reflection of their progressive integration in world financial markets as well as the strength of these countries' macroeconomic fundamentals.[3]

One of the challenges that this growing integration brought on the macroeconomic front, was that domestic macroeconomic cycles were validated and exacerbated by movements in private capital flows. In fact, in general, private capital flows are likely to move in tandem with domestic economic cycles for several reasons (see Box 1.1). However, what increased the pro-cyclicality of these inflows, and ultimately contributed to the build up of vulnerability – in the form of a rapid build-up of short-term, unhedged, external liabilities – was the policy mix that these countries used in dealing with the macroeconomic cycles and capital flows.

Box 1.1 Private capital flows and domestic macroeconomic cycles

In principle, private capital flows can both generate and exacerbate domestic macroeconomic cycles through various channels.

- First, in a more integrated setting, domestic demand pressures can be accommodated more easily by *borrowing abroad* – that is, private capital flows can validate excess demand pressures. If this excess demand falls primarily on the tradeables sector, it is likely to be manifested in a widening of the current account deficit, while if it falls on non-tradeable goods, it will lead to domestic inflationary pressures.

- Second, a country that has become relatively more attractive to investors (whether owing to higher domestic returns and improved prospects or to decline in returns elsewhere) will receive inflows of *private capital* which, in turn, can lead to problems of domestic absorption and 'overheating' pressures – even if these flows are financing investments, since in general, there is lead time involved before these investments translate into productive capacity. Again, this will be manifested in a widening of the current account deficit and/or inflationary pressures.

- Third, to the extent that the excess demand falls on domestic assets it will contribute to *asset price* inflation. In turn, such asset price increases and attendant increases in financial wealth can further contribute to a consumption boom – that is, private capital flows can contribute to a consumption boom and macroeconomic over-heating *indirectly* as well.

In fact, capital flows have tended to move very much in tandem with domestic macroeconomic cycles – particularly in Indonesia, Korea and Malaysia. In Thailand, although there was less of a correspondence between the capital inflows and demand pressures in the early 1990s, from the mid-1990s onwards, capital inflows have moved with the domestic macroeconomic cycle (see table 1.5).

Table 1.5   *Correlation between private capital flows and changes in excess demand pressures, 1990–1996*

Country	Correlation coefficient[a,b]
Indonesia	0.86
Korea	0.47
Philippines	0.95
Malaysia	0.79
Thailand	0.23

Notes:
[a] Correlation coefficient between private capital flows and changes in excess demand pressures 1990–6.
[b] Excess demand measured as deviations in output from a (Hodrick–Prescott) trend.

In particular, in dealing with over-heating pressures resulting from an upturn in domestic demand and capital inflows, the East Asian countries relied primarily on monetary policy. Monetary tightening, of course, served to increase interest rates and the differential between domestic and international interest rates. Upward pressures on domestic interest rates were exacerbated by the stance of fiscal policy. While remaining relatively conservative in a medium-term structural sense, fiscal policy actually turned expansionary – in cyclically adjusted terms – at a time when the domestic economy was over-heating.

The increased differential between domestic and international interest rates, in turn, provided further impetus for capital inflows. In fact, with growing integration, resulting from a breakdown of barriers to capital inflows and increasing familiarity of investors with emerging markets, domestic assets in these countries were becoming closer substitutes for international assets. In other words, the interest-sensitivity of capital inflows to these countries increased during the 1990s. The implication of this was that monetary policy became less effective as an instrument to deal with over-heating and capital inflows – and was in fact serving to encourage further inflows and hence the rapid accumulation of external liabilities. And since short-term flows tend to be the most sensitive to interest differentials, a large proportion of the inflows took the form of short-term obligations. Thus, when, during 1994–6, all four countries experienced an upturn in the economic cycle and domestic demand pressures (although the timing of the cycles varied across countries), the use of this policy mix resulted in a rapid increase in *short-term* external liabilities. Indeed, the two countries where this policy mix was most pronounced – Indonesia and Thailand – saw the most significant increase in short-term external obligations.

The final element in the macroeconomic policy mix that contributed to the rapid accumulation of external liabilities – contributing not only to their short-term, but also the *unhedged*, nature – was the exchange rate policy followed. The East Asian countries, having adopted an export-led growth strategy, were keen to avoid an appreciation of their real exchange rates – and thus avoid the potential vulnerability arising from large and sustained real exchange rate appreciation. In this, however, their main strategy was to avoid a large appreciation of their nominal rates. However, while the magnitudes were not huge, these countries did see an appreciation of their real exchange rates during 1994–6; they were thus not able to prevent their real exchange rates from appreciating, despite their attempts to prevent nominal exchange rate appreciations. On the other hand, it could be argued that allowing a greater degree of nominal exchange rate appreciation may have reduced the incentives to borrow abroad – in as much as an appreciation of the nominal exchange rate increases expectations of a future depreciation. Moreover, allowing an appreciation of the nominal exchange rate reduces the magnitude of the capital inflows, and hence further pressures of over-heating that these inflows could potentially cause, thus obviating some of the need to tighten monetary policy. In other words, allowing greater nominal exchange rate appreciation would have reduced the cycle of tight monetary policy, capital inflows and further tightening of monetary policy, and led to a less rapid accumulation of external obligations. As discussed below, these exchange rate policies also implied relatively *predictable* nominal rates. Not only was the movement of the central rate relatively small, but the fluctuations around the central rate were also limited. In turn, by reducing the perceptions of exchange rate risks, the relatively narrow range of nominal exchange rate fluctuations encouraged the accumulation of external liabilities in the form of *unhedged* obligations. It also helped skew the liabilities towards a short-term maturity structure. Wider fluctuations around the central parity would have dampened the incentives for short-term flows somewhat – since short-term flows are more affected by fluctuations around the central parity – whereas long-term flows, such as FDI, are more affected by movements in the central parity itself.

In sum, domestic interest rates (adjusted for actual exchange rate movements) rose as a result of domestic demand pressures and were exacerbated by the tightening of monetary policy and more expansionary fiscal policy (in cyclically adjusted terms). These high interest rates were sustained through sterilisation efforts during 1994–6 which, in turn, encouraged further short-term, unhedged, inflows of capital.[4] In other words, the policy mix employed during the period of domestic over-heating and capital inflows served as a major incentive – at the macroeconomic level – for the rapid accumulation of short-term unhedged external liabilities, thereby increasing countries' vulnerability along this dimension. However, the extent to which this policy mix was used did vary across the four countries – as did the degree of vulnerability arising from the accumulation of short-term unhedged external liabilities. This story is examined in greater detail below.

4.1 Domestic demand pressures 1994–1996

Although the timing of the domestic economic cycles varied, all four countries saw a pick-up in domestic demand pressures during 1994–6. In Korea, the growth of domestic demand picked up sharply in 1994 and 1995, with its contribution to GDP growth averaging around 9 per cent, from 4 per cent in 1993. In Malaysia, the contribution of domestic demand to GDP growth had already accelerated in 1993 from 3.5 per cent the previous year to 9 per cent. In 1994, the contribution of domestic demand to GDP growth increased further, to around 13 per cent. Similarly, Thailand which had already seen a 2-percentage point pick-up in the contribution of domestic demand to GDP growth in 1993, saw a further pick-up in the contribution of domestic demand in 1994 and 1995. Indonesia saw acceleration in the growth of domestic demand slightly later, which was sustained in 1995 and into 1996. In all four countries, the acceleration in the growth of domestic demand reflected a pick-up in the growth of both investment and consumption, although the relative importance of the two differed across countries. Also, in all four countries, with the sharp pick-up in the contribution of domestic demand, the contribution of the external sector to GDP growth turned negative during the period (see figure 1.11).

The demand pressures were manifested primarily in a widening of the current account deficit, although in Thailand there was a small increase in inflation as well. Malaysia's current account deficit widened by around 5 percentage points from 3.7 per cent of GDP at end-1992 to 8.5 per cent of GDP in 1995, while Thailand's – which had been high throughout the 1990s – increased by 3 percentage points during the over-heating period, from 5.0 per cent of GDP in 1993 to 8 per cent in 1995. Although Korea ran very small current account deficits throughout the 1990s, the change in current account position since 1993 was significant – from a small surplus of 0.1 per cent of GDP in 1993 to a deficit of 1.2 per cent of GDP in 1994. This increased further to 2 per cent of GDP in 1995. In Indonesia, the current account deficit widened from 1.6 per cent of GDP in 1994 to 3.4 per cent in 1995, and further to 3.6 per cent in 1996 (table 1.6).

Figure 1.11   *GDP growth and its components, 1989–1997*

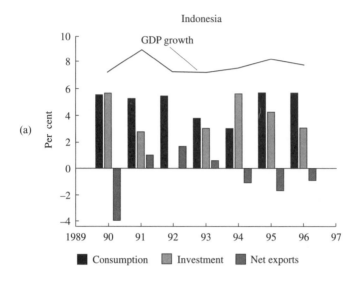

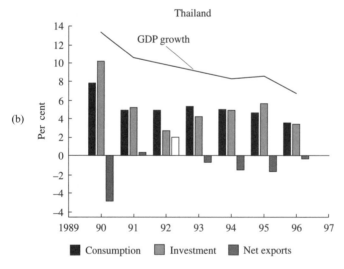

4.2 Monetary policy

As can be seen in table 1.5 (p. 33), private capital flows tended to move in tandem with domestic economic cycles. In doing so, they also served to amplify the degree of overheating in the domestic economy that occurred

Figure 1.11   (*cont.*)

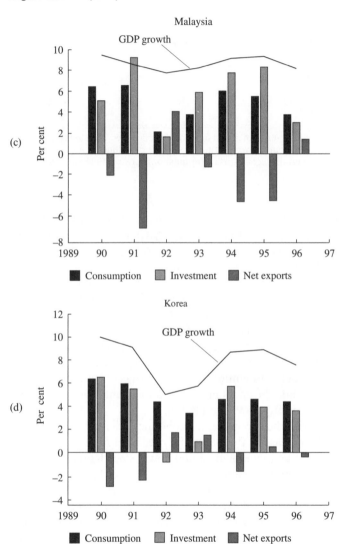

(c)

(d)

Source: World Bank.

during 1994–6. In responding to the capital inflows and over-heating pressures, the East Asian countries relied primarily on monetary tightening and sterilisation of the inflows.[5]

In Indonesia, albeit to a lesser extent than during the previous bout of macroeconomic over-heating (during 1990–1), relatively heavy reliance was

Table 1.6   *Symptoms of macroeconomic over-heating, 1993–1996*

Country	Period of over-heating	Increase in current account deficit[a] (per cent of GDP)	Increase in inflation (percentage points)[a]
Indonesia	1995–6	1.76	−0.064
Korea	1994–5	1.76	−0.068
Malaysia	1993–5	4.76	−0.28
Thailand	1994–5	2.99	0.68

Note: [a] Changes in current account deficit and inflation are calculated from the end of period preceding the bout of over-heating. In the case of Indonesia, for example, it is the change in the current account deficit (or inflation) between 1994 and 1996.

placed on monetary policy in dealing with the demand pressures in 1995–6. Following a rapid growth in monetary aggregates in 1994, based on an expansion of domestic credit, monetary policy was tightened significantly by mid-1995. In 1996, the increase in net foreign assets would thus have contributed to a growth in reserve money of 73 per cent, had the tightening of domestic credit not imparted a decline of 37 per cent; on net, therefore, reserve money growth was contained to 36 per cent that year. The primary form of monetary management was OMOs, using SBIs (Bank Indonesia certificates of deposits), but use of discount operations was also made. This was reinforced by measures to control the growth of bank credit more directly. In particular, BI emphasised 'moral suasion', and banks were required to submit annual business plans and implementation reports and to set guidelines for credit policy formulation.

In Korea, along with the expansion in economic activity during 1994–5, there was a sizable increase in the Bank of Korea's net foreign asset position, largely reflecting an increase in capital flows. Since Korea was essentially following a monetary targeting policy, the Bank of Korea responded to the inflows of capital that took place in 1994 by sterilising through the issuance of large amounts of Monetary Stabilisation Bonds (MSBs). However, as discussed below, Korea's nominal exchange rate also appreciated (by about 4 per cent), which helped to reduce potential over-heating pressures and some of the need for tightening monetary policy.

In Malaysia, monetary policy played a much less important role in dealing with the macroeconomic upturn and capital inflows during 1994–5 than it had in the previous economic cycle. In fact, Malaysia sterilised very heavily in 1992 and 1993, when it received large capital inflows. By comparison, in the policy response in the latter period, there was less reliance on monetary tightening and the nominal exchange rate played a greater role in absorbing some of the potential over-heating pressures. Malaysia also imposed capital controls to deal with capital inflows in early 1994. Nonetheless, monetary policy was also tightened progressively from late 1995 to mid-1996. In more recent years, changes in the statutory reserve requirements (SRR), direct borrowing from, or lending to, the banking system, and the transfer of government and Employees Provident Fund (EPF) deposits to the central bank had become the main instruments of monetary management. These mechanisms were supported by sales of government securities and Bank Negara bills. In 1996, the statutory reserve requirements were increased twice (in February and March) to 13½ per cent of eligible liabilities. In addition, over 1995–6, Malaysia introduced a number of credit-control measures, both in order to reduce banks' credit expansion (i.e. for monetary policy purposes) and for prudential reasons.

Finally, Thailand, like Indonesia, relied quite heavily on monetary policy and sterilised interventions in responding to the growing demand pressures. As mentioned above, Thailand began to see the emergence of excess demand pressures in 1995. Monetary policy was tightened progressively during the course of the year. Despite very substantial increases in net foreign assets in 1995 (which would have resulted in an increase in reserve money of 52 per cent), the contraction in domestic credit extended by BOT succeeded in containing reserve money growth to 22 per cent per annum. One of the constraints to undertaking OMOs was the scarcity of high-grade securities, and an important measure taken in 1995 was the introduction of BOT bonds. In addition, BOT introduced a series of administrative measures designed to reduce credit growth of banks and finance companies. These measures included extending the credit-monitoring scheme in late 1994 to include finance companies with assets over B20 billion, requiring that reserves for non-resident baht deposits be held entirely as non-remunerated deposits at the central bank, and tightening the limits on financial institutions' foreign exchange position in 1995. During the first half of 1996, when private capital inflows were sustained, BOT continued to sterilise – both through repurchase operations and increased issuance of BOT bonds. The emphasis on the use of monetary policy is corroborated in the estimates of monetary policy reaction functions. Table 1.7 reports the results for Indonesia and Thailand, which are the two countries that are found to have relied quite heavily on the use of monetary policy.

The following specification of the reaction function was estimated for Indonesia:

$$\Delta dc_t = \beta_0 + \beta_1 \Delta nfa_t + \beta_2 ygap_t + \beta_3 \Delta reer_t + d1 + d2 + d3$$

where *dc* and *nfa* is domestic credit and net foreign assets of the central bank, respectively, *reer* is the real effective exchange rate, *ygap* is the output

Table 1.7   *Estimates^a of monetary policy reaction functions*

Country	Constant	nfa	ygap	reer
Indonesia	−820	−0.74	−0.05	−19495
		(−2.69)**	(−1.88)	(−2.08)**
				adjusted R^2 0.73
Thailand	−19.8	−1.04)**	−3038.12)*	0.016)
		(−4.57)**	(1.12)*	(0.006)

Notes: ^a Estimates obtained using two-stage least squares, owing to the possible simultaneity bias.
* Significant at 5 per cent level; ** significant at 1 per cent level.

gap and $d1$, $d2$, $d3$ are seasonal dummies. The output gap is measured as actual *minus* potential GDP over actual GDP, where the potential GDP is obtained using a Hodrick–Prescott filter.

For Thailand, the reaction function estimated was

$$\Delta dc_t = \beta_0 + \beta_1 \Delta nfa_t + \beta_2 \Delta \log y_t + \beta_3 \Delta reer_t.$$

As can be seen, the coefficients on both the change in net foreign assets and the output gap are negative and significant in Indonesia. This corroborates the observation that monetary policy was used to deal with domestic over-heating and that a large proportion of the expansion of net foreign assets associated with capital inflows was sterilised. In Indonesia, around three-quarters of the increase in net foreign assets were thus offset through a contraction in domestic credit. A coefficient close to − 1 on the change in net foreign assets for Thailand, indicates an almost one-for-one contraction in domestic credit in response to an increase in net foreign assets.

With progressive integration, however, monetary policy was becoming increasingly less effective, so that in raising interest rates these countries were simply providing an impetus for further capital inflows.

In general, when the exchange rate is pegged, and international capital movements are sensitive to interest rate differentials, changes in domestic credit will tend to be offset by movements in capital flows. The degree to which a tightening of domestic credit will induce further private capital inflows will depend on the degree of capital mobility and the extent to which domestic assets are considered substitutes for foreign assets. The closer the degree of substitutability between domestic and foreign assets and the greater the mobility of capital, the larger will be the response of private capital flows to any changes in domestic credit (i.e. the larger will be the 'offset').

Offset coefficients were calculated for Indonesia and Thailand, using the approach of Cumby and Obstfeld (1981). This requires estimating a money demand, money supply and net liabilities function as follows:

Table 1.8 *Estimates of the offset coefficient*

Country	per cent	
Indonesia	40 (1988–93)	60 (1990–6)
Thailand	47 (1988–91)	54 (1992–6)

$$\log(m/p)^d = \gamma_0 + \gamma_1 \log \gamma_1 + \gamma_2 r_t + d1 + d2 + d3$$

$$\log(m/p)^s = \delta_0 + \delta_1 r_r + \delta_2 \log(ba/p) + d1 + d2 + d3$$

$$\log(ep/p) = \beta_0 + \beta_1 \log \gamma_1 + \beta_2 r + \beta_3 r^* + d1 + d2 + d3$$

where m is the stock of M1, p is the domestic price level (CPI), y is domestic output, r is the domestic interest rate, r^* is the foreign interest rate (US LIBOR) and $d1$, $d2$, $d3$ are seasonal dummies.

The 'offset' coefficient, or extent to which domestic credit contraction (expansion) is offset by further inflows (outflows) of capital, is given by:

$$\beta_2 \delta_2 / [(\delta_1 - \gamma_2) + (\beta_2 \delta_2)].$$

As table 1.8 shows, the degree of offset had increased during the 1990s – a reflection of increased capital mobility and increasing substitutability of home and foreign assets, resulting from growing investor familiarity. Around 60 per cent of a contraction in domestic credit was offset through further inflows in the case of Indonesia, and around 54 per cent was offset in the case of Thailand.

4.3 Fiscal policy

While monetary policy was being tightened, fiscal policy actually turned procyclical in all four countries. Although the underlying fiscal positions remained strong, fiscal policy was not sufficiently contractionary – in view of the over-heating – to result in a cyclically neutral position. Rather it imparted a positive impulse and as a result added to the pressures on domestic interest rates and widened the differential between domestic and foreign rates.

Fiscal management had been a major element in the government's success in adjusting to the large external shocks that Indonesia experienced in the 1980s, and Indonesia's fiscal accounts continued to show improvements during the 1990s. In fact, since 1994 Indonesia had recorded fiscal surpluses – generated in part by privatisation – which Indonesia had used to repay external public debt and improve its debt indicators.[6] In both 1995 and 1996 the conservative fiscal position allowed a sizable build-up in government deposits with BI, which served as a moderating influence on reserve-money growth. Despite the conservative fiscal position however, fiscal policy behaved procyclically in 1996. In particular, while the fiscal stance (which measures the difference between the cyclically neutral and the actual balance) remained contractionary, it became less contractionary. That is to say, the fiscal impulse (change in the fiscal stance) was positive at the time that demand pressures had intensified.[7]

In Korea, fiscal policy has often tended to be procyclical. This is in large part because policy has generally been formulated within a medium-term framework, subject to the constraint that outlays remain broadly in line with revenues. While this has helped maintain a conservative fiscal position, the focus on expenditure objectives has meant that fiscal policy has often been procyclical. In 1994, the fiscal stance, while remaining contractionary, was slightly procyclical, although relative to previous economic cycles, fiscal policy behaved less procyclically during the 1994 over-heating bout.

As in the other East Asian countries, the fiscal restructuring and consolidation that Malaysia implemented resulted in significant improvements in the fiscal balance during the 1990s. In 1995, however, while still achieving a surplus, the federal government position registered a sharp decline from 3 per cent of GDP in 1994 to 1.3 per cent. (The slower pace of growth of revenues was in part due to income tax cuts and reductions in import duties.) The budget surplus declined again marginally to 1.1 per cent of GDP in 1996 and although, as in Indonesia, the fiscal stance remained contractionary in 1995 and 1996 it became less contractionary. In particular, the fiscal impulse was sizably expansionary in 1995 when the economy was experiencing strong demand pressures.

Thailand had also succeeded in eliminating fiscal deficits following the fiscal consolidation undertaken during the Sixth Development Plan (1987–91), and Thailand's fiscal position remained conservative throughout the 1990–6. Although fiscal surpluses had declined during the Seventh Development Plan (1992–6) – as the focus of fiscal policy shifted towards addressing the infrastructure bottlenecks – they remained around 2 per cent of GDP during 1992–4. In 1995, the fiscal surplus rose to 2.5 per cent of GDP. However, the fiscal stance which had been expansionary in 1994 (and hence had been countercyclical given that the economy was not experiencing over-heating pressures), turned slightly more expansionary in 1995 (so that the fiscal impulse was expansionary) when excess demand pressures emerged. In 1996, the fiscal surplus declined to 1.6 per cent of GDP, entailing a strongly expansionary fiscal impulse – although the growth of

Table 1.9 *Correlation between the fiscal impulse*
and excess demand pressures

Country	Correlation coefficient[a,b,c]		
	1990–1996	*1990–1993*	*1993–1996*
Indonesia	0.86	0.91	0.87
Korea	0.88	0.93	0.91
Malaysia	−0.75	−0.86	0.82
Thailand	−0.23	−0.32	0.13

Notes: [a] Correlation coefficient between fiscal impulse and
excess demand pressures.
[b] Excess demand measured as deviations in output
from a (Hodrick–Prescott) trend.
[c] Fiscal impulse is the change in fiscal stance.

economic activity had also slowed slightly, and demand pressures were lower than in 1995. In both years therefore fiscal policy was procyclical.

Table 1.9 shows the correlation between the fiscal impulse and excess demand pressures in these countries during 1990–6. As can be seen, in Korea, Indonesia and Malaysia, fiscal policy has tended to operate in a procyclical fashion. In Thailand, fiscal policy turned procyclical in the latter period, including during the period of domestic over-heating.

In sum, while the fiscal stance remained conservative in all four countries, fiscal policy imparted a positive impulse to the domestic demand pressures, thereby aggravating pressures on interest rates.

4.4 Exchange rate policy

The final element in the policy mix that contributed to the rapid build-up of short-term unhedged, external liabilities was the exchange rate policies followed in these four countries. As mentioned above, concerned with preventing an appreciation of their real exchange rates, the East Asian countries maintained pegged exchange rate systems – with the authorities intervening in the foreign exchange markets to maintain the peg in the face of the large capital inflows.[8] By preventing the nominal exchange rate from appreciating very much, and by adopting exchange rate policies that resulted in fairly predictable nominal exchange rate movements, however, these countries increased the incentives for unhedged, short-term inflows.

During the period, Indonesia maintained a managed float, in which BI set the central rate and intervened in the foreign exchange market at a band

Table 1.10   *Magnitude of the variability*
in the nominal exchange rate

Country	Magnitude[a]
Indonesia	0.002
Korea	0.007
Malaysia	0.013
Thailand	0.005

Note: [a] Magnitude of the average unpredictable
component of the monthly change in the
nominal exchange rate during 1990–6
(per cent).

around it. The band was relatively narrow for most of the period, although it was widened progressively from 1994 onwards. (In January 1994 the band was widened to about 1 per cent, and by June 1995 it had been widened to 2 per cent, and to 8 per cent by September 1996.) Although the central rate was set against a basket of currencies, in practice, Indonesia appeared to have been targeting the real exchange rate within a relatively narrow range by depreciating the nominal band *vis-à-vis* the US dollar to broadly offset the inflation differentials between the two countries. This was particularly the case during the early to mid-1990s. Even during the 1994–6 period, however, there is evidence to suggest that there was some targeting of the real exchange rate. Thus, the nominal exchange rate was depreciated on a relatively constant basis. This is corroborated in the estimates of the nominal exchange rate on time

$$\log(nexch)_t = 7.48 = 0.01 \; time$$
$$\underset{(906)}{} \quad \underset{(28.22)}{}$$

$$\text{adj. } R^2 = 0.98$$

where *nexch* is the nominal exchange rate *vis-à-vis* the US dollar and t is a time trend.

The fact that this policy of depreciating the central rate *vis-à-vis* the US dollar resulted in relatively *predictable* exchange rate movements is borne out in the fact that the standard deviation of the error term from this regression (reported in table 1.10) is very low – indeed, the lowest of the four countries.

Under Korea's Market Average Rate (MAR) system, the nominal exchange rate *vis-à-vis* the US dollar was allowed to float in the interbank market within a daily range around the weighted average of the previous day's interbank rate for spot transactions. Overall, therefore, the predictability of the nominal exchange rate – while lower than that of Indonesia and Thailand – remained greater than that of the Malaysian ringgit.

Malaysia's exchange rate policy was a managed float, but the nominal exchange rate was allowed to appreciate by 7 per cent from beginning of 1994 to end-1996. The ringgit also demonstrated the greatest degree of unpredictability overall, as reported in table 1.10.

Thailand also attempted to limit movements in its real exchange. While it did not actually depreciate the nominal rate in order to target the real rate, it kept the nominal rate *vis-à-vis* the US dollar more or less constant, in an effort to limit real exchange rate appreciation during 1994–6. This is borne out in the following estimates, which suggest that the nominal exchange rate did not vary significantly over time

$$\log(nexch)_t = 3.2 + 0.0009 \, time$$
$$\quad\quad\quad (165) \quad\quad (1.09)$$

$$\text{adj. } R^2 = 0.01$$

where *nexch* is the nominal exchange rate *vis-à-vis* the US dollar and *t* is a time trend.

As a result, though, like the Indonesian rupiah, the average unpredictable component of the monthly change in the Thai baht was extremely very small, as can be seen from table 1.10.

4.5 The role of the overall policy mix

In general, therefore, relatively greater reliance was placed on tightening monetary policy and sterilisation as means of dealing with the overheating pressures, although this was less pronounced in Malaysia and Korea. Rather than alleviate the pressures on domestic interest rates, fiscal policy imparted a positive impulse in all four countries. In conjunction with the relatively predictable nominal exchange rates, this encouraged the accumulation of unhedged short-term external liabilities. Of course, the degree to which this policy was employed, did differ somewhat across the four countries, as summarised in table 1.11. And as can be seen, the two countries that most relied on this policy mix – Thailand and Indonesia – saw the largest build-up in external short-term liabilities during 1994–6.

Table 1.11 *Summary of policy mix*

Country	Tightening of monetary policy and sterilisation	Positive fiscal impulse	Predictable exchange rates	Share of short-term to total external debt accumulation[a]
Indonesia	xxx	xx	xxx	47
Korea	xx	xx	xx	34
Malaysia	x	xx	x	25
Thailand	xxx	xx	xxx	43

Notes: [a] 1993–6 (per cent).
   xx = medium usage.
   xxx = strong usage.

The contribution of the policy mix to the build-up of short-term external liabilities is also borne out in the results of a panel regression. In particular, a panel regression of the share of short-term external debt to total debt was run on the magnitude and sign of the fiscal impulse, the degree of sterilisation and the relative unpredicability of the exchange rate, which yielded the following results:

$$D^s\!/D^t = 21.46 + 3.95\,fi + 12.33\,st - 5.62\,e^u - 64d$$
$${\scriptstyle(5.60)}\quad{\scriptstyle(2.39)}\qquad{\scriptstyle(2.54)}\qquad{\scriptstyle(-2.51)}\quad{\scriptstyle-(1.27)}$$

adj. $R^2 = 0.26$

where D^s/D^t is the ratio of short-term debt to total debt, fi is magnitude of the fiscal impulse (as a percentage of GDP), st is dummy capturing whether the country undertook heavy sterilisation that year or not and e^u is the unpredictability of the nominal exchange rate given by the estimation of an ARCH model of the nominal exchange rate on a constant and a time trend. d is an multiplicative variable capturing the interactive effects of low sterilisation, extent of exchange rate appreciation and degree of unpredictability of the exchange rate.

The coefficients are all of the expected signs and all, except the interactive variable, d, are significant at the 2 per cent level. That is, a positive fiscal impulse and monetary tightening raises the ratio of short-term to total debt (through their effects on the domestic interest rates) while greater unpredictability of the exchange rate has a negative impact on the ratio of short-term to total debt. The coefficient on the multiplicative variable is expected to be negative – i.e. less sterilisation, a greater degree of nominal appreciation and greater unpredicablity of the nominal exchange rate, are expected to lead to a lower ratio of short-term unhedged to total obligations.

5 Institutional weaknesses and macro–financial fragility in East Asia's financial sectors

This section analyses the weaknesses in the financial and corporate sectors that arose from moral hazard and incentive problems – owing to institutional and regulatory weaknesses – lack of transparency and weaknesses in corporate governance. These weaknesses are worth studying since an important explanation for the failure of aggregate macroeconomic policies to stem capital inflows, alter their composition or adequately minimise their adverse consequences, lay in the quality of domestic financial intermediation and the governance of private firms. Indeed, those East Asian countries which received foreign capital mostly intermediated through the domestic banking system or lent directly to the corporate sector (in the form of bonds, loans and short-term paper) became more vulnerable than countries which had received flows mostly in the form of FDI.[9]

Several microeconomic factors were important in facilitating this process, in particular, implicit insurance provided to financial institutions and certain specific institutional changes in the 1990s in some East Asian countries. All these interacted with a weak supervisory and regulatory framework for banks and led to increased financial fragility. On the demand side of the credit market, corporate governance was weak because of excessive ownership concentration with links with financial institutions, inadequate transparency and disclosure and lack of minority shareholder protection. Below we analyse each of these factors in some detail.

5.1 Implicit insurance

The (implicit or explicit) insurance on liabilities provided by the government to the financial system, as well as implicit guarantees provided to the corporate sector, has been an important factor in motivating excessive risk-taking, including large foreign exchange risks (McKinnon and Pill, 1997, provide an analytical model). As some of the cost of a default of an individual borrower (or the negative impact of a general financial crisis on a borrower) were expected to be passed on to the rest of the domestic economy, risks were under-priced. As discussed above, the pegging to the dollar at a (quasi-) constant level for a long period represents an implicit guarantee against the risk of devaluation (a contingent liability for the government). This happened in the case of Chile in the late 1970s, in Mexico in the early 1990s and has been an important factor in the case of Thailand and Korea.

5.2 Specific institutional changes

Specific institutional changes played a role in encouraging foreign inflows. Important among these was the creation of offshore financial markets where local financial institutions were to provide clients in nearby countries with financial services. Malaysia, for example, promoted Labuan as a financial centre, and the Philippines developed an offshore euro-peso market. These markets were often given regulatory and tax advantages over domestic markets. Because of the regulatory and tax advantages, much external financing was channelled through these centres.[10] They also put pressures to reform and deregulate local markets, as firms would otherwise switch to the offshore market. The offshore markets, however, created adverse dynamics, mainly as they ended up servicing domestic firms ('out–in' transactions) rather than firms in nearby countries ('out–out' transactions). Put differently, the offshore centres became vehicles for funding domestic firms, rather than vehicles to provide financial services regionally, and encouraged more offshore borrowings. This bias was most severe in Thailand (see Box 1.2).

Box 1.2: Offshore centres: the case of Thailand[11]

Thailand's Bangkok International Banking Facility (BIBF) special incentives contributed to a great degree to the crisis. In March 1993, permission was given to 46 (domestic and foreign) commercial banks to operate international banking business in Bangkok. In 1994, further privileges were granted to BIBF-based banks including the right to open branches outside Bangkok and issue negotiable CDs. Due to special incentives, the BIBF provided an important channel for the domestic financial sector to raise short-term funds ('out–in' lending). Because of bilateral tax treaties between Japan and Thailand, Japanese banks could offset withholding taxes levied on foreign exchange borrowings by Thai companies against their other income in Japan. As a result, Japanese banks, which had about one-quarter of the BIBF-market, were willing to absorb the withholding tax and lend at very low spreads to Thai companies.

The supply of funds was further boosted by the incentive for foreign BIBFs to become full bank branches, the approval of which was made dependent on the volume of loans. Historically low international interest rates, especially on Japanese yen, were another factor in the large financing available and low spreads charged. As a result, out–in lending boomed between 1993 and 1996 (from 126 bn baht to 331 bn baht). Reflecting the rapid growth of BIBF out–in lending, Thai commercial banks' foreign currency loans rose at the end of 1996 to $31.5 bn, or 17 per cent of private sector loans, while commercial banks' short-term external liabilities surged.

5.3 Weak regulatory and institutional framework

Weaknesses in financial systems were probably the single most important factor contributing to vulnerability in East Asian economies (see Claessens and Glaessner, 1997). Insufficient capital adequacy ratios, inadequate legal lending limits on single borrowers or group of related borrowers, inadequate asset classification systems and poor provisioning for possible losses, poor disclosure and transparency of bank operations and lack of provisions for an exit policy of troubled financial institutions, all contributed to banking fragility in many East Asian countries. Relative to other developing countries, a limited role of foreign banks in local markets (Claessens and Glaessner, 1998) also reduced the ability of banking systems to absorb shocks and, more generally, inhibited the institutional development of banks. Thus, as a whole, as of June 1997, just before the Thai crisis erupted, banking sectors throughout East Asia appeared more fragile than those in developed (and some developing) countries. (Figure 1.12). It is worth noting that fragility indicators of financial systems in East Asia do not show any worsening between June 1996 and December 1997, implying that the weaknesses in their banking systems were more the cause rather than the consequence to the crisis (see, 1998, p. 36).

Underpinning the financial fragility in East Asia there was a domestic and external financial – capital account – liberalisation process, which led to increased lending and greater competition in banking, but which proceeded without an adequate upgrade in the regulatory and supervisory framework. While increased competition may be desirable in the long run, it may induce banks to pursue risky investment strategies in the short run – because of the erosion in the banks' franchise value. However, the ultimate reason why banks can grow and become more fragile is the lack of a

Figure 1.12   *Banking sector fragility in Asia, June 1997*

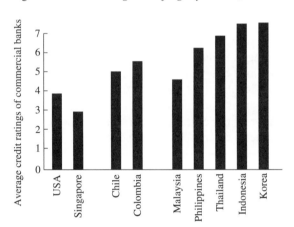

regulatory and supervisory framework that can adequately monitor them. Indeed, as shown in figure 1.13, a destabilising financial liberalisation process (along with a lending boom) has been singled out as one of the factors that led to increased financial fragility in Asia during the 1990s, especially in the cases of Korea and Thailand.

The argument above does not imply that countries in Asia did not attempt to improve their regulatory and supervisory frameworks during the 1990s. On the contrary, in several cases the authorities made significant progress in this regard. Nevertheless, developments since mid-1997 have shown that the measures implemented were 'too little, too late'. It is important to note, however, that this outcome is not specific to Asia during the 1990s. Indeed, many financial liberalisation episodes in the past have led to a lending boom, increased financial fragility and a crisis. Examples of this are Mexico in 1994–5, Chile and the USA in the early 1980s, and the Nordic countries in the mid- and late 1980s among others.

Among the most critical flaws in banking regulation in East Asian countries were insufficient capital adequacy ratios, lax restrictions for lending to risky sectors, poor provisioning for non-performing loans and future losses and poor transparency and disclosure to enhance market discipline.

5.3.1 Capital adequacy requirements

The 1988 Basle Capital Accord guidelines established that internationally active banks should have capital (Tier one *plus* Tier two)[12] equal to at least 8 per cent of their (risk-weighted) assets. However, these are minimum levels of capital, and countries have sovereign discretion to modify them to

Figure 1.13   *Financial fragility in Asia, 1997: contributing factors – destabilising credit*

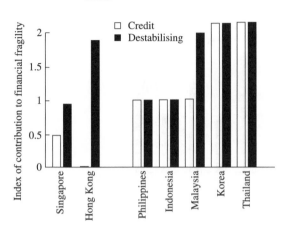

Note: The bars indicate the extent to which the specific factor contributed to banking sector fragility; a value of zero indicates no contribution, of 1 indicates some contribution, of 2 an important contribution.
Source: Goldman-Sachs (December 1997).

local circumstances. In fact, a number of articles have suggested that the capital ratios for banks in developing countries should be higher.[13]

Although several East Asian countries – Indonesia, Malaysia and Thailand – applied the minimum standard of 8 per cent risk-based capital/assets ratio (CAR) early in the 1990s, developments since 1995 have shown that these cushions were insufficient to protect depositors' money. Indeed, when compared *vis-à-vis* the stock of non-performing loans, as of September 1997 banks appeared to be relatively well capitalised in the Philippines, Malaysia, and Indonesia, but insufficiently capitalised in Korea, and Thailand[15] (figure 1.14a). Nevertheless, as the crisis unfolded it became clear that non-performing loans were underreported and capital had been lost in all crisis countries (figure 1.14b).

5.3.2 Legal lending limits

The risk associated with excessive exposure to a single related entity or connected group of borrowers has been documented in the literature as one of the prime micro culprits leading to financial crisis. Thus, since related parties' transactions present possible conflicts of interests, banks should extend credit to related companies and individuals on an arm's-length

Figure 1.14   *Capital/asset ratio, NPLs and recapitalisation need, 1998*

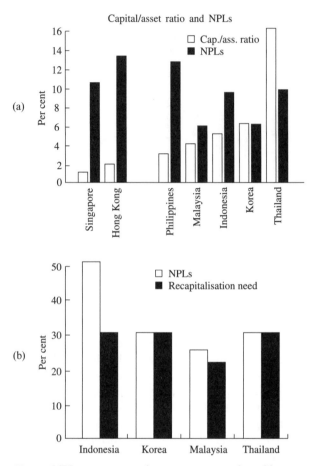

Notes: [a] NPLs are expressed as a percentage of total loans.
    [b] Recapitalisation need is expressed as a percentage of GDP.
Source: JP Morgan, *Asian Financial Markets*, 3rd quarter (July 17 1998).

basis. Similarly, industry concentration also presents a significant risk for
banks, especially in the case of economic sectors – such as real-estate – that
are susceptible to experience boom–bust cycles.[15] To prevent banks from
becoming excessively exposed to one particular industry and abuses from
related parties' lending, bank supervisors place requirements in the form of
lending ceilings, usually expressed in terms of a percentage of banks'
capital.

Similar to the capital adequacy requirements, the measures implemented in recent years regarding legal lending limits in East Asian countries proved to be insufficient to contain the exposure of banks to the risks referred above. For example, and as shown in figure 1.6, as of September 1997, banking sectors in Indonesia, Malaysia, Thailand and to some extent in the Philippines, showed a large exposure to real-estate, a sector prone to experience large boom–bust cycles. Excessive lending to related parties has also been singled out as an important source of financial fragility in the crisis countries (see below).

5.3.3 Non-performing loans and provisions for future losses

Adequate loan loss provisions complement capital in providing a safeguard against risks and potential losses. To build these provisions an asset-classification system is needed. This usually classifies assets as Pass, Special Mention, Substandard, Doubtful or Loss, with the latter three categories collectively regarded as 'classified assets'. For each category a reserve for potential future losses is required. However, as of mid-1997, the asset-classification system in East Asian countries appeared inadequate in that they were not 'forward-looking' – instead of addressing the underlying credit quality or the borrower's capacity to repay, they tended to rely on length of delinquency. In contrast, the US classification system differs in using a more judgemental approach to determine delinquencies.[16] Furthermore, some countries in the region were too liberal in the permissible length of delinquency before assets were classified. For example, in Thailand (unsecured) loans could be in arrears for up to 12 months before they were classified. The timebased formula, if not complemented by credit-evaluation judgement, can encourage the rolling over of bad loans and lead to under-provisioning ('evergreening').

Figure 1.15 is indicative of the problem. Indeed, loan loss provisions in a sample of banks in the countries under study – 0.54 per cent of assets during 1988–95 – appear to be insufficient. Although differences in asset quality could possibly justify provisions of about half those in banks in Latin America and the Caribbean or in Sub-Saharan Africa, it could hardly justify lower provisions than in high-income countries – the average for the latter group was 0.63 per cent of assets.

In addition, the asset classification and provisioning guidelines in the region, as of mid-1997, relied excessively on a liberal treatment of collateral. Indeed, in Indonesia, Malaysia, the Philippines and Thailand, the level of provision depends on appraised collateral value, which provides incentives for banks to over-state collateral values to lessen provisioning needs (and, as a result, to over-state the book value of their assets).[17]

Figure 1.15   *Loan loss provisions, 1988–1995*

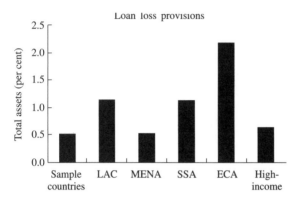

Note: Bars represent the average over 1988–95 for each bank in the sample, then
averaged for each country and then for each region or country group.
Sources: Demirgüç-Kunt and Huizinga (1997); Claessens, Demirgüç-Kunt and
Huizinga (1997).

5.3.4 Transparency

In order for market forces to work effectively, foreign counterparts, depositors and shareholders, need to be provided with relevant, reliable and comparable information on a timely basis in order to assess the condition of
banks. Banks are therefore usually required to disclose to the public information regarding their activities, and provide a true and fair view of their
financial position. Transparency comprises the following: (a) consistent
and accurate accounting standards, (b) satisfactory standards for financial
reporting and (c) timely disclosure of information.

Overall, as shown in figure 1.16 below, banks in countries throughout
the region rank poorly in overall transparency-disclosure *vis-à-vis* banks
in the USA or Hong Kong (taken as the benchmark for comparison purposes).

Finally, figure 1.16 illustrates these weaknesses as perceived by the
market in the fall of 1997. Among the aspects that were not discussed previously were the rapidly growing NBFIs, which were an additional important source of competition for banks, especially in Korea and Thailand.
Furthermore, as NBFIs were generally less regulated and subject to
weaker supervision than banks, their growth directly exacerbated fragility
in these countries. Although each of these elements considered on their
own may not lead to financial distress, together and in combination with

Figure 1.16   *Transparency and quality of disclosure, 1997: overall rating*

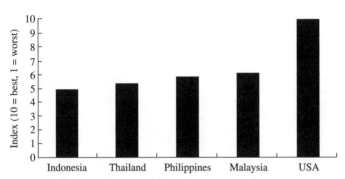

Note: Sample size used to construct bars differs from country to country.
Source: Goldman-Sachs (January and September 1997).

other weaknesses and policies, they can lead to or exacerbate a crisis. Figure 1.17 also shows that there were considerable differences among countries in terms of financial fragility, with the Philippines, for example, being considerably less fragile than the other East Asian Economies, except for Hong Kong and Singapore.

5.4 Weak corporate governance

Corporate governance was impaired in East Asia, and contributed to excessive borrowing in the years preceding the crisis, reduced incentives for monitoring and was also a factor behind the inefficient investment and declining profitability. There were four related problems in corporate governance: concentrated ownership; weak incentives; poor protection of minority shareholders; weak information standards. But, most of these problems were no more severe in East Asia than in many developing countries.

5.4.1 Concentrated ownership

High ownership concentration is typically both a symptom and a cause of weak corporate governance. It is a symptom because in the face of weak legal and regulatory protection against abuse by corporate insiders, ownership concentration is a means for investors to be better able to monitor and

Figure 1.17   Financial fragility in Asia, 1997: contributing factors – lending, disclosure and compliance.

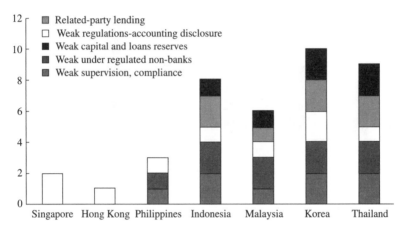

Source: Ramos (1997a).

control management. It is a cause because as owners gain control and wealth, they may also pursue both empire-building strategies and other benefits of control and excessive risk-taking behaviour. Morck, Shleifer and Vishny (1988) have found evidence of an inverted U-shape relationship between concentration and profitability. It is also a cause because large, presumably politically powerful, shareholders will try to delay improvements in disclosure and governance, as those may erode their control and insider benefits.

Asian firms are generally closely held and managed by majority, often family, interests, and there is some supporting empirical evidence of the problems associated with concentrated ownership. On average, excluding Korea, the three largest shareholders own some 50 per cent of the shares of the 10 largest non-financial private firms.[18] Alba, Claessens and Djankov (1998) found evidence of an inverted U-shape relationship between profitability and ownership in Thailand. They also found that between 1992 and 1996 the decline in profitability was sharper in the Thai firms with more concentrated ownership. This result may reflect that family owner/managers may be less able and/or willing than professional managers to change behaviour and adapt to changing circumstances. It may also reflect the desire to expand their businesses, frequently beyond efficient levels without more professional management. Finally, there is also anecdotal evidence of the strong resistance by large shareholders in Asia to improvements in corporate governance mechanisms

5.4.2 Weak market incentives

The incentives to improve disclosure and governance, either at the individual-firm or at the country level, were limited in many countries. Many firms had comfortable relations with banks and other financial intermediaries and were able to raise equity through new stock issues. This lack of market discipline appears caused by five factors:

- First, the interlocking ownership between financial intermediaries and corporates, as in Chile during the early 1980s, as well as other relationships played a role. Korea is a good example of how inter-relationships between banks and corporates reduced market discipline. In Thailand, Alba, Claessens and Djankov (1998) found a significant and strong relationship between ownership concentration and leverage, suggesting perhaps interlocking ownership between financial institutions and corporations.

- Second, the rapid and large increase in stock prices in the early 1990s throughout emerging Asia may have reduced the sensitivity of equity investors to company disclosure and governance.

- Third, the requirement in some countries for government approval of new equity issues (and their prices), government ownership and contingent government support (for example, in large infrastructure projects) may have also comforted investors.

- Fourth, there are few, well governed domestic institutional investors in the region. Privately managed institutional investors are rare and the large publicly controlled funds and investment banks have been mostly passive players in corporate matters.

- And, fifth, key market institutions that play a crucial role in facilitating and creating the incentives for market discipline to work in industrial countries are not fully developed in the region. Credit-rating agencies, for example, have only recently been introduced in many countries. The nascent regulatory framework further aggravated the lack of market institutions.

5.4.3 Protecting minority shareholders

The legal and regulatory systems of many countries in the region include a relatively wide set of provisions to protect shareholders from abuse by insiders. Table 1.12 (based on La Porta *et al.*, 1997, 1998) compares the investor and creditor protection in East Asia with other regions. The table shows that shareholder and creditor protection is stronger in Asia than in

Table 1.12 *Investor protection in Asia and Latin America*

	Investor Protection[a]	Creditor Protection[b]	Judicial Enforcement[c]		Investor Protection[a]	Creditor Protection[b]	Judicial Enforcement[c]
India	2	4	6.1	Argentina	4	1	5.6
Indonesia	2	4	4.4	Brazil	4	1	6.5
Malaysia	4	4	7.7	Chile	4	2	6.8
Pakistan	5	4	4.3	Colombia	1	0	5.7
Philippines	4	0	4.1	Mexico	0	0	6.0
Sri Lanka	2	3	5.0	Venezuela	1	—	6.2
Thailand	3	3	5.9	Average	2.2	0.8	6.1
Average	3.1	3.1	5.4				

Notes: [a] An index of how well the legal framework protects equity investors. It will equal 6 when (1) shareholders are allowed to vote by mail; (2) shareholders are not required to deposit share in advance of a meeting; (3) cumulative voting is allowed; (4) the minimum per centage of share capital required to call a meeting is less than 10 per cent; (5) an oppressed minority mechanism is in place; and (6) legislation mandates one vote per share for all shares (or equivalent).
[b] An index of how well the legal framework protects secured creditors. It will equal 4 when: (1) there are minimum restrictions (e.g. creditors' consent) for firms to file for reorganisation; (2) there is no automatic stay on collateral; (3) debtors lose control of the firm during a reorganisation; and (4) secured creditors are given priority during a reorganisation.
[c] An index measuring the quality of judicial enforcement ranging from 1 to 10 (best) equal to the average of five subindexes measuring: (1) efficiency of the judicial system; (2) rule of law; (3) corruption; (4) risk of expropriation; (5) risk of contract repudiation.
— Not available.
Source: La Porta *et al.* (1997, 1998).

Latin America. In enforcement of property rights, however, the region (especially Indonesia and the Philippines) scores much below Latin America, meaning that shareholders could not fully use their legal protecting mechanisms. Furthermore, weak disclosure meant that shareholders often did not have the information to judge corporate performance and insider behaviour.

5.4.4 Accounting standards and practices

Accounting and auditing standards in the region are generally consistent with those issued by the International Accounting Standards Committee,[19] and Malaysia and Thailand have strong reporting standards.[20] The Philippines' standards, however, appear weaker. There is strong anecdotal evidence, however, that accounting *practices* in the region were not yet up to international standards. Compliance with accounting rules was also hampered by weaknesses in industry self-regulatory organisations. In Indonesia, for instance, in the absence of strong professional associations, the official capital market regulatory agency licenses legal and accounting professionals to work in the securities areas. An additional problem has been a shortage of well qualified accountants and auditors, especially in Indonesia, the Philippines and Thailand. The impact of this shortage was compounded by restrictions on the activities of foreign accounting firms in many countries in the region (e.g. Indonesia).

6 Conclusions

This chapter has attempted to identify the key factors that led to the financial crisis in East Asia. In this, the chapter focuses primarily on domestic factors, although surges and the rapid withdrawal of international lending contributed to increased vulnerability and to the precipitation of the crisis. The chapter also does not focus on the dynamics of the onset and the deepening of the crisis, although many of the attributes that led to increased vulnerability were also responsible for making the crisis in East Asia more severe and protracted than originally anticipated.

The roots of increased vulnerability lie in East Asia's success in attracting private capital flows, based on strong macroeconomic fundamentals and structural reforms of the 1980s. In the initial phase, East Asia was quite successful in managing inflows so as to avoid increased vulnerability. In the more recent period, there was a shift in the pace and pattern of investment, and in the structure of financing, that led to a surprisingly rapid build-up of vulnerability. Investment rates rose from already very high levels, and were directed increasingly towards non-traded and potentially risky sectors, with evidence of falling productivity. Although domestic savings continued to provide the bulk of the financing, current account deficits widened, reaching quite high levels in some countries. More pertinently, there was a very heavy reliance on debt finance from domestic and foreign intermediaries, and in the most vulnerable cases, much of this was short-term and unhedged.

The chapter uses a simple analytical framework to argue that it was the reinforcing dynamics between macroeconomic policies and microeconomic policies and conditions in a more integrated setting that led to the build-up of vulnerability. Growing financial integration and the segmentation of domestic credit markets acted as a magnifier of domestic macroeconomic cycles. Against this backdrop, three key domestic factors contributed:

• First, although macroeconomic policies generally remained prudent throughout this period, the macroeconomic policy mix used to moderate excess demand pressures, arising in part from large capital inflows, accentuated incentives for excessive borrowing, and for the accumulation of short-term and unhedged liabilities in particular.

- Second, financial sector weaknesses – including implicit guarantees, weak institutional capacity and poor lending practices – combined with inappropriate financial sector liberalisation and ineffective regulation, led to excessive and risky lending and generally poor management of balance sheet risks by both banks and non-bank financial intermediaries.

- Third, poor governance and disclosure on the part of corporates, and implicit and explicit guarantees of private and public enterprises on the part of government, fuelled excessive borrowing and lending. These domestic factors were abetted by inadequate due diligence and risk pricing by foreign lenders, and investor-herding during the boom period. All of these factors reinforced each other through macro-financial linkages, and cumulatively added to growing macroeconomic and financial vulnerability.

As a result, the countries that were eventually prone to crisis, became vulnerable in three ways: (1) increased banking sector fragility associated with lending and asset booms and rising exposure to risky sectors; (2) high leverage both at the economywide level and in many individual firms; and (3) currency and maturity mismatches that left some economies highly vulnerable to reversals in capital flows. These weaknesses were inadequately recognised prior to the loss of investor confidence, in part because of poor disclosure and transparency, but also because of the euphoria of the boom period. These structural weaknesses, however, meant that these countries were highly vulnerable to sharp reversals in capital flows, and that these reversals could have large and devastating effects on the balance sheets of financial institutions and corporates. In turn, these losses led to large increases in government contingent liabilities, and a potential downward spiral.

NOTES
Revision of a paper presented at the CEPR/World Bank conference: 'Financial Crises: Contagion and Market Volatility' (London, 8–9 May). We would like to thank Peter Montiel and Michael Pomerleano for very useful contributions, Michael Dooley, the discussant, and seminar participants for comments. This chapter draws on and extends the analysis in the joint World Bank–ADB study: *Managing Global Financial Integration In Asia: Emerging Lessons and Prospective Challenges* (March 1998). The opinions expressed do not necessarily reflect those of the World Bank or of the Central Bank of Chile.
   1. Eichengreen and Mody (1998), for example, find that observable issuer characteristics do not fully explain changes over time in the volume and spreads of

new bond issues. Similarly, Cline and Barnes (1997) show that spreads for emerging markets fell more after the Mexico crisis than can be explained by improvements in fundamentals and improved international ratings.

2. Fiscal adjustment took place later in the Philippines.
3. Regressions of the determinants of private capital flows to Indonesia and Thailand, for example, find that, in addition to differentials between domestic and foreign interest rates, domestic macroeconomic variables – such as GDP growth, export growth and low inflation – are statistically very significant.
4. The relationship between monetary tightening and sterilisation and short-term capital inflows is also borne out empirically in cross-country analysis (see, for example, Montiel and Reinhart, 1999).
5. Although 'sterilised' interventions are often taken to refer solely to open-market operations (OMOs), we are referring here to the tightening of monetary policy in response to an accumulation of net foreign assets in the central bank – whether through OMOs or by other means.
6. Prepayment was also used as a means of reducing the net inflows of capital and domestic over-heating problems.
7. The fiscal impulse is analysed with respect to non-oil fiscal balance and demand pressures in the non-oil sector.
8. The effective pegging to the US dollar did not in fact, *ex post*, prevent an appreciation of Indonesia's real exchange rates during 1995–6, because there were large cross-currency movements between the US dollar and the currencies of their other trading partners (notably Japan) during the period.
9. Kaminsky and Reinhart (1996) confirm this finding for a wider set of countries.
10. The net financing gain in unclear, however, as it depends on the degree of substitutability: if foreign or domestic investment simply moves from the domestic market to the offshore market, there will be no net financing gain and only a loss of tax and regulatory coverage.
11. See also Kawai and Iwatsubo (1998).
12. Tier 1 capital includes issued and paid-up share capital, non-cumulative preferred stock and disclosed reserves from post-tax retained earnings. Tier 2 capital can include a range of other items such as undisclosed reserves that have passed through the profit and loss account, conservatively valued revaluation reserves, revaluation of equities held at historical cost (at a discount), some hybrid debt instruments, general loan loss reserves (up to 1.25 per cent of risk-weighted assets) and subordinated term debt.
13. See Gavin and Hausmann (1996).
14. Non-performing loans are measured as a share of total loans.
15. See World Bank (1997).
16. Although some classification guidelines in the region state that in all instances the judgement of the examiners supersedes the time-delinquency classifications, there is a concern regarding the underlying credit analysis going into the classifications.

In contrast, the US regulatory agencies classify corporate and commercial loans in a more judgemental way based on four different categories which correspond to levels of risk: Loans 'Especially Mentioned', Substandard, Doubtful and Loss. Loans Especially Mentioned include loans which do not warrant being classified as Substandard but which are potentially weak as a result of lack of collateral, credit information or documentation. Loans may be included on this list if repayment may be endangered by economic or market conditions affecting the borrower or if the borrower is facing economic or financial difficulties and likely to have repayment problems. 'Substandard' loans are loans which are believed present a substantial and unreasonable degree of risk, although a loan should not be classified as Substandard if repayment seems reasonably assured. Substandard loans should have a definitive weakness that jeopardises repayment, such as adverse financial, management, economic or political conditions affecting the borrower or a significant weakness in collateral. 'Doubtful' loans are those loans or portions of loans which would normally be classified as Substandard but additional characteristics exist which make collection highly improbable. For partly secured loans that otherwise would have been classified as Substandard, the portion of such loan which is unsecured would be classified as Doubtful (split classification). 'Loss' loans are loans or portions of loans which are considered non-collectable or worthless and of such little value that it is not practical to defer writing-off the loan even though partial recovery may be possible.

17. In the USA it has been established that irresponsible appraisals contributed to the asset bubble of the late 1980s. As a result, in a movement to regulate the appraisal profession, the Financial Institutions Reform, Recovery and Enforcement Act of 1989 (FIRREA), authorised each state to certify, license, and supervise real-estate appraisers within its jurisdiction. Furthermore, starting in January 1993, FIRREA required all federally regulated financial institutions to use state licensed or certified real-estate appraisers, as appropriate, to perform appraisals in federally related transactions.

18. Not corrected for shareholder affiliation and cross-shareholding between firms (see further La Porta *et. al.*, 1998). In Korea, *chaebols* dominated their groups through interlocking ownership between firms.

19. Malaysia, for instance, has adopted 24 of the 31 International Accounting Standards (IASs) without alteration, while the others are generally consistent with international standards (World Bank, 1997).

20. The Center for International Analysis and Research is an investment advisor located in the USA. The index is based on the reporting practices of major domestic corporates with regard to 85 disclosure variables.

REFERENCES

Akerlof, G. and P. Romer (1993). 'Looting: The Economic Underworld of Bankruptcy for Profit', *Brookings Papers on Economic Activity*, **2**, 1–73

Alba, P., S. Claessens and S. Djankov (1998). 'Thailand's Corporate Financing and Governance Structures: Impact on Firms' Competitiveness', *Policy and Research Working Paper* **0**, The World Bank (November)

Asian Development Bank and World Bank (1998). 'Managing Global Financial Integration In Asia: Emerging Lessons and Prospective Challenges', 10–12 March

Blanchard, O. and M. Watson (1982). 'Bubbles, Rational Expectations and Financial Markets', in P. Wachtel (ed.), *Crises in the Economic and Financial Structure*, Lexington: Lexington Books

Claessens, S. and T. Glaessner (1997). *'Are Financial Sector Weaknesses Undermining the East Asian Miracle?'*, *Directions in Development*, World bank (September)

(1998). 'Internationalisation of Financial Services in Asia', *Working Paper*, **1911**, World Bank

Claessens, S., S. Djankov and L. Lang (1998). 'East Asian Corporates: Growth, Financing and Risks over the Last Decade', World Bank (September), mimeo

Claessens, S. A. Demirgüç-Kunt and H. Huizinga (1997) 'How Does Foreign Entry Affect the Domestic Banking Market?', *Policy and Research Working Paper*, **1918**, Washington, DC: World Bank

Cline, W. R. and N. J. S. Barnes (1997). 'Spreads and Risk in Emerging Market Lending', *Research Paper*, **97–1** (December), Washington, DC: Institute of International Finance

Corbo, V. and L. Hernandez (1996). 'Macroeconomic Adjustment to Capital Flows: Lessons from Recent Latin American and East Asian Experience', *The World Bank Research Observer*, **11(1)** (February): 61–85

Corsetti, G., P. Pesenti and N. Roubini (1998), 'What Caused the Asian Currency and Financial Crisis?', New York University, mimeo

Cumby, R. and M. Obstfeld (1981). 'Capital Mobility and the Scope for Sterilisation: Mexico in the 1970s', *National Bureau of Economic Research Working Paper*, **770** (September): 1–10

Demigüç-Kunt, A. and H. Huizinga (1997) 'Determinants of Commercial Bank Interest Margins and Profitability: Some International Evidence', *Policy and Research Working Paper*, **1990**, Washington, DC: World Bank

Eichengreen, B., and A. Mody (1998). 'What Explains Changing Spreads on Emerging-Market Debt: Fundamentals or Market Sentiment?', IMF and World Bank, paper prepared for NBER conference 'Capital Inflows to Emerging Markets', (20–21 February 1998), mimeo; printed in S. Edwards (ed.), *The Economics of International Capital Flows*, Chicago: University of Chicago Press (1998), and *NBER Working paper*, **6408**

Feldstein, M. (1998). 'Refocusing the IMF', *Foreign Affairs*, **77** (March–April): 20–33

Gavin, D. and R. Hausmann (1996). 'The Roots of Banking Crises: The Macoreconomic Context', in R. Hausmann and L. Rojas-Suarez (eds.), *Banking Crises in Latin America*, Baltimore, Johns Hopkins University Press

IMF (1997) *World Economic Outlook*, Washington, DC: IMF (December)

Kawai, M. and K. Iwatsubo (1998). 'The Thai Financial System and the Baht Crisis: Processes, Causes and Lessons', Institute of Social Science, University of Tokyo, mimeo

Kaminsky, G., and C. Reinhart (1996). 'The Twin Crises: The Causes of Banking and Balance-of-payments Problems', *International Finance Discussion Paper*, **544**, Board of Governors of the Federal Reserve System

Krugman, P. (1979). 'A Model of Balance-of-payments Crises', *Journal of Money, Credit and Banking*, **11**: 311–25

(1998). 'Firesale FDI', MIT, paper prepared for NBER conference 'Capital Inflows to Emerging Markets', mimeo

La Porta, R., F. Lopez-de-Silanes, A. Shleifer, and R. W. Vishny (1997). 'Legal Determinants of External Finance', *Journal of Finance*, **52(3)** (July)

(1998). 'Law and Finance', *Journal of Political Economy*, **106** (December): 1113–55

McKinnon, R. I. and H. Pill (1997). 'Credible Liberalisations and International Capital Flows: The Over-Borrowing Syndrome', *American Economic Review, Papers and Proceedings*, **87(2)**: (May): 189–93

Montes, M. F. (1998). *The Currency Crisis in South East Asia*, Singapore: Institute of South East Asian Studies

Monteil, P. and C. Reinhart (1999). 'The Dynamics of Capital Movements to Emerging Economies During the 1990s' in S. Griffith-Jones, M. Montes and A. Nasution (eds.), *Short-term Capital Movements and Economic Crises*, Oxford: Oxford University Press

Morck, R., A. Shleifer and R. W. Vishny (1988). 'Management Ownership and Market Valuation', *Journal of Financial Economics* **20**: 237–65

Pomerleano, M. L. (1998). 'The East Asia Crisis and Corporate Finances', World Bank (August), mimeo

Radelet, S. and J. Sachs (1998a). 'The Onset of the East Asian Financial Crisis', updated, 30 March

(1998b). 'The East Asian Financial Crisis: Diagnosis, Remedies, Prospects', *Brookings Papers on Economic Activity*, Panel, Washington, D.C., 26–27 March, 1998

Ramos, R. (1997a). 'Asian Banks at Risk: Solidity, Fragility', *Banking Research*, Goldman-Sachs (September)

(1997b). '1998: Issues and Outlook: Cyclical Slowdowns, Structural Ills and the Odds for Recovery', *Banking Research*, Goldman Sachs (December)

Sachs, J., A. Tornell and A. Velasco (1996). 'Financial Crises in Emerging Markets: The Lessons from 1995', *Brookings Papers in Economic Activity*, **1**: 147–214

Sarel, M. (1997). 'Growth and Productivity in ASEAN Countries', *IMF Working Paper*, **WP/97/97**

World Bank (1997). *Private Capital Flows to Developing Countries*, Washington, DC: World Bank

(1998). *Global Development Finance*, Washington, DC: World Bank

Discussion
Sule Ozler

I congratulate the authors of chapter 1 on their taxonomy of the Asian crises. They make a very complete coverage of the nature and sources of vulnerabilities in the East Asian countries that have experienced the most recent financial crisis. In most discussions of international financial crises

– the present as well as the historical – a central debate concerns whether the crises are due to domestic or external factors. Conclusions often lean in the direction of a crisis being generated as a consequence of a combination of domestic as well external factors, but opinions differ on their relative importance. In their chapter 1, the authors deny that they are undertaking any discussion of international aspects of the crisis. Instead, the chapter is an attempt to identify the nature and the sources of vulnerabilities in the East Asian economies.

Having narrowed the focus to an analysis of domestic factors leaves the task of identifying which domestic factors were behind the crisis. Historical experience and economic theory tell us that short-term macroeconomic policies, as much as structural microeconomic attributes, institutional setting and inevitably their interaction deserve attention. The chapter starts with the assertion that 'the build-up of financial vulnerabilities in East Asia was associated with reinforcing dynamics between capital flows, macro policies and weak financial and corporate sector institutions.' Put this way, I find very little to disagree with the authors' analysis, and find that they present a highly informative and valuable overview.

The build-up of vulnerabilities is deemed to have led to three key weaknesses in East Asia: an increase in banking fragility prior to the crisis; a vulnerable corporate structure caused by increased leverage, among other causes; and an increase in maturity mismatches. The macroeconomic policy mix gets some of the blame in the build-up of these weaknesses for having led to an increased flow of foreign capital in the wake of domestic overheating. These weaknesses are argued to be due to the presence of implicit insurance of the financial system by the government, specific institutional changes which encouraged foreign inflows (such as the creation of offshore financial centres that had regulatory and tax advantages over domestic markets), a weak regulatory institutional framework concerning financial institutions, lack of transparency on bank conditions and finally weak corporate governance.

A voluminous amount has been written on the East Asian crisis: its origins, its typology and the interactions between domestic and external factors. All this leaves one wondering what features of this crisis distinguish it from others and why academic economists are so surprised and think that there are new lessons to be learned. The authors, consistent with the consensus view, identify the distinguishing features of this crisis to be weaknesses in domestic financial systems and destabilising liberalisation processes. In other words, the crisis does not have its roots in government improvidence but involves the private sector, and is much more microeconomic than macroeconomic. Furthermore, the fundamentals of Asian economies were different in that high levels of investment were supported by high levels of national savings preceding the surge of international capital.

Nevertheless, the timing and sequence of liberalisation has long been under debate. Many prominent and influential economists have argued that capital account liberalisation should follow not only fiscal prudence but also domestic financial liberalisation and an appropriate regulatory framework. In particular since the early 1990s, most economists and international organisations have advocated government intervention in building market-friendly development strategies. The question has not been about whether governments should intervene, but about how much, when, and where. It is widely recognised today that economies of a large set of countries, especially those in the developing world, are riddled with various sorts of market imperfections. Hence the solution for the difficulties of the Asian economies is sought not only in short-term macroeconomic reforms but also in long term microeconomic changes and institutional reforms. It is also recognised since the dismal social consequences of the Latin American adjustment programmes that followed the commercial bank debt crisis of the 1980s that improving the quality of social safety nets increases the long-term economic return of development strategies. Reform programmes that hamper human development and political stability have proven to be unsustainable.

Overall, then chapter 1 does an excellent job in giving an overview of the interplay between macro policies, the domestic financial sector and corporate governance in Asian economies in making them vulnerable to crisis. The lessons to be learned from this taxonomy are not new: these issues have been known to economists for a long time and have been discussed in the context of the operation of financial markets. The key fact of life today is that changes in information and communications technology have given rise to highly mobile capital. The speed with which high levels of capital cross borders makes the task of knowing when and how much to adjust a lot harder, and regulation of these flows very necessary. Not only domestic institutions in developing countries, but also international institutions, need reform to rise to the task of adjustment in today's global economy.

2 The Asian crisis: lessons from the collapse of financial systems, exchange rates and macroeconomic policy

JENNY CORBETT AND DAVID VINES

1 Introduction

The East Asian financial crisis plunged the most rapidly growing and successful economies in the world into financial chaos and deep depression. At the time of writing, 18 months from its onset, neither the events themselves nor the appropriate policy responses are properly understood; but the outlines of a picture are becoming clear.

We see the Asian crisis – as many others do – as the outcome of a flawed process of financial liberalisation. But the trouble with that diagnosis is that it has often been served up accompanied by a rather loose list of mistakes, and buttressed by no very clear argument. Accordingly, the question which we set ourselves is a precise one: why was the crisis so bad?[1] In other words, why did 'crisis' turn into 'collapse'?[2] Our answer to this question is that it was because of the inter-relationship between currency crises and financial crisis. Our argument proceeds in four stages, which are set out schematically in figure 2.1.

(1) We argue that *vulnerability* was created *both* by liberalisation in the presence of a bank-based financial regime (which contained implicit promises of bail-out if its balance sheet deteriorated), and by liberalisation in the presence of a monetary policy regime based on pegged exchange rates (which led to boom and bust). These vulnerabilities were interconnected, and led to a risk of currency and financial collapse (levels 1 and 2 in figure 2.1).

(2) *Negative shocks* precipitated *both* financial crisis and currency crisis. They imposed significant losses on the financial system which, because of its vulnerability, triggered obligations for the government to bail out the financial sector. They also precipitated currency devaluation in the face of the vulnerability to currency crisis (levels 3 and 4 in figure 2.1).

67

Figure 2.1   *Inter-relationship between currency crises and financial crisis: the four stages of currency collapse*

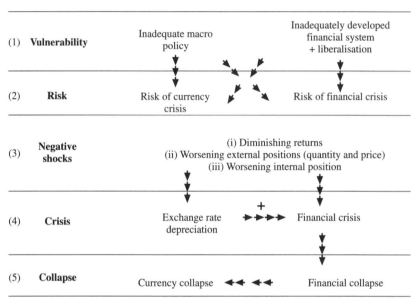

Source: Corbett and Vines (October 1999).

(3) *Collapse* resulted from the interaction of a currency and a financial crisis. The critical linkage was that currency depreciation led to a worsening of financial crisis. This was because of the particular feature to which the fixed exchange rate regime had led – massive unhedged borrowing in foreign currency. Devaluation became sufficiently large that those who had lent to the financial system came to believe that government guarantees to it could not be honoured, and this triggered financial collapse. The resulting fears of sovereign insolvency in turn led to currency collapse (level 5 in figure 2.1).

(4) *Macroeconomic policy making* then disintegrated[3] because policy makers failed to treat the right problem. They applied rather conventional policies appropriate for macroeconomic imbalances, instead of the policies which would have been appropriate for financial and currency collapse.

We have written this chapter, and we wrote our earlier account (Corbett and Vines, 1999) because we were not satisfied with the accounts of the crisis which become available early on. Krugman has offered two different insights, first suggesting that the crisis was due to 'Panglossian' over-investment (a 'fundamentals' explanation, see Krugman, 1998a), and then suggesting that panic might have been important (a 'non-fundamentals' explanation, see Krugman 1998b, 1998c), without offering any very clear guidance on how to choose between them. Radelet and Sachs (1998) list five possible ways of understanding the crisis: as a macroeconomic policy-induced crisis (which includes currency crisis as a category), as financial panic, as bubble collapse, as moral hazard crisis and as 'disorderly work-out'. Although the authors come down firmly on the side of financial panic and disorderly work-out, they also argue that all of the crisis features 'may in fact be intertwined in any particular historical episode', and yet they never give a clear indication of how this 'intertwining' is meant to work. Corsetti, Pesenti and Roubini (1998) believe that there is a choice between fundamentals-based explanations (citing Krugman, 1998a) and financial panic-based explanations (citing Radelet and Sachs, 1998); they opt for the former, but it is not at all clear why. (See also Corsetti, Pesenti and Roubini, Chapter 4 in this volume).

There are, however, a number of analyses now available which point in a similar direction to ours. Chapter 1 in this volume (Alba *et al.*, 1999), provides a very helpful overall account of what happened, and reaches a conclusion rather like our own, but does so less formally. Indeed their chapter, which mobilises the ample research resources of the World Bank, may be read as providing an incredibly useful empirical buttressing of the necessarily less well documented claims in the present chapter. Chang and Velasco (1997) provide a formal model which shares a number of the features which we emphasise. Eichengreen (1999) presents proposals for the reform of the global financial architecture which are motivated by an analysis very like our own. And there are similarities, too, with the chapter on the 'Asian Financial Crisis' to be found in Soros (1998).

The layout of the chapter is as follows. Sections 2–4 argue that the Asian economies were vulnerable to *financial crises* and to *currency crises*. Section 5 argues that the reason for *collapse* was the particular way in which currency crisis and financial crisis became intertwined and caused *both financial and currency collapse*. Section 6 shows how this twin collapse led to a *disintegration in macroeconomic policy making,* because policy makers applied policies which were inappropriate for currency and financial collapse. Sections 7 and 8 discuss, in the light of our analysis of collapse, the critical unresolved issue for global financial architecture: the lack of a mechanism for debt work-outs. A final section, section 9, places our analysis in historical perspective.

2 Vulnerability

The concept of 'vulnerability' is central to our account of the Asian crisis. It is an idea which is intrinsically non-linear. Dornbusch makes its meaning vividly, if imprecisely, clear when he says '[v]ulnerability means that if something goes wrong, then suddenly a lot goes wrong' (Dornbusch, 1997, p. 21). But vulnerability turns out to be an idea which is surprisingly difficult to pin down.

In this chapter we adopt a multiple-equilibrium interpretation. Seminal analyses are to be found in Diamond and Dybvig (1983) and Obstfeld (1986, 1991, 1994, 1995). These papers analyse, respectively, bank runs and exchange rate crises and use very different kinds of analysis to analyse these two different problems. But they share the generic idea that one can locate vulnerability in multiple equilibria. More than this, they locate the multiple equilibrium in the following 'problem': if participants in some shared activity (being bank depositors, or holders of a currency) expect a good outcome (no bank run, no currency crisis) then they may do things which bring this good outcome about. But if they expect a bad outcome (bank run, currency collapse) then they may do things which bring that about. In these generically similar accounts, vulnerability consists in the possibility that the economy may flip from the good equilibrium to the bad one.[4]

3 Asian vulnerabilities

We believe that, in Asia, vulnerability to crisis was created in two different ways, both a consequence of insufficient institutional development in the region during the 'miracle' boom period. The first kind of vulnerability was created by the continuation, into the era of liberalisation, of a financial system containing implicit guarantees. The second kind of vulnerability was created by the continuation, into the era of liberalisation, of a macroeconomic policy based around fixed exchange rates.

3.1 Finance

3.1.1 The vulnerability in Asian underdeveloped financial systems

Vulnerability was created in Asia by liberalisation of both trade and finance in the presence of an unreformed financial system. The previous financial system in Asia was designed for the channelling of domestic savings into investment and growth, largely through the banking system. It appears that much of the investment was covered by guarantees, either implicit or explicit.[5] The process of credit allocation appears to have involved extension of bank loans, often under state direction, the collateral for which often appears to have been little more than expected revenue growth, or even just the name of the borrower. Many firms were very highly geared, and banks were thus highly vulnerable to a revenue downturn; in aggregate the whole of the financial system was similarly vulnerable. In countries experiencing very rapid growth the risks of such a downturn were probably heavily discounted. But – importantly here – it appears that the financial system was implicitly guaranteed against these risks, as a quid pro quo of its acceptance of state direction of finance. This was essentially a financial system in which corporate finance was managed through a guaranteed banking system with the purpose of channelling of domestic credit to domestic firms.

Liberalisation had two effects on this financial system:

- First, it *increased the return on capital*. Pre-liberalisation economies can be characterised as capital-scarce, low-wage economies in which the risk-adjusted productivity of capital is initially low, even although capital is scarce. As a result, returns to investment are low and investment is low. But reforming and opening changes this. The process involves putting in place sound macroeconomic policies, which provide a guarantee of stability. This reduces the risk premium on investment.[6] Furthermore, the process of trade liberalisation can lead to an increase in the rate of return on capital – although the economy specialises in exports of labour-intensive manufactures – as a result of achieving economies of scale in production for world markets, and as a result of technology transfer into the liberalising economy.

- Second, it meant that investment, which became less risky and more profitable, could be *financed from abroad*. The mistake, which led to the vulnerability of the financial system, appears to be that the guarantees of the old-style financial system continued to be extended to much of the foreign-financed investment. This had the implication that the stock of implicit guarantees to the financial system rose markedly. Accounts of what happened in the region suggest that financial intermediaries systematically downplayed the risks associated in the expansion of their balance sheets in this manner.

This is the world which Krugman described in his by-now-famous account, released on the Web very early into the crisis (Krugman, 1998a). He argued that the problem with such financial intermediaries – institutions whose liabilities were perceived as having an implicit government guarantee – is that they were subject to severe moral hazard problems. In his analysis such intermediaries will 'almost always' require a bail-out (see below). For our purposes, we actually need to say less than this, merely that continuation of this form of financial system created guarantees which, if optimistic expectations were not fulfilled, would need to be honoured.[7] If the amount of these guarantees were to become too large then there was a risk that they could not be honoured. More precisely, the risk was that governments would trade off the cost to them of honouring the guarantees against the cost of not doing so, and would choose the latter (or would do so once the first few had been honoured) either because raising the necessary tax revenue became too costly or because risk premia would rise in international markets, forcing up the cost of honouring them. Economies then became vulnerable to the risk of a financial collapse: losses to the asset side of the balance sheet of the financial system so large that the government becomes unable – or unwilling – to cover them.

3.1.2 The risk of financial collapse

We now explain this risk in more detail. Krugman's paper presented to the world his idea of 'Pangloss over-investment'. He suggested that we think of a representative Asian country as having a downward-sloping demand curve for capital, and facing a given world interest rate. He then proposed that we model Asian 'crony capitalism' as government guarantees which ensure bail-outs for investments that make losses. In the absence of such guarantees, investors would add to the capital stock to the point where the marginal product of capital had fallen to the world interest rate. But in the presence of guarantees, investors would over-invest, to the point where the marginal product of capital *in the best state of the world* had fallen to the world interest rate. The reason for this is that unexploited profit opportunities would remain if investment was not pushed this far: in a bad state of the world investors would stand to lose nothing (because of the bail-out provision), but in a good state investors would make profits in excess of their interest obligations.

This clear and simple idea was the central contribution of the Krugman paper.[8] There is one big problem with it: that is that it does not help us to understand the Asian collapse. Pangloss over-investment is quite consistent with an equilibrium in which crony capitalism continues on its merry way. There *are* financial crises; one occurs whenever a firm owned by a crony goes bust. But, as long as taxpayers go on paying for the bail-outs to the cronies, then the system can continue for a long time, and possibly forever.

In a prescient paper presented in late 1993 (Dooley, 1994, included in a revised form as chapter 3 in this volume, see Dooley, 1999a), Michael Dooley supplied the missing link. He argued that the Asian miracle was – as the above story suggests – organised theft by international investors, but also that it might end in tears. Dooley suggested that Asian governments had set themselves up to pay out on the kind of guarantees which Krugman later described (although he did not specify the downward-sloping demand for capital as Krugman later did). But – in addition – he suggested that the amount available for such payouts was limited, and that adjustment costs would mean that investors could not steal the money straight away. In the end, but not immediately, he reasoned, investors would find a way to set up enough projects with negative expected returns to enable them to walk away with the state's capacity to pay out rewards. When that happened, there would be a crisis.

Irwin and Vines (1999) show how the ideas of Krugman and Dooley – taken together – can lead to a story of financial collapse. There are Krugman-style investors. There is a government with a limited capacity (or willingness) to pay up on guarantees if things go bad. They model stochastic shocks in the environment – as Krugman implicitly suggested was necessary – in order to capture the idea that the arrival of a negative external shock is an essential part of the story of the Asia crisis.[9] The Krugman investors have rational expectations; they thus understand the government's problem, and they build a risk premium into the price at which they lend to the country. (They do this because, as Dooley suggests, there is a probability that the government will not be able or willing to bail them out.)

In such a setup it is possible to describe the evolution of the financial crises in Asia as follows. Initially there were no guarantees, and investment was risky to investors. As a result, the initial level of the capital stock was low. In the mid-to-late 1980s Asian governments began offering implicitly to bail out people whose investments went wrong. This means that at the given world interest rate the expected average profitability of investment rose (after allowing for the fact that bail-outs would cushion losses). As a result capital accumulated, moving towards Krugman's 'Pangloss' equilibrium, at which point the marginal product in the best state of the world would be equal to the world interest rate.[10]

It is possible that this 'Pangloss equilibrium' could have been the long-run equilibrium of the system: if the government was able – or willing – to afford all of the losses which would be incurred in bad states. Alternatively if this implicit fiscal obligation became too large, rational foreign lenders might have built a premium into the interest rate which they demanded over and above the world interest rate; as a result the long-run equilibrium of the capital stock would have been less high. Irwin and Vines characterise the long-run equilibrium of the resulting system, showing how it depends on the willingness to bail out and other parameters.

Vulnerability in such a system arises as follows. Because of the short-run inflexibility of the stock of capital – owing to adjustment costs – there is the following multiple-equilibrium problem. The economy has at any point of time a particular stock of capital, and in the good equilibrium, the interest rate is equal to the world rate. Suppose that the economy experiences a negative productivity shock, but that the government can afford to pay the guarantees: there is then no risk of default, which is why the interest rate can be in equilibrium at the low world level. However, there may also be another bad equilibrium with a much higher interest rate. At such a high interest rate there are a range of productivity shocks bad enough to provoke an inability on the part of the government to pay up on its guarantees, and so to provoke a crisis. This is why this high interest rate can be an equilibrium. Thus in this setup there is a short-run 'bank-run' problem. With low interest rates no productivity shock can be bad enough to cause the government not to pay up on its guarantees. But with high interest rates it is much more difficult for the government to pay up on its guarantees, so the probability of not being able to do so is much greater, thus validating the risk premium which is the reason for the high interest rate. Thus this model has a self-fulfilling multiple-equilibrium property. The reason for this is because of the endogeneity of the risk premium on loans to the country. This enters non-linearly into the model, in such a way as to give the possibility of two equilibria.[11]

3.2 Currency

3.2.1 The vulnerability of Asian fixed exchange rate systems

Vulnerability was created in Asia by liberalisation of both trade and finance and the rapid growth which this caused, in the presence of a monetary policy regime based on pegged exchange rates. At the time, the dangers involved were not understood. This is illustrated by a paper on Thailand published by the IMF in 1990 (Robinson *et al.*, 1990) which described – with admiration – how Thailand's macroeconomic framework had been jointly based upon a fixed nominal exchange rate (to provide the necessary nominal anchor) and fiscal prudence (to make room for its export-led expansion). Such a strategy, it was said, had served Thailand very well through to the late 1980s, and had been the basis for behaviour which was regarded as little short of miraculous. Praise for this strategy was strongly echoed in an IMF paper published as late as December 1996 (Kochar, Dicks-Mireaux and Horvath, 1996).

Yet it now appears that this macroeconomic strategy was entirely inadequate for the 1990s, both for Thailand and elsewhere. In our view this strategy, which might have served Asian countries well in the past, ceased to do so for two reasons. Again we consider the Thai example, but the points are relevant to the other Asia crisis countries as well.

- The first reason is well known. The textbook Mundell–Fleming model shows that the trilogy of fixed exchange rates, autonomous national monetary policy and open international capital markets is inconsistent.[12] What had happened in the decade between 1985 and 1995 was the *opening of Thai capital markets to capital inflows*. Nevertheless, the Thai authorities tried to damp the boom in the first part of the 1990s by raising interest rates, even though the Thai baht was pegged to the dollar. The effect was to stimulate capital inflow, as Thai companies and banks borrowed abroad at lower dollar interest rates, and to leave the economy with a large outstanding stock of unhedged foreign debt, without succeeding in dampening the boom in the economy. Such a policy may even have fuelled the boom: with credit constraints within the domestic economy, higher interest rates on domestic credit actually encouraged financial intermediaries to borrow abroad and to increase the supply of lending.[13] Similar errors appear to have been made in Indonesian and Korean macroeconomic policy, although to a lesser extent. It appears that policy authorities were continuing to use an approach to monetary policy which was appropriate only to the earlier period of much lower capital mobility.

- The second reason is less well understood and is to do with fiscal policy. In Thailand, the fiscal stance appeared, by conventional deficit measures, to be very tight. A budgetary law, which constrained any year's fiscal expenditure to lie within a small margin above the previous year's tax revenue, prevented the emergence of fiscal deficits, and from the late 1980s produced small surpluses of 2 or 3 per cent of GDP because revenue was growing so rapidly (see Warr and Nidhiprabha, 1996). Yet fiscal balance, or even surpluses of this size, may be an insufficiently restrictive policy when a country experiences a large boom, if monetary policy is *immobilised by a fixed exchange rate*.

The experience of Thailand and of other Asian countries in the past decade has shown that a large boom is precisely what one would expect at a time of liberalisation.[14] We have already described how a liberalising economy is likely to experience a large investment boom; but it is also likely to cause a consumption boom, because liberalisation characteristically involves the removal of liquidity constraints.[15] Thus an overall boom in demand is the particular problem which macroeconomic management is likely to face in an emerging, liberalising, economy. It is our view that the inflexibility of monetary policy imposed by a fixed exchange rate is dangerous in these circumstances, especially if fiscal policy is inadequately contractionary.

The way in which this can lead to macroeconomic vulnerability has been documented by Warr (1998) and Warr and Vines (1999) for the case of Thailand. Warr shows how the boom which preceded the crisis was not choked off by an appreciating exchange rate precisely because of the exchange rate peg. He then argues that the consequence of this boom was that cost price increases were unchecked, making the export sector increasingly uncompetitive. This is an intrinsically sequential story. It suggests that, under fixed exchange rates and inflexible monetary policy, there will be an excessive investment boom (and perhaps also consumption boom) in an initial phase, and that the consequences will be an erosion of the profitability of the investment projects in a subsequent phase.[16] It seems plausible that this argument applies in the other Asian countries, at least in part.

With a commitment to a fixed exchange rate the difficulties which emerge in the period following the boom cannot be alleviated by means of subsequent currency depreciation if the value of the currency peg is to be maintained. In this subsequent phase the economy becomes vulnerable to a currency crisis, particularly in the face of exogenous shocks. It is thus possible to say that the maintenance of a fixed exchange rate rendered the Asia Pacific economies vulnerable to a currency crisis in the face of any significant worsening of the external environment. [17]

3.2.2 The risk of exchange rate crisis

We now explain this vulnerability to currency crisis in more detail.

The currency crisis literature descends from Krugman (1979). The original canonical Krugman model describes a balance of payments crisis in which a loss of foreign exchange reserves leads to a collapse of a pegged exchange rate and currency depreciation. This arises when domestic credit expansion by the central bank is inconsistent with the pegged exchange rate. The credit expansion results from the monetisation of budget deficits; foreign exchange reserves fall gradually until the central bank is vulnerable to a sudden run, which exhausts the remaining reserves and pushes the economy to a floating rate. This original Krugman model was a fundamentals model – the fundamental which caused the crisis was domestic credit. Subsequent developments of this type of model (e.g. Masson, 1998) treat the fundamental which causes reserves to fall as a shock to exports hitting the trade balance.

Such models can be generalised so as to have self-fulfilling possibilities, and so can describe situations of vulnerability. For example the Masson

(1998) model also incorporates foreign indebtedness, which raises the possibility of a risk that reserves will run out, leading to a risk premium on this debt, a rise in the interest rate which must be paid on it and so to a further fall in reserves and to an increased likelihood of crisis. Feedbacks of this kind are what enable these models to describe the effects of vulnerability: the possibility of self-fulfilling crisis outcomes in which a switch from a non-crisis outcome to a crisis can happen independently of any change in the fundamentals.

The operation of these currency-crisis models depends fundamentally, however, on a reserve constraint. They are unable to answer the question: how can a crisis arise in a world of very high capital mobility? This is the relevant question for the Asia crisis. The second-generation models of Obstfeld answer this challenge. In those models, currency crisis arises because of conflict between the macroeconomic policy objectives of government and the maintenance of a fixed exchange rate. (See Obstfeld 1986, 1991, 1994, 1995; Ozkan and Sutherland 1993, 1994, 1995; Davies and Vines, 1998). Such models enable one to understand the kinds of problems which can arise with open international capital markets – when it is not the case that the government actually runs out of reserves. Instead, the models focus on the fact that a fixed exchange rate constitutes a constraint on macroeconomic policy which is abandoned when the constraint becomes too costly for policy makers to sustain it. For example, a negative shock to aggregate demand can cause a recession so deep that it is optimal for a government to depart from a fixed exchange rate, even although it will lose credibility by doing so.

These models also describe circumstances of vulnerability. In them, fear that a fixed currency peg will be abandoned can lead to a risk premium being attached to holding the currency, with the consequence that interest rates rise, thus making the maintenance of a fixed exchange rate all the more costly. This feature can enable these models to produce self-fulfilling crisis outcomes, in which a switch from a non-crisis outcome to a crisis can actually be induced by a rise in the risk premium associated with the fear that this might happen.

3.3 Interconnection between the types of vulnerability

It appears that in Asia these two forms of vulnerability were interconnected. Inadequate macroeconomic policy increased the vulnerability of the economy to financial crisis, as well as to currency crisis. The fixed exchange rate system enabled borrowing in international currency with an implicit guarantee of a fixed exchange rate, which became particularly attractive when monetary policy erroneously attempted to combine a fixed exchange rate with higher domestic interest rates. This meant that there was a very large build-up of a stock of debt denominated in foreign currency. It thus appears that domestic financial intermediaries not only underestimated the risks to the asset side of their balance sheets, but also disregarded the risks involved to the liability side in borrowing from abroad. They appear to have believed that they were to a large extent guaranteed against *both* of these risks.

In addition, it appears that an inadequately developed financial system increased the vulnerability of the economy to currency, as well as to financial, crisis. The effect of the guarantees to the financial system was to unduly lower the risk premium on investment, further stimulating the investment boom discussed on p. 75 with its consequent inflation. This further increased the subsequent vulnerability of the economy to currency crisis.

4 Negative shocks

Both the financial-crisis and the currency-crisis models surveyed above give an important role to negative external shocks. We now provide a general review of such shocks for the Asian economies.

4.1 Diminishing returns to investment

Well before the signs of crisis in the East Asian economies there had been a debate about their productivity growth record and whether there had been 'too much' investment. Krugman (1994) likened their capital-intensive growth to that of the Soviet Union.[18] He pointed out that 'if growth in East Asia has been primarily investment driven' then it was likely that 'capital piling up there is beginning to yield diminishing returns'.[19] It is worth noting that such falls in the rate of return will not explain crisis, since response to them could have been smooth and gradual, but they do constitute a negative shock, albeit a slow-acting one.

4.2 Worsening external position

Current account deficits had increased in all the countries except Singapore but the degree of problem varied. The only country with a really large deficit was Thailand (8 per cent of GDP). Malaysia, at 6 per cent of GDP, had reversed a worsening trend. However it is impossible to read much from *ex post* current account deficits because it is not possible to determine whether these were the consequence of benign inward FDI, or high domestic absorption, or a negative external shock. In the face of this lack of conclusiveness about causality it is important to look for more direct signs of external weakness.

One explanation of this story notes that competitiveness, measured by real exchange rates, worsened in most countries. There are a number of possible reasons for this. It may have been a result of changes in nominal exchange rates, and in particular an appreciation of the dollar (to which most of these countries' currencies were pegged) relative to the yen. Or it may have been due to a fall in dollar export prices. Or it may actually have been due to rises in domestic costs and prices of the kinds discussed above. The evidence is itself inconclusive; for many countries the amounts appear to have been small; the only countries where competitiveness appeared to have declined by more than 10 per cent from 1990 were Indonesia, the Philippines and Hong Kong. In Singapore, Malaysia and Thailand the declines appear to have been close to 10 per cent, and Korea and Taiwan appear to have had virtually no decline.[20] However, these figures – which use relative prices in computing the real exchange rate – appear to miss the rise in domestic costs described above for Thailand (and there is a suspicion that they may do so for other countries too).

Other versions of the story seek more specific explanations. One of these looks to the weakness of the market for electronic goods, perhaps caused by large increases in supply from the countries under consideration. Another version of the negative shock story attributes it to market crowding as a result of increased exports from China. Here the idea is that, until the mid-1990s, China had internal difficulties (and perhaps also an overvalued exchange rate) which held back export expansion. The resolution of those difficulties (and the devaluation of the yuan in 1994) enabled China to increase exports of manufactures competitive with those produced in the Asian economies. This had effects equivalent to a negative productivity shock in the other Asian 'Tigers', which faced falling quantity demand and/or a falling price for their exports. Yet another variety of this story notes the prolonged recession in Japan, and the shock caused by the devaluation of the yen. Japan acts not as an export competitor from these countries but as an import market, and so recession in Japan acted as a significant export market shock.[21]

Perhaps most persuasively, it does appear that almost all countries in the region experienced significant declines in both export revenues and in export volumes in 1996 (IMF, *World Economic Outlook*, October 1997, figures 7, 8). This does appear to be significant evidence of a negative external shock in that year, although it does not discriminate as between the origins of this shock.

5 Crises and collapse

5.1 The initial financial crises and currency crises

5.1.1 Finance

It appears that, for all of the Asian economies, the negative shocks which we have just described led to problems for the financial system. The negative shocks reduced the value of the assets of the banking system, requiring government bail-outs for the financial system. This clearly led to an onset of financial crisis in all countries, long before the summer of 1997. In both Thailand[22] and Korea, the stock market had begun to fall by 1995 and by 1996 large swathes of the economy were in trouble. It is our interpretation that, but for one feature of the circumstances, all the Asia-Pacific economies might have withstood the need for these bail-outs without the financial crisis turning into a financial collapse. We argue that, but for what is to be described immediately below, the 'bad equilibrium' described on p. 74 could have been avoided.

5.1.2 Currency

For all countries, the negative shocks described above appear to have been important for macroeconomic policy. In Thailand in particular,[23] vulnerability also appears to have resulted from the rise in costs and prices which followed from the boom phase, which led to a rise in real wages and an appreciation of the real exchange rate. In Thailand, the negative shocks were already, by 1996, causing recession. The appropriate monetary policy in the face of this would have been expansion. But the government was committed to a fixed exchange rate, departure from which, through a more expansionary monetary policy, would have involved a loss of credibility. Nevertheless, the depression of the economy by the negative shocks gave an incentive to devalue. Our argument is that the recession in the economy caused by the negative external shock – and made worse because of the already existing lack of export sector competitiveness – meant that the costs of holding onto the peg became too great.

It is thus possible to argue that in Thailand – where the Asian crisis first hit – the situation was quite similar in form to the ERM crisis of 1992, in which the 'crisis' led to a floating exchange rate, with the intention of achieving a controlled devaluation sufficient both to take the pressure off the export competing sector and to lead to a domestic recovery. It does appear that not to have devalued would have been very costly, even independently of any increase in the interest rate. As long as there are limits to the government's willingness to impose these costs on the export sector and domestic economy, one can argue that it was a rational choice to allow the currency to devalue.

5.3.1 Discussion

We would like to make a number of observations on this account about the onset of the crisis. We begin with Thailand:

- First, we attribute the devaluation to a *conflict between the macroeconomic policy objectives and negative shocks*. The devaluation was not, we argue, due to a shortage of reserves, or to a mismatch between reserves and short-term liabilities. The reason for this is that in a world of highly mobile capital it is not reserves which matter but private capital flows. It is always possible to induce these by a sufficiently high interest rate – the question is whether that becomes too costly. Our argument is that in a fragile economy, with inflated costs as a consequence of the previous boom, the government was not prepared to raise the interest rate sufficiently to defend the currency. [24]

- Second, there does not appear to be a need to appeal to self-fulfilling crisis (equals multiple-equilibrium) ideas in order to explain Thailand's original devaluation. We can say that the devaluation was provoked by the *external shocks imposed on an economy* which had a cost position worsened by the previous boom. It does not appear to be helpful to argue that if only the risk premium had not risen then the devaluation would not have happened. [25]

- Third, we have to ask: would the authorities have devalued if they had known what was coming? Would not continuing on a fixed exchange rate have been preferable to unleashing the crisis which followed? It is implicit in this analysis that what the Thai authorities – and their IMF advisers – thought would be achieved by departing from the fixed exchange rate was the *macroeconomic benefits of a modest depreciation*. It does not appear to us that they anticipated that this might be a step along the road towards overall collapse. [26]

- Finally, we have to ask: what did determine the extent of the depreciation in the early stages of the currency crisis? We have to admit that there is no very good analysis in the theory of currency crisis of how far the currency devalues if the peg is abandoned. The Ozkan and Sutherland models referred to above (p. 77) suppose that if the currency devalues, the resulting devaluation will be real (i.e. the background to the model is one of absolute nominal stickiness) and that the extent of depreciation will be an amount sufficient to remove the negative effects of the demand shock. Most other analyses treat the extent of the resulting depreciation as exogenous. But it clearly depends on the nature of the *policy regime*. Once the devaluation came, there was great uncertainty about the ability of the Thai authorities to take the necessary corrective action even in the early stages of the crisis. In particular – as we argue below – it was not clear what the new nominal anchor would be, and thus what real depreciation would result from any particular nominal depreciation. This is consistent with the initial depreciation in the summer of 1997 being much larger than was expected.

In none of the other economies were inflated costs, and the recession caused by the boom, as serious as in the Thai economy. It thus appears to us that one may well need to locate the onset of currency crisis in Korea, Indonesia, Malaysia and the Philippines in a process of contagion: an increasing risk premium leading to the costs of defending the exchange rate being more than those which were politically acceptable. (See Masson's chapter 8 in this volume, and Weber's discussion of it (p. 280), both of which argue this point persuasively.) For these economies, there does appear to be a need to appeal to self-fulfilling currency-crisis ideas in order to explain their initial devaluations. For these economies, it does appear to be possible to argue that if only the risk premium had not risen, then the devaluation would not have happened.

Again, for these other economies, we have to ask whether the authorities would have devalued if they had known what was coming. Here again it does not appear that they understood that allowing the currency to devalue might – given the financial structure which had developed under fixed exchange rates – provoke a process which ended in financial collapse.[27]

5.2 Collapse: the effect of currency crisis on financial crisis

It is our argument that, in each of the Asia-Pacific countries, it was the *depreciation of the currency* which turned financial crisis into financial collapse. This was a result of the particular feature, already noted, to which the fixed exchange rate regime had led: foreign currency liabilities as a result of massive unhedged borrowings in foreign currency. Devaluation increased the local currency value of these liabilities. Financial collapse resulted when currency devaluations were sufficiently large that those who had lent to the financial system came to believe that government guarantees could not be honoured. This triggered fears of sovereign insolvency.

This is our interpretation of how collapse first developed in Thailand. The devaluation of the baht in the middle of 1997 made the financial crisis worse by increasing the value of the outstanding obligations on dollar borrowings. As already noted, firms had built up large unhedged foreign borrowings in dollars. The larger was the devaluation of the baht, the larger became the local currency value of these borrowings following the depreciation. As a consequence, depreciation increased the size of the required bail-outs for the financial system. There came a point where these became too large, *or were thought to have become too large*. At this point, panic set in, followed by financial collapse. This is a story about a 'flip to a bad equilibrium' in the financial system happening *after* the currency devaluation.

It is clear to us that financial collapse can lead to the currency falling further – that is, to currency crisis eventually turning into currency collapse. Once there is sovereign insolvency, then this is likely to lead to difficulty in controlling money expansion. This is likely to lead immediately to an expectation that any nominal anchor has been abandoned, which will immediately cause the currency to plummet. The mere *fear of sovereign insolvency* can give rise to the same outcome.

This process may well be unstable. The further the currency collapses, the larger the bail-out obligations of the government to the financial system become.

Notice that the effect of currency depreciation in this situation, in which there are large foreign borrowings denominated in foreign currency, appears to be inherently non-linear. If it is small enough it acts in an 'orthodox way' – helping to relieve the macroeconomic downturn created by vulnerability and negative shocks. But if the devaluation is large enough to trigger bail-outs which in turn are large enough to trigger sovereign insolvency, *or the fear of it,* then the effect is clearly, and potentially massively, negative. It is possible to argue that the critical policy mistake in the handling of the crises was to allow a currency depreciation which became sufficiently large to broach this non-linear threshold. But our view is that it was not at all well understood where this threshold was. And for the Indonesian, Korean, Philippines and Malaysian economies hit by contagion it became almost impossible to prevent degrees of currency depreciation which, *ex post*, appear to have broached this threshold.

This sequential story is how we interpret what happened not only in

Thailand, but in all of the crisis-hit Asia-Pacific countries. We have some circumstantial evidence in favour of this interpretation for Korea, as a result of private conversations with one of the major rating agencies. These have suggested to us that in rating Korean banks, for example, rating agencies knew that the banks were in financial difficulty but did not downgrade ratings because they still regarded the government commitment to bail out banks as firm. But in making this judgement they took into account the growing cost of the bail-outs only so far as it concerned the cost of injecting enough capital to shore up the banks' adequacy ratios. This they considered to be well within the government's budget capacity. It appears that if the rating agencies had been aware of the possibility of a large currency depreciation and had had to factor in the cost to the government of honouring all of the banks' foreign liabilities in depreciated currencies, then they would have considered that the budget deficit could not have stood it. That binding budget constraint would, it appears, have led to a revision of their estimate of the likelihood of support for the banks and a consequent downgrading of bank ratings.

The above argument suggests the following tentative hypothesis about the Asian crisis. Estimates of the financial fragility of the banking sector before the currency crisis appear not to have been enough to trigger a crisis. Markets (or, at least, the rating agencies which supply them with information) do appear to calculate the probabilities of banks' rescue and consider government budget constraints important. These probabilities change when budget constraints change. Estimates of sovereign risk may well take into account the likelihood of bank failure, but in this case it appears that the currency crisis had to come first before the failures became so large as to threaten sovereign insolvency and create financial collapse. We might be able to assume that the style of analysis was similar in the markets themselves. Information about how one aspect of crisis – the currency crisis – is likely to affect another – the financial crisis – may not have been perfect, and understanding this may play a crucial role in explaining how the crisis developed.

Notice how complex the contagion process becomes when there is the possibility of collapse of both the financial system and the currency. The mere fear that *financial* crisis will turn into collapse is enough to provoke an expectation of currency depreciation. If that is strong enough to make the currency peg unsustainable, then the currency depreciation can trigger the financial collapse which had been feared. That financial collapse in turn might be enough to trigger currency collapse, because of its effects in causing sovereign insolvency. And that would validate the initial fears of currency depreciation.

6 The disintegration of macroeconomic policy making[28]

The problem for macroeconomic policy in the collapsing economies, identified above, is that financial collapse, or the fear of it (in turn, caused by currency depreciation) led to fears of sovereign insolvency, and so to currency collapse. The critical problem was to halt this currency collapse. For at least the first nine months the IMF argued that halting and reversing currency collapse was a precondition of crisis resolution, and that traditional monetary and fiscal policies were essential for that purpose because there was no effective alternative.[29]

Dornbusch (1997, p. 55), writing early on in the crisis, said

> it is not over until the fat lady sings. What Yogi Berra said of opera also applies to currency operettas. Until the IMF is in with a very traditional program – budget, flexibilized currency, bank workout, and monetary program – there is no reason to expect stabilization. Once a currency is seriously under attack it will stay in meltdown mode until the full treatment is applied. Between the IMF team arriving and the full reality check there is always a difficult moment – politics won't allow this or that. [But g]o right to the end of the book: the IMF program will be accepted, the currency stabilizes, the stock market picks up. The only question is how much of a financial devastation and growth setback has happened on the way.

But the answer to this question depends on what tune the fat lady sings.

In 'orthodox' crises the problems are those of excess domestic absorption and a lack of national competitiveness. The correct remedies are those advocated and routinely applied by the IMF: tight fiscal and monetary policies which curb excess absorption, and which steer the exchange rate to the modest level of depreciation required to achieve expenditure through the promotion of net exports. It is now a commonplace to say that Asian crises have been very different from the orthodox balance of payments crisis with which the IMF is used to dealing. But our detailed analysis in the sections above has been designed to go much further than this broad remark, and to tie this difference firmly to the intertwining of currency and financial crises.

We believe that the application of tight monetary policies to Asia reduced, rather than improved, the creditworthiness of indebted firms and exaggerated the financial collapse. We believe that fiscal contraction, by exacerbating the downturn, caused firms' revenues to fall and also worsened the collapse. And we believe that our analysis enables one to see how – and in what way – different policies were needed. In the following two subsections we defend these claims.[30]

6.1 The interest rate defence: was monetary policy too tight or mismanaged?

It can be – and has been – argued that interest rates were pushed to much too high a level, and kept too high, in all the Asian-Pacific countries under the discipline of IMF programmes.

One way of arguing this point is to note that in all of Korea, Thailand and Indonesia, non-traded goods price inflation has been negative. This is most simply demonstrated by comparing the extent of exchange rate depreciation with the extent of CPI inflation. Normally one would expect CPI inflation, after lags had washed out, to be roughly equal to the exchange rate depreciation *times* the import content of output and expenditures, *plus* any domestic demand effects. In all of these countries CPI inflation has been significantly less than this. Thus what we have observed is rapidly rising import costs, much less rapidly rising prices in the consumption basket, and a *negative* increase in the price of the domestic content of the consumption basket. One can argue that constant non-traded goods prices would be an indicator of tight monetary policy. Given the very great difficulty of actually depressing prices, one can then argue that a monetary policy which caused falling non-traded goods prices was certainly very tight.[31]

The combination of falling non-traded goods prices and long-lasting high interest rates effectively destroyed all capitalists who had borrowed in the non-traded goods sector.

The response to this argument is that – with a huge foreign debt overhang – the currency depreciation destroyed or was destroying all those who borrowed abroad. The Fund could reply – and did reply – that it could not have done any better. It was trying, so the Fund's argument went, to prevent the worse outcome of uncontrolled currency depreciation.

Our own view is different. We believe that a better outcome could have been achieved in the form of less depreciation for any given increase in the interest rate. The best way of approaching this point is by means of a comparison with what was done when the UK and Italy were thrown out of the ERM of the EMS in 1992. After the UK's exit, the Treasury immediately announced a new form of nominal anchor, namely an inflation target. This was presented to the public within a matter of days of the exchange rate collapse, and provided a trajectory for prices which it was the intention of monetary policy to follow. It was made clear that the interest rate would be manipulated in order to steer prices onto this trajectory. The important thing is that such a 'UK' strategy effectively has two instruments rather than just one. The first instrument is of course the interest rate; but the second 'instrument' is the announced target for prices towards which the interest rate is aiming to steer the economy. This second instrument is a critical part of this strategy. It is useful for domestic price and wage-setters. But it is also crucially important for the foreign exchange market by providing a partial anchor for the long-run nominal exchange rate.[32] Once this second element of the strategy is safely in place, interest rates can be cut to low levels without endangering the exchange rate.

The outcome in the UK may be contrasted with what happened after Italy was ejected from the EMS. In that country there was an unsatisfactory period, lasting nearly a year, in which it was not at all clear what the new strategy would be. As a result, confidence took much longer to return.[33]

What happened in Asia is much worse than what happened in Italy. In Asia, when the fixed-rate peg disintegrated the authorities did not, decisively, do what the British did. Instead they attempted – with the IMF's encouragement – to use only the interest rate to prevent currency collapse. But markets had no idea whether the authorities were attempting to stabilise prices around the level which would involve little or no slippage (which is what, as we have seen, eventually emerged) or whether, instead, the authorities were really reconciled to having 'let prices go'. Markets thus had no idea whether the long-run equilibrium exchange rate was consistent with no slippage or consistent with huge slippage. Without that guidance, markets took the reasonable view that what they were being offered was (on average) something in between – namely, large slippage. That precipitated a large currency depreciation – an outcome somewhere between no depreciation and a huge depreciation.[34] The interest rate increases were motivated by trying directly to counter this. But countering such fears of currency fall with interest rate increases can be very, very costly.[35] As a consequence, it appears to be the case that the policy authorities, (and the Fund) saw high interest rates partly also as a way of *signalling* that the policy of the country was that it would not let prices go. But we also know that the sending of such signals about type can be very costly, or ineffective, or both.[36] In fact, it seems to have been both. Far better would have been – in the language of signalling theory – for the countries to 'reveal' their type, by announcing an inflation target strategy like that announced in Britain.[37]

As a result of not following the British example the Asian economies appear to have got the worst of all worlds: high interest rates and – because they had no new secure nominal anchor – large currency depreciation. The effects of this bad outcome were just as disastrous on the domestic economy as they were on the exchange rate. Because markets had no idea whether the authorities were attempting to stabilise prices around a level involving not very much slippage, or whether they were, instead, reconciled to having 'let prices go', markets had no idea whether the high nominal interest rates which were being offered within the domestic economy were high real interest rates or low real interest rates. As a result, borrowing and lending dried up, loans were recalled, large parts of the economies went bankrupt, and credit collapsed.

The effect of this credit collapse was savage. Firms were unable to obtain working capital and so production, particularly for export, collapsed, too. The collapse in exports actually made the foreign exchange situation worse.

6.2 Fiscal errors

The monetary errors described above were compounded by inappropriate fiscal strategy. In the absence of a fully credible nominal anchor, one can see why the IMF continued to push for fiscal stringency. A central part of the reasoning behind this strategy was a signalling one – to make it clear that the policy makers were not the type who would 'let prices go'.

But this fiscal policy turned out to be quite inappropriate. Indeed, in Indonesia one can argue that it was the *cause* of the collapse observed in early 1998. In the last two months of 1997 the IMF was still pushing the standard line – that fiscal deficits should not rise during an adjustment pro-gramme. Indeed because of the costs of the bank bail-outs the IMF was pushing for a 1 per cent *surplus*, in order to pay for the extra-budget bail-out costs (see Fischer, 1998). It has been claimed that, by November 1997, after the dust settled from the bank-closure fiasco,[38] the technocrats were back in control and indeed were working hard to assert their authority against Suharto and the *ancien régime*. In these two months, they tried their best fiscally. But it became clear that the budget due at the end of the first week of 1998 would achieve only a surplus of minus -1.5 or -2 per cent of GDP. With the aid of economic theory, one might have argued then that this tightness was the best that could be done, and perhaps even that such tightness was all that was actually desirable. Indeed, with hindsight, the draft budget which the technocrats were offering now looks as if it would have been an amazingly competent fiscal strategy.

The IMF, and the Washington policy community, then faced a choice. Even without jettisoning their deficit concerns they could then have said – 'this budget is the best possible under the circumstances, Indonesia needs our help, we are working with them, etc.'. They chose the alternative course. They comprehensively trashed the new budget in Washington when it was presented. Until that point the rupea had gone from 2.5k to the dollar to 4k to the dollar – that is, despite Indonesia's travails, Indonesia's currency had hardly fared any worse than that of Korea and Thailand. But in the after-math of the public renunciation in Washington of what was happening in

Jakarta, the markets turned on Indonesia. By the end of January the rupea stood at 7.5k to the dollar. Although it subsequently recovered, this was the moment at which the gravity of the Indonesian outcome diverged from that in the rest of the crisis countries. There is thus a plausible line that the Washington policy community, because of the choice that they took, *caused* the Indonesian hyperinflation.[39]

The fiscal errors in Indonesia were by far the worst. But elsewhere the same kinds of mistakes were made. There was an initial move towards fiscal tightening, so as to build up a 'war chest', to pay for the costs of bailing out and restructuring the financial sector. This was coupled with a refusal to let the automatic stabilisers operate as output plummeted.[40] One can thus certainly argue that, elsewhere too, fiscal austerity worsened the depressions. But, more than this, one can argue that the – predictable – failure to meet the fiscal targets added to the air of crisis, making adjustment harder, not easier. Of course eventually fiscal positions were greatly relaxed, but too late.

6.3 The disintegration of macroeconomic policy making, and its reconstruction

The implication of the analysis earlier in this chapter is that the critical core requirement for reversing the collapse of the Asian currencies was to remove the fear of sovereign insolvency. This fear led to a fear of budget deficits, money creation, currency collapse, and that fed into further financial collapse and further fear of sovereign collapse. We thus suggest that by proposing high interest rates and fiscal austerity the IMF was: (1) not properly addressing the core issue – namely, how best to remove the fear of sovereign insolvency; (2) doing things which actually made addressing this core issue more difficult; and (3) doing things which could have been avoided if this core issue had been properly addressed.

Only when the fear of sovereign insolvency is removed is it possible to safely organise monetary policy around an inflation target, in the knowledge that sovereign debt will not be inflated away. The organising of monetary policy around such an inflation-target framework – immediately after Asian exchange rates had collapsed – would have removed the fear of further currency collapse and removed the need for high interest rates, both of which would have – in turn – made it much easier to remove fear of sovereign insolvency.[41]

Furthermore, once this fear has in fact been removed then all else can follow. Like the UK, post-ERM, the country can then not only revert quickly to a low-interest rate regime, but it can also allow temporary budget deficits to cushion the crisis in the short term. The clear implication is that the removal of the threat of sovereign insolvency and the adoption of the inflation target, *together and of themselves,* provide the means whereby one does *not* need to soldier on with high interest rates and fiscal cuts as the crisis develops.

Of course there will need to be a contingent threat of higher interest rates, and higher tax rates, in the background, to guard against a take-off in inflation or an excessive rise in the deficit.[42] But at the time of crisis countries will already have a deep recession – for reasons extensively discussed. Thus to argue – as the IMF did – that more of the medicine was necessary as the crisis developed is – we believe – deeply misguided.[43]

7 The precondition for a reconstruction of macroeconomic policy: resolution of sovereign solvency crises

The implication of our analysis is that the Asian crisis has posed a completely new problem in crisis management. Our analysis has been that: (1) crisis became collapse because financial guarantees to the banking system became larger than the government could honour, or because this was feared to be the case; (2) a major reason for this was because of large foreign exchange-denominated obligations of the banking system which become unexpectedly onerous as a result of currency devaluation. The collapse suddenly caused a large number of losses: debts which could not be repaid immediately (and which may never be repayable). These initially fell upon the banks, and have (explicitly and implicitly) become partly or even completely socialised as a result of the state guarantees offered to the banking system. The crucial new task of crisis management was to allocate these wealth losses which originated in the private sector, and to do so in such a way which would remove the threat of sovereign insolvency.

There are two questions which must be answered about these wealth losses. How are the outstanding foreign creditors of the sovereign debtor to be treated? And how are the remaining creditors of the domestic private sector to be treated?

7.1 Lessons from earlier sovereign debt crises

In approaching these two questions, it is helpful to consider two earlier crises, the Mexican crisis of 1994–5 and the Latin American crisis of the 1980s. In these two cases the crisis was that of sovereign debt.

7.1.1 The Mexico solution

In this scenario the crisis was that of sovereign debt, the foreign creditors of the sovereign were to be repaid and taxpayers were to meet the bill. This 'Mexico solution' can be quick. If the sovereign's creditors are indeed to be repaid, then there will be no sovereign insolvency. All that is required is to organise liquidity financing and to reassure international creditors that indeed all debts will be repaid in full, so that a continuing orderly rollover of debts can proceed. The role of the IMF in such circumstances is clear and circumscribed. It is to stand behind the government saying 'we believe that every cent will be repaid', and then to organise a lender-of-last-resort (LOLR) liquidity lifeboat until the market comes to believe that this claim is true.

The task of this liquidity lifeboat is to enable immediately outstanding debts to be rolled over. In the Mexico crisis of 1995, Mexico received a $17.8 billion stand-by programme (amounting to what was then an unprecedented 688 per cent of Mexico's quota in the IMF), in combination with $20 billion from the US Stabilisation Fund and $10 billion from the G-10. But this funding enabled Mexico's debts to be rolled over in full, and the loans are in the process of being paid *in full*. Mexico quickly regained access to private capital markets and economic growth has been resumed.

When the Mexico crisis hit at the end of 1994 it was hailed as the first crisis of the twenty-first century, and everyone believed that a major task had been accomplished in dealing with it. But in retrospect solving the Mexico crisis looks to have been easy. This is because the problematic debts were sovereign debts; the solution of deciding to honour these sovereign debts, and promising to raise the revenue to do so through taxation looks, with three years of hindsight, to have been a very simple one to manage.

7.1.2 The Latin American debt crisis scenario

Such a benign outcome is not – of course – the inevitable outturn of a sovereign debt crisis. If the foreign debts of the sovereign cannot be repaid and are not to be repaid, then the above strategy falls apart, on day one. The IMF cannot stand behind the government and give the required assurance. Instead, a work-out is required of the sovereign insolvency. During this period (1) capital markets will seize up and also (2) as implied by the analysis on p. 89, it will be almost impossible to run good macroeconomic policy in the face of fears of recourse to the printing press and hyperinflation. The Latin American crisis of the 1980s showed how miserable the resulting work-out can be if it is, in Radelet and Sachs' terms 'disorderly'. Partial default and subsequent rescheduling led to a problem which took 10 years to solve: Latin America's 'lost decade' of low investment and greatly increased poverty. A solution to the work-out problem is difficult and may take much time: it involves a stay on payments to private creditors, an injection of liquidity financing in the short term and an orderly writing-down of debts. If all three parts of the package are not available then liquidity injection, from the IMF or anywhere else, will simply finance capital flight, as creditors scramble to be first in obtaining what settlement of claims they can. Resolution of the Latin American debt crisis took so long both because of free-rider problems – each creditor seeking to profit from concessions made by other creditors – and because creditors held out for an injection of funding from the governments of advanced countries.

7.2 Resolving the Asian sovereign and private sector debt crises

If the debt problem has been a private debt problem, and if – because these debts fell upon the financial system, or otherwise – the state has taken over some or perhaps even a large proportion of these debts, then there is a sovereign debt problem. But, of course, there are also creditors of the private sector debtors to deal with. There are thus our two questions: How are the outstanding foreign creditors of the sovereign to be treated? And how are the creditors of the domestic private sector to be dealt with?

7.2.1 The Korean and Thailand solution

We may call the Korean (and the Thailand) solution the one in which foreign creditors of the sovereign *are* to be repaid in full. The role of the IMF in such circumstances is again – like that in Mexico – clear and circumscribed. As in that case, this role is to stand behind the government saying 'we believe that every cent will be repaid', and then to organise a LOLR liquidity lifeboat, until the market comes to believe that this claim is true. It appears that this is what has been going on in Korea, since early 1998. Foreign confidence in the country is returning. As Dornbusch (1997) says: 'the currency stabilises and the stock market turns. Recovery begins.'

But this is not the end of the question – within the country there remains a need for a domestic debt workout.

(1) Which of the bankrupt parts of the financial system are to be closed, and which parts are to be rescued and recapitalised with bail-outs? (Almost complete bail-out is what happened, for example, in the case

of the Savings and Loan (S&L) crisis in the USA in the early 1980s.) Should political pressures against closure from the bombed-out parts of the financial system be resisted? Can it be? How much of these bail-outs will be paid for by current taxpayers, and how much by government borrowing? How is the bail-out process going to be organised?

(2) And how are bankrupt private sector firms to be dealt with? Efficient and speedy bankruptcy procedures are needed to resolve the financial position of the distressed parts of the private sector, so as to enable closure of some activities and the rescue and recapitalisation of others. Rescue packages at the firm level must involve a stay on payments to private creditors and an injection of liquidity financing in the short run *plus* an orderly writing-down of debts.[44]

Many in Korea have complained that they have been ill-treated in that capital inflows have not resumed, even though the country has been scrupulous in honouring its foreign debts. But the reorganisation of banks, and the shutting of bankrupt *chaebol*, takes time, and until it is done, it is not clear which firms and which banks are financially viable and which are attractive to foreigners to continue to own or to purchase through inward investment.[45] Large-scale capital inflow, the rolling over of private debts and the resumption of rapid investment and growth cannot happen until decisive steps are taken to resolve these private sector uncertainties. Thus the 'Korea–Thailand solution' is much harder to organise than the Mexico solution.

There is a further difficulty in the resolution of such a crisis. This is that the solution of the crisis and the value of the currency are inter-connected. It is clear that it has been difficult to work out how much bankrupt firms are worth without having a clear idea how much the Korean real exchange rate will rebound in an upwards direction after the initial collapse, and this has remained uncertain. Yet, that should be possible to clarify, at least in principle, once the desired time profile for the repayment of foreign debt has been determined, and in early 1999 this was becoming clear. Once that is known the necessary pattern of current account surpluses – and the required real exchange rate – becomes reasonably clear.

Failing decisive clarification and resolution of the position of bankrupt firms, the country will need to grow its way out of the debts. This is the route which both Korea and Thailand attempted in 1998. This requires the generation of a large flow of profits into the corporate sector – which in turn requires very large current account surpluses. The intention is to recapitalise firms by growing their revenues rather than to shut them. It requires a very great sacrifice. It is also likely to take a long time.

7.2.2 The Indonesian debt crisis scenario

In the final case to be described, foreign creditors of the sovereign are *not* to be repaid *and* a bankruptcy and crisis resolution procedure is required domestically. This is by far the most difficult case to organise.

As in the case of the Latin American debt crisis the IMF cannot stand behind the government and give the assurances which foreign creditors require. Because the state has been obliged – for one reason or another – to take over such a large amount of private sector debts, there is a sovereign debt problem; a work-out will be required of the sovereign insolvency. As in the Latin American debt crisis, a full solution must involve a stay on payments to foreign creditors, an injection of liquidity financing in the short term, and an orderly writing-down of debts. Again, as in the Latin American case, if three parts of the package are not available then liquidity injection, from the IMF or anywhere else, will simply finance capital flight, as creditors scramble to be first in maintaining what settlement of claims they can.

But as in the case of Korea, this is not the end of the question – within the country there remains a need for a domestic debt work-out. It is necessary to know (1) which of the bankrupt parts of the financial system are to be closed, and which parts are to be rescued and recapitalised with bail-outs and (2) how bankrupt private sector firms are to be dealt with. As in the case of Korea, bankruptcy procedures are needed. Rescue packages at the firm level must involve a stay on payments to private creditors and an injection of liquidity financing in the short run plus an orderly writing-down of debts.

What is required is, however, much more demanding than in the Korean case. It appears that, in these circumstances the government needs to assume some, *but not all,* of the private sector debt, and to take upon itself the task to repay some, *but not all* of the debt which it owes to foreign creditors. What proportion of the loss will be taken by shareholders, domestic taxpayers and foreign creditors banks (and perhaps foreign taxpayers) becomes an extremely difficult bargaining problem. The resolution of this, with at least three sides, may take years. As well as the free-riding and hold-up problems which plagued the solution to the Latin American problem, lenders will be reluctant to initiate rescheduling because of fears that offering concessions to one private sector debtor will encourage others to demand similar treatment. This problem of bargaining coordination amongst the debtors adds a further layer of difficulties to those which arose because of coordination difficulties among creditors in the Latin American crisis.

Two further factors add additional layers of difficulty to the problem.

First, it will be almost impossible to determine how much bankrupt firms are worth independently of the resolution of the sovereign debt crisis, and vice versa. This is because the value of firms will depend on where the real exchange rate will settle, which will depend on how the sovereign debt resolution process proceeds, which in turn will depend on the value of bankrupt firms.[46] Second, even putting this point aside, with a large part of the private sector bankrupt, it will not be possible to know how much one part is worth without knowing how much other parts are worth.

What is probably required in these circumstances is an aggregate, if crude, economywide bankruptcy procedure in which *all corporate debts are converted to equity at the same time as sovereign debt is written down.* This corporate equity will immediately then trade at a discount – enforcing a write-down – but it will be saleable, thus enabling creditors to exit and so removing the log-jam of unresolved claims.[47]

8 Challenges for the IMF

Two or three years ago one might have argued that the IMF was the most successful global institution in history (see Evans, 1997). The Asian crisis has enormously damaged the Fund's credibility and authority. In rebuilding its reputation, the Fund faces three key tasks, not all of which appear easily soluble, or even soluble at all.

8.1 Avoiding macroeconomic vulnerability: macro policy design, surveillance and the IMF

The IMF's surveillance mechanisms have been found wanting by this crisis. Internal studies within the Fund have described how the IMF was drawing attention to macroeconomic imbalances in Thailand, but that it did not foresee the severity of the impending crisis. More seriously, the Fund was essentially caught unawares by the crisis in Korea. There are also tasks for the Fund in modernising its advice on policy design. Advising countries about the need for, and the way to achieve, central bank credibility and the management of macroeconomic policy with floating exchange rates so as to produce a stable low-inflation environment is an enormous task. One has only to think, for example, about the enormous amount of intellectual energy which has been expended on just this task in Britain, New Zealand, Australia and other OECD countries.

8.2 Financial restructuring and surveillance and the IMF

There are large tasks ahead in risk management for the regulators of international banks in the lending countries, to discourage risky lending of the kind that international banks engaged in during the run-up to the Asian crisis. If, as it appears from both the earlier Mexican episode and from the Asian crisis, banks do not take due care in the lending process, it is up to regulators to impose very significant risk weightings in lending to these markets so as to make lending more costly to them and discourage it. (See Fane, 1998, and the discussion by Turner in the Round Table (chapter 13).) These issues are of relevance to the Fund – in as much as it ends up involved in overseeing financial regulation in borrowing countries – since if the supply of lending to these countries is more carefully controlled then the regulation of financial markets there will be made easier.

There are also enormous tasks ahead in designing this regulation so as to produce transparent, properly regulated financial systems that curtail demands for funds for risky speculative investments. These tasks present a difficulty for the division of labour between the IMF and the World Bank. The Bank is essentially responsible for microeconomic development issues and the Fund for macroeconomic policy, but these macro–micro demarcations are essentially blurred when dealing with the banking and financial sectors. Historically the Bank has been the institution which has concentrated on financial sector institution-building and it has had much more financial sector expertise than the Fund. It has now been suggested that the IMF expand its activities to deal with monitoring, surveillance and short-run crisis resolution, leaving the Bank to deal with financial reconstruction and longer-term structural reform. However these tasks are so inter-related that any division along these lines appears to be artificial. As a result suggestions have been made that *all* of the financial sector expertise of the IMF and the Bank should be concentrated in the IMF.[48]

But that, too, has problems. To concentrate global financial supervision and regulation within the IMF bundles such functions together in an institution which has global LOLR-type obligations. By contrast, debundling is the rule within national jurisdictions. This is so for good reasons – there are conflicts of interest in concentrating these two different kinds of work within the one institution. This is an issue that will need clearer resolution in the next few months and years.

8.3 Crisis management and the international architecture

Finally, and even more difficult, the crisis has thrown up a gap in the *international architecture of crisis management*. There is an especial need for new international institutions of crisis management in the case where foreign creditors are not all to be repaid. (This case has been forcefully argued recently by such unlikely bedfellows as US Treasury Secretary Rubin, and George Soros, 1998.) At present, we have argued, the IMF is confined of necessity to the twin role (1) as guarantor that countries' international debts will be honoured and (2) as provider of liquidity financing to debtor countries, during the time that the market takes to believe this guarantee. This was the case in the Mexican crisis where the sovereign debts were dealt with and have been honoured by the Mexican taxpayer. It also appears to be the likely outcome of the Korean crisis, where the Korean taxpayers will pick up the responsibility of servicing the debts of foreign banks.

But when this is not possible, because the existing debts are too large, a rescue package must involve a stay on payments to private creditors (for both public sector and private sector debtors), an orderly writing-down of both public and private debts and an injection of liquidity financing in the short term. As we described on p. 94, what is required is exceptionally demanding. There is not the international architecture to make this possible; in particular, if countries were to do what was described above, both their sovereign and their corporate sector would need international legal protection of a kind not currently available.

The IMF is thus in a very difficult position. There are very significant obstacles – including serious legal ones – to organising the necessary international bankruptcy process. And there is no clear agreement that the Fund is the right institution to oversee it, since it would be required both to oversee the procedure and to advise and assist indebted countries. Nevertheless some process of this kind seems essential, in order that a failure to repay in full does not lead to an extended period of debt deadlock, both in Indonesia and in similar circumstances in the future.[49]

If such a work-out process is not established, then it will go on being possible to argue, as has been argued in the case of Korea and Thailand, that repayment is a less bad outcome than deadlock. Significant moral hazard will then remain in the international system: lenders, continuing to point to the dire difficulties associated with debt deadlock, will continue to expect to be bailed out, and they will continue not to take sufficient care in lending. There is no doubt that the consequence of the Mexican rescue was to increase this kind of moral hazard in the international system.[50] If a similar lesson is drawn from the Asian crisis – that satisfactory, speedy crisis resolution is available only if *all* international debts are honoured – then this will further worsen the moral hazard problem. In these circumstances the IMF will inevitably come – has already come – to be seen as a debt-collecting agency. This cannot be – and has not been – good for the legitimacy of the IMF as an international institution.

9 Conclusion: a historical context

The present chapter has offered a framework for understanding the Asian crisis. In conclusion, it is possible to step back a little. We have come to see the crisis as a problem relating to the transition between two types of capitalism.[51] There is, we would argue, what might be called 'Gershenkron-capitalism': an economy which is largely closed, in which what is produced and consumed is all pretty basic stuff. In such economies what really matters for rapid growth and development is the mobilisation of savings. The 'Asian values' of thrift and hard work are of central importance; efficiency, variety, choice and quality are all second-order virtues. This is what the Asian economies looked like in their growth phase, up to the mid-1980s, before the 'Asian miracle' was a household phrase.

Then there is capitalism as we know it in the most advanced OECD countries – open, consumer-oriented, quality-conscious and subject to globalising competition in goods and especially capital markets. No two OECD countries are identical, of course. But there is a generic similarity at this level of generality. How can a country graduate out of the first category and into the second, as the Asian economies attempted to do from the mid-1980s onwards?

Much of modern growth literature seems to mislead here. It can be read as suggesting that what is involved is a process of capital accumulation, leading to 'catch-up', which is continuous and smooth. Instead we see the transition between these two forms of capitalism as a traverse which is pretty difficult to manage. There are important and deep problems of institution design in the financial sector, and in macroeconomic policy making, which must be managed to make this traverse go well. Viewed from this broad sweep, understanding the Asian crisis then becomes rather straightforward: the Asian economies made serious mistakes on the traverse. Others, for example in Latin America, have made mistakes before. The warning is that others, in the future, will be in danger of doing so again.

APPENDIX: THAILAND, A STYLISED CHRONOLOGY

Pre-crisis
1 **1988–96** boom – growth at 10 per cent p.a.
2 Small but increasing contribution from TFP growth – i.e. boom not only from factor supplies (Warr, 1998).
3 Monetary policy operated through the Exchange Equalisation Fund (EEF), kept the exchange rate stable and inflation low.
4 **Early 1990s** relaxation of controls on foreign capital flows (along with deregulation of interest rates between 1989 and 1992).
5 Banking licence issue became looser, number of finance companies and other non-bank financial intermediaries increased and assets in the financial sector increased fourfold from 1990 to 1996 (Menkoff, 1998). Bangkok International Banking Facility (BIBF) established in 1993 with intention to develop regional financial centre – added to inflow of short-term capital. IMF view that 'The perception of implicit guarantees was probably strengthened by the bailouts in the resolution of earlier banking crises [Thailand 1983–7]' (IMF, 1998, p. 35).
6 As foreign capital inflow increased BOT tried to sterilise; rising domestic nominal interest rates resulted.
7 Sterilisation was incomplete, resulting in
   • increased levels of foreign exchange reserves
   • high current account deficits
   • increases in prices of non-tradeables relative to tradeables (a real appreciation)
   • increased capital inflows (Warr, 1998).
8 Fiscal policy was regarded as fairly conservative, maintaining a slight budget surplus of 1–2 per cent p.a. and committing to a budget rule which tied increases in spending to a small margin above the previous year's tax revenues.
9 Stock market price bubble developed from 1993, though other asset price rises were moderate (IMF, 1998).

The triggers
1 Export growth collapsed in 1995–6. Falls greatest in exports to Japan, NAFTA and China (Warr, 1998). Current account deficits increased.
2 Real wages grew at 9 per cent from 1990 to 1994 (Warr, 1998).
3 **1996**, speculative attacks against the baht began.
4 **January 1997** the first Thai company (Somprasong) defaults on foreign debt.
5 **March 1997–May 1997** revelations about the size of bad loans at finance companies, government sets up agency to resolve property-loan problems,

government promises to buy a large quantity ($3.9bn) of property bad loans but reneges. Financial Institution Development Fund promises to buy $2.3bn of sub-standard debts from Bangkok Bank of Commerce for $1.85bn. Move to save Finance One (largest finance company) fails.

6 **May 1997** attempts to impose capital controls.

7 **June 1997** Bank of Thailand suspends operations of 16 finance companies.

All these hint at a growing problems for the government if it is to honour its implicit guarantees.

The crisis

1 **2 July 1997** government announces a 'managed float' of the baht (baht devalues by 15 per cent, and 20 per cent in offshore markets) apparently still believing that a moderate, ERM-type outcome could be achieved.

2 **August 1997** 42 more troubled finance companies suspended. IMF package of $3.9 bn standby credit and $12.7bn international lending agreed.

3 **August–January 1998** baht continues to fall to a low point in January by which time depreciation had reached approximately 50 per cent. Currency recovers and stabilises in March 1998 when the depreciation is about 35 per cent.

4 **October 1997** Finance Minister resigns.

5 **October 1997** spreads on Brady bonds begin to widen markedly. In May they had increased by only 13 basis points, and June by only a further 3. By September the cumulative widening of spreads had still only reached 100 basis points. Spreads peaked in January 1998 at 555 basis points. This indicates that fears of sovereign default came well after the initial currency attacks.

6 **November 1997** new government takes office and issues Letter of Intent.

8 **December 1997** government closes 56 out of 58 suspended finance companies.

The policy response

1 The first IMF package (**August 1997**) requires financial sector restructuring (closing non-viable institutions, intervening in weakest banks, recapitalising the banking sector) tight fiscal measures (fiscal deficit to 3 per cent to give 1 per cent surplus) and 'new framework for monetary policy', which involved raising interest rates, but only to 12 per cent at this stage.

2 Short-term nominal interest rates rise to over 20 per cent, fall briefly but continue to rise to 25 per cent by end-1997 and stay at this kind of level until May 1998.

3 IMF programme modified to tighten fiscal policy further in November 1997.

4 **December 1997** IMF reviews standby credit and makes package more stringent.

4 **February 1998** IMF programme modified to allow 2 per cent of GDP budget deficit in order to facilitate recovery, but Fund still demands tight monetary stance.

5 **May 1998** IMF programme modified to allow target of 3 per cent of GDP budget deficit and 'somewhat higher monetary growth' with 'cautious reductions in interest rates'. At this date the money market rate is still about 17 per cent; only by December 1998 does it fall to 3 per cent.

6 **August 1998** the Compehensive Financial Restructuring Programme announced by Thai government.

7 GDP in 1998 is estimated to have fallen 8 per cent.

NOTES

An early version of this chapter appeared as Corbett and Vines (1999). We are grateful for comments from participants at the Warwick conference on 'International Capital Markets and International Financial Crises' (24 and 25 July 1998); from participants at a seminar in the Department of Economics, RSPAS, Australian National University (September 1998) (in particular by Ross McLeod, Ross Garnaut and Bhanupong Nidhiprabha); and from Richard Agénor, Barry Eichengreen and Marcus Miller. We would also like to acknowledge helpful conversations in Washington in November 1998 with Timothy Lane, Charles Adams and Paul Masson (IMF), Amar Bhattacharya and Joe Stiglitz (World Bank) and Caroline Atkinson (US Treasury), none of whom will agree with all of what we have to say. The debts which we owe to our colleagues Gregor Irwin, Gordon Menzies, Hwe Loo Tan and Peter Warr will be clear to them, and we have been strongly influenced by Crafts (1998). We also want to acknowledge valuable research assistance by Catherine Downard.

1. As we write it appears that Korea and Thailand are recovering – for reasons which are similar – and that Indonesia and Malaysia are not – also for reasons which have similarities. But no one would deny our use of the term 'almost complete collapse' to describe what happened in even Korea and Thailand, from which circumstances these two countries have made almost superhuman recovery.

2. Richard Portes has suggested use of the term 'financial crisis' for what we call 'collapse' (p. 158). As will be apparent, we find it necessary to have two separate terms.

3. It will become apparent that we are using the words 'disintegrated'/'disintegration' in a way which is different from our use of the word 'collapse', and we think it helpful to have a different term.

4. The vulnerability issue has been re-examined in an important pair of papers by Morris and Shin (1998, 1999). In these models, strategic interactions between

speculators can give rise to 'break-points': on one side of a particular level of the 'fundamentals' a system is safe, but immediately beyond this level the system spectacularly collapses. The essential insight in their models comes from a strategic complementarity between speculators: the expected profitability to one speculator from selling depends positively on the number of other speculators who are also selling. The onset of a crisis happens when the fundamentals evolve to the point where a 'break' happens. Morris and Shin are critical of the multiple-equilibrium analysis of vulnerability which we use; they argue (and they are right) that there is no good theory of why and when flips happen from one equilibrium to the other. They instead want to model vulnerability using their break-point ideas. Our problem with the Morris and Shin approach – with which we have much sympathy – is that so far it has been applied only in a model with very sparsely specified economic features. Including an endogenous risk premium – which is at the centre of our treatment – within the strategic interactions of their model at present looks as if it would be ferociously difficult. But if this could be done, then the resulting analysis could be very useful.

5. Stiglitz (1996) discusses ways in which the system worked and cautions against forgetting just how well it worked.

6. McKibbin (1994) estimated the implicit reduction in the risk premium when Mexico joined NAFTA, and showed that it was large enough to cause a significant boom.

7. It is often quite difficult to disentangle moral hazard from over-optimism.

8. It is a theory of 'crony capitalism' in as much as the emergence of bad states is the consequence of 'off-balance sheet payments' to cronies, rather than just the consequence of pure risk (or incompetence).

9. By doing this, Irwin and Vines answer in the affirmative the question posed by Kletzer (1999) in his comment on Dooley's chapter 3 (p. 122). Kletzer called for formalisation of the chapter in order to see if the Dooley story requires, for completeness, to be located in a stochastic world. We think that it does.

10. At the same time, liberalisation increased the marginal product of capital, which also induced capital accumulation for non-problematic reasons (see Portes and Vines, 1997).

11. It enters in exactly the same way that expectations of exchange rate collapse enter into the multiple-equilibria currency-crisis models. It is worth noting that this multiple-equilibrium feature of the model is a feature of short-run but not of long-run equilibria. In the long run, high interest rates mean that much less capital is invested in the country, and this effect is strong enough to mean that the costs of paying out on the guarantees in the high interest case would be no higher than in the low-interest rate case, thus removing the problem. But the realistic assumption that there is a 'short run' – in which risk premia can be instantly adjusted but in which the capital stock is effectively predetermined – means that the model is one which is vulnerable to a multiple-equilibrium problem.

12. Many other countries, before the recent experience in Asia, have failed to learn this lesson. For example, monetary policy in the UK in the late 1980s and early 1990s contained contradictions of a very similar kind. An attempt was made

both to control inflation and to peg the exchange rate at a low level in the mid-1980s. Then an attempt was made both to promote a recovery from recession and to maintain a fixed exchange rate within the ERM link in the early 1990s. Both attempts ended in fiasco.

13. See Dooley (1994)
14. Portes and Vines (1997) argued strongly, in a paper written during 1996, that this was the lesson to learn from the Mexican experience of 1994–5. Jeffrey Sachs had been saying this since immediately after the Mexico crisis.
15. In addition, the investment boom is likely be associated with an increase in stock market valuations, and that can add to the forces causing the consumption boom, as consumers who are more wealthy spend some of their gains.
16. This sequential argument makes two realistic assumptions. The first of these is that wage and price adjustment lags behind output, with the dual implication that wage and price adjustment fails to choke off the boom in the first period, and that wages and prices rise so far in the second as to throw the boom into reverse. The second assumption is that investors are not sufficiently forward-looking as to see what is coming and so damp investment in the first period. Irwin and Vines (1995) developed this argument in some detail in an unpublished paper on the Mexican crisis. Notice that this story has much similarity to the theory proposed by Aghion, Bacchetta and Banerjee in chapter 5 of this volume. That chapter has flexible prices; the stickiness comes from 'time-to-build' in the supply-side effects of capital investment. For a while, increases in investment lead to increases in supply which can go hand-in-hand, sequentially, with increases in collateral and so further increases in investment. But eventually rises in non-traded goods prices squeeze profitability and cause a reverse. Edison, Luangaram and Miller (1998) have also produced a model to analyse this issue, concentrating in the possibilities for boom, and subsequent bust, in the price of a non-traded asset, namely land.
17. But notice that currency crisis could also be precipitated simply by the downturn which follows the ending of the boom itself, for example, as the stock market falls. It is thus also possible to argue that the fixed exchange rate rendered these economies vulnerable to a process of boom and bust, in which the bust itself caused a currency crisis.
18. In this, he was quoting the work of Young (1995).
19. That interpretation is challenged by (among others) Radelet and Sachs (1997).

> Good economic policies and a favourable economic structure raise the returns to capital and thereby stimulate rapid investments in capital. Without [these] ... the returns to capital would be much less, so that capital accumulation would be much lower, and overall growth would be much slower as a result.

However they agree that

> If ... most ... growth is the result of capital accumulation ... growth will slow down as capital deepening takes place (that is, as the capital-labour ratio rises sharply in the economy) since capital deepening will be associated with a declining rate of return to new investments. This is in fact the case in East Asia: as capital accumulation has progressed, rates of return on capital have declined, suggesting that indeed both capital accumulation and growth will taper off in the future.

> Radelet and Sachs (1997) cite OECD data that the
>
> rate of return on capital in Korea declined gradually from around 22 percent in the mid 1980s to about 14 percent in 1994. In Singapore, a comparable indicator – the rates of return on US foreign direct investment – fell from 27 percent in the late 1980s to 19 percent in the mid-1990s. In Hong Kong and Taipei, China rates of return fell from around 21 percent to 15 percent. While these declines do confirm the neo-classical prediction of declining returns to investment, and are consistent with the rapid accumulation of capital documented by Young ... the important point is that they are still well above the world-wide average returns on US foreign direct investment of 11 percent.

20. These figures are taken from IMF (1997).
21. See Diwan and Hoekman, chapter 10 in this volume.
22. For a stylised account of the crisis in Thailand, see the appendix (p. 99).
23. For further details of the Thai experience, see the appendix (p. 99).
24. This is not to deny the fact that, as the crisis broke, the Thai authorities had exhausted their reserves and were unable to obtain access to sufficient foreign capital to continue to defend the currency. As a crisis breaks it may be rational for lenders to refuse to lend at almost any interest rate, because of the strong possibility that the currency will be devalued. Even if the government attempts to borrow in foreign currency in order to intervene, lenders to the government may perceive the near-certainty of devaluation and the resulting capital loss which the government would face on its borrowing, and may begin to build such large probability of default into the risk premium as to make further borrowing impossible.
25. See the discussion of related issues, in the context of the Mexico crisis, in Agénor and Masson (1999).
26. We would like to acknowledge a helpful discussion on this point with Pierre-Richard Agénor, who does not agree with us. We accept that we have no decisive evidence on this point, but the 'mistake' which it implies is a central part of our interpretation of the crisis. (If the authorities had understood that the outcome would be so bad, then the only way to preserve our overall interpretation would be to argue that the costs of defending the fixed exchange rate peg had become even higher than this.)
27. The remarks in n. 26 are relevant here, too.
28. Recall that we are using the term 'collapse' more loosely in this section than in the previous two. We would like to thank Gordon Menzies for very helpful comments on an initial draft of this section.
29. One forum in which these arguments were presented with vigour was a meeting in London in February 1998 which the authors attended and whose proceedings are described in Chote (1998); there were many others.
30. In this we are on the side of Stiglitz (1998a, 1998b) (see also chapter 12 in this volume). Our arguments are designed, by carefully specifying alternative policies, to bolster Stiglitz's position
31. This argument is more persuasive than an alternative one, which gives ambiguous results. This alternative argument claims that high nominal interest rates – 20 or 30 per cent in Korea and Thailand for a long period, above 70 per cent in Indonesia for a long period – implied very high real interest rate in terms of

non-traded goods. The problem with this argument is that the real interest rates in terms of traded goods was, in all these cases, and for a significant period of time, negative. When relative prices move very significantly, so that one measure of real interest rates in highly positive, and another measure of real interest rates is highly negative, it is quite hard to make a case about the looseness or tightness of monetary policy using real interest rates. More work in this area is clearly needed, applying the ideas about 'monetary policy stress' developed by Clarida, Jordi and Gertler (1998).

32. Such a target cannot entirely remove uncertainty about the long-run nominal exchange rate. This is because it does not remove uncertainty about the long-run real exchange rate but only uncertainty about the price level at which this real exchange rate will be reached.

33. This is clear from the results shown in Clarida, Jordi and Gertler (1998).

34. Suppose that speculators do not know whether the country is of the kind (which we call type a) in which policy makers will keep its nominal exchange rate in a year's time exactly the same as at present, or of a kind (which we call type b) in which policy makers will let the currency fall all the way to a quarter of its present value. Suppose that speculators believe that there is a 50 per cent probability that the country under consideration is of type b. Let interest rates not be raised above the world rate. Then if speculators are risk-neutral the exchange rate of the country will immediately fall to only five-eighths of its current value (a fall to the halfway point between a 'no-change' outcome and a fall to 25 per cent of its current value).

35. In the example described in n. 34, if the probability of the country being a type-b country remains at 50 per cent, the interest rate increase required to entirely prevent any fall would have been enormous – namely 37.5 per cent per annum above world rates. (To compensate holders of a currency which was expected to fall next period to 62.5 per cent of current value would require a coupon yield that much above world yields.)

36. In the example described in nn. 34 and 35, a type-a country would need to set an interest rate so high that a type-b country would find it too costly to mimic. If the costs which the two types of countries attached to interest rate increases were not very different, a very high interest rate increase would be needed for this purpose. (We are grateful to Hwee Loo Tan, MPhil. student at Oxford University, for discussing these issues with us.)

37. It is interesting to note that by late 1998 Thailand began debating both independence for the Bank of Thailand and inflation targeting, and it is now likely to adopt an institutional structure for monetary policy which is similar to that in the UK (including a monetary policy committee with outside members).

38. In dealing with the Indonesian crisis the IMF was forced to take rapid action and closed 16 banks. But it took this action without being able to say whether those banks which remained open were candidates for closure in the longer-term reform process, and the result was widespread panic.

39. An alternative, more prevalent, view is that the meltdown was inevitable because the crisis coincided with the sunset of the Suharto regime, which began at least as early as December 1997. But we believe that this view provides too

much cover for those who committed policy mistakes; and, in our view, there could have been a less dreadful outcome than the one which emerged as 1998 wore on.

40. By the middle of 1999 this view has come to be widely held. It is not adequate to argue that there was some, gradual, adjustment of the programmes as the severity of the downturn became apparent.
41. See Burnside, Eichenbaum and Rebello (1998).
42. The former threat is a central feature of inflation targeting.
43. We would like to acknowledge a helpful discussion on this issue with Martin Wolf. For scepticism, see Eichengreen (1998).
44. There is an extended discussion of these issues in Eichengreen (1999); Eichengreen *et al.* (1999).
45. Krugman (1998b) fails to make this point.
46. In particular, the equilibrium real exchange rate will depend on how much of the foreign debt is to be honoured.
47. We are grateful to discussion with Martin Wolf on this issue. We do not think that Eichengreen (1999), much as we admire his discussion, faces up to it.
48. One reason given for this is the importance of sound financial systems for effective macroeconomic policy. Another possibility might be the 'goal-overload' from which the Bank already suffers. See Gilbert, Powell and Vines (1999).
49. See Miller and Zhang (1998), and chapter 11 by Bhattacharya and Miller in this volume, for extended discussion of these issues.
50. This is the conclusion that Richard Portes draws in his discussion in the Round Table (chapter 13).
51. We owe the idea in this conclusion to Crafts (1998). He does not quite use our labels, although they are implicit in what he says.

REFERENCES

Agénor, P.-R. and P. Masson (1999). 'Credibility, Reputation, and the Mexican Peso Crisis', *Journal of Money, Credit, and Banking* **31(1)**: 70–84

Alba, P., A. Bhattacharya, S. Claessens, S. Ghosh, and L. Hernandez (1999). 'The Role of Macroeconomic and Financial Sector Linkages in East Asia's Economic Crisis', chapter 1 in this volume

Bhattacharya, A., P. Alba, S. Claessens, S. Ghosh and L. Hernandez (1998). 'Volatility and Contagion in a Financially Integrated World: Lessons from East Asia's Recent Experience', World Bank, mimeo

Bhattacharya, A. and M. Miller (1999). 'Coping with Crises: Is there a "Silver Bullet?"', chapter 11 in this volume

Burnside, C., M. Eichenbaum, and S. Rebello (1998). 'Prospective Deficits and the Asian Currency Crises', *NBER Working Paper* **6758**

Chang, R and A. Velasco (1997). 'Financial Fragility and the Exchange Rate Regime', Federal Reserve Bank of Atlanta, *Working Paper*, **97–16**

Chote, R. (1998). 'Financial Crises and Asia', in Centre for Economic Policy Research, *Financial Crises and Asia*, CEPR Conference Report, **6**

Clarida, R., J. Jordi and M. Gertler (1998). 'Monetary Policy Rules in Practice: Some International Evidence', *European Economic Review*; **42**(6): 1033–67

Corbett, J. and D. Vines (1999). 'Asian Currency and Financial Crises: Lessons from Vulnerability, Crisis, and Collapse', *World Economy,* January

Corden, W. M (1997). 'Is There a Way Out? Are the IMF Prescriptions Right?', Notes from a Lecture given in Singapore (5 August), mimeo.

Corsetti, G. P. Pesenti and N. Roubini (1998). 'What Caused the East Asian Financial Crisis?', New York University, mimeo; see also chapter 4 in this volume

Crafts, N. (1998). 'East Asian Growth Before and After the Crisis', London School of Economics (July), mimeo

Davies, G. and D. Vines (1998). 'Ripe for Attack and Attackable: When are Self-fulfilling Currency Crises Possible?', Institute of Economics and Statistics, Oxford, mimeo

Diamond, D. and P. Dybvig (1983). 'Bank Runs, Deposit Insurance, and Liquidity', *Journal of Political Economy* **91**: 401–19

Diwan, I and B. Hoekman (1999). 'Competition, Complementarity and Contagion in East Asia', chapter 10 in this volume

Dooley, M. P. (1994). 'Are Recent Capital Inflows to Developing Countries a Vote for or Against Economic Policy Reforms?', *Working Paper*, **295**, University of California Santa Cruz; published in W. Gruben, D. Gould and C. Zarazaga (eds.), *Exchange Rates, Capital Flows, and Monetary Policy in a Changing World Economy*, Boston: Kluiver Academic (1997); reprinted in revised form as Chapter 3 in this volume

  (1997). 'A Model of Crisis in Emerging Markets', University of California, Santa Cruz, mimeo; *NBER Working Paper*, **6300** (December)

  (1999a). 'Are Capital Inflows to Developing Countries a Vote for or Against Economic Policy Reforms?', chapter 3 in this volume

  (1999b). 'A Model of Crisis in Emerging Markets' *Economic Journal*, forthcoming

Dornbusch, R. (1997). 'A Thai–Mexico Primer', *The International Economy*, **55** (September–October): 20–23

Edison, H., P. Luangaram and M. Miller (1998). 'Asset Bubbles, Domino Effects, and 'Life Boats': Elements of the East Asian Crisis', *Working Paper*, Warwick University

Eichengreen, B. (1998). 'Exiting from a Fixed Exchange Regime without Precipitating a Crisis', delivered as the Alexandre Kafka Lecture, Rio de Janeiro (December)

  (1999). *Towards a New International Financial Architecture: A Practical Post-Asia Agenda,* Washington, DC: Institute for International Economics

Eichengreen, B., P. Masson, M. Savastano and S. Sharma (1999). 'Transition Strategies and Nominal Anchors on the Road to Greater Exchange Rate Flexibility', IMF (2 February), mimeo

Eichengreen, B. and R. Portes (1995). *Crisis, What Crisis? Orderly Workouts for Sovereign Debtors*, London: Centre for Economic Policy Research

Evans, H. (1997). 'The Bretton Woods Institutions: A View from the Boards', *Global Economic Institutions*: CEPR *Discussion Paper*, **32**, London

Evans, K. (1998) 'The Economy', *Indonesia Update 1988,* Economics Division, RSPAS, Australian National University (24 September), mimeo

Fane, G. (1998). ' The Role of Prudential Regulation', chapter 17 in R. McLeod and R. Garnaut, *East Asia in Crisis*, London: Routledge

Fischer, S. (1998). 'The Asian Crisis: A View from the IMF', address to the Midwinter Conference of the Bankers' Association for Foreign Trade (22 January); available at http://www.imf.org/external/np/speeches/1998/012298.htm

    (1999). 'On the need for an International Lender of Last Resort', paper presented to the annual meetings of the American Economic Association; available at http://www.imf.org/external/np/speeches/1999/010399.htm

Gilbert, C., A. Powell and D. Vines (1999). 'Positioning the World Bank', *Economic Journal*, features section (November)

IMF (1997). *World Economic Outlook.*, Washington, DC: International Monetary Fund (September)

    (1998). *International Capital Markets,* Washington, DC: International Monetary Fund

Irwin, G. and D. Vines (1995). 'The Macroeconomics of the Mexican Crisis: A Simple Two-period Model', *CEPR Discussion Paper*, **124** (September)

    (1998). 'A Model of Moral Hazard and Financial Crisis', Oxford University, mimeo

    (1999). 'A Krugman–Dooley–Sachs Multiple Equilibrium Model of the Asian Financial Crisis', *CEPR Discussion Paper*, **2149** (April)

Kim, J. and L. Lau (1994). 'The Sources of Economic Growth of the East Asian Newly Industrialised Countries', *Journal of the Japanese and International Economies*, **8**: 235–71

Kletzer, K. (1999). 'Discussion of Dooley (1999a), p. 000 in this volume

Kochhar, K., L. Dicks-Mireaux and B. Horvath (1996). 'Thailand: The Road to Sustained Growth', *IMF Occasional Paper*, **146**

Krugman, P. (1979). 'A Model of Balance-of-payments Crises', *Journal of Money, Credit, and Banking*, **11**: 311–25

    (1994). 'The Myth of Asia's Miracle', *Foreign Affairs* **73**: 62–78.

    (1996). 'Are Currency Crises Self-Fulfilling?', in B. S. Bernanke, and J. J. Rotemberg (eds.), *NBER Macroeconomics Annual*, Cambridge, Mass. and London: MIT Press: 345–78

    (1998a). 'Whatever Happened to Asia?', http://web.mit.edu/krugman/www/DISINTER.html

    (1998b). 'Firesale FDI', http://web.mit.edu/krugman/www/FIRESALE.htm

    (1999c). 'Saving Asia: Its Time to get Radical', *Fortune Investor*; (September 7): 33–8 available at http://www.pathfinder.com/fortune/investor/1998/980907/sol.html

Masson, P. (1998). 'Contagion: Monsoonal Effects, Spillovers, and Jumps between Multiple Equilibria', *IMF Working Paper*, **WP/98/142**; see also chapter 8 in this volume

MacLeod, R. and R. Garnaut (1998). *East Asia in Crisis*, London: Routledge

McKibbin, W. (1994). 'The Macroeconomic Consequences of NAFTA', Australian National University, mimeo
  (1998). 'The Economic Crisis in Asia: An Empirical Analysis', *Discussion Paper in International Economics*, **136**; Washington, DC: Brookings Institution
McKibbin, W. and W. Martin (1998). 'The East Asian Crisis: Empirical Causes; mimeo, available from http://www.msgpl.com.au/msgpl/msghome.htm
Menkoff, L. (1998), 'Thailand's Financial Institutions and Their Current Crisis', in L. Menkoff and B. Reszat, *Asian Financial Markets – Structure, Policy Issues and Prospects*, Baden-Baden: Nomos Verlagsgesellschaft
Miller, M. and L. Zhang (1998). 'Sovereign Liquidity Crises: The Strategic Case for a Payments Standstill', *CEPR Discussion Paper*, **1820** (February)
Morris, S. and H. S. Shin (1998). 'Unique Equilibrium in a Model of Self-fulfilling Currency Attacks', *American Economic Review*, **88**: 587–97
  (1999). 'A Theory of the Onset of Currency Attacks', chapter 7 in this volume
Obstfeld, M. (1986). 'Rational and Self-fulfilling Balance-of-payments Crises', *American Economic Review*, **76**: 72–81
  (1991). 'The Destabilising Effects of Exchange Rate Escape Clauses', *NBER Working Paper*, **3603**
  (1994). 'The Logic of Currency Crises', *NBER Working Paper*, **4640**
  (1995). 'Models of Currency Crises with Self-fulfilling Features', *NBER Working Paper*, **5285**
Ozkan, F. G. and A. Sutherland (1993). 'A Model of the ERM Crisis', University of York, mimeo
  (1994). 'A Currency Crisis Model with an Optimising Government', University of York, mimeo
  (1995). 'Policy Options for a Currency Crisis', *Economic Journal*, **105**: 510–19
Portes, R. and D. Vines (1997). *Coping with International Capital Flows*, London: Commonwealth Secretariat
Radelet, S. and J. Sachs (1997). 'Asia's Re-emergence', *Foreign Affairs*, **76(6)**: 44–59
  (1998). 'The East Asia Crisis: Diagnosis, Remedies, Prospects'. *Brookings Papers on Economic Activity*, **1**: 1–74
Robinson, D. Y. Byeon, R. Teja and W. Tseng (1990). 'Thailand: Adjusting to Success: Current Policy Issues', IMF *Occasional Paper*, **85**
Sachs, J. (1995) 'Do we Need a Lender of Last Resort?', Frank D. Graham Lecture, Princeton University (April)
  (1996). 'Alternative Approaches to Financial Crises in Emerging Markets', *Revista de Economia Politica*, **16(2)**, (April–June): 40–52
Sadli, M (1988). 'The Indonesian Crisis', *Asia-Pacific Economic Literature* (May)
Soros, G. (1998). *The Crisis of Global Capitalism: Open Society Endangered.*, London: Little Brown
Stiglitz, J. (1996). 'Some Lessons from the East Asian Miracle', *World Bank Research Observer*, **11 (2)**: 151–77
  (1998a). 'Macroeconomic Dimensions of the East Asian Crisis', in Centre for Economic Policy Research, *Financial Crises and Asia*, CEPR Conference Report, **6**

(1998b). 'Sound Finance and Sustainable Development in Asia', Keynote Address to the Asia Development Forum, Manila (12 March 1998); available at http://www.worldbank.org/html/extdr/extme/jssp031298.htm

Warr, P. (1998.) 'Thailand', chapter 3 in R. McLeod and R. Garnaut *East Asia in Crisis*, London: Routledge

Warr, P. and B. Nidhiprabha (1996). *Thailand's Economic Miracle.*, Washington, DC: World Bank and Oxford University Press

Warr, P. and D. Vines (1999), 'How Boom Turned to Bust: A Macroeconometric Analysis of Thailand's Economic Crisis', mimeo

Young, A. (1995). 'The Tyranny of Numbers: Confronting the Statistical Realities of the East Asian Growth Experience', *Quarterly Journal of Economics*, **110(3)**: 641–80

Discussion
Christopher Bliss

While I was preparing my discussion of chapter 2, I had a strange dream. Some of you may think that this shows a shameful lack of concentration on my part. Be that as it may, the dream was striking. I dreamed that I was about to mark a large number of essays written by history undergraduates. The evident absurdity of this idea was not felt in the dream. The essays were concerned with the causes of the First World War. My first task was to map out a marking scheme, and my dream self felt entirely confident of my ability to do that.

One thing was clear. I would give low marks to any answer which advocated any single cause. Especially low marks would go to an essay which claimed that the war was caused by the assassination of the Arch-Duke in Sarajevo. The idea that the assassination of any individual, however prominent, could inescapably entail the outbreak of a Europewide war is completely ridiculous. Of course, a good answer could describe how the assassination triggered general conflict by being the occasion of a war between Austro-Hungary and Russia, which dragged in many other countries via the system of interlocking alliances which had maintained peace in Europe for over 40 years. The best answer would have to address that long peace, because one cannot reasonably claim that Europe's alliances made war inevitable in 1914, without explaining why very similar alliances had maintained peace for a length of time without precedent in modern Europe.

I shall leave my dream now, but I shall bring one thing from it to the Corbett–Vines chapter: my marking scheme. Corbett and Vines get good marks for avoiding a unicausal account of the crises. Theirs is a subtle and analytically sharp analysis. Their assassin is financial liberalisation. Yet they make it clear that by itself this could have been innocuous, as it was to a considerable extent in OECD countries. What proved to be unstable was the imposition of the assassin's bullet on economic systems characterised by inflexible exchange rates and fiscal rigidity.

For this to make an intellectually satisfying case, it is important that financial liberalisation of the critical kind should be quite a recent arrival on the Southeast Asian scene. Otherwise the story is vulnerable to the objection, which tells heavily against some other accounts of the crises (cronyism, non-transparency, over-valued exchange rates, etc.): why did these factors not cause collapse much earlier? I have to believe these distinguished experts if they claim that financial liberalisation was quite a recent arrival in the several countries concerned. I would have liked to read more on this point.

Although it is always easier to explain things with the benefit of hindsight, the Corbett–Vines account suggests that it would have been possible to forecast crisis for the affected countries given their institutions and their thrust towards financial liberalisation. The failure of the economics profession to make those forecasts must be counted as a singular failure, comparable in size to the failure to come up with consistent and useful policy recommendations for ex-socialist countries in their transition to capitalism.

3 Are capital inflows to developing countries a vote for or against economic policy reforms?

MICHAEL P. DOOLEY

In the summer of 1993 the World Bank Economic Development Institute asked me to prepare a paper for a conference evaluating the remarkable capital inflows that were then seen as both a problem and a blessing for developing countries in Latin America and Asia. The audience comprised senior officials from central banks and finance ministries in the emerging market countries. A revised version of that presentation is the foundation for this chapter.[1] The argument presented is that capital inflows to emerging markets were motivated by a three-part government insurance policies. The three ingredients were fixed exchange rates, lender-of-last-resort (LOLR) commitments and open capital markets. The paper warned that one of the three links in the insurance chain would have to be broken: if not broken voluntarily, the market would eventually force a regime change. With the benefit of hindsight it appears that these warnings were closer to the mark than the author, much less the audience, imagined.

The key analytic point raised by the paper is that a sequence of capital inflows followed by sudden reversals is entirely consistent with rational investor behaviour. So-called 'convergence play' inflows to European countries before the crises in 1992, and deposit inflows into US Savings and Loans (S&Ls) before the crisis, are cited as examples of episodes in which investors moved into a country, or financial intermediary, with every intention of moving out under the umbrella of free government insurance. Moreover, the build-up of implicit government liabilities would eventually generate a successful speculative attack that would end the regime.

These issues remain at the heart of arguments over reform of the international monetary system examined in this volume. If the approach advocated here is correct, we have not seen the last of capital inflow/crisis sequences in developing countries. I have recently attempted to make these ideas in a more formal framework, (Dooley, 1997), but believe that this attempt to explain the problem to a non-technical audience remains a useful introduction to the subject.[2]

In the early 1990s, private capital inflows were a widespread and surprising problem for macroeconomic policy in a variety of developing countries. Although sustained private capital inflows were something that most governments would have been happy to live with, there was concern that what flowed in for reasons we do not fully understand could flow out for those same reasons. While capital inflows can be inconvenient, unexpected reversals of access to foreign capital can, as we learned after 1982, have disastrous and lasting effects.

In most cases, developing countries (DCs) have attempted to offset the domestic effects of capital inflows through some combination of sterilised exchange market intervention, exchange rate appreciation and, in some cases, restrictions on non-residents' access to domestic investments. Early in 1994, for example, Malaysia imposed restrictions on capital inflows reminiscent of the control programme launched in Germany and other European countries with 'strong' currencies in the waning days of the Bretton Woods System of fixed exchange rates. In other cases capital market liberalisation has been put on hold or slowed substantially.[3]

In this chapter we develop the argument that there are very good reasons for governments to be concerned about what we will call 'arbitrage capital flows'. Such capital inflows share the unfortunate properties of capital inflows to US S&Ls in the 1980s and are likely to have the same consequences for taxpayers in developing countries.

The basic motivation behind these capital flows is the opportunity to exploit a government subsidy or guarantee. They do not reflect confidence in the investment climate in the country but in the government's ability to give away money. The only lasting way to deal with this type of capital inflow is to remove the subsidy or guarantee. As discussed below, this involves difficult choices for countries that have graduated to the ranks of nations that participate fully in the international financial system.

1 What lies behind private capital inflows?

Conventional pessimists argue that capital inflows after 1989 were mainly the result of the depressed yields available in industrial countries.[4] Really dedicated pessimists allege that low yields in the industrial countries 'pushed' poorly informed investors to reach for higher returns available in emerging markets without understanding the risks involved. Once underway, resulting booms in 'emerging' equity and other financial markets generated speculative inflows that seemed to be unrelated to the fundamental value of the securities traded. Such inflows are a misguided vote of confidence for economic policies in recipient countries.[5]

The conventional optimistic interpretation is that private capital inflows reflect fundamentally improved risk-adjusted expected returns on investments in recipient countries. In this case net capital inflows, and the associated current account deficits, help reallocate real capital formation to countries where risk-adjusted returns have improved. Such inflows are naturally limited by the supply of superior investment opportunities. Inflows of this type are clearly a vote of confidence for economic policies in recipient countries.

In this chapter we argue that neither of these arguments helps much in understanding the scale of private capital inflows to emerging markets after 1989. Both sides of the debate have focused on the incentives for *net* investment in emerging markets. It is thus natural that the focus is on real or imagined opportunities to add to the productive capital stock of countries receiving capital inflows.

The view developed is that large capital inflows reflect private investors' efforts to exploit financial arbitrage opportunities generated by governments of developing countries. Two ingredients are necessary for these types of capital flows. First, the government must be wealthy enough to credibly offer a subsidy or support a guarantee. Second, emerging markets must be accessible to international investors. If these two conditions are met, the size of the position taken by private investors for arbitrage incentives that may have been around for a long time will grow explosively.

Such inflows do not reflect investors' confidence in the economic performance of the recipient economies but in the ability of their governments to guarantee abnormal rates of return (at the governments' expense) for a limited but predictable period of time. In many ways, recent inflows into emerging markets are analogous to the spectacular inflows to US S&Ls before 1989 or the 'convergence play' inflows to high-inflation EMS currencies before the exchange market crisis of 1992.

2 Recent private capital inflows into developing countries

In 1988, a prevalent view was that DCs that had trouble servicing external debt in the 1980s would not re-enter international capital markets for a generation. The useful life of this prediction was even shorter than the average for economic predictions, as very large inflows to developing countries in Asia, Latin America and the Middle East were widespread after 1989.

Table 3.1 shows private capital flows into developing countries in Asia and the Western Hemisphere expressed as a percentage of the recipient country's GDP. In some respects the experience of the two regions has been remarkably similar. For the Western Hemisphere private capital inflows were reduced dramatically following the 1982 debt crisis as eight of 10 countries experienced private capital outflows from 1984 to 1989. In contrast, from 1992 to 1993 nine of 10 of the Latin countries shown experienced private capital inflows. For Asian DCs private inflows were less affected by the debt crisis but here, too, inflows increased sharply after 1989 with six of the eight countries listed experiencing sizable inflows from 1989 to 1993.

The counterparts of these private inflows can be divided into official capital outflows, conventionally measured by increases in international reserves, and current account deficits. This is an interesting division because reserve gains probably have minor implications for the real economy while current account deficits measure the contribution of foreign savings to real domestic consumption and capital formation.

For the Western Hemisphere small private inflows before 1989 financed current account deficits. From 1990 to 1993 much larger private inflows were matched by current account deficits of about $100 billion and reserve accumulations of about $60 billion.

For Asia, almost all the private inflow before 1989 was matched by reserve accumulations. The much larger private inflows since then have increasingly supported larger current account deficits since 1994 the reserve build-up has accounted for two-thirds of the private inflow.

In summary, a widespread response to capital inflows has been official intervention in foreign exchange markets and increases in international reserve assets. This response suggests that differences in formal exchange rate arrangements may be less important than governments' attitudes toward the effects of inflows on exchange rates and the monetary base. Second, renewed access to international capital markets has allowed many countries to increase investment and/or consumption relative to GDP. Finally, a sudden reversal of private capital inflows constitutes a significant shock to a majority of the countries in these two regions.

3 Arbitrage capital flows

It would be a mistake, however, to conclude that investors care what the DCs are doing with the capital inflows. The key to understanding such inflows is a careful evaluation of the contingent liabilities taken on by governments. These implicit liabilities can create powerful incentives for private financial transactions.

Table 3.1   Private capital inflows as percentage of GDP, 1970–1993

Asia

	Indonesia	Korea	Malaysia	Philippines	Singapore	Sri Lanka	Taiwan	Thailand
1970	2.70	5.58	−1.87	−0.36	74.37	1.72	0.54	2.66
1971	2.30	6.40	1.97	−0.52	87.07	1.18	0.32	3.42
1972	6.49	3.81	4.60	0.80	48.60	1.62	0.67	4.03
1973	5.17	4.51	−1.25	2.06	28.77	1.31	−6.06	2.16
1974	−0.86	9.38	6.43	4.75	41.48	2.77	8.38	4.91
1975	−3.22	8.74	4.28	4.43	24.52	1.70	2.72	5.23
1976	3.23	4.53	−0.64	5.00	15.11	1.55	−0.39	3.12
1977	1.95	3.52	−3.37	2.75	9.27	2.12	−6.08	6.00
1978	4.05	−0.39	−1.73	7.54	15.58	1.98	−6.39	3.75
1979	0.86	5.55	−2.15	5.50	15.96	9.60	−1.20	7.49
1980	−0.75	5.51	0.29	4.30	24.48	8.99	3.60	5.23
1981	−0.63	4.13	5.80	1.02	18.66	9.36	8.61	7.84
1982	−1.19	2.02	10.94	3.40	17.28	12.55	−2.74	0.70
1983	9.16	−0.42	10.38	0.96	5.04	9.61	−2.72	7.93
1984	3.74	0.27	3.81	−1.38	11.91	6.12	−5.76	6.59
1985	2.20	0.42	5.70	−4.48	11.21	4.58	−3.90	3.78
1986	−2.25	−4.08	4.58	−5.05	4.97	5.92	9.25	2.53
1987	1.58	−6.41	−3.75	−5.45	10.05	3.31	9.67	3.10
1988	−0.76	−3.10	−8.22	−2.19	2.23	5.08	−9.55	7.00
1989	1.17	−0.57	3.88	0.58	−3.50	4.56	−8.31	10.29
1990	8.71	−0.40	8.47	1.93	0.23	4.72	−9.35	14.87
1991	8.11	2.94	12.10	2.12	−7.84	5.20	−1.32	12.56
1992	6.64	2.70	15.04	−1.27	−6.40	2.66	−3.15	8.76
1993	3.42	1.22	4.89	2.70	−11.05	4.26	−0.06	7.87
Average								
1984–8	0.9	−2.6	0.4	−3.7	8.1	5.0	−0.1	4.6
1989–93	6.7	1.6	10.1	1.4	−6.3	4.2	−3.5	11.0

Source: IMF. International Monetary Fund.

Western Hemisphere

	Argentina	Bolivia	Brazil	Chile	Colombia	Ecuador	Mexico	Peru	Uruguay	Venezuela
1970	0.98	-3.46	2.48	1.16	3.94	6.89	3.40	-2.56	-0.79	1.19
1971	-0.09	-4.83	3.26	-0.90	6.66	3.21	2.39	-0.01	-0.96	1.84
1972	0.46	-4.97	6.11	-0.13	5.17	7.90	2.72	-0.70	-5.85	3.71
1973	0.28	-6.06	5.20	-0.69	2.73	4.37	1.90	2.86	-3.43	-3.00
1974	-0.02	-4.00	5.58	-3.49	1.92	1.86	3.13	7.84	-0.93	-8.13
1975	0.52	1.32	4.32	-0.51	1.51	8.13	3.17	4.62	0.88	3.05
1976	0.09	-0.91	5.76	1.90	4.16	5.37	-0.48	-0.09	3.90	-1.07
1977	-0.15	-0.47	2.94	5.96	1.90	11.06	2.91	2.97	8.62	6.74
1978	-4.27	-1.36	5.32	11.15	1.77	10.55	3.19	-0.23	5.95	12.49
1979	2.30	5.78	3.50	10.56	5.87	7.02	4.59	-0.94	5.88	5.97
1980	-2.22	-26.27	3.82	11.95	5.35	8.36	5.50	0.35	9.16	0.03
1981	-3.27	-6.31	4.59	15.23	5.55	0.65	3.94	5.55	4.39	-3.12
1982	-7.50	-11.04	3.18	3.48	7.91	5.79	-4.73	5.32	-4.01	-9.13
1983	-1.17	-19.63	-1.26	-2.32	3.73	-16.90	-3.24	-5.99	-5.87	-8.18
1984	0.43	0.68	1.36	6.79	1.45	-7.21	-2.71	-8.80	-0.50	8.57
1985	-0.84	-1.94	-4.36	-0.62	4.70	-9.55	-2.53	-8.65	-2.95	-4.27
1986	-1.61	5.45	-3.16	-8.58	1.76	-13.06	0.10	-5.45	-2.06	-5.19
1987	-3.86	-0.67	-2.95	-6.02	-0.39	-6.84	2.46	-5.86	-2.84	1.60
1988	-0.12	7.46	-3.37	-7.22	1.64	-1.30	-1.71	-5.98	-4.87	2.17
1989	-7.11	2.35	-1.38	-2.08	1.01	-5.45	1.74	-4.02	-4.29	-3.00
1990	-0.93	4.52	-1.00	4.74	0.01	-4.28	2.73	-2.09	-1.37	-10.21
1991	-1.38	3.48	-0.81	4.49	-0.73	-2.68	7.27	3.50	-3.61	3.15
1992	5.05	7.04	1.34	8.63	1.04	-7.91	7.64	1.26	3.67	3.39
1993	7.33	5.36	-1.16	5.71	2.53	0.15	6.75	0.19	-1.51	2.92
Averages										
1984-8	-2.2	2.2	-2.3	-3.0	1.7	-7.2	-0.4	-6.5	-2.9	-2.9
1989-93	2.5	5.1	-0.4	5.9	0.7	-3.7	6.1	0.7	-0.7	-0.2

Source: IMF. *International Monetary Fund.*

In a tightly controlled financial system government guarantees are difficult to exploit. But as capital markets become more integrated and direct controls on financial transactions break down, investors will find new and better ways to take advantage of explicit or implicit government guarantees. The volume of such capital flows may have little to do with the economic fundamental we usually associate with private capital flows. Instead, the scale of transactions is determined by the resources available to support the government guarantee. The important difference between this and a speculative bubble is that, when a bubble bursts, some private speculators lose to others. When an implicit guarantee is called, the government loses.

One can find dramatic examples of this process in both developed countries and DCs. The combination of deposit insurance and a relaxation of controls over deposit rates and portfolio selection in the USA led to explosive growth in inflows into S&Ls and to their eventual collapse. The problem, clear in retrospect, was that the contingent liability of the US government provided the private investor with a virtual guarantee that high yields offered by savings and loan deposits would not be matched by *depositors'* losses. Depositors did not question the ability of some S&Ls to offer deposit rates 200–400 basis points over the market. As long as depositors were 'probably' guaranteed, there was little downside risk.

The important lesson is that the *size of the capital inflow* to the S&Ls did not depend on the fundamental quality of the assets they were acquiring. To extend the analogy with a DC, depositors did not care if the S&L bought a junk bond (international reserves), a shopping centre (domestic investment), or a new car for the bank president (imports of consumer durables). Depositors were protected by the very considerable ability of the US government to bail them out. Moreover, the interest rate offered by S&Ls did not accurately reflect anyone's expected rate of return on the assets, although the S&L executives probably thought their boats, cars and vacation homes were extremely good investments. For these reasons it was a mistake to interpret the 'capital inflow' to S&Ls as reflecting either a rational or irrational evaluation of their solvency.

In DCs a similar process helped generate the debt crisis of 1982. In this case, the government of debtor countries offered guarantees of the dollar value of residents' liabilities. The rapid build-up of private external debt in the 1970s was matched by a build-up of *contingent* liabilities of the government. This contingent liability became an important – but at the time, little noticed – part of the DC government's overall position. To some extent the offer of the guarantee *caused* the private capital inflow. Perhaps more important, the usual market checks to private inflows were short-circuited by the government guarantee.

About half of the private capital inflow before 1982 was recycled to international markets through unrecorded private capital outflows, what *ex post* has been labelled 'capital flight'. The other half was matched by current account deficits, a pattern quite similar to the balance of payments of DCs today.

The most recent example of arbitrage capital flows was the so-called 'convergence play' inflows to high-inflation EMS countries from 1987 to 1991. Over this period an estimated $300 bn flowed into 'high-yield' EMS member countries as investors calculated that the governments' commitment to maintain the exchange rate arrangement was credible for long enough so that they could reverse their positions *before* the exchange rate peg was abandoned. At the same time, the central banks of the countries receiving inflows resisted the fall in nominal interest rates that would have occurred if inflows were permitted to augment the money supply. As argued below, this is exactly the problem facing monetary authorities in emerging markets. With the benefit of hindsight it is easy to see that the huge losses suffered by EMS governments as the exchange rate arrangement was abandoned in 1992 justified private investors' faith in the guarantee rather than the economic policies of the governments involved.

4   Capital flows in 1994–1998

Is it possible that such a process is again at work in international capital markets? It is interesting to note that the 'over-lending' hypothesis for the build-up of external debt of DCs is often associated with the view that a bubble can occur once in every generation of investors. Thus, as the story goes, memory of the widespread defaults by DCs in the 1930s died out with the bankers of the 1930s and set the stage for irrational, follow-the-leader, lending to the same countries of the 1970s. A repeat of the same argument to explain recent widespread inflows to DCs implies a dramatic reduction in the half-life of investors, or at least their memories. In this business one learns not to rule out an explanation simply because it assumes a high level of incompetence, but in the current circumstances I believe there is a much better and more important lesson to be learned.

The alternative explanation is that a combination of fundamentals and arbitrage transactions are again at work. First, the fundamentals clearly favour a repatriation of funds to many debtor countries. Fiscal reform has been impressive in many countries; debt restructuring has been put in place; privatisation, in fact as well as intention, has been remarkably successful. At the same time, interest rates available in industrial countries are at their lowest levels in many years. All these factors make a net private capital inflow to DCs unsurprising. But are these factors sufficient to explain the large private capital inflows in recent years? I have serious doubts.

It seems likely that once again private capital inflows are being sustained not only by the more favourable investment climate but also by arbitrage opportunities generated by the governments of DCs. The form of the incentive is a little different as compared to the external debt/capital flight pattern that led up to the 1982 debt crisis. But in one important respect the recent private capital inflows are similar in that they are sustained by a contingent claim on the government. The distinguishing feature this time is that private capital inflows to DCs have taken the form of domestic currency-denominated instruments including equities, corporate bonds, bank deposits and government securities.[6] This is certainly different from the dollar-denominated, government-guaranteed, syndicated credits that comprised the build-up in debt before 1982.

In the current pattern of capital flows it is not obvious that the government of the borrowing country has provided a guarantee. However an *implicit guarantee* is provided by the increasingly popular use of the exchange rate as an anchor for inflationary expectations. In basing its credibility on the maintenance of a fixed or managed exchange rate the government, in effect, provides an exchange rate guarantee for the investor in domestic currency-denominated instruments similar to that offered by high-inflation EMS countries.

This, of course, seems to leave the investor with a credit risk. But in most emerging markets the government is very likely to provide a credit as well as exchange rate guarantee. In cases where international investors buy government securities, the guarantee is explicit. Commercial bank deposits are also guaranteed, especially where the deposit is denominated in domestic currency.

Finally, even the liabilities of domestic non-financial corporations carry a strong government back-up. This is because such firms are heavily indebted to the domestic banking system. If non-resident creditors want out these firms can be expected to ask for and receive credit from the domestic banks: to refuse to do so would depress the market value of the banks' existing claims on the domestic firms and call into question the solvency of the domestic banking system.

What limits this process? As long as the DC central bank maintains domestic nominal interest rates at levels above those available on similar foreign assets there is, in principle, no limit to the private capital inflows generated. Of course, in reality the government's resources are limited. At some point the market will begin to doubt the government's ability to maintain the exchange rate peg and the negative carry resulting from the low return earned on reserves relative to that paid on the domestic liabilities issued in sterilised exchange market intervention. But the scale of private capital inflows necessary to exhaust the central bank's expected net worth can be very large indeed.

5 Solutions?

The only solution is to break the chain of guarantees now being offered to international investors. The chain has several links:

- The first is the commitment to allow free access of international investors to domestic financial markets.

- The second is the commitment to a nominal exchange rate target.

- The third is the commitment to sterilise the monetary effects of capital inflows in order to resist declines in domestic interest rates and over-heating the domestic economy.

- The fourth is the implicit guarantee of deposits and solvency of the domestic banking system.

If any one of this chain of guarantees is broken, the losing position now being taken by governments will evaporate; but none of the links can be broken without cost.

A threat to withdraw the guarantee of bank deposits or the solvency of the banking system is unlikely to be credible. The historical involvement of the governments of DCs with their banking systems makes the threat to allow bank failures a hollow one. Authorities in DCs recognise the dangers of external borrowing by their commercial banks – for example, the government of Mexico has had some success in limiting their banks' borrowing in international markets and this has forced investors to acquire direct claims on non-financial firms. But, as argued above, investors expect the firms to call on their banks during a crisis and the banks are expected to provide funds that will allow a profitable exit for the foreign investor.

Another option that is probably not feasible is to turn back the clock on capital market integration. Experience in the industrial countries suggests that once private investors have 'found' a market and incurred the fixed costs of operating in that market governments are not able to materially restrict access to profitable investments. For DCs that retain effective controls, as appears to be the case in some Asian DCs, a slowing or reversal of liberalisation might be a short-term option.

By default, this leaves the exchange rate–monetary policy regime as the only option. Unfortunately, there are no easy answers here, either. A flexible exchange rate regime would allow an independent monetary policy but seems to be associated with excessive volatility in real exchange rates. Recent research on the behaviour of flexible rates for industrial countries is not encouraging, in that there seems to be no correspondence between the variance of the fundamentals and the variance of the real exchange rate. The prospect of an 'unnecessary' real exchange rate appreciation is not attractive to countries that have prospered with export-led growth.

A few emerging market countries will find it feasible to fix the exchange rate and allow capital flows to influence domestic monetary conditions. But this is a particularly difficult policy choice for most DCs. For economies that are attempting to reduce entrenched inflation and inflationary expectations, a capital inflow that is not sterilised means an increase in the monetary base and a fall in domestic interest rates. This is not the normal recipe for a successful stabilisation programme. While a few very open economies will find it optimal to fix the exchange rate and import monetary policy, most will find the complete loss of control over monetary policy unacceptable.

Our view is that relinquishing the exchange rate target is the best of a nasty list of choices for most DCs. Although the exchange rate is a powerful way for the government to signal its *intention* to fight inflation, a nominal exchange rate target does not contribute to credibility of those intentions in an environment where private expectations for the real equilibrium exchange rates change rapidly. DCs engaged in important stabilisation and reform programmes are those for which we have relatively little *ex ante* information on the equilibrium real exchange rate. Greater exchange rate flexibility will not greatly affect the *net* private capital inflow that is fully justified by the economic reform packages that have been put in place in many DCs. It will stop the 'arbitrage' capital flows that have recently dominated the economic environment. The collapse of the EMS in 1992 should be a reminder that as much as we might yearn for stability in everything, the reality seems to be that difficult choices are necessary.

NOTES

1. Conference presentation is in 'Financial Sector Reforms, Economic Growth, and Stability: Experiences in Selected Asian and Latin American Countries', in *Economic Development Institute Seminar Series* (Washington, DC: World Bank, 1994). A revised version appeared as a *UCSC Working Paper*, 'Are Recent Capital Inflows to Developing Countries a Vote for or Against Economic Policy Reforms?' (1994), *Working Paper*, **295** (University of California, Santa Cruz) and reprinted as an appendix to 'International Capital Flows : Direct v. Portfolio Investment' in Gruben, Gould and Zarazaga (1997).
2. See Dooley (1997).

3. Mathieson and Rojas-Suarez (1992).
4. Calvo, Leiderman and Reinhart (1993).
5. The sharp declines in prices in emerging equity markets and markets for sovereign debt are apparently related to the rebound in interest rates in industrial countries that began late in 1993. See Dooley, Kletzer and Fernandez-Arias (1994).
6. Gooptu (1993).

REFERENCES

Calvo, G., L. Leiderman and C. Reinhart (1993). 'Capital Inflows to Latin America: The Role of External Factors', *IMF Staff Papers*, **40**

Dooley, M. (1997). 'A Model of Crises in Emerging Markets', *NBER Working Paper*, **6300** (December)

Dooley, M., K. Kletzer and E. Fernandez-Arias (1994). 'Recent Private Capital Flows to Developing Countries: Is the Debt Crisis History?', National Bureau of Economic Research, *Working Paper*, **4792** (July)

Gooptu, S. (1993). 'Portfolio Investment Flows to Emerging Markets', *Finance and Development*, **30(1)** (March): 9–12

Gruben, W., D. Gould and C. Zarazaga (eds.) (1997). *Exchange Rates, Capital Flows, and Monetary Policy in a Changing World Economy*, Boston: Kluwer Academic

Mathieson, D. and L. Rojas-Suarez (1992). 'Liberalisation of the Capital Account: Experiences and Issues', *IMF Working Paper*, **WP/92/46**

Discussion
Kenneth Kletzer

In chapter 3 and a companion paper (Dooley, 1997), Michael Dooley outlines an argument that various distortionary domestic policies are, to a significant degree, responsible for large financial capital inflows and subsequent financial and currency crises in the 1990s. This argument is an application of the broad truth that inflows of foreign financial capital can have undesirable welfare consequences in the presence of distortionary domestic policies, which is itself an application of the general theory of the second best. Dooley observes that many government policies toward financial intermediation provide implicit contingent insurance for asset holders. The distribution of the benefits of these implicit insurance subsidies can differ between foreign and domestic holders of claims on domestic debt service or dividends. Because of its basis in market and policy-induced distortions, this approach directly links welfare consequences to speculative capital inflows and currency crises.

Explicit and implicit insurance schemes are used by governments to avoid the real costs of domestic liquidity crises. Potential financial market intervention can distort the pattern of investment when such insurance is subsidised by the government, leading to excessive borrowing, investment or risk-taking. In the presence of international capital mobility, foreign purchasers of various domestic assets can partake of the benefits of these insurance schemes, including any implicit subsidies. This leads to the policy-created international capital market arbitrage opportunities Dooley mentions. It seems sensible to think that opportunities for private market participants to raid the public coffers are more acute for countries undergoing financial market development and liberalisation than for countries with fairly established institutions for regulating financial market activity. This statement allows for even the richest of countries to undergo periods of unintended distortionary transfers from the public to the private sector. Dooley makes this point nicely, giving us the examples of the 1992 Savings and Loan (S&L) débâcle for the USA and the EMS crisis of 1992 for Europe.

One consequence, central to Dooley's argument, is that the consolidated government incurs state-contingent liabilities as foreign capital flows into the country. The cumulative inflow of such 'policy-arbitrage' capital will be limited by the net present value (NPV) of the subsidies the government is expected to pay in equilibrium. This depends on both public sector solvency and the credibility of the government to honour such guarantees in various contingencies. Chapter 3's title derives from this observation based on the implied public sector budget identity. Economic reforms can raise the efficiency of capital in the recipient country, leading to a larger current account deficit as investment responds to a higher marginal productivity of capital and consumption to higher levels of permanent income. Dooley points out that because reforms can increase the fiscal capacity of the government, capital may flow in to take advantage of the government's greater ability to pay future subsidies to financial claims. In this case, economic reforms lead to an increase in the contingent liabilities of the public sector and the potential welfare loss increase in this instance.

In Dooley's argument, financial capital inflows are linked to subsequent currency crises through an extension of the Krugman (1979) model. In the simple version of the speculative-attack model, public debt follows an exogenous process and is monetised. In this version, public sector liabilities are contingent and endogenous. Public debt (contingent) rises as capital flows into the country under implicit guarantees, and it is assumed that this increase in public debt will be monetised in the event that the guarantees are called. This potential future increase in the equilibrium money supply growth rate is inconsistent with the exchange rate peg, allowing a speculative attack to occur.

Chapter 3 and its companion emphasise the importance of policy-created distortions that lead to endogenously increasing public sector liabilities. I agree with Dooley that the accumulation of implicit state-contingent public sector liabilities is an important feature of recent capital inflows to industrialising nations undergoing policy reforms and deserves the attention of economists and respect of policy makers. I also appreciate the emphasis on a mechanism for generating currency crises that is directly linked to welfare economics. The chapter has its shortcomings. The major one is the absence of a mathematical model so that a demonstration of the claims with appropriate necessary assumptions is missing. Both chapter 3 and Dooley (1997) need a fully articulated dynamic model to examine the important ambiguities that are possible here.

One reason is that time-consistency must play an important role in an equilibrium analysis of the story told. The anticipated future response of the government is essential for formulating creditors' asset demands, hence the accumulation of public sector liabilities. The particular policies taken by the government determine the rate at which creditors can accumulate implicit claims against it. If the subsidies can be generated by two-way capital flows, then opening capital markets can lead to an instantaneous rise in public sector debt. Anticipated future monetisation of future public sector deficits can also lead to a speculative attack before any contingent liabilities are realised. Do we even need an adverse realisation to get a currency crisis or triggering of contingent government transfers in the Dooley story? An analytical model, such as the one by Burnside, Eichenbaum and Rebello (1998), is needed to answer such a question. An analytical model allows us to study the dynamics of investment, consumption and relative prices, the variables that enter a welfare analysis of possible policy solutions.

A second issue is that the adverse incentives created by public subsidies can distort the pattern of investment so that the probability that government guarantees are called is endogenous (as in the US S&L crisis). The importance of overinvestment in the presence of moral hazard for understanding the Asian crisis has been stressed by Paul Krugman (1998). This first creates a source of ambiguity for the capital inflow and currency crisis dynamics – under some conditions, a financial crisis could be inevitable. It also leads to the importance of modelling the microeconomics of the domestic credit market and the incentives created by deposit insurance and related policies. Different versions of how imperfect monitoring leads to implicit subsidisation and capital inflows allow different conclusions about which policies are helpful and which are not. This is well known from the application of adverse-selection models of credit market imperfections in the Washington policy debate after the Asian currency crises. It could be important for discussing possible *ex ante* policy reforms because the dynamics of capital inflows and endogenous public sector contingent liabilities could turn out to be quite different under alternative models of the credit market.

REFERENCES

Burnside, C., M. Eichenbaum and S. Rebello (1998). 'Prospective Deficits and the Asian Currency Crisis', Northwestern University Department of Economics (September), mimeo; *NBER Working Paper*, **6758**

Dooley, M. P. (1997). 'A Model of Crises in Emerging Markets', *NBER Working Paper*, **6300** (December)

Krugman, P. R. (1979). 'A Model of Balance-of-Payments Crises,' *Journal of Money, Credit, and Banking*, **11**: 311–25.

(1998). 'Whatever Happened to Asia?', http://web.mit.edu/krugman/www/DISINTER.html

4 The Asian crisis: an overview of the empirical evidence and policy debate

GIANCARLO CORSETTI, PAOLO PESENTI AND
NOURIEL ROUBINI

1 Introduction

Was the Asian crisis caused by fundamental weaknesses and policy mistakes, or was it due to a financial 'panic' (encompassing phenomena such as 'fickle investors', volatile hot money, multiple instantaneous equilibria, speculative capital flights and bank runs)? An analysis of the causes of the crisis is important because, depending on one's view, conclusions may differ as regards what could have been done differently to prevent the crisis and its global contagion, and what can be done in the future to reduce the risk of financial turmoil.

Yet, the two 'views' of the crisis are not completely inconsistent with each other. On the one hand, the possibility of multiple instantaneous equilibria – underlying interpretations based on self-fulfilling attacks – arises only when economic fundamentals are 'weak enough' – i.e. some deterioration of fundamentals is a necessary condition preceding a panic. On the other hand, the view that the crisis is initially triggered by fundamental factors does not necessarily rule out the possibility that, after the crisis, movements of asset prices (exchange rates and stock market indexes) and capital flow reversals may be excessive and not warranted by fundamentals.

Challenging the readings of the 1997-8 events that downplay the role of structural factors, in the first part of this chapter we attempt to document the extent to which the Asian crisis was related to fundamental imbalances. We argue that, beneath apparently strong economic performances (low budget deficits, low public debt/GDP ratios, single-digit inflation rates, high economic growth and high savings and investment rates) lay institutional weaknesses, policy inconsistencies and severe structural distortions. We provide a cohesive interpretive framework to understand why these weaknesses made the Asian countries vulnerable to the crisis that eventually burst out in the summer of 1997.

In the second part of this chapter, we delve into a discussion of two sets of normative issues. The first concerns the role of the International

Monetary Fund (IMF) rescue and stabilisation packages. Did the IMF make mistakes in the design and implementation of its plans? Was the monetary and fiscal conditionality too tight? Were the IMF conditions for structural reform beyond the bounds of what standard IMF package should have included? Were the bank runs observed in some countries related to IMF policy prescriptions?

The second set of issues concerns the role played by the liberalisation of the capital account in making the East Asian countries more vulnerable to a financial crisis. Some have argued that, because of the weaknesses in the financial sector, the pace of liberalisation should have been more gradual and cautious. Others favour outright and widespread controls on capital outflows as a way to stem financial instability and allow countries to resume growth without suffering disruptive effects on their asset markets. Others again stress the desirability of controls on capital inflows (as opposed to outflows), especially targeted against short-term 'hot money' inflows, regarded as highly volatile and possibly destabilising.

The chapter is structured as follows. In section 2 we set out our interpretation of the crisis, which emphasises moral hazard as the common source of over-investment, excessive external borrowing and current account deficits. In section 3 we present empirical tests of the role of fundamentals in the crisis, using a cross-section analysis of 24 emerging economies. We provide evidence that weak cyclical performances, low foreign exchange reserves and financial sector weaknesses resulting in high shares of non-performing loans were at the core of the Asian crisis. In section 4, we consider the policy strategies used to address the crisis, in particular, the critiques of the IMF stabilisation packages in East Asia, and present an overview of the debate on those issues. In section 5, we consider the debate on capital account liberalisation and capital controls. We discuss the arguments in favour and against by drawing a distinction among different types of controls, as well as by addressing the issue of the optimal sequencing and speed of capital account liberalisation. Section 6 concludes with a discussion of some open issues.

2 Interpreting the Asian crisis

In a number of studies (Corsetti, Pesenti and Roubini, 1998a, 1998b, 1998c) we have emphasised the relevance of the moral hazard problem in a comprehensive interpretation of the Asian meltdown. In our view, the role of moral hazard was that of magnifying the financial vulnerability of the region during the process of financial market liberalisation in the 1990s, and exposing its fragility *vis-à-vis* the macroeconomic and financial shocks that occurred in the period 1995-7. In this section, we provide a synthetic exposition of our thesis.[1]

In interpreting the Asian crises, one should consider three different, yet strictly inter-related dimensions of the moral hazard problem at the corporate, financial and international level. At the *corporate* level, political pressures to maintain high rates of economic growth had led to a long tradition of public guarantees to private projects, some of which were effectively undertaken under government control, directly subsidised, or supported by policies of directed credit to favoured firms and/or industries.[2] In the light of the record of past government intervention, the production plans and strategies of the corporate sector largely overlooked the costs and riskiness of the underlying investment projects.[3] With financial and industrial policy enmeshed within a widespread business sector network of personal and political favouritism, and with governments that appeared willing to intervene in favour of troubled firms, markets operated under the impression that the return on investment was somewhat 'insured' against adverse shocks.

Such pressures and beliefs accompanied a sustained process of capital accumulation, resulting in persistent and sizable current account deficits. While common wisdom holds that borrowing from abroad to finance domestic investment should not raise concerns about external solvency – it could actually be the optimal course of action for under-capitalised economies with good investment opportunities – the evidence for the Asian countries in the mid-1990s highlights that the profitability of new investment projects was low.[4]

Investment rates and capital inflows in Asia remained high even after the negative signals sent by the indicators of profitability.[5] Consistent with the *financial* side of the moral hazard problem in Asia, the crucial factor underlying the sustained investment rates was excessive borrowing by national banks abroad, corresponding to high and excessive investment at home. Financial intermediation played a key role in channelling funds toward projects that were marginal if not outright unprofitable.[6]

The adverse consequences of these distortions were crucially magnified by the rapid process of capital account liberalisation and financial market deregulation in the region during the 1990s, which increased the supply elasticity of funds from abroad.[7] The extensive liberalisation of capital markets was consistent with the policy goal of providing a large supply of low-cost funds to national financial institutions and the domestic corporate sector. The same goal motivated exchange rate policies aimed at reducing the volatility of the domestic currency in terms of the US dollar, thus lowering the risk premium on dollar-denominated debt.

The *international* dimension of the moral hazard problem hinged upon the behaviour of international banks, which over the period leading to the crisis had lent large amounts of funds to the region's domestic intermediaries, with apparent neglect of the standards for sound risk assessment.[8] Underlying such an over-lending syndrome may have been the presumption that short-term interbank cross-border liabilities would be effectively guaranteed by either a direct government intervention in favour of the financial debtors, or by an indirect bail-out through IMF support programmes. A very large fraction of foreign debt accumulation was in the form of bank-related short-term, unhedged, foreign currency-denominated liabilities: by the end of 1996, a share of short-term liabilities in total liabilities above 50 per cent was the norm in the region. Moreover, the ratio of short-term external liabilities to foreign reserves – a widely used indicator of financial fragility – was above 100 per cent in Korea, Indonesia and Thailand.

The core implication of moral hazard is that an adverse shock to profitability does not induce financial intermediaries to be more cautious in lending, and to follow financial strategies reducing the overall riskiness of their portfolios. Quite the opposite: in the face of negative circumstances the anticipation of a future bail-out provides a strong incentive to take on even more risk – that is, as Krugman (1998a) writes, 'to play a game of heads I win, tails the taxpayer loses.' In this respect, a number of country-specific and global shocks contributed to severely weaken the overall economic outlook in the Asian region, exacerbating the distortions already in place. In particular, the long period of stagnation of the Japanese economy in the 1990s led to a significant export slowdown from the Asian countries; in the months preceding the eruption of the crisis the hopes for a Japanese recovery were shattered by a sudden decline in economic activity. Sector-specific shocks such as the fall in the demand for semi-conductors in 1996, and adverse terms of trade fluctuations also contributed to the worsening of the trade balances in the region between 1996 and 1997.

The sharp appreciation of the US dollar relative to the Japanese yen and the European currencies since the second half of 1995 led to deteriorating cost competitiveness in most Asian countries whose currencies were effectively pegged to the dollar. Based on standard real exchange rate measures, many Asian currencies appreciated in the 1990s, although the degree of real appreciation was not as large as in previous episodes of currency collapses (such as Mexico in 1994). In general, competitive pressures were enhanced by the increasing weight of China in total export from the region.

As a result of the cumulative effects of the financial and real imbalances considered above, by 1997 the Asian countries appeared quite vulnerable to financial crises, either related to sudden switches in market confidence and sentiment, or driven by deteriorating expectations about the poor state of fundamentals. In 1997, the drop of the real estate and stock markets – where sustained speculative trends were in part fuelled by foreign capital inflows – led to the emergence of wide losses and outright defaults in the corporate and financial sectors. Policy uncertainty stemming from the lack of commitment to structural reforms by the domestic authorities worsened the overall climate. From the summer of 1997 onward, rapid reversals of financial capital inflows led to the collapse of regional currencies amid domestic and international investor panic.

3 The empirical evidence: a first look

This section presents some preliminary evidence on the determinants of the crises in Asia, testing for the empirical relevance of a set of macroeconomic factors that are consistent with our interpretation of the 1997-8 events. In our tests we compare the performance of all the Asian countries that were subject to pressures in 1997 with the performance of other emerging economies, for a total sample of 24 countries whose selection has been determined by data availability.[9] Following the methodology suggested in previous studies,[10] we first construct a 'crisis index' as a measure of speculative pressure on a country's currency, and then regress this variable on a set of indexes of financial fragility, external imbalances, official reserves adequacy and fundamental performance.

3.1 The crisis index

Our crisis index (IND) is a weighted average of the percentage rate of exchange rate depreciation relative to the US dollar – if such depreciation can be deemed abnormal, as explained below – and the percentage rate of change in foreign reserves between the end of December 1996 and the end of December 1997.[11] The logic underlying the index IND is quite simple. A speculative attack against a currency is signalled either by a sharp depreciation of the exchange rate or by a contraction in foreign reserves which prevents a devaluation.[12] We present the values for IND in table 4.1: a large negative value for IND corresponds to a high devaluation rate and/or a large fall in foreign reserves – i.e. a more severe currency crisis.

In evaluating the crisis index we need to control for the fact that, in some countries, a high rate of depreciation in 1997 may reflect a past trend rather than severe speculative pressures. For example, the fact that the Turkish currency depreciated by over 50 per cent in 1997 should not be interpreted as a signal of 'crisis,' as chronically high inflation rates in Turkey over the 1990s have been associated with 'normally' high depreciation rates.[13]

Table 4.1   *Crisis and economic indicators, December 1996–December 1997*

Country	Crisis index (IND)	Real appreciation (RER)	Current account (CA)	Lending boom (LB)	Non-performing Loans (NPL)	Reserves adequacy (M2/RES)	Reserves adequacy (M1/RES)	Reserves adequacy (STD/RES)
Argentina	4.9	38.6	−1.9	16.5	9.4	351.0	108.2	147.8
Brazil	−0.5	75.8	−2.0	−26.3	5.8	345.9	66.8	78.3
Chile	−1.4	37.5	−1.7	24.1	1.0	188.2	41.9	53.3
China	7.6	4.9	0.8	6.9	14.0	828.9	334.0	26.7
Colombia	−9.1	26.6	−5.0	35.0	4.6	209.4	104.3	73.9
Czech Rep.	−19.5	50.7	−4.4	22.7	12.0	356.9	139.5	42.9
Hong Kong	5.7	31.8	−1.6	25.5	3.4	411.9	34.2	20.0
Hungary	−1.6	−38.8	−6.5	−56.5	3.2	167.1	83.3	52.3
India	5.7	−29.1	−1.2	−2.3	17.3	860.0	296.5	37.2
Indonesia	−38.3	17.5	−2.9	9.6	12.9	614.8	114.3	188.9
Jordan	9.8	6.1	−4.5	1.4	6.0	437.8	141.4	33.9
Korea	−38.6	11.1	−2.5	11.2	8.4	665.4	147.6	217.0
Malaysia	−38.8	19.9	−6.4	31.1	9.9	364.8	115.6	45.3
Mexico	10.9	8.9	−2.7	−10.9	12.5	444.8	129.3	142.9
Pakistan	11.4	−2.0	−5.3	−3.7	17.5	3369.9	1822.8	399.0
Peru	0.7	−20.4	−6.2	177.2	5.1	123.6	32.4	61.6
Philippines	−29.8	38.9	−4.6	150.8	14.0	465.6	91.8	849.3
Poland	3.5	30.0	0.9	38.5	6.0	262.3	95.9	14.2
Singapore	−15.7	4.7	16.5	16.7	4.0	103.5	25.0	20.0
Sri Lanka	−1.0	17.7	−5.7	28.4	5.0	236.4	72.9	26.8
Taiwan	−11.4	−7.0	2.9	43.4	3.9	575.1	141.0	22.8
Thailand	−47.8	20.0	−7.2	58.0	13.3	380.5	43.3	121.5
Turkey	4.3	−16.1	−0.1	43.2	0.8	302.6	48.9	76.0
Venezuela	4.9	2.2	6.8	−51.5	3.8	102.4	58.5	28.2

There is no obvious way to purge the sample of the effects of trend depreciations not associated with a crisis. In this study, we take the following approach: if a currency in 1997 has fallen in value by less than its average depreciation rate in the 1994-6 period, we consider this as being part of a trend depreciation and set the 1997 depreciation rate equal to zero in constructing the index.[14] In our sample, such screening procedure leads to a significant re-sizing of the crisis index for two high-depreciation countries: Turkey and Venezuela.

As table 4.1 shows, the countries that in 1997 appear to have been hit by the most severe crises are, in order, Thailand, Malaysia, Korea, Indonesia, the Philippines and the Czech Republic. Among Asian countries, the currencies of Singapore and Taiwan were also moderately devalued in 1997, but these two countries were not subject to such extensive and dramatic financial turmoils as the ones affecting other East Asian economies. Conversely, outside the Asian region the Czech Republic appears as a crisis country since its currency, which had been pegged since 1992, suffered a severe speculative attack in the spring of 1997 leading to a devaluation.[15]

3.2 Indexes of financial fragility

Measures of banking system weakness are provided by the stock of nonperforming loans as a share of total assets in 1996 (NPL)[16] and an index of 'lending boom' (LB), defined as the growth of commercial bank loans to the private sector (as percentage of GDP) in the period 1990-6. The latter is an indirect measure of financial fragility suggested by Sachs, Tornell and Velasco (1996).[17] Both variables (NPL and LB) are reported in table 4.1.

We adopt two indicators of domestic financial fragility. The first one encompasses the information in both NPL (non-performing loans) and LB (lending boom) and is defined as follows: if the sign of the lending boom in the 1990s is positive, we assign to the new indicator $NPLB$ the original value of NPL; if the lending boom in the 1990s is negative, we set $NPLB$ equal to zero:[18]

$$NPLB = \begin{cases} NPL & \text{if } LB > 0 \\ 0 & \text{if } LB \leq 0. \end{cases}$$

As regards the second indicator, note that according to the theoretical model presented in Corsetti, Pesenti and Roubini (1998a) the vulnerability of a country to currency and financial crises increases with the implicit fiscal costs of financial bail-outs. Under the maintained hypothesis that the time series of *NPL* provides information about the size of the overall bail-out in the event of a crisis, we can obtain a statistical *proxy* for the associated fiscal costs by taking the ratio of non-performing loans to GDP in 1996.

Such series is denoted *NPLY*, and is defined as the product of *NPL* and commercial bank loans to the private sector as a share of GDP in 1996. This variable allows us to properly assess the performance of those countries with low ratios of bank loans to GDP but relatively large non-performing loans as a share of banking assets (e.g. India and Pakistan). In those countries, the contingent fiscal liabilities related to bail-out costs are smaller relative to countries with a similar *NPL*, but have a higher ratio of bank lending to GDP.

3.3 Indexes of current account imbalances

Table 4.1 reports the average current account balance as a share of GDP in the 1994-6 period (*CA*) and the real exchange rate appreciation in the 1990s (*RER*). There is no simple way to assess when a current account balance is sustainable (e.g. when it is driven by investment in sound projects) and when it is not (e.g. when it reflects a structural loss of competitiveness), or to what extent a real appreciation is due to misalignment, as opposed to an appreciation of the fundamental equilibrium real exchange rate. However, the consensus in the empirical literature on crisis episodes is that the *combination* of a sizable current account deficit and a significant real appreciation represents a worrisome signal of external imbalance.

Consistent with this view, we construct an index of *current account imbalance, CAI,* defined as follows: if the rate of real exchange rate appreciation is above a given threshold, *T*, *CAI* is equal to the current account balance (as a share of GDP); if the real appreciation is below the threshold (or there is a real depreciation), *CAI* is set equal to zero:[19]

$$CAI = \begin{cases} CA & \text{if } RER \text{ appreciates by more than } T \\ & (T = 0, 10 \text{ per cent}) \\ 0 & \text{otherwise.} \end{cases}$$

3.4 Indexes of foreign reserves adequacy and fundamentals' performance

In section 6 (p. 154), we are interested in testing whether the effects of external imbalances and financial fragility are magnified by the inadequate availability of foreign exchange reserves and by the weak performance of other fundamental variables. Other things being equal, the vulnerability of a country to a currency crisis is higher when reserves are low relative to some measure of domestic liquid assets or short-term foreign debt. To assess the role played by reserves availability, we construct three different measures: the ratio of $M1$ to foreign exchange reserves ($M1/RES$), the ratio of $M2$ to foreign reserves ($M2/RES$), and the ratio of the foreign debt service burden (i.e. short-term foreign debt *plus* interest payments on foreign debt) to foreign reserves (STD/RES). The values of these variables are reported in table 4.1.

To test for the joint role of fundamentals and foreign reserves in determining a currency crisis, we classify the countries in our sample as being *strong* or *weak* with regard to these two dimensions using dummy variables. Regarding foreign reserves, we use a broad classification according to which a country is 'strong' if the ratio of $M2$ to reserves is in the lowest quartile of the sample. The resulting dummy variable for low reserves, $D2^{LR}$, is defined as:

$$D2^{LR} = \begin{cases} 1 & \text{if } M2/RES \text{ above lowest sample quartile} \\ 0 & \text{otherwise.} \end{cases}$$

Similar dummies are created by replacing $M2/RES$ with $M1/RES$ and STD/RES per cent ; such dummy variables are labelled $D1^{LR}$ and $D3^{LR}$.

With regard to fundamentals, we focus on current account imbalances and financial fragility. Countries are classified as being *strong* or *weak* according to the scheme:

$$D^{WF} = \begin{cases} 1 & \text{if either } CAI \text{ in highest sample quartile} \\ & \text{or } NPLB \text{ in lowest sample quartile} \\ 0 & \text{otherwise.} \end{cases}$$

A similar dummy can be obtained by replacing $NPLB$ with $NPLY$.[20]

3.5 Testing for the role of fundamentals' imbalances in the crisis

3.5.1 Financial fragility and external imbalances

The results of the regression of IND on CAI and $NPLB$ are shown in column (1) of table 4.2. The coefficients of the two regressors have the expected sign and are statistically significant at the 5 per cent level: both a large current account deficit associated with a real appreciation and a larger rate of non-performing loans associated with a lending boom worsen the

Table 4.2   *Explaining the crisis index^a: basic regressions*

Estimated coefficient and summary statistic	Independent variable	(1)	Regression with M2/RES (2)	Regression with M1/RES (3)	Regression with STD2/RES (4)
β_1	Constant	6.877	7.073	7.437	5.324
		(3.755)	(4.094)	(3.956)	(3.552)
β_2	CAI	3.768	0.849	2.210	0.569
		(1.254)	(2.869)	(3.677)	(1.971)
β_3	NPLB	−1.338	−2.888	−2.805	−0.476
		(0.605)	(2.073)	(1.946)	(0.782)
β_4	$CAI \times D2^{LR}$		3.613		
			(3.191)		
β_5	$NPLB \times D2^{LR}$		1.761		
			(2.035)		
β_4	$CAI \times D1^{LR}$			1.467	
				(3.982)	
β_5	$NPLB \times D1^{LR}$			1.534	
				(1.929)	
β_4	$CAI \times D3^{LR}$				3.571
					(2.564)
β_5	$NPLB \times D3^{LR}$				−0.864
					(0.986)
Summary statistic					
$\bar{R}^2$		0.555	0.541	0.536	0.622
R^2		0.594	0.621	0.616	0.688
Addendum: *Wald-tests* Null hypothesis		*p*-values	*p*-values	*p*-values	*p*-values
$\beta_2 + \beta_4 = 0$			0.005	0.018	0.023
$\beta_3 + \beta_5 = 0$			0.099	0.057	0.091

Note: ^{a} The dependent variable is the crisis index, *IND*. See table 4.1 and appendix (p. 155) for definition of variables. Standard errors are shown in parentheses.

crisis index. In columns (2)–(4) we interact the two regressors with the dummies for low reserves.

The coefficients β_2 and β_3 measure the effects of *CAI* and *NPLB* on the crisis index in countries with high reserves ($D^{LR} = 0$); conversely, the sums of the coefficients $\beta_2 + \beta_4$ and $\beta_3 + \beta_5$ measure the impact of fundamental imbalances on the crisis index in countries with low reserves ($D^{LR} = 1$).

Looking at the regression results shown in columns (2)–(4), the coefficients β_2 and β_3 are not significant on their own, but rather only when reserves are low. In fact, for the case in which we use the reserve dummy $D2^{LR}$, based on $M2$ data, the Wald-tests indicate that the hypotheses $\beta_2 + \beta_4 = 0$ and $\beta_3 + \beta_5 = 0$ can be rejected at the 1 per cent and 10 per cent significance levels.[21] Similar or stronger results are obtained when we use the other two low-reserves dummies, $D1^{LR}$ and $D3^{LR}$. As a whole, these results suggest that structural imbalances (current account deficits/currency appreciation and non-performing loans/lending boom) play a role in the onset of a crisis to the extent that there is insufficient availability of foreign reserves – that is, in the light of both fundamental and non-fundamental models of currency crises, low reserves enhance the vulnerability of the economy to speculative attacks.

In table 4.3 we test whether the effects of current account imbalances CAI on the crisis index depend on weak fundamentals D^{WF} and low reserves $D2^{LR}$. Relative to column (2) of table 4.2, in column (1) of table 4.3 we consider an additional regressor, namely an interaction term equal to $CAI \times D2^{LR} \times D^{WF}$. In this case, the sum of the coefficients $\beta_2 + \beta_4 + \beta_6$ captures the effects of current account imbalances on the crisis index in countries with low reserves and weak fundamentals. If $\beta_2 + \beta_4 + \beta_6$ is positive while $\beta_2 + \beta_4$ is not significantly different from zero, the crisis index worsens when a high-deficit country with an appreciated currency meets both 'weak-fundamentals' and 'low-reserves' criteria, but the crisis index does not respond to the reserves indicator if such a country is in the 'strong-fundamentals' region. The results of the Wald-tests show that $\beta_2 + \beta_4 + \beta_6$ is indeed significantly positive at the 1 per cent significance level, while $\beta_2 + \beta_4$ is not significantly different from zero.[22]

Column (2) of table 4.3 includes a similar test for the role of non-performing loans. Here we add an additional regressor to those of column (2) in table 4.2, which is an interaction term equal to $NPLB \times D2^{LR} \times D^{WF}$. The sum of the coefficients $\beta_3 + \beta_5 + \beta_7$ thus captures the effects of non-performing loans on the crisis index in countries that meet both 'low-reserves' and 'weak fundamentals' criteria. Our tests show that $\beta_3 + \beta_5 + \beta_7$ is negative at the 5 per cent significance level while $\beta_3 + \beta_5$ is not significantly different from zero. The crisis index depends on non-performing loans in countries with weak fundamentals and weak reserves, but not in countries with strong fundamentals and weak reserves. The implication of these results is that a crisis need not be related to current account imbalances or bad loans *per se*: such imbalances represent a source of severe tension only when they are observed in parallel with fundamental *and* reserve weaknesses.[23]

3.5.2 Fiscal implications of financial fragility

Next, in tables 4.4 and 4.5 we perform regressions similar to those in tables 4.2 and 4.3, but now we move our focus away from financial fragility *per se*,

Table 4.3   *Explaining the crisis index[a]: the role of fundamentals and reserves*

Estimated coefficient and summary statistic	Independent variable	(1)	(2)	(3)
β_1	Constant	− 2.861	5.535	5.602
		(2.138)	(3.887)	(4.082)
β_2	CAI	0.841	0.762	0.766
		(2.946)	(2.694)	(2.771)
β_3	NPLB	− 1.338	− 2.569	− 2.583
		(0.605)	(1.954)	(2.017)
β_4	$CAI \times D2^{LR}$	2.851	1.118	1.559
		(6.650)	(3.274)	(6.293)
β_5	$NPLB \times D2^{LR}$	1.769	2.448	2.446
		(2.091)	(1.945)	(2.000)
β_6	$CAI \times D2^{LR} \times D^{WF}$	0.834		− 0.497
		(6.337)		(6.004)
β_7	$NPLB \times D2^{LR} \times D^{WF}$		− 2.120	− 2.131
			(1.123)	(1.164)
Summary statistic				
$\bar{R}^2$		0.516	0.596	0.572
R^2		0.621	0.684	0.683
Addendum: *Wald-tests* Null hypothesis		*p*-values	*p*-values	*p*-values
$\beta_2 + \beta_4 = 0$		0.547	0.337	0.688
$\beta_2 + \beta_4 + \beta_6 = 0$		0.009		0.388
$\beta_3 + \beta_5 = 0$		0.146	0.883	0.875
$\beta_3 + \beta_5 + \beta_7 = 0$			0.017	0.026

Note: [a] The dependent variable is the crisis index, *IND*. See table 4.1 and appendix (p. 155) for definition of variables. Standard errors are shown in parentheses.

and on to the role of the fiscal implications of financial fragility. We therefore substitute *NPLB* – the non-performing loans ratio adjusted to account for the lending boom – with *NPLY* – a more direct *proxy* for the implicit fiscal costs of banking sector bail-outs.

The results are very similar and, if anything, even stronger than those obtained in tables 4.2 and 4.3. First, as table 4.4, column (1) shows, both *NPLY* and *CAI* are statistically significant regressors of the crisis index (at the 5 per cent level and 1 per cent level respectively). Second, columns (2)–(4) of Table 4.4 confirm that the effects of current account deficits are more relevant when reserves are low.[24] The results of columns (2)-(3) in

Table 4.4   *Explaining the crisis index[a]: fiscal implications of financial fragility*

Estimated coefficient and summary statistic	Independent variable	Regression with M2/RES (1)	Regression with M1/RES (2)	Regression with STD2/RES (3)
β_1	Constant	6.682	8.142	6.289	5.491
		(3.699)	(3.951)	(3.789)	(3.492)
β_2	CAI	4.156	2.288	−1.402	0.845
		(1.158)	(2.394)	(4.511)	(1.963)
β_3	NPLB	−1.630	−6.579	−4.817	−0.597
		(0.724)	(3.263)	(2.419)	(0.874)
β_4	$CAI \times D2^{LR}$		2.594		
			(2.657)		
β_5	$NPLY \times D2^{LR}$		5.133		
			(3.170)		
β_4	$CAI \times D1^{LR}$			5.760	
				(4.660)	
β_5	$NPLY \times D1^{LR}$			3.481	
				(2.497)	
β_4	$CAI \times D3^{LR}$				3.487
					(2.530)
β_5	$NPLY \times D3^{LR}$				−1.185
					(1.248)
Summary statistic					
$\bar{R}^2$		0.558	0.578	0.634	0.618
R^2		0.596	0.651	0.557	0.684
Addendum: *Wald-tests* Null hypothesis		*p*-values	*p*-values	*p*-values	*p*-values
$\beta_2 + \beta_4 = 0$			0.001	0.002	0.016
$\beta_3 + \beta_5 = 0$			0.074	0.105	0.107

Note: [a] The dependent variable is the crisis index, *IND*. See table 4.1 and appendix (p. 155) for definition of variables. Standard errors are shown in parentheses.

table 4.4 are worth emphasising. Note that the coefficient on *NPLY*, β_3, maintains the predicted sign and is statistically significant on its own at the 5 per cent level. This suggests that non-performing loans as a share of GDP – that is, as a measure of the intrinsic fiscal burden – affect the crisis index regardless of whether reserves are low or high.

In table 4.5 we present results of regressions equivalent to those in table 4.3, again using *NPLY* instead of *NPLB*. Once again, current account deficits and non-performing loans matter if both reserves and fundamentals

Table 4.5   *Explaining the crisis index[a]: bail-out costs, fundamentals and reserves*

Estimated coefficient and summary statistic	Independent variable	(1)	(2)	(3)
β_1	Constant	9.060	3.754	3.677
		(4.233)	(2.731)	(3.026)
β_2	CAI	2.438	1.570	1.557
		(2.439)	(1.577)	(1.633)
β_3	NPLB	− 6.912	− 4.985	− 4.957
		(3.347)	(2.164)	(2.263)
β_4	$CAI \times D2^{LR}$	− 7.295	− 2.753	− 2.085
		(14.900)	(2.033)	(9.972)
β_5	$NPLB \times D2^{LR}$	5.425	5.287	5.267
		(3.246)	(2.081)	(2.160)
β_6	$CAI \times D2^{LR} \times D^{WF}$	9.905		− 0.685
		(14.676)		(10.005)
β_7	$NPLB \times D2^{LR} \times D^{WF}$		− 5.420	− 5.436
			(1.060)	(1.117)
Summary statistic				
$\bar{R}^2$		0.566	0.818	0.808
R^2		0.660	0.858	0.858
Addendum: Wald-tests Null hypothesis		*p*-values	*p*-values	*p*-values
$\beta_2 + \beta_4 = 0$		0.741	0.424	0.957
$\beta_2 + \beta_4 + \beta_6 = 0$		0.001		0.633
$\beta_3 + \beta_5 = 0$		0.073	0.626	0.445
$\beta_3 + \beta_5 + \beta_7 = 0$			0.000	0.000

Note: [a] The dependent variable is the crisis index, *IND*. See table 4.1 and appendix (p. 155) for definition of variables. Standard errors are shown in parentheses.

are weak.[25] However, observe that the coefficient on *NPLY* tends to maintain the expected sign and be statistically significant on its own, affecting the crisis index *regardless* of whether reserves are low or high, as well as *regardless* of whether fundamentals are weak or not.[26]

3.5.3 Real and financial weaknesses

Finally, we attempt to test whether direct measures of capital productivity have explanatory power as regressors of the crisis index. Conventional wisdom holds in that borrowing from abroad is less 'dangerous' for external sustainability if it finances new investment (leading to increased productive capacity and to higher future export receipts) rather than consumption (which implies lower saving). For these reasons, a current account deficit that is accompanied by a fall in savings rates is regarded as more problematic than a deficit accompanied by rising investment rates.

Underlying such 'conventional' conclusions, however, is the implicit assumption that the return on investment is at least as high as the cost of the borrowed funds.[27] As evidence on the profitability of the investment projects we employ a standard measure of investment efficiency, the $ICOR$ or 'incremental capital output ratio' defined as the ratio between the investment rate and the output growth rate. In Corsetti, Pesenti and Roubini (1998b), we document that, for all the Asian countries except Indonesia and the Philippines, the $ICOR$ had increased sharply in the 1993–6 period relative to the years 1987–92. This evidence suggests that the efficiency of investments in South East Asia was already falling in the four years prior to the 1997 crisis.

Here, we derive a measure of the $ICOR$ for all the countries in our sample in the period 1993–6. We then test for its significance in our basic regression model.[28] We find that the $ICOR$ variable is generally not significant; however, a simple transformation of the $ICOR$ is significant in some regressions. We then define a new variable, $ICORLB$, which is equal to the original $ICOR$ when the lending boom variable is positive, and is equal to zero when the lending boom is negative. The idea here is that low capital profitability is not problematic in itself if the corporate and financial sectors are able to properly assess the characteristics of the investment projects, but may significantly contribute to the build-up of tensions in the financial markets if there is a lending boom and excessive credit growth – perhaps driven by moral hazard and implicit guarantees on investment by the public sector. When we regress the crisis index on the $ICORLB$ variable and $NPLY$ we find that both variables have the expected sign and are statistically significant.[29]

The results of our empirical analysis provide evidence in support of the thesis that crises are systematically related to the fundamental weaknesses in the real and financial sectors of the economy. The recent turmoil in Asia does not seem to represent an exception in this respect. External imbalances, as measured by the current account deficits associated with real exchange rate appreciation, are significantly correlated with the crisis index. So are measures of financial fragility (non-performing loans in the presence of a lending boom) and measures of the fiscal costs associated with financial bail-outs (non-performing loans as a share of GDP). The effects of these variables on the crisis index are found to be stronger in countries with low reserves.

4 Strategies to recover from the crisis

The last sections of our overview are devoted to a brief assessment of the current debate on the policy strategies to recover from the crisis.[30] This section focuses on the divergent views of the role played by the IMF in dampening – or exacerbating – the impact of the crisis. Section 5 discusses the case for limiting international capital mobility as a crisis management strategy.

The philosophy of IMF involvement in Asia has been synthesised as follows by the Managing Director of the IMF, Michel Camdessus:

As soon as it was called upon, the IMF moved quickly to help Thailand, then Indonesia, and then Korea formulate reform programs aimed at tackling the roots of their problems and restoring investor confidence. In view of the nature of the crisis, these programs had to go far beyond addressing the major fiscal, monetary, or external balances. Their aim is to strengthen financial systems, improve governance and transparency, restore economic competitiveness, and modernise the legal and regulatory environment.[31]

As a condition for the loans, the recipes of the IMF hinged substantially upon two key postulates: the need to reform the economies, with particular emphasis on fiscal discipline and banking sector restructuring, and the requirement to maintain high interest rates to avoid capital outflows and currency attacks. Box 4.1 reports the chronology of the agreements between the IMF and the Asian countries between July 1997 and August 1998. The chronology makes it clear that the targets and the tactics of the Fund did not remain unchanged over time: as the situation in Asia progressively deteriorated, the requests of the IMF became less and less restrictive over time. The Indonesian case provides a striking example of such modifications. The first aid package of October 1997 encompassed strict fiscal discipline, while the agreement of June 1998 allowed the country to limit the budget *deficit* – as opposed to target a budgetary surplus – below 8.5 per cent of GDP.[32] To some observers, such evolution represents an unequivocal sign of flexibility and open-mindedness. To others, these changes occurred too late.

Box 4.1 Chronology of IMF Intervention in Asia,
July 1997–August 1998

1997
2 July *Thailand* announces a managed float of the baht and IMF
negotiations begin.

14 July   The *Philippines* extends and augments its existing IMF-support programme of 1997, and arranges a stand-by facility in 1998. IMF offers Philippines USD 1.1bn loan package.

20 August   IMF approves a USD 3.9bn credit for *Thailand*. The plan assumes a positive growth of 2.5 per cent in 1997 and 3.5 per cent in 1998; and calls for maintaining gross financial reserves at the equivalent of 4.2 months of imports in 1997 and 4.4 months in 1998; limiting the end-period rate of inflation to 9.5 per cent in 1997 and 5 per cent in 1998; targeting a small overall fiscal surplus by 1998 through an increase in the rate of the value-added tax (VAT), and selective expenditure cuts; initiating a credible and up-front restructuring of the financial sector, focused on the identification and closure of unviable financial institutions (56 finance companies).

8 October   *Indonesian* government agrees to request help from IMF.

31 October   The IMF announces a USD23 bn multilateral financial package involving the World Bank and Asian Development Bank to help *Indonesia* stabilise its financial system.

5 November   The IMF approves a USD 10bn stand-by credit for *Indonesia* and releases a disbursement of USD 3bn. Measures include financial sector restructuring, with the closure of 16 insolvent banks; structural reforms to enhance economic efficiency and transparency, with the liberalisation of foreign trade and investment, the dismantling of monopolies, and privatisation; stabilising the rupiah through a tight monetary policy; implementing fiscal measures equivalent to 1 per cent of GDP in 1997/8, and 2 per cent in 1998/9, to yield a 1 per cent of GDP surplus in both years.

21 November   *Korea* requests IMF assistance.

25 November   In light of a larger than expected depreciation of the baht, a second IMF package for *Thailand* is approved. The new plan includes additional measures to maintain the targeted fiscal surplus of 1 per cent of GDP, the establishment of a timetable for financial sector restructuring, and plans to protect the weaker sectors of society.

4 December   IMF approves a USD 21bn stand-by credit for *Korea*, and releases a disbursement of USD 5.6bn. The initial programme assumes GDP growth in 1998 of 2.5 per cent and features comprehensive financial sector restructuring, including central bank independence, strong market and supervisory discipline, and the suspension of nine insolvent banks. Fiscal measures equivalent to 2 per cent of GDP make room for the cost of financial restructuring, consistently with a balanced budget target. The plan calls for

Box 4.1 (*cont.*)

efforts to dismantle the non-transparent and inefficient ties among government banks and business; for the implementation of trade and capital account liberalisation measures, as well as of labour market reforms; for the publication and dissemination of key economic and financial data.

8 December   Disbursement of USD 810mn to *Thailand*.

16 December   *Korean* government allows won to float.

18 December   Disbursement of USD 3.5bn to *Korea*.

24 December   *Korea* issues a letter of intent pointing at the need for an acceleration of the programme as the situation deteriorates. The plan includes further monetary tightening, the abolition of the daily exchange rate band, the lifting of all capital account restrictions. Financial sector reform and market liberalisation, as well as trade liberalisation, are expedited. The IMF also announces that a debt rescheduling by international commercial banks is critical to *Korea*'s recovery.

30 December   Disbursement of USD 2bn to *Korea*.

1998

15 January   Disbursement of USD 2bn to *Korea*.

15 January   A second package for *Indonesia* is agreed upon. The plan allows for a relaxation of the previous fiscal targets, that is now a budget deficit equal to 1 per cent of GDP. Previous IMF conditions not fulfilled but reiterated in the second package include: dismantling of government monopolies, postponing infrastructure projects, and closing insolvent banks.

16 January   International lenders agree on plan to officially roll over short-term debt

7 February   *Korea* agrees to third IMF programme. GDP growth projections are lowered to 1 per cent. The letter of intent includes additional measures to target fiscal deficit to 1 per cent of GDP, increasing the amount of financial instruments available to foreign investors, and broadening the financial sector reform strategy to accommodate stabilisation of short-term debt payments.

17 February   Disbursement of USD 2bn to *Korea*.

24 February   The *Thai* plan is further modified. The fiscal policy target is adjusted from a surplus of 1 per cent of GDP to a deficit of 2 per cent of GDP.

4 March   Disbursement of USD 270mn to *Thailand*.

10 April   *Indonesia* issues a Supplementary Memorandum of Economic and Financial Policies on additional measures. These include strong monetary policy, accelerated bank restructuring, a comprehensive agenda of structural reforms. The IMF allows *Indonesia* to continue its fuel and power subsidies. In the light of the failure of the first two packages, the IMF will resort to a stricter enforcement of provisions.

2 May *Korean* authorities update the programme of economic reforms. Growth forecasts for 1998 are further revised downward to -2 per cent. The letter of intent includes the accommodation of a larger fiscal deficit of about 2 per cent of GDP in 1998, measures to strengthen and expand the social safety net, the loosening of restrictions on foreign exchange transactions, and the formation of an appraisal committee to evaluate recapitalisation plans by under-capitalised banks.

4 May Disbursement of USD 1bn to *Indonesia*.

26 May Fourth IMF programme agreed to by *Thailand*. The main priority is to prevent any further slowdown of the economy and foster an early recovery. The modified programme calls for cautious and gradual reductions of interest rates, higher monetary growth rates, a looser fiscal deficit target at 3 per cent of GDP, and accelerated corporate debt restructuring with financial sector reforms.

29 May Disbursement of USD 2bn to *Korea*.

10 June Disbursement of USD 135mn to *Thailand*.

24 June Additional IMF reforms agreed to by *Indonesia* in light of changing political climate and worsening economic situation. Provisions include an increase in social expenditures (7.5 per cent of GDP), a budget deficit target at 8.5 per cent of GDP, the closure, merging or recapitalisation of weak banks, and the establishment of a bankruptcy system.

15 July Disbursement of USD 1bn to *Indonesia*. The IMF increases financing by USD 1.4bn.

15 July A new letter of intent by *Korea* announces a further easing of macroeconomic policies. The letter includes the accommodation of a larger fiscal deficit for 1998 (5 per cent of GDP), and measures to bolster the social expenditure programme.

29 July The *Indonesian* government requests the cancellation of the existing arrangement with the IMF and its replacement with a new extended arrangement, including new measures on bank and corporate restructuring and improvements in the distribution system.

25 August Disbursement of USD 1bn to *Indonesia*. The IMF approves an extended facility with a longer repayment period.

25 August The *Thai* programme is modified to incorporate a more comprehensive approach to bank and corporate restructuring.

Box 4.1 (*cont.*)
The fiscal deficit target is still at 3 per cent of GDP, for both 1998 and 1999, but this target excludes the costs of financial sector restructuring.
25 August   IMF disburses USD 1bn to Korea.

4.1 Did tight monetary policies and high interest rates worsen the crisis?

Several analysts have argued that the high interest rates prescribed by the IMF to limit currency depreciation had severe repercussions on the economies of the Asian countries. According to the critics of the IMF recipes, interest rates hikes were not effective in slowing down currency depreciation, but rather worsened the extent of the crisis by leading to widespread banking and corporate bankruptcies. The effects of these policies have been described in terms of a vicious circle: the credit crunch imparted severe financial losses to otherwise solvent companies; the widespread fall in profitability translated into higher levels of non-performing loans and credit risk, exacerbating the crisis-induced recessions and, in turn, causing a further contraction in the supply of credit.

In the light of these considerations, the appropriate policy response to the crisis should have been one of loose money and low interest rates – the same strategy adopted by Japan to deal with its internal crisis. According to an extreme version of this argument, during the crisis there were conditions for a currency/interest rate 'Laffer curve': a *fall* – not a rise – of interest rates would have strengthened the economy and restored confidence, causing the Asian currencies to appreciate.

The above criticisms, however, have been challenged on a key issue. Loose monetary policies in the early stages of a currency crisis contribute to exacerbating the extent of the depreciation, increasing the burden of foreign currency-denominated liabilities issued by banks and firms. In the presence of large external net liabilities, a monetary expansion could actually produce financial distress and bankruptcies, setting in motion the same vicious circle described above.[33] Consistent with this argument is the view that the severity of the Asian crisis could in part be attributed to the unwillingness of governments to undertake the appropriate restrictive measures at the right time: the case of low interest rate policies in Malaysia after the runs on the Thai baht is a fitting example. By the same token, Japan's policy response to its internal crisis could not be considered suitable for other Asian countries. As Japan is a large net foreign creditor with sizeable current account surpluses, the effects of a weaker yen on the Japanese economy are qualitatively and quantitatively different from the effects of low interest rates and exchange rate depreciation in countries with a large external debt denominated in foreign currency. As regards the 'Laffer curve' argument, it is – in the words of Paul Krugman (1998b) – 'as silly as it sounds'.

While the appropriate interest rate policy at the onset of the crisis is still subject to a widespread debate, at the time of this writing – and in the light of the large recessions experienced by the Asian economies in 1998 – most observers seem to agree that high interest rates maintained beyond an 'emergency scenario' can have destabilising consequences. Indeed, by the summer of 1998 interest rates in the East Asian region had significantly fallen and, in Korea and Thailand, were back to pre-crisis levels. Yet, these countries are exhibiting a credit crunch which does not appear to be related to the level of interest rates; rather, it has more to do with the inability of financially distressed banks to lend to a corporate sector labouring under the weight of a severe debt overhang.

4.2 Did the IMF plans require unnecessary fiscal adjustments?

Several commentators have argued that the fiscal policy requirements included in the IMF plans were unnecessarily – and harmfully – strict. At the onset of the crisis, the Asian countries under attack were running low budget deficits or fiscal surpluses, and were characterised by relatively low ratios of public debt to GDP, unlike the typical interlocutors of the IMF in past crisis episodes. Excessively tight fiscal discipline made the crisis-induced recession worse.

In support of the 'discipline' view, it has been contended that loose fiscal policies at the onset of the crisis would have raised doubts about the policy makers' commitment to reduce the outstanding current account imbalances, jeopardising the credibility of their plans. Also, while fiscal deficits and debt were typically low before the crisis, in several Asian countries the projected fiscal costs of post-crisis financial bail-outs are estimated to be in the range of 20–30 per cent of GDP. As these extra public liabilities translate into a permanent increase in the interest bill paid by Asian governments of 2–4 per cent of GDP per year, fiscal balances must be appropriately adjusted. In this respect, the IMF has reiterated that, on a country-by-country basis, fiscal plans were targeted to raise the necessary revenues to meet these extra interest costs. Quoting a speech by Stanley Fischer (1998a) in January:

the fiscal programs vary from country to country. In each case, the IMF asked for a fiscal adjustment that would cover the carrying costs of financial sector restructuring – the full cost of which is being spread over many years – and to help restore a sustainable balance of payments. In Thailand, this translated into an initial fiscal adjustment of 3 percent of GDP; in Korea, 1½ percent of GDP; and in Indonesia, 1 percent of GDP, much of which will be achieved by reducing public investment in projects with low economic returns.

One year after the eruption of the Thai crisis, some observers shared the view that the IMF might have been too slow in revising its approach to fiscal policy in the crisis countries. It was only when recessions rapidly materialised in the course of 1998 that the IMF progressively loosened its fiscal conditions to allow for cyclically adjusted fiscal deficits. However, it should be acknowledged that over the entire year of 1998, news about the size and depth of the recessionary effects of the crisis came as a shocking surprise not only to the Asian governments and the IMF, but also to a vast majority of country analysts.

4.3   Did the IMF 'stick to its knitting'?

The breadth of the restructuring efforts required by the IMF have raised a concern that the IMF has been playing an excessively intrusive role in domestic affairs. The criticism that, by including in the programmes a number of structural elements, the IMF was moving beyond its traditional macro-adjustment-related areas of competence (monetary and fiscal tasks) was first made by Martin Feldstein (1998). Similar arguments were echoed by regional commentators, resentful of what they perceived as an imposition of major structural reforms (in areas as heterogeneous as financial and labour markets, competition policy, trade relations) and an interference with the jurisdiction of a sovereign government.

The main counter-arguments were spelled out by Stanley Fischer (1998c) in his reply to Feldstein. To the extent that the Asian meltdown was attributable to structural problems rather than the traditional macroeconomic imbalances, an effective rescue strategy was bound to address the issues at the very core of the crisis. IMF lending to the Asian region would serve no purpose if the weaknesses of the financial sector (ranging from poor bank supervision and regulation to murky relations among governments, banks and corporations) were not removed by the appropriate structural reforms. Similarly, the insistence on good governance and the avoidance of 'crony capitalism' represented a precondition to avoid future crises, as half-hearted reform efforts would not help to re-establish market confidence. Fischer (1998c) concluded that:

the basic approach of the IMF to these crises has been appropriate – not perfect, to be sure, but far better than if the structural elements had been ignored or the Fund had not been involved.

4.4 Did plans to close insolvent banks lead to runs on solvent banks?

The possibility that IMF plans to close insolvent banks led to runs on financially healthy banks has been pointed out, among others, by Jeffrey Sachs. In his comments on the first IMF plan for Indonesia, which called for the closing of 16 banks, Sachs (1998) stated:

In my view, although it's a minority opinion, the IMF did a lot of confidence-reducing measures. In particular, I blame the IMF for abruptly closing financial institutions throughout Asia, sending a remarkably abrupt, unprepared and dangerous signal . . . that you had better take your money out or you might lose it.

The advocates of the opposite view point out that the IMF was not at fault if measures of prevention of bank runs – such as incentive-compatible deposit insurance schemes – were not in place in Indonesia. Moreover, when the IMF requirement partly backfired and an unexpected run occurred, President Suharto's government bore responsibility for failing to enact promised reforms in exchange for the $40 bn international rescue effort. In support of this view is the fact that the requirements imposed on Indonesia by the IMF, including the closing of insolvent banks, were similar to those demanded of Thailand and Korea; yet, neither country experienced bank runs of the same magnitude as those hitting Indonesia. It has also been argued that, in the Indonesian case, more rather than less should have been done: as early as September 1997, widely circulated documents listed more than 16 Indonesian banks experiencing financial difficulties. Instead, the prompt re-opening of a closed bank owned by one of President Suharto's sons contributed to reducing the confidence of the public on the overall rescue plan.

4.5 Did IMF intervention enhance worldwide moral hazard?

Many authors have expressed concern with the possibility that IMF-led rescue packages may risk a moral hazard. This is because expectations of a bail-out can lead investors and creditors to refrain from effectively monitoring their investment and lending strategies. Also, officials in debtor countries may pursue excessively risky courses of action, leaving a country more vulnerable to sudden shocks to fundamentals and shifts in market sentiment. While the residents of the country hit by a crisis suffer because of the crisis-induced recession, to the extent that the creditors are bailed out they do not bear a fair share of the burden of the crisis.

Unquestionably, the risks of creating moral hazard will be thoroughly assessed within the future debate on international policy design and crisis prevention in emerging markets. Yet, several objections have been voiced against a simplistic reading of the problem. First, there is no direct evidence that the surge in capital flows to Asia after 1995 were related to expectations of international bail-outs in the aftermath of the Mexican rescue package. The second objection concerns the issue of who bears the costs of the crisis. The IMF has repeatedly pointed out that a majority of private creditors, especially bond holders and equity investors, took a huge hit during the crisis. By the end of 1997, foreign equity investors had nearly lost three-quarters of their equity holdings in some Asian markets. Nonetheless, commercial banks were to some extent spared; for instance, foreign banks operating in Korea demanded public guarantees on bank loans as a precondition for rolling over the existing loans, without forgiving any amounts due,[34] a point highlighted by Litan (1998).

The third objection goes against the argument that countries which rely on international support when things go out of control will follow unsound policies. As put by Fischer (1998c, p. 106), countries try to avoid going to the Fund; policy makers whose countries end up in trouble generally do not survive politically. In this regard, attaching conditions to assistance gives policy makers incentives to do the right thing.

A fourth, and more substantial point, is that moral hazard may be the lesser evil, as the alternative response to a crisis – to leave countries and creditors to sort out their debts – may have much more dramatic and distortionary consequences. The lessons from the inter-war period and the 1980s demonstrate that such a strategy requires complex negotiations over a long period of time, during which access to international markets is curtailed and long-term growth drastically lowered. The experience of the 1990s also suggests that highly interdependent economies can be subject to the rapid transmission and the 'contagious' spread of speculative waves and financial panic. In this scenario, a delay in taming a local crisis through the appropriate programme of international assistance – and the failure to promptly restore market confidence – would greatly increase the chances of a systemic chain reaction across countries.

5 The Asian crisis and the debate on capital controls

Vis-à-vis the persistent and pervasive nature of the current crisis, the terms of the current debate have progressively encompassed such items as the reform of multilateral institutions, the future of economic and financial cooperation and, most importantly, the desirability of deregulation and liberalisation of international capital markets. The crucial question in this debate is whether exchange controls and limited capital mobility should become elements of an overall strategy of international crisis management and global restructuring.[35]

In order to discuss this topic, one needs to distinguish among three related issues: (a) the case for controls on short-term capital inflows; (b) the case for controls on capital outflows in the event of a crisis; and (c) the optimal speed and sequencing of capital account liberalisation.

Concerning the first issue, it has been argued that restrictions on short-term inflows may be part of an appropriate policy strategy to prevent a crisis, as they discourage volatile short-term portfolio investment and therefore insulate the country from the disruptive effects of sudden reversals in market sentiment. The experiences with capital controls on short-term inflows of Chile,[36] Colombia and Slovenia are often mentioned in support of this view.

Restrictions on short-term capital inflows may take the form of cross-border controls on bank lending and borrowing only, or be extended to all short-term flows. The case for controls on short-term cross-border interbank flows is less controversial than the alternative. It is usually couched in terms of prudential banking standards, rather than in terms of restrictions on capital flows. The case for regulating interbank lending and borrowing hinges upon the evidence on the disruptive effects of highly volatile flows, such as the case when creditor banks suddenly refused to renew their loans to firms and banks in Korea, Thailand and Indonesia.

In principle, restrictions and controls on interbank flows could be imposed on either lending banks or borrowing banks. Regarding the former possibility, it should be stressed that, under the current Basle capital adequacy standards, lending banks have a clear incentive to supply short-term rather than long-term loans to banks in emerging markets. This is because risk weights are lower on short-term than long-term bank loans. After the Asian crisis, there is a growing consensus in favour of changing these standards, so as to penalise short-term bank lending to emerging markets through a revision of risk weights (this issue has been tackled in a BIS review of the capital adequacy standards).

As regards restrictions on the borrower side, the consensus view is that effective prudential regulation of banks in emerging economies requires higher reserve requirement ratios on liabilities representing cross-border interbank loans and deposits. Note that, as highlighted from our discussion, possible restrictions on short-term cross border banks flows are debated within the context of prudential regulation and supervision of financial institutions.

The case for broader controls on all short-term capital inflows (including also portfolio investments and equities) is more controversial. The main argument in its favour is that controls on interbank flows may not be sufficient to shield a country from the high volatility of 'hot money' flows. To the extent that corporate firms also respond to distorted incentives leading them to excessive borrowing, controls on corporate foreign liabilities, especially short term, may be warranted. In Asia during the early 1990s, for example, corporate firms directly undertook risky cross-border borrowing on a large scale. In Indonesia corporate borrowing was massive, over $70 bn, and much larger than foreign borrowing by banks. The scale of corporate borrowing was very large also in the other crisis countries.

The available empirical evidence from Chile and other countries that have imposed controls on a broad range of short-term capital inflows is mixed. Controls do appear to affect the composition of inflows (in favour of long-term loans and FDI) but do not appear to affect the overall volume of inflows. Moreover, controls become less effective over time, because of evasion and leakages (especially via trade credits). Finally, there is some evidence that the Chilean controls have favoured large corporations over small and medium ones. It has been argued that the apparent success of Chile in avoiding major currency crises should be attributed to an effective prudential regulation and supervision of the financial system, more than to the presence of controls on short-term inflows. In this respect, it is worth emphasising that, during the financial turmoil, Chile – along with Colombia and Brazil – did actually phase out controls, with the goal of stimulating much-needed capital inflows, and reduce the pressure on the currency.

The case for controls on capital outflows, especially in the aftermath of a currency crisis, appears much more controversial in the ongoing academic and policy debate.[37] The logic of the argument in favour of outflow controls is laid out by Krugman (1998c). The economic recovery in Asia is hampered by high interest rates, but, under perfect capital mobility, a reduction in these rates would further depreciate the exchange rate. For countries with a high stock of liabilities denominated in foreign currency, a depreciation would then be recessionary, via the increasing burden of foreign debt. Controls on capital flows allow domestic policy makers to break the links between interest rates and exchange rates, so that interest rates can be lowered without incurring the cost of a currency devaluation.

Krugman (1998c), stresses the effectiveness of capital controls with the following provocative characterisation of the successful performance of the Chinese economy in 1997–8:[38]

think about China right now: a country whose crony capitalism makes Thailand look like Switzerland and whose bankers make Suharto's son look like JP Morgan. Why hasn't China been nearly as badly hit as its neighbours? Because it has been able to cut, not raise, interest rates in this crisis, despite maintaining a fixed exchange rate; and the reason it is able to do that is that it has an inconvertible currency, a.k.a. exchange controls. Those controls are often evaded, and they are the source of lots of corruption, but they still give China a degree of policy leeway that the rest of Asia desperately wishes it had.

Is the short-run relief that capital controls give to policy makers offset by their long-run costs (higher inflation, higher risk premium, efficiency costs owing to a distorted allocation, etc.)? Some authors argue that there is no compelling empirical evidence that countries which implement capital account convertibility are systematically associated with better macroeconomic performances in the long run. For instance, Rodrik (1998, p. 61) has shown that, in a large sample of countries,

the data provide no evidence that countries without capital controls have grown faster, invested more, or experienced lower inflation. Capital controls are essentially uncorrelated with long-term performance once we control for other determinants.

Advocates of the opposite view highlight several arguments against such controls on capital outflows. First, imposing capital controls and limiting capital mobility – they argue – is no 'solution' to the structural problems underlying the Asian crisis. Rather, policy interventions should aim at making the financial system sound, well regulated and effectively supervised (see, for example. Dornbusch, 1998b). The second argument is based on the experience with capital controls in Latin America in the aftermath of the 1980s' debt crisis, which was quite dismal. Controls tended to be ineffective, a tool of financial repression associated with negative real interest rates. For these reasons, they eventually led to more, rather than less, capital flight.

The third argument stresses the role of 'political risk' in international financial instability. While the implementation of capital controls may help fight a crisis and buy time to organise a policy response to speculative flows, the anticipation (or the possibility) of controls may actually accelerate it. In this respect, the fact that some countries impose controls may lead to a perverse international contagion on other countries. The news of capital controls imposed by Russia and Malaysia in August 1998 was arguably an important factor in the contagious spread of financial panic to Latin America and other emerging markets.

Finally, capital controls are not implemented and managed by the ideally 'benevolent' policy makers of economic theory, but by governments that are potential sources of distortions and moral hazard. This implies the possibility of a political use (or misuse) of such controls, the risk of creating incentives to rent-seeking, and the temptation to use controls to avoid and or delay necessary reforms.

While the arguments in favour of capital controls, especially during a crisis, are controversial, the views on the third issue presented above, the optimal speed and sequencing of capital account liberalisation, reflect a widespread and explicit consensus. This consensus view (expressed formally even within the G-7 group and the IMF: see, for example, Camdessus, 1998) stresses that, while a progressive liberalisation of the capital account may be warranted over time, policy makers should be very careful about doing it in a gradual and orderly way. As long as financial systems are weak, poorly regulated and subject to political distortions, a hasty rush to capital account liberalisation may be unwise and produce destabilising effects. The benefits of free capital flows are numerous and, provided that financial systems are strong, the arguments in favour of free capital mobility are compelling. In the transition to a system with desirable characteristics, however, capital account liberalisation will have to be cautious, gradual and carefully managed. The transition process will have to prevent large foreign debt accumulation, excessive borrowing and lending and a mismatch in the maturities and currency denomination of assets and liabilities of financial institutions and corporate firms, which have proven to be so destabilizing in many recent and less recent episodes of financial and currency crises.

6 Open issues

In the light of the most recent developments in the region, we find it appropriate to conclude our study by briefly highlighting some open issues regarding the implications of the crisis. Some of the crisis countries, notably Indonesia, Korea and Thailand, are currently experiencing a harsh economic contraction. Many corporations have little access to working capital and are burdened by a massive stock of liabilities. Corporate debt/equity ratios that were already high before the crisis have grown higher, to levels that can hardly be deemed sustainable (400 per cent in Thailand, over 500 per cent in Korea, an even higher ratio for Indonesia).

Banks are under extreme stress. Partly as the result of high interest rates (which increase the rate of non-performing loans), and partly owing to the attempt to recapitalise financial intermediaries at a rapid pace, the net worth of the banking system of Korea, Thailand and Indonesia has drastically deteriorated. It should be emphasised that, in terms of actual disbursement, official financial assistance has been significantly lower than announced and reported by newspaper headlines. Financial means from official sources have not alleviated the liquidity squeeze in capital markets.

In such context of financial distress and debt overhang, banks have been severely cutting credit to firms. In some cases, this has been a decisive factor in inducing bankruptcy of corporations that in all likelihood would have been solvent in normal conditions. Contractions in trade credit are particularly painful, as such cuts undermine the firms' ability to import intermediate inputs, and to produce and export domestic goods. An important indicator supporting this statement is the fact that, in spite of massive real depreciations, exports from the crisis countries have not significantly increased in volume.

Over the summer of 1998, interest rates in Asia fell significantly relative to the peaks of the crisis, and in Korea they were back to pre-crisis levels. In spite of this, the credit crunch is still severe in most countries: while the price of credit has been falling, banks that are effectively bankrupt or experience financial distress are unwilling to lend to corporate firms suffering from debt overhang, so that loans are still drastically rationed. In such a situation, capital controls leading to lower interest rates do little to ease the credit crunch, and it is far from clear whether they help to remove structural impediments to recovery.

While the need for a more decisive expansionary policy has been widely recognised, several observers have emphasised that an effective way to help the Asian countries to start producing and exporting again might consist of an accelerated debt restructuring process that would recapitalise banks, reduce corporate debt overhang and provide firms with debt moratoria and new priority financing of working capital and trade. In this regard, it can be argued that a gradual, voluntary and market-based work-out of foreign and domestic debts is not the most effective strategy to address this issue, since a market-based process of debt restructuring may be too slow. The longer the process takes, the larger the number of otherwise solvent firms that become insolvent, and the worse the collapse of economic activity. Suggestions for a comprehensive approach to bank and corporate restructuring with a more active role of governments may have to be considered.

APPENDIX

In this appendix we describe in detail the construction of the variables used in the empirical analysis.

Crisis index (IND)
The index is a weighted average of the percentage rate of exchange rate depreciation relative to the US dollar and the percentage rate of change in foreign reserves between end-December 1996 and end-December 1997. A large negative value for *IND* corresponds to a high devaluation rate and/or a fall in foreign reserves – i.e. a more severe currency crisis. All data are from the International Financial Statistics of the International Monetary Fund (*IFS*-IMF).

Real exchange rate appreciation
This variable measures the percentage rate of change of the real exchange rate between end 1996 and an average over the 1988–90 period. The real exchange rate measure is based on wholesale price indexes, using trade weights of OECD countries (excluding Mexico and Korea). For the three transition economies – the Czech Republic, Hungary and Poland – whose real exchange rates exhibited large fluctuations in the early transition years, the appreciation is calculated between 1996 and 1992. For Argentina, whose real exchange rate experienced large swings in the hyper-inflation period, the real exchange rate is computed between 1996 and end-1990.

Current account deficits and the CAI index
The current account deficit as a share of GDP is an average over the 1994–6 period. Data are from *IFS*. The index of current account imbalances CAI is computed as follows: for countries where the real exchange rate appreciated more than 10 per cent over the period defined above, *CAI* takes the value of the average 1994–6 current account balance (as a share of GDP); for all other countries, *CAI* is set equal to zero.

Lending boom (LB)
This variable is the rate of growth between 1990 and 1996 of the ratio between the claims on the private sector of the deposit money banks (line 22d in *IFS*) and nominal GDP. All data are from *IFS*. In the case of transition economies where either data since 1990 are not available or the ratio is very unstable in the early transition years, we take 1992 (rather than 1990) as the starting date.

Non-performing loans as a share of total bank assets (NPL).
As there are no homogeneous series for non-performing loans, we need to build our data set relying on several sources. For most of the Asian countries in our sample (Korea, Indonesia, Hong Kong, Taiwan, Malaysia, Thailand) there are two available estimates of *NPL* in 1996; one from the

1997 BIS *Annual Report*, the other from Jardine Fleming. Both estimates are biased: the former under-estimates non-performing loans before the onset of the crisis (for instance, the end-1996 figure for Korea is 0.8 per cent); the latter is based on data from the third quarter of 1997, when non-performing loans were already reflecting the consequences of the currency crises on the financial conditions of banks and corporate firms (for instance, Korean non-performing loans are estimated to be 16 per cent). We take the average of the two figures as a reasonable estimate of the non-performing loans before the onset of the crisis – i.e. end-1996–early-1997. For the remaining countries, we proceed as follows: for India, Argentina, Brazil, Chile, Colombia, Mexico, Peru and Venezuela we use the estimates for 1996 in the 1997 BIS *Annual Report*. For China, Singapore and the Philippines, we use estimates from Jardine Fleming. For the other countries in the sample, we rely on information derived from IMF country reports. It is worth emphasising that our estimates do not appear to be systematically biased towards the countries that suffered a crisis in 1997. Note in fact that non-crisis countries such as Mexico, China, India and Pakistan all show a very large fraction of non-performing loans (over 10 per cent of total loans).

Fiscal cost of the bail-out of the banking system as a share of GDP (NPLY)
This variable is computed as follows. We take the estimate of the non-performing loans as a share of banks' assets (NPL) derived above and we multiply it by the ratio to GDP of claims on the private sector by deposit money banks at the end of 1996. The latter variable is computed from IFS data.

The NPLB index
In deriving *NPLB*, we interact the lending-boom variable with the non-performing-loans variable: for countries where the sign of the lending-boom variable is positive, we set *NPL2* equal to *NPL*; for countries with a negative lending boom, we set *NPLB* equal to zero.

Reserve adequacy ratios
We compute three ratios for reserve adequacy at end 1996. The first is the ratio of $M1$ to foreign exchange reserves ($M1/RES$); the second is the ratio of $M2$ to foreign reserves ($M2/RES$); the third is the ratio of the foreign debt service burden (i.e. short-term foreign debt *plus* interest payments on foreign debt) to foreign reserves (STD/RES). Foreign exchange reserve data are from *IFS* (line 11.d). Data on short-term debt and interest payments on foreign debt are from Datastream.

Taiwan

Taiwan is not included in the IMF data base. Our data for Taiwan are from Datastream and rely on Taiwan national data sources.

NOTES

We thank Rudi Dornbusch, Linda Goldberg, Paul Krugman, Jacques Olivier, Richard Portes, Roberto Rigobon, Andrew Scott, Harald Uhlig, Jaume Ventura and seminar participants at Boston University, Dartmouth, IMF, MIT and Yale for helpful comments. Michele Cavallo and Andrew Tiffin have provided excellent research assistance. The views expressed here are those of the authors, and do not necessarily reflect those of the Federal Reserve Bank of New York or any other institution with which the authors are affiliated.

1 A partial list of recent studies providing empirical evidence on the Asian crisis includes Alba *et al.* (1998), Dornbusch (1998a); Goldstein (1998); IMF (1998); OECD (1998); Pomerleano (1998); Radelet and Sachs (1998). The role of moral hazard in the onset of the Asian crisis has been discussed by a number of authors. See, for example, Fischer (1998b); Greenspan (1998); Krugman (1998a). A large number of contributions on the crisis are available online on Nouriel Roubini's Asian Crisis Homepage at www.stern.nyu.edu/ ˜nroubini/asia/AsiaHomepage.html

2 See IMF (1997).

3 See Pomerleano (1998) for a thorough assessment of the corporate roots of the financial crisis in Asia.

4 For instance, in Korea, 20 of the largest 30 conglomerates displayed in 1996 a rate of return on invested capital below the cost of capital. In 1997, before the crisis, as many as seven of the 30 largest conglomerates could be considered effectively bankrupt. OECD (1998) stresses that Korean *chaebols* were performing poorly since the second half of the 1980s.

5 In part, this may have occurred because the interest rate fall in industrial countries (especially in Japan) lowered the cost of capital for firms and motivated large financial flows into the Asian countries.

6 The literature has focused on a long list of structural distortions in the pre-crisis Asian financial and banking sectors: lax supervision and weak regulation; low capital adequacy ratios; lack of incentive-compatible deposit-insurance schemes; insufficient expertise in the regulatory institutions; distorted incentives for project selection and monitoring; outright corrupt lending practices; non-market criteria of credit allocation, according to a model of relationship banking that emphasises semi-monopolistic relations between banks and firms, somehow downplaying price signals. All these factors contributed to the build-up of severe weaknesses in the under-capitalised financial system, whose most visible manifestation was eventually a growing share of non-performing loans.

7 See, for example, McKinnon and Pill (1996).

8 See, for example, Stiglitz (1998).

9 The countries are Argentina, Brazil, Chile, China, Colombia, Czech Republic, Hong Kong, Hungary, India, Indonesia, Jordan, Korea, Malaysia, Mexico,

Pakistan, Peru, the Philippines, Poland, Singapore, Sri Lanka, Taiwan, Thailand, Turkey and Venezuela.

10 See, for example, Eichengreen, Rose and Wyplosz (1996); Sachs, Tornell and Velasco (1996); Kaminsky, Lizondo and Reinhart (1998).

11 The weights assigned to exchange rate and reserves changes in IND are, respectively, 0.75 and 0.25. For the purpose of sensitivity analysis, we consider alternative crisis indexes with different weights, and find that the choice of the weight coefficients is not crucial to our results. Alternative tests with different samples of shorter size provide similar results. All tests are available upon request from the authors.

12 While of course an increase in domestic interest rates may also signal a frustrated speculative attack, our crisis index excludes changes in interest rates. This is because an increase in interest rates in the presence of speculative pressures is highly correlated with non-sterilised foreign exchange intervention, leading to a fall in reserves.

13 Note that Turkey exhibited a satisfactory economic performance in 1997, with GDP growing over 6 per cent and its stock market being a leading performer among emerging countries.

14 Other authors use a different approach to the same problem. For example, Sachs, Tornell and Velasco (1996) control for the variance of the exchange rate and reserves in the last 10 years.

15 The Czech Republic shared many symptoms with the Asian crisis countries: a fixed-exchange rate regime maintained for too long, a severe real appreciation, a dramatic worsening of the current account and a weak banking system with large shares of non-performing loans.

16 In the appendix (p. 156) we describe in detail our methodology to estimate the series NPL.

17 These authors argue that such a measure is a proxy for financial fragility as the quality of bank loans is likely to deteriorate significantly – and a large fraction is likely to become non-performing – when bank lending grows at a rapid pace in a relatively short period of time.

18 The logic of the $NPLB$ variable is straightforward: non-performing loans represent a source of severe tension only when observed in tandem with excessive bank lending that enhances the vulnerability of the country to a crisis.

19 In tables 4.2–4.5, we present regression results for the 10 per cent threshold, but similar results are obtained for the zero threshold.

20 In this case, the dummy variable would be equal to 0 for countries with our index of current account imbalance (CAI) in the highest quartile of the sample, or with a rate of non-performing loans as a share of GDP (i.e. $NPLY$) in the lowest quartile of the sample; it would be equal to 1 otherwise.

21 Their p-values are 0.005 and 0.09, respectively.

22 Note also that the coefficient on $NPLB$ (β_3) is still significantly different from zero in this regression.

23 In column (3) of table 4.3, we consider interactions of both CAI and $NPLB$ with the dummies for weak fundamentals and low reserves. The results for $NPLB$

are similar to those in column (2). For the current account, instead, we fail to reject the hypothesis that both $\beta_2 + \beta_4 + \beta_6$ and $\beta_2 + \beta_4$ are equal to zero. Formal tests such as the variance inflation test suggest that this is due to multi-collinearity between the two interaction terms: when they both appear in a regression, the effects of CAI are swamped by those of $NPLB$.

24   The p-values on the Wald-tests for $\beta_2 + \beta_4 = 0$ are 0.001, 0.002 and 0.016, respectively in columns (2), (3) and (4), under the three different measures of low reserves.

25   These are the implications of the Wald-tests on $\beta_2 + \beta_4 + \beta_6 = 0$ in column (1) and $\beta_3 + \beta_5 + \beta_7 = 0$ in columns (2) and (3). The failure to reject $\beta_2 + \beta_4 + \beta_6 = 0$ in column (3) is again due to multicollinearity between '$CAI \times D2^{LR} \times D^{WF}$' and '$NPLY \times D2^{LR} \times DWF$'.

26   To test for the robustness of our results we perform a number of other tests. First, we use two other indicators of crisis that give more weight to reserve losses relative to exchange rate depreciation; our qualitative results remain the same. As reported in tables 4.2–4.5, the results are also robust to the use of three alternative definitions of low reserves. Next, we test whether the significance of CAI is sensitive to the threshold for the real exchange rate appreciation; instead of a 10 per cent trigger we use a 0 trigger and obtain the same qualitative results. The significance of the two non-performing loans measures, $NPLB$ and $NPLY$, is also invariant with respect to modification of the definitions of these variables. All these results are available upon request from the authors.

27   Also implicit is the assumption that high investment rates contribute to the enhancement of productive capacity in the traded sector. If the investment boom is confined to the non-traded sector (commercial and residential construction, as well as inward-oriented services), in terms of sustainability analysis the contribution of such investment projects to future trade surpluses – and thus to the ability of the country to repay its external debt obligations – is limited to their indirect impact on the productivity of the traded sector. The two 'implicit' assumptions above need not hold in the Asian case.

28   Recall that the $ICOR$ measures the ratio of the share of investment in GDP to the growth rate of output.

29   Specifically, our regression yields:

$$IND = \begin{array}{cccc} 11.3 & - & 2.21 & NPLY & - & 2.94 & ICORLB \ R^2 & = & 0.48. \\ (5.28) & & (0.77) & & & (1.25) & & \end{array}$$

30   Needless to say, our survey is meant to provide only a synthetic introduction to the multi-faceted issues under discussion since the summer of 1997. For a wider window on the debate, the reader is referred to Roubini's Asian Crisis Homepage (see p. 160).

31   Camdessus (1998).

32   At the time of writing, the IMF plans also allow for a fiscal deficit of 4 per cent in Korea and 2 per cent in Thailand.

33   A loose monetary policy could of course also ignite inflationary expectations.

34   To be sure, some of the banks have added modestly to their loan reserves to account for possible future write-offs, while claiming to be charging interest rates that do not fully reflect the risk of the loans rolled over.

35 For an overview of the debate since the Halifax Summit of 1995 see Kenen (1996).
36 For an assessment of the Chilean experience, see Massad (1998).
37 By the Fall of 1998, a number of countries were assessing costs and benefits of the recourse to capital controls as a strategy to mitigate the extent of a crisis. At the beginning of September 1998, the Malaysian central bank announced the introduction of capital controls, requiring official approval for repatriation and withdrawal of ringgit from external accounts, imposing that all settlements of exports and imports be made in foreign currency, limiting the sale and purchase of ringgit-denominated financial assets to transactions through authorised depository institutions and restricting the export of foreign currency by resident travellers. More drastic controls were introduced in Russia following the 17 August decision to devalue the ruble.
38 In a subsequent 'open letter to Prime Minister Mahathir', Krugman suggests four 'guiding principles' for an exchange controls policy to succeed: first, the actual implementation of controls should aim to disrupt ordinary business as little as possible; second, the distortions they impose on the economy should not be overlooked; third, currency controls should not be used to defend an over-valued currency; fourth, controls must serve as an aid to reform, not an alternative.

REFERENCES
Alba, P., A. Bhattacharya, S. Claessens, S. Ghosh and L. Hernandez (1998). 'Volatility and Contagion in a Financially-Integrated World: Lessons from East Asia's Recent Experience', paper presented at the PAFTAD 24 conference 'Asia Pacific Financial Liberalisation and Reform' (Chiangmai, Thailand) (May 20–22)
Camdessus, M. (1998). 'The IMF's Role in Today's Globalised World', address to the IMF–Bundesbank Symposium (Frankfurt) Germany (2 July)
Corsetti, G., P. Pesenti and N. Roubini (1998a). 'Paper Tigers? A Model of the Asian Crisis', *NBER Working Paper*, **6783** (November)
    (1998b). 'What Caused the Asian Currency and Financial Crisis? Part I: A Macroeconomic Overview', Yale University, mimeo
    (1998c). 'What Caused the Asian Currency and Financial Crisis? Part II: The Policy Debate', Yale University, mimeo
Dornbusch, R. (1998a). 'Asian Crisis Themes', MIT (February), mimeo
    (1998b). 'Capital Controls: An Idea Whose Time is Past', in S. Fischer *et al.*, 'Should the IMF Pursue Capital-Account Liberalisation?', *Essays in International Finance*, **207**, International Finance Section, Princeton University (May)
Eichengreen, B., A. K. Rose and C. Wyplosz (1996). 'Contagious Currency Crises', *NBER Working Paper*, **5681** (July)
Feldstein, M. (1998). 'Refocusing the IMF'. *Foreign Affairs*, **77(2)** (March-April)
Fischer, S. (1998a). 'The Asian Crisis: A View from the IMF', address at the Midwinter Conference of the Bankers' Association for Foreign Trade (Washington, DC) (22 January)

(1998b). 'The IMF and the Asian Crisis'. Forum Funds Lecture at UCLA (Los Angeles) (20 March)

(1998c). 'In Defense of the IMF. Specialised Tools for a Specialised Task', *Foreign Affairs*, **77**(4)

Goldstein, M. (1998). 'The Asian Financial Crisis: Causes, Cures, and Systemic Implications', *Policy Analyses in International Economics*, **55**, Washington, DC: Institute for International Economics

Greenspan, A. (1998). 'Remarks before the 34th Annual Conference on Bank Structure and Competition', Federal Reserve Bank of Chicago (7 May)

International Monetary Fund (1997). *World Economic Outlook. Interim Assessment*, Washington, DC: International Monetary Fund (December)

(1998). *World Economic Outlook*, Washington, DC: International Monetary Fund (May)

Kaminsky, G., S. Lizondo and C. M. Reinhart (1998). 'Leading Indicators of Currency Crises'. *IMF Staff Papers* (March)

Kenen, P. B. (ed.) (1996). 'From Halifax to Lyons: What has been Done about Crisis Management?', *Essays in International Finance*, **200**, International Finance Section, Princeton University (October)

Krugman, P. (1998a). 'What Happened to Asia?', MIT, mimeo

(1998b). 'Will Asia Bounce Back?', speech for Credit Suisse First Boston, Hong Kong (March)

(1998c). 'Saving Asia: It's Time to Get Radical', *Fortune Investor* (September 7): 33–8; available at Lttp://www.pathfinder.com/fortune/investor/1998/98097/sol./html

Litan, R. E. (1998). 'A Three-Step Remedy for Asia's Financial Flu', *Brookings Policy Brief* **30** (February)

Massad, C. (1998). 'The Liberalisation of the Capital Account: Chile in the 1990s', in S. Fischer *et al.*, 'Should the IMF Pursue Capital-account Liberalisation?', *Essays in International Finance*, **207**, International Finance Section, Princeton University (May)

McKinnon, R. and H. Pill (1996). 'Credible Economic Liberalisations and International Capital Flows: The 'Overborrowing Syndrome', in T. Ito and A. O. Kruger (eds.), *Financial Deregulation and Integration in East Asia*, Chicago: University of Chicago Press: 7–42

OECD (1998). *Economic Survey of Korea 1997-98*, Paris: OECD

Pomerleano, M. (1998). 'The East Asia Crisis and Corporate Finances – The Untold Micro Story.' *Emerging Markets Quarterly*, winter: 14–27

Radelet, S. and J. Sachs (1998). 'The Onset of the East Asian Financial Crisis,' *NBER Working Paper*, **6680** (August)

Rodrik, D. (1998). 'Who Needs Capital-account Convertibility?,' in S.Fischer *et al.*, 'Should the IMF Pursue Capital-account Liberalisation?', *Essays in International Finance*, **207**, International Finance Section, Princeton University (May)

Sachs, J. (1998). 'To Stop the Money Panic', interview, *Asia Week* (February 13)

Sachs, J., A. Tornell and A. Velasco (1996). 'Financial Crises in Emerging Markets: The Lessons from 1995', *Brookings Papers on Economic Activity*, **1**: 147-217

Stiglitz, J. (1998). 'The Role of International Financial Institutions in the Current Global Economy', address to the Chicago Council on Foreign Relations, Chicago (27 February)

Discussion
Richard Portes

A financial crisis is a disturbance to financial markets that disrupts the market's capacity to allocate capital – financial intermediation and hence investment come to a halt. The term 'financial crisis' is used too loosely, often to denote either a banking crisis, or a debt crisis, or a foreign exchange market crisis. It is perhaps preferable to invoke it only for the 'big one': a generalised, international financial crisis. This is a nexus of foreign exchange market disturbances, debt defaults (sovereign or private) and banking system failures: a triple crisis, in which the interactions are the key to causality, depth and persistence (Eichengreen and Portes, 1987).

The widespread securitisation of debt in recent years has not changed the picture – after all, one of the major historical examples is the 1930s crisis of defaults on sovereign bonds. Nor has it diminished the importance of banking sector fragility in provoking and exacerbating financial crises.

In chapter 4, a financial crisis is interpreted as a *financial sector* crisis. The stress is on banks and non-performing loans and the ultimate need for government bail-outs. This drives the story – and it provokes the exchange rate and debt crises. The framework includes explicit discussion of the impact of bail-outs on income distribution and the fiscal position. This is new and important. But my brief comments focus on the limitations of the analysis.

Insofar as bail-outs are expected – and indeed here the crisis is a consequence of anticipated bail-out costs – moral hazard is central. But its origin here is only agents' expectations of the reaction of the domestic government – not that of the international financial institutions. There is no bail-out from abroad, yet it is reasonable to believe that the bail-out of Mexico in early 1995 led by the IMF and the USA did play a significant role in stimulating over-lending to the Asian crisis countries. Krugman's 'Pangloss' model (1998) also focuses on the domestically generated moral hazard, but I believe this emphasis is misplaced. Unfortunately, it is very difficult to construct an empirical test for either form of moral hazard, and if we cannot verify their existence, it is even harder to distinguish between them.

What about the other factors behind the crises? The authors' treatment of foreign borrowing ignores its maturity structure, whereas many observers argue that vulnerability to attack depends significantly on the size of short-run debt in relation to foreign exchange reserves. The authors also ignore the supply-side (foreign) factors in the capital inflow – in effect, they assume that up to the crisis, funds are infinitely elastic at a given interest rate. Indeed, in the model all investment is financed externally – and this is supposed to characterise economies whose domestic savings rates were among the highest in the world. The authors criticise 'second-generation' models of speculative attacks because they too require weak fundamentals, at least weak enough to set the stage for rational, self-fulfilling shifts in market expectations. And it is common ground that the Asian economies did not exhibit weak macroeconomic fundamentals. Yet their empirical work includes financial fragility among the fundamentals – and this was the key Asian weakness, which inhibited the use of the interest rate defence against speculative pressure.

In the model, the crisis is the consequence of anticipated bail-out costs and distributional conflicts, which give rise to expectations of monetisation of future fiscal deficits. I find it difficult to believe, however, that agents really estimate the extent of the bail-out that might be required. The empirical work in the chapter seems to me unsafe and unsatisfactory – in fact, distinctly ad hoc. There is a proliferation of dummy variables and interaction terms (which change – not surprisingly – from one version of the study to the next). 'Preliminary tests' are used to reject some variables, but not within any explicit 'general-to-specific' hypothesis testing framework. The original version of the chapter reported 14 regressions on a cross-section of 24 countries, each regression having typically 18–19 degrees of freedom; there were clearly many unreported regressions that had been run. All this comes too close to data-mining for my taste, and I would suspect that the results would not be robust: either to alternative specifications, or as indicators or interpretations of the next round of crises.

That said, there are important insights in the chapter's analysis. It reflects an exceptionally thorough study of the Asian crisis, and it certainly widens and deepens our understanding of an extraordinarily complex set of phenomena.

REFERENCES

Eichengreen, B. and R. Portes (1987). 'The Anatomy of Financial Crises', in R. Portes and S. Swoboda (eds.), *Threats to International Financial Stability*, Cambridge: Cambridge University Press: 10–58

Krugman, P. (1998). 'What Happened to Asia?', MIT, mimeo

Part Two

Theoretical Contributions

5 Capital markets and the instability of open economies

PHILIPPE AGHION, PHILIPPE BACCHETTA AND
ABHIJIT BANERJEE

1 Introduction

The world has in recent months been captivated by the sight of the 'miracle' economies of a few months ago tumbling first into a financial crisis and then into a full-scale macroeconomic collapse. Not surprisingly, several potential explanations for why this happened are already in the air: some argue that it was pure happenstance (a 'panic');[1] others blame the peculiarities of the financial sector in these economies ('crony capitalism').[2]

This chapter takes a somewhat contrarian position with respect to this debate. Specifically it argues that what happened in East and Southeast Asia is not necessarily an aberration requiring a special explanation. In the years before the crisis hit, these economies had been going through a process of rapid change. The financial sector was being liberalised, making it easier for domestic firms to borrow. Partly as a result of this liberalisation, capital was flowing into these economies in large quantities, causing a real currency appreciation, rapid growth in lending and a boom in investment. When the crisis came it is these forces that got reversed – capital flowed out, the currency fell, lending stopped and investment collapsed.[3]

This pattern of a boom accompanied by capital inflows and a real appreciation followed by a dramatic collapse with capital outflows and rapid depreciation is by no means unknown in other middle-income countries. Very much the same thing happened in Mexico in 1994 and in the Southern Cone in the early 1980s.[4]

Perhaps more importantly, this pattern of growth and collapse may be a natural feature of economies at an intermediate level of financial development, especially those with a liberalised financial sector. The primary objective of this chapter is to substantiate this claim. To this end, it develops a simple model of a small open economy with a tradeable good produced using a non-tradeable input (which may be thought of as real estate or skilled labour). To this it adds the assumption that the capital markets

167

are imperfect, in the sense that a firm's creditworthiness, and therefore the amount it can borrow and invest, depends on its current cash flow situation.[5]

In such a model the process of growth is driven by a combination of two forces: on one side, more investment leads to more output and, *ceteris paribus*, to higher profits. Higher profits improve creditworthiness and fuel more borrowing, which leads to more investment. Capital flows into the country to finance this boom. At the same time, the boom in investment increases the demand for the non-tradeable input and raises its price relative to the tradeable good (unless the supply of the non-tradeable input is extremely elastic). This rise in prices leads to lower profits in the tradeable goods sector and, therefore, reduced creditworthiness, less borrowing and less investment. Of course once investment falls all these forces get reversed and eventually the price of non-tradeable inputs may fall enough to raise profits and start off another boom.

The interplay of these two forces, we show, can under certain conditions lead the economy to have stable cycles where the economy alternates between investment booms with high prices of non-tradeable inputs and large capital inflows and slumps where non-tradeable inputs are cheap and capital inflows are sharply reduced or even reversed. Moreover, even in the case where the economy does not permanently cycle, in a wide class of cases the economy will respond to a shock (such as the liberalisation of the domestic capital market) by going through several booms and slumps before converging to its steady state.[6]

When a monetary dimension is added to this model, the variations in the relative price of the non-tradeable input are mirrored by movements in either the nominal exchange rate or the level of central bank's reserves. With a fixed exchange rate, the phase of capital inflows and high investment is also a phase of reserves' accumulation and when the economy collapses, reserves may be depleted and the fixed-exchange rate policy abandoned.

We examine a liberalisation of capital movements and show that an economy that was hitherto completely stable can become volatile and start to go through cycles of explosive booms and deep slumps. These results, however, do not apply to foreign direct investment (FDI). FDI differs from foreign lending in not depending on the creditworthiness of the domestic firms. When, in a slump, cash flow is low in the domestic economy, foreign direct investors may actually prefer to come in to profit from the low price of non-tradeable inputs.

Our results are not inconsistent with alternative explanations of the crisis. Indeed, it is hard to deny that corruption played a role in the recent vicissitudes of the financial sector in East and Southeast Asia. It is also likely that panic selling had something to do with the speed with which the currencies crashed. The question that remains, however, is whether a crisis would have hit these economies even in the absence of these factors. Our model suggests that it probably would have done.[7] Recognising this possibility does more than change our perspective on the current crisis: it also informs what our response to the crisis ought to be. Discussion of these policy issues is postponed to the concluding section.

2 A simple framework

We consider a small open economy with two goods, respectively tradeable and non-tradeable. While the tradeable good can serve both as a capital input and as a consumption good, the non-tradeable good can serve only as an input in the production of the tradeable good. One should typically think of the non-tradeable good in this economy as input services such as real estate, (skilled) labour, . . . Until we introduce monetary considerations into the analysis, we take the tradeable good as the numeraire and we denote by p the price of the non-tradeable input when expressed in units of the tradeable good. We assume that the non-tradeable input is not used for consumption.[8]

There are two distinct categories of individuals in the economy. First, the *lenders* who cannot directly invest in production, but yet can lend their initial wealth endowments at the international market-clearing gross interest rate, r. Second, the *investors* (or *borrowers*) who also have the opportunity to invest in production. The production function for the tradeable good is given by:

$$y_T = f(K, z_N) \tag{5.1}$$

where K (resp. z_N) denotes the current tradeable (resp. non-tradeable) investments and y_T denotes the current domestic flow of tradeable output. (The production function f obeys the usual concavity assumptions.)

2.1 Credit market imperfections

Because of standard agency (moral hazard) considerations, an investor with initial wealth W can invest at most $\frac{1}{\nu}W$, where $\frac{1}{\nu} > 1$ is a credit multiplier which reflects the degree of capital market imperfections.[9] Credit constraints vanish as ν tends towards 0, while $\nu = 1$ corresponds to the polar

Figure 5.1   *The timing of events*

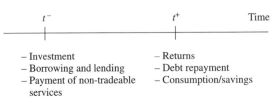

case where the credit market collapses and investors can invest only their own wealth. As we shall argue below, volatility is most likely to occur for intermediate values of the parameter v, in other words for intermediate degrees of financial development.

2.2 Production decision

Investors with total initial wealth, W_B, will choose a non-tradeable investment, z_N $\left(\text{with corresponding tradeable investment } K = \dfrac{W_B}{v} - p \cdot z_N\right)$ to maximise current profits, i.e. to solve:

$$\max_{z_N} f\left(\underbrace{\frac{W_B}{v} - p \cdot z_N, z_N}_{K}\right) - p \cdot z_N$$

where $z_N \leq y_N$ (endowment of non-tradeable good). The equilibrium price of the non-tradeable input, p, will then be simply determined as the price such that the demand for non-tradeable input, z_N (defined as the solution to the above maximisation programme) is equal to the fixed supply, y_N, of the non-tradeable good. This equilibrium price is the key variable whose movements over time will produce output cycles.

2.3 The timing of events

The timing of events within each period t is depicted in figure 5.1. Investment, borrowing and lending takes place at the *beginning* of the period (which we denote by t^-); investors also pay the non-tradeable good services, $p \cdot z_N$, to the owners of non-tradeable goods. Everything else occurs at the *end* of the period (which we denote by t^+): first, the returns to investments are realised; second, the debt repayment, $r\left(\frac{W_B}{\nu} - W_B\right)$, from borrowers to lenders; third, the consumption and the savings decisions, which in turn will determine the initial wealth of borrowers at the beginning of the next period (i.e. at $(t + 1)^-$).

2.4 Savings behaviour

For simplicity, we assume a linear savings behaviour: all agents save a fixed fraction $(1 - \alpha)$ of their total end-of-period wealth and consume a fixed fraction α.[10]

Now that the basic model has been laid out, we can analyse the dynamics of the economy and in particular try to understand why open economies with imperfect credit markets may experience macroeconomic volatility. As we focus on output, it is sufficient to examine the evolution of investors' behaviour. Let W_B^{t+1} denote the disposable wealth of investors (borrowers) at the beginning of period $(t + 1)$. The dynamic evolution of W_B (and therefore of investment and total output) between two successive periods, is simply described by the equation:

$$W_B^{t+1} = (1 - \alpha)\left[f\left(\overbrace{\frac{W_B^t}{\nu} - p^t \cdot z_N}^{\substack{\text{Cost of non-} \\ \text{tradeable services}}}, z_N\right) - \overbrace{r\frac{W_B^t}{\nu} - W_B^t}^{\text{Debt repayment}} \right] \quad (5.2)$$

where p^t is the market-clearing price of the non-tradeable input at time t. The expression in brackets is the *net* end-of-period t revenue of investors. The net disposable wealth of investors at the beginning of period $(t + 1)$ is what is left of this net end-of-period return after consumption, hence the multiplying factor $(1 - \alpha)$ on the RHS of (5.2).

Looking at (5.2) one can immediately see that an increase in investors' last-period wealth, W_B^t. has an ambiguous effect on their current wealth, W_B^{t+1}. On the one hand, for a given price of the non-tradeable good, p^t a higher-wealth W_B^t means a higher level of investment, $\frac{W_B^t}{\nu}$ in period t which, everything also remaining equal, should produce higher revenues and therefore generate higher wealth at the beginning of period $(t + 1)$. (This we might call a *wealth effect*.) On the other hand, more investment in period t also implies a bigger demand for the non-tradeable good and therefore an increase in the price, p^t, of that good during that period, which in turn will have a detrimental effect on period t revenues and therefore on period $(t + 1)$

Figure 5.2   *Wealth and price effects*

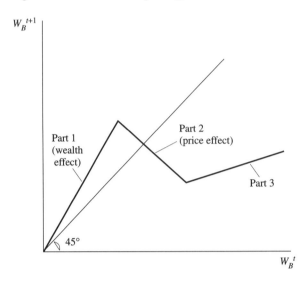

wealth, W_B^{t+1}. And the less substitutable the two inputs are in the production of tradeable output, the stronger this latter *price effect* turns out to be.[11]

Figure 5.2 depicts the evolution of W_B^{t+1} as a function of W_B^t in the Leontief case where $f(K, z_n) = \left(\dfrac{K}{a}, z_n\right)$. (Similar patterns can be derived by simulating the CES case: $f(K, z_N) = (K^\rho + z_N^\rho)^{\frac{1}{\rho}}$, see Aghion, Bacchetta, and Banerjee, 1998.) On the left-hand part of the curve (part 1) the *wealth effect* dominates the *price effect*: the middle part of the curve (part 2) corresponds to the *price effect* becoming stronger than the *wealth effect*; finally the right-hand part of the curve (part 3) follows from the fact that investors will eventually not borrow the full amount proposed by lenders, as a result of the price effect. In other words, investors are not constrained on the third part of the curve. This happens when production becomes insufficiently profitable compared to lending all their wealth at rate r, i.e. $y_T - r\left(\dfrac{W_B}{\nu} - W_B\right) - r W_B$. In that case the evolution of investors' wealth is simply given by:

$$W_B^{t+1} = (1 - \alpha) r W_B^t. \tag{5.3}$$

Now, when the overall curve, $W_B^{t+1}(W_B^t)$, intersects the 45° line on its *downward*-sloping part (part 2) in which the price effect dominates and yet investors choose to borrow and produce, one can obtain output cycles in

Figure 5.3   *An endogenous cycle*

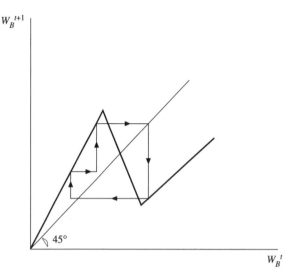

which a debt build-up period – during which the price of non-tradeable input increases – eventually leads to a credit crunch and thereby to a recession. Figure 5.3 depicts an endogenous cycle driven by endogenous fluctuations in the price of the non-tradeable input. Intuitively, the story goes as follows: during a boom the domestic demand for non-tradeable input goes up as (high-yield) investments build up, and thus so does the price of non-tradeables relative to that of tradeables. This, together with the accumulation of debt that still goes on during booms will eventually squeeze investors' borrowing capacity and therefore the demand for the non-tradeable goods. At this point, the economy experiences a slump and two things occur: the price of non-tradeable collapses (i.e. it falls relative to that of tradeables), while a fraction of the non-tradeable assets on offer is not purchased as there are not enough investment funds. The collapse in the price of non-tradeables thus corresponds to a contraction of the tradeable goods sector and of the level of real output. Of course, the low price of non-tradeables will eventually lead to higher profits in the tradeable sector and therefore more investment. A new boom and new cycle then begins.

Even where such a stable endogenous cycle is not a possible outcome, the convergence to the steady state after a shock may exhibit cycle-like behaviour in the sense there may be several booms and slumps before the economy settles down. In this case, as well as where there are genuine limit cycles, slumps are the result of booms which are in a sense too successful and raise the price of the non-tradeable too high. In this sense, the model is suggesting that a tendency towards occasional slumps may be inevitable in a certain type of economy.

In appendix 1 we analyse this model in more detail in the case where the production technology takes the Leontief form.[12] For this special case we derive necessary conditions for long-run macroeconomic volatility. Interestingly, these conditions involve the parameter ν (which measures the degree of credit market imperfection) being neither too small nor too close to 1. In other words, long-run output volatility of the kind analysed above is inconsistent with both full financial development ($\nu \sim 0$) and also with the total absence of credit markets ($\nu \sim 1$): in the former case the increasing price of non-tradeable inputs will not affect borrowing (and therefore investment) capacity; in the latter case, the absence of credit opportunities will maintain an upper bound on the demand for (and therefore the price of) non-tradeable inputs. It is thus not so surprising that financial fluctuations with real output effects have been primarily experienced by middle-income countries (e.g. in Latin America or in Southeast Asia) with intermediate degrees of financial development.

3 Financial liberalisation and macroeconomic volatility

While an easier access to foreign capital should in principle favour sustained growth, we show in this section that opening an emerging market economy to unrestricted foreign lending and borrowing (i.e. to foreign 'indirect' investment) may actually be destabilising.[13] We also show that this is not the case for FDI. The experiment we consider is simply the opening up to foreign borrowing and lending of a closed economy where saving, equals investment. Assume that the quantity of domestic saving $W_B + W_L$, is initially lower than the demand for investment, $\frac{W_B}{\nu}$. The opening up of the economy will then result in net capital inflows as investors can satisfy their excess demand in international capital markets. The corresponding increase in borrowings will increase the scope for bidding up the price of the non-tradeable input, thereby inducing permanent fluctuations in p, W_B and aggregate output.[14]

While other configurations are also possible, the situation depicted in figure 5.4 fits well the stylised facts mentioned in the Introduction. After a liberalisation capital inflows increase, leading to an investment boom and/or consumption boom. After several periods of expansion, the price of the non-tradeable input experiences substantial increases, which in turn is reflected in a real exchange rate appreciation. This change in relative prices

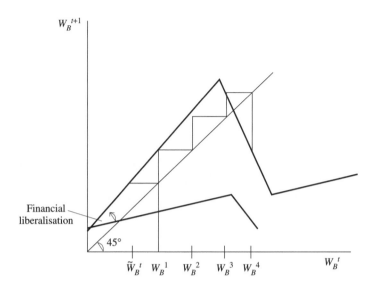

Figure 5.4   *Capital inflows after a liberalisation*
$\tilde{W}_B$ refers to the stable steady-state level of borrowers' wealth
before the economy opens up to foreign borrowing and lending.
This initial value is assumed to be sufficiently small that the non-
tradeable input is not fully employed in domestic production in
the absence of borrowing and lending, so that $p = 0$ initially.
After the liberalisation, borrowers' wealth, W_B, progressively
increases as capital inflows allow investors to increase their
borrowing, investments and profits. During the first two periods
following the liberalisation the demand for the non-tradeable
input remains sufficiently low that $p = 0$. In period 3 (at W^3_B) the
non-tradeable input's p increases but we still have growth.
However, in period 4 (at W^4_B) the *price effect* of the liberalisation
becomes sufficiently strong as to lead to a recession accompanied
by a subsequent drop in the non-tradeable input price, p.
Thereafter, the economy ends up experiencing permanent
fluctuations of the kind described on p. 173.

eventually squeezes out investors' net worth and thereby leads to a recession. At that point, aggregate lending drops, capital flows out and the real
exchange depreciates. The resulting gain in competitiveness allows firms to
rebuild their net worth so that growth can eventually resume.

We should stress that the dynamics in figure 5.4 occur only for *intermediate* levels of financial development. As we mentioned earlier, when ν is too
low there is no volatility.[15] When ν is high, investment capacity is likely to

be smaller than saving in the closed economy (i.e. $\frac{W_B}{\nu} < W_B + W_L$). In this case, a financial opening will not help investment and no capital inflow will occur, so that there will be no upward pressure on relative prices.[16] It is obviously desirable for a country to lower its ν – i.e. to liberalise the domestic financial sector – *before* fully opening up to foreign lending.

Whilst a full financial liberalisation can have destabilising effects on economies with intermediate levels of financial development, those economies are unlikely to become volatile as a result of opening up to foreign *direct* investments alone. We distinguish FDI from other flows by assuming that it is part of firms' equity and that FDI investors have full information about firms.[17] Furthermore, we restrict our analysis to the benchmark case where the supply of FDI is infinitely elastic at some fixed price greater than the world interest rate, r.[18]

Then, starting from a situation in which domestic cash flows are small and therefore domestic investment cannot fully absorb the supply of non-tradeable inputs, foreign direct investors are likely to come in to profit from the low price of the non-tradeable inputs. This price will eventually increase and it may even fluctuate as a result of FDI. But these price fluctuations will affect only the distribution of profits between domestic and foreign investors, not aggregate output. For example, in the Leontief case, with FDI aggregate output will stabilise at a level equal to the supply of non-tradeable resources y_N, whereas the same economy may end up being destabilised if fully open to foreign *indirect* investment (i.e. to foreign lending).

4 Monetary and exchange rate policy

Our analysis so far has focused on the real sector of the economy. However, nominal and monetary factors are often an integral part of financial crises and volatile environments. For example, policies of pegged nominal exchange rates and subsequent speculative attacks are often blamed as being responsible for crises. The impact of devaluations on firms' finances and the optimal policy response after a crisis are also crucial issues.

Our basic framework can easily be extended to incorporate a nominal sector. Here we sketch a simple model with money neutrality. We show that a flexible exchange rate would mirror fluctuations in the relative price of the non-tradeable input, p. With a fixed exchange rate, it is the level of central banks' foreign exchange reserves that mirrors fluctuations in p. We first introduce nominal prices: p_T for the output good and p_N for the non-tradeable input good. The relative price of the non-tradeable input is $p = p_N/p_T$.

We assume that money must be held in advance to buy either the tradeable good or the non-tradeable input and that the seller's currency is used by convention. If the aggregate quantity of money is M, in equilibrium we simply have

$$M = p_T y_T + p_N y_N \tag{5.4}$$

(the cash-in-advance constraint is binding since interest rates are positive). Let s be the nominal exchange rate, defined as the quantity of domestic currency per unit of the foreign currency. Assuming Purchasing Power Parity (PPP) on traded goods and foreign prices for that good equal to unity – i.e. $p_T = s$ – a flexible exchange rate (using (5.4), the PPP assumption and the definition of p) is given by:

$$s = \frac{M}{y_T + p y_N}. \tag{5.5}$$

In the Leontief case, y_T and y_N are constant so that s depends only on M and p. Movements in the relative price of the non-tradeable input are then fully reflected in the nominal exchange rate (a decrease in s reflecting an appreciation of the domestic currency).

Consider now a fixed-exchange rate policy. In this case, s is fixed at $\bar{s}$ and M is endogenously determined by money demand. What is most interesting is the evolution of foreign exchange reserves at the central bank. The central bank's balance sheet is described by the equation $M = DC + IR$, where DC represents domestic credit and IR international reserves. Assume that DC consists exclusively of existing government debt and is fixed at $\overline{DC}$. From (5.4), the evolution of IR is given by

$$IR = \bar{s}(y_T + p y_N) - \overline{DC}. \tag{5.6}$$

International reserves move in parallel with the non-tradeable's price, p, so that periods of capital inflows (outflows) are reflected by increases (decreases) in both p and IR. In particular, the fall in p during slumps will correspond to a decline in international currency reserves. This decline in international reserves may in turn become critical: in line with the speculative-attack literature, there may typically be a lower limit of reserves at which the central bank is forced to abandon the fixed exchange rate. Consequently, downturns in lending at the end of booms will be associated with a depletion of reserves and the abandonment of the fixed-exchange rate policy. Interestingly, the kind of currency crisis we are describing is not caused by inconsistent policies as argued in most of the speculative-attack literature, but rather by the endogenous changes in firms' financial health.[19]

5 Policy conclusions

What is our model telling us about what should be done *ex post*, for example, in the Asian economies that are currently in crisis? A first implication of our model is that slumps should be seen as part of the normal process in economies like these which are both at an intermediate level of financial development and in the process of liberalising their financial sectors. This clearly warns us against seeing these emerging market economies as ones which have lost their way and are beyond repair and therefore must undertake in haste a radical overhauling of their economic system.[20]

Second, policies which allow firms to rebuild their creditworthiness quickly will at the same time contribute to a prompt recovery of the overall economy. In this context it is worth considering the role for monetary policy and, more generally, for policies which affect the credit market. While our model in its present form cannot be *directly* used for this purpose since money is neutral and in any case the interest rate is fixed by the world interest rate, it is not hard to extend this model to allow for both monetary non-neutrality and a less infinitely elastic supply of foreign loans. Once we take the model in this direction it quickly becomes clear that a low interest rate policy is *not* necessarily the right answer *even in a slump that is induced by a credit crunch*. The problem is that while such an interest rate reduction may be good in the sense that it will help restore the financial health (and therefore the investment capacity) of enterprises, if at the same time it leads to a devaluation of the domestic currency, the net obligations of those who have borrowed in foreign currency will also go up. The optimal interest rate policy *ex post* during a financial crisis, therefore cannot be determined without knowing more about the details of the currency composition of the existing debt obligations of domestic enterprises.

This emphasis on creditworthiness as the key element in the recovery from the slump also suggests that a policy of never bailing out insolvent banks (or that of closing down a large number of banks), runs the danger of making firms less able to borrow (because of the comparative advantage of banks in monitoring firms' activities[21]) and of thereby prolonging the slump.[22] If banks are to be shut down, there should be an effort to preserve their expertise and monitoring experience about the relevant firms and industries.

Our model also delivers policy implications *ex ante* for emerging market economies which are *not yet* in the middle of a financial crisis:

- First, our analysis suggests that an unrestricted financial liberalisation may actually *destabilise* the economy and bring about a slump that would not have happened otherwise. If a major slump is likely to be costly even in the long run (because, for example, it sets in process political forces which are destabilising – as in Indonesia in 1998–9), fully liberalising foreign capital flows and fully opening the economy to foreign lending may not be a good idea at least until the domestic financial sector is sufficiently well developed (i.e. ν becomes sufficiently small).

- Second, in our model, foreign *direct* investment does *not* destabilise. Indeed, as we have argued above, FDI is most likely to come in during slumps when the price of the non-tradeable input is low; furthermore, even if this price ends up fluctuating when the economy is open to FDI, these fluctuations will affect only the distribution of profits between domestic and foreign investors but not aggregate output. There is therefore no cost *a priori* to allowing FDI even at low levels of financial development.[23]

- Third, what brings about financial crises in our model is precisely the *rise in the price of non-tradeables*. If one specific non-tradeable good (say, real estate) could be identified as playing a key role in the emergence of a financial crisis, there could be an argument for controlling its price, either directly or though controlling the speculative demand for that good using suitable fiscal deterrents.

- Finally, there may be a role for monetary policies *ex ante* to prevent the occurrence of a financial crisis – i.e. to avoid slumps. One option is to sterilise capital inflows while maintaining a fixed exchange rate so as to keep the prices of non-tradeables down. The problem is that such a sterilisation may also increase the interest rate to an extent which may again result in domestic firms' net cash revenues being squeezed down, thereby also leading to an investment slump. This, and other important aspects in the design of stabilisation policies for emerging market economies, awaits future elaborations of the framework developed here.

APPENDIX 1: SOLVING THE MODEL IN THE LEONTIEF CASE

In appendix 1 we analyse the model of section 2 in the special case where the production technology for the tradeable good is Leontief, given by:

$$y_T = \min\left\{\frac{K}{a}, z_N\right\} \tag{5A.1}$$

where K is the investment in tradeable input, z_N is the investment in non-tradeable input, $z_N \leq y_N$ (where y_N is the endowment flow of non-tradeable good), and $\alpha < 1$. We thus assume a maximum degree of complementarity between the two kinds of investments.[24]

Since total investment at the beginning of period t is equal to $\frac{W_B^t}{v}$, then the investment in tradeable input is simply equal to:

$$K^t = \frac{W_B^t}{v} - p^t \cdot z_N^t. \tag{5A.2}$$

In the Leontief case p^t and z_N^t are simply determined as follows:

(a) If $\frac{W_B^t}{v} < ay_N$, the demand for non-tradeable inputs under the Leontief technology is strictly less than the supply of non-tradeable input $y_N \left(z_N^t = \frac{K^t}{a} = \frac{1}{a} \cdot \frac{W_B^t}{v} \le y_N \right)$. The equilibrium price for the non-tradeable input, p^t is consequently equal to 0; it follows from (5A.2) that $K^t = \frac{W_B^t}{v}$ and $z_N^t = \frac{K^t}{a} = \frac{1}{a} \frac{W_B^t}{v}$.

(b) If $\frac{W_B^t}{v} \ge ay_N$ there is full employment of the non-tradeable input, namely $z_N^t = y_N$. Now, since $z_N^t = \frac{K^t}{a}$ and K^t always satisfies (5A.2), the equilibrium price of the non-tradeable input, p^t, is now positive and equal to:

$$p^t = \frac{W_B^t/v - ay_N}{y_N}. \tag{5A.3}$$

The dynamics of borrowers' wealth can now be simply re-expressed in each of cases (a) and (b). If we assume that all individuals in the economy receive a (small) endowment of tradeable good, z, at the beginning of each period,[25] then we have:

• In case (a), where $\frac{W_B^t}{v} < ay_N$:

$$W_B^{t+1} = (1-\alpha)\left[z + \frac{1}{a} \cdot \frac{W_B^t}{v} - r\frac{1-v}{v} W_B^t \right]. \tag{5.I}$$

We implicitly assume that $\frac{1}{a} \cdot \frac{1}{v} - r\frac{1-v}{v} > r$ (or, equivalently, that $\frac{1}{a} > r$), otherwise investors would always choose *not* to produce and instead to lend all their inherited wealth at the international interest rate r. The curve $W_B^{t+1}(W_B^t)$ defined by (5.I) is upward-sloping. This is hardly surprising: insofar as there is an excess supply of non-tradeable input the price p^t remains equal to zero which in turn implies that a small increase in investors' wealth, W_B^t, will have *no price effect* but only a positive wealth effect on their disposable wealth in the following period, W_B^{t+1}.

• In case (b), where $\frac{W_B^t}{v} \ge ay_N$, the wealth effect disappears owing to the fact that investment (and therefore output) is now constrained by the fixed

Figure 5A.1   *Permanent cycles*

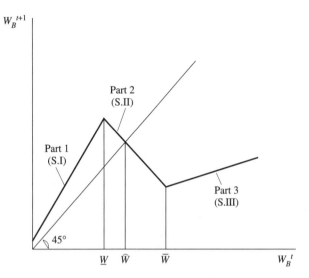

supply of non-tradeable input and therefore can no longer increase with investors' wealth W_B^t. The dynamics of borrowers' wealth is then determined by the downward-sloping curve:

$$W_B^{t+1} = (1 - \alpha)\left[z + y_N - r\frac{1 - v}{v}W_B^t\right]. \tag{5.II}$$

The downward-sloping linear relationship between W_B^t and W_B^{t+1} when $\frac{W_B^t}{v} \geq a y_N$ implies also that for W_B^t sufficiently large investors will choose not to borrow the full amount when the profit rate is lower than the international interest rate, r. This in turn implies that for W_B^t sufficiently large the dynamics of investors' wealth is simply determined by the upward-sloping relationship:

$$W_B^{t+1} = (1 - \alpha)[z + r \cdot W_B^t]. \tag{5.III}$$

Let $\underline{W}$, $\widehat{W}$ and $\overline{W}$ denote the intersections of the downward-sloping curve (5.II), respectively with curve (5.I), the 45° line and curve (5.III),[26] (see figure 5A.1). A necessary condition for permanent cycles is simply that:

(i) $\underline{W}$, $\widehat{W}$ and $\overline{W}$

(ii) $\left|\dfrac{dW_B^{t+1}}{dW_B^t}\right|_{(II)} = (1 - \alpha)(\tfrac{1}{v} - 1)r > 1.$

(The reader can indeed graphically verify that whenever (i) or (ii) is violated the economy converges to a steady-state level of investors' wealth, W_B^*, to which correspond stationary levels of investment and aggregate output.)

Condition (ii) is clearly violated when ν is close to 1, in other words when credit markets are too undeveloped: in that case, the price effect of an increase in investors' wealth remains too small (owing to the tight constraint imposed by the unavailability of credit on the demand for the non-tradeable input) to sustain permanent fluctuations in investors' wealth.

The second part of condition (i) is violated when ν is close to zero – i.e. when capital markets are (almost) perfect. (W ends up being less than $\widehat{W}$ when $\nu \rightarrow 0$.) This is also not so surprising: when $\nu \rightarrow 0$, the investors' wealth, W_B^t, must remain sufficiently small for the price of the non-tradeable input not to reach a level where investors are unconstrained. This means that except for small values of W_B the dynamics of investors' wealth is described by (5.III), which in turn rules out permanent fluctuations in W_B and aggregate output in the long run. That the economy should stabilise as $\nu \rightarrow 0$ appears to be robust to the choice of production technology: either the tradeable and non-tradeable inputs are substitutable in the production of tradeable good, in which case we have already argued in section 2 that the economy is quite unlikely to produce long-run sustained fluctuations, or the two kinds of inputs are complementary, in which case the limited supply of non-tradeable input limits the fraction of borrowings, $\frac{W_B}{\nu}$, that can be invested in production, which in turn implies that most savings will end up being lent on the international credit market when $\nu \rightarrow 0$, which also stabilises the economy.

APPENDIX 2: WHY FULL FINANCIAL LIBERALISATION – UNLIKE FOREIGN *DIRECT* INVESTMENT – MAY DESTABILISE AN EMERGING MARKET ECONOMY

In Appendix 2 we construct an example of an emerging market economy (i.e. an economy with an intermediate degree of capital market imperfection) which, in the absence of foreign borrowing and lending, would be stable and actually converge to a permanent boom, but which becomes permanently volatile once fully open to foreign borrowing and lending. We then argue that such an economy would have remained stable had it been open to foreign *direct* investment only.

More formally, consider an economy whose financial markets are initially closed to foreign capital inflows so that the aggregate supply of funds available to domestic investors, I^t, is now equal to the min of the investment capacity, $\frac{W_B^t}{\nu}$, and of total domestic savings, $W_B^t + W_L^t$ where W_L^t denotes the disposable wealth of *domestic* lenders at the beginning of date t. That is:

$$I^t = \min\left\{\frac{W_B^t}{\nu}, W_B^t + W_L^t\right\}.$$

Following the same steps as before but with $K^t = I^t - p^t y_N$, we again have two cases:

(a) $I^t < a y_N$: then $p^t = 0$ and the dynamics of investors' wealth is given by:

$$W_B^{t+1} = (1-\alpha)\left[z + \frac{1}{a}I^t - \tilde{r}(I^t - W_B^t)\right] \tag{5.I}$$

where $\tilde{r}$ is the domestic interest rate, equal to $\frac{1}{a}$ if $\frac{W_B}{\nu} > W_B + W_L$ (i.e. if investment capacity is greater than savings) and equal to the opportunity cost of lending (say, $\tilde{r} = \varrho$) if $\frac{W_B}{\nu} < W_B + W_L$.

(b) $I^t > a y_N$: then $p^t = \frac{I_t - a y_N}{y_N}$ and the dynamics of investors' wealth is expressed by:

$$W_B^{t+1} = (1-\alpha)[z + y_N - \tilde{r}(I^t - W_B^t)] \tag{5.II}$$

Since total funds to investors, I^t, now depend on domestic lenders' wealth, W_L^t, we need to specify the dynamic equation for W_L^t. If non-tradeable resources entirely belong to domestic lenders, and taking $z \approx 0$ for simplicity, we have:

$$W_L^{t+1} = (1-\alpha)[p^t y_N + \tilde{r} W_L^t].$$

Now, one can show the existence of parameter values for which this economy with closed financial markets converges to a permanent 'boom'[27] (with $\tilde{r} = \frac{1}{a}$ and $p^t = 0$) even though the two necessary conditions (i) and (ii) are satisfied for the economy to experience persistent cycles once financial markets are fully liberalised – i.e. open to foreign borrowing and lending.

More formally, during a 'boom' $\left(\text{i.e. when } \frac{W_B^t}{\nu} > W_B + W_L\right)$ $p^t = 0$, the dynamics of domestic investors' and domestic leaders' wealth endowments, respectively W_B^t and W_L^t is governed by:

$$W_B^{t+1} = (1-\alpha)\left[\frac{1}{a}(W_B^t + W_L^t) - \frac{1}{a}W_L^t\right]$$

$$W_L^{t+1} = (1-\alpha)\frac{1}{a}W_L^t. \tag{5B.1}$$

Notice that we need $(1 - \alpha)\frac{1}{a} \leq 1$ to have a stationary value for W_L. If q_t $= \frac{W_B^t}{W_L^t}$ denotes the ratio between domestic investors' and lenders' wealth endowments at date t, then during 'booms':

$$q^{t+1} = q^t = q^0$$

where $\left(\frac{1}{\nu} - 1\right)q^0 > 1.^{28}$

During a 'slump' ($\frac{W_B^t}{\nu} < W_B^t + W_L^t$), the dynamic equations for W_B^t and W_L^t become:

$$W_B^{t+1} = (1 - \alpha)\left[\frac{1}{a\nu} - \underline{\sigma}\left(\frac{1}{\nu} - 1\right)\right]W_B^t$$

$$W_L^{t+1} = (1 - \alpha)\underline{\sigma}W_L^t. \tag{5B.2}$$

Hence during slumps:

$$q^{t+1} = \left[\frac{1}{a\nu\underline{\sigma}} - \left(\frac{1}{\nu} - 1\right)\right]q^t.$$

A sufficient condition for the economy to converge to a permanent boom is $\frac{1}{a\underline{\sigma}} > 1$; and for this permanent 'boom' to be consistent with $p^t \equiv 0$ we need that

$$W_B^{t+1} + W_L^{t+1} = I^{t+1} < ay_N \text{ for all } t.$$

Consider an example where $1 - \alpha = a = \left(\left(\frac{1}{\nu} - 1\right)r + \varepsilon\right)^{-1}$, with $\varepsilon > 0$ and small, $\underline{\sigma} = 1$ and $r = \frac{1}{\nu}$. The reader can check that in this example for z sufficiently small the *closed* economy converges to a permanent 'boom' with $p^t \equiv 0$, whilst the same economy, once *fully* open to foreign lending and borrowing, satisfies the necessary conditions (i) and (ii) for *permanent fluctuations*.

Now, we want to show that the closed economy considered above *cannot* be destabilised by foreign *direct* investment alone. Here, the argument is very simple: with its supply being infinitely elastic at a fixed price between the world interest rate, r, and the rate of return on the domestic production technology, $\frac{1}{a}$, FDI will automatically come in when non-tradeable resources are partly idle – i.e. when upon opening the closed economy to FDI, domestic investment $I^t = W_B^t + W_L^t < ay_N$. In other words, FDI will be attracted by the price of the non-tradeable input being low (equal to zero) and it will cease as soon as non-tradeable resources become fully employed in domestic production activities – i.e. when aggregate production equals the supply of non-tradeable inputs, y_N. This implies that, starting from a closed economy (with no FDI) in a permanent boom $\left(\text{i.e. } \frac{W_B^t}{\nu} > W_B^t + W_L^t \right)$ and with $p^t = 0$, FDI cannot cause permanent fluctuations in aggregate output.

This vindicates our claim that whilst an emerging market economy may be destabilised as a result of a full financial liberalisation, it should not be destabilised as a result of being open to FDI alone.

NOTES
1   See for example, Radelet and Sachs (1998).
2   Krugman (1998), for example.
3   For evidence of what happened in East Asia, see Corsetti, Pesenti and Roubini (1998); Radelet and Sachs (1998).
4   For a description of the 1994 Mexican crisis which brings out this kind of picture, see Edwards (1997). For the Southern Cone crises see Corbo, de Melo and Tybout (1986). See also World Bank (1997); Milesi-Ferretti and Razin (1998) for more systematic descriptions of capital flows reversals and currency crises. In several cases, consumption growth is also observed in boom periods.
5   The fact that firm-level cash flows are a key determinant of aggregate investment is now widely recognised even for advanced economies such as the USA (see Bernanke, Gertler and Gilchrist, 1997). Macroeconomic models which emphasise the role of firm-level cash flow in determining investment, include Bernanke and Gertler (1989); Gertler and Rogoff (1990); Bacchetta and Caminal (1999); and Aghion, Banerjee and Piketty (1997). Gertler and Rogoff (1990) introduce credit constraints into an open-economy model. However, they consider neither business-cycle fluctuations nor relative prices movements. The emphasis on cash flows distinguishes this whole literature from models based on the effect of collateral on investment (for example, Kiyotaki and Moore, 1997).
6   The key condition for output volatility is that cash flow should be important for investment but not excessively so. We view this as a typical situation of economies which are at an intermediate level of financial development. Better financial sector institutions, like better credit-rating facilities, better bankruptcy laws and better disclosure laws, presumably make borrowing easier and therefore cash flow less important for investment.
7   Direct evidence on the basic mechanism we analyse is thin since data on profits and relative prices is scarce. However, several papers show that profits in the tradeable sector sharply deteriorated with the increase in the price of non-tradeables in the Southern Cone experience (see Galvez and Tybout, 1985; Petrei and Tybout, 1985; De Melo, Pascale and Tybout, 1985). Moreover, there is also

clear evidence of a strong correlation between capital inflows and real estate prices (for example see Guerra de Luna, 1997).

8 Allowing for consumption of the non-tradeable will not substantially affect the analysis as long as it is not a strong substitute for the tradeable good.

9 See Aghion, Bacchetta and Banerjee (1998) for an explicit microeconomic derivation of this credit multiplier based on a simple model of moral hazard in the credit market.

10 Such a saving behaviour can be 'rationalised' by bequest models with Cobb–Douglas 'warm-glow' preferences that have been used by the recent theoretical literature on income distribution and credit constraints. The intertemporal decisions of lenders are of no consequence for input in such an open economy since investors can borrow in international capital markets. It will, however, affect net capital flows.

11 In particular, while p^t remains proportional to W_B^t in the case where the technology f is Cobb–Douglas (so that in this case W_B^{t+1}/W_B^t remains constant and therefore no output cycles can occur over time), in the case where the production function f is CES (or *a fortiori* Leontief) the price p^t becomes a non-linear function of W_B^t. We show in Appendix 1 (p. 179) that whilst the wealth effect of an increase in W_B^t dominates for small values of W_B^t the price effect dominates for higher values of W_B^t.

12 More general functions are analysed in Aghion, Bacchetta and Banerjee (1998).

13 In a different context, Bacchetta and van Wincoop (1998) also show that a liberalisation leads to volatility when there are installation costs to capital and imperfect information about return properties of firms.

14 See Appendix 2 (p. 182) where we construct an explicit example of an economy which, in the absence of foreign investments and lending, converges to a permanent boom with $p \equiv 0$, but which experiences permanent fluctuations in p, W_B and aggregate output once fully open to foreign borrowing and lending.

15 When several developed countries did liberalise their capital movements in the 1970s and 1980s periods of high instability could not be observed. However, in some countries with initially protected financial systems, such as Spain in the late 1980s, dynamic evolutions similar to that depicted in figure 5.4 could be observed.

16 This may be the case in some of the poorer African and Asian countries.

17 Typically, measured FDI implies participations of more than 10 per cent in a firm's capital so this appears to be a reasonable assumption. Razin, Sadka and Yuen (1998) make a similar distinction about FDI.

18 This, in turn, implies that in our model FDI is a substitute to domestic investment. The effects of FDI on macroeconomic volatility when domestic and foreign investments are complementary is examined in Aghion, Bacchetta, and Banerjee (1998).

19 The optimal monetary policy response to financial crises cannot be directly analysed using the above model where money is neutral. However, if prices were rigid and money demand depended negatively on the interest rate, it would be possible to analyse the impact of unexpected monetary shocks. By extending our framework in such a direction, we can get the standard textbook result that

an expansionary monetary policy decreases the nominal interest rate and makes the currency depreciate. A decline in the nominal interest rate, i, clearly has a positive impact on profits as it has the direct effect of increasing firms' creditworthiness. We can assume that interest rates are flexible. This appears a realistic assumption in emerging markets, where debt tends to be short run. On the other hand, it may also induce a currency depreciation with opposite effects on investors' wealth, W_B. Assume, for example, that the monetary expansion takes place just before firms' debt is to be repaid. This obviously induces a loss for domestic borrowers who borrow in foreign currency as the value of the debt increases. To assess the overall real effect of an expansionary monetary policy, it is therefore important to take into account the proportion of foreign currency debt in firms' balance sheets. Unexpected devaluations can also have important effects, as emphasised by Mishkin (1996). We need, however, to introduce uncertainty in the model; this is left for future research.

20 Indeed, if our model is right, the slump sets in motion forces which, even with little interference, should eventually bring growth back to these economies. The risk is that by trying to overhaul the system in a panic, one may actually undermine those forces of recovery instead of stimulating them. This is not to deny that there is a lot that needs changing in these economies, especially on the institutional side with the establishment and enforcement of disciplinary rules in credit and banking activities. For example, as argued by Aghion, Armendariz and Rey (1998), unregulated banks often try to to pre-empt potential competitors in booming sectors by investing excessively and too early – that is, before they have acquired the necessary information and expertise – into those sectors. In the context of our model, banks may typically engage in pre-emptive lending to speculators in non-tradeable inputs and/or to tradeable good producers during booms. This in turn will further increase output volatility whenever inadequate monitoring and expertise acquisition by banks increases aggregate risk and therefore the interest rate imposed upon domestic producers.

21 See Diamond (1984).

22 The conservative view among policy makers, is precisely that governments should commit to a '*no bail-out*' policy towards insolvent banks as a way to overcome moral hazard problems in the banking sector, the argument being that it is the very prospect of future bail-outs that encourages investors and banks to indulge in excessive risk-taking. Aghion, Bolton and Fries (1998) argue instead that when banks have private information about the proportion of non-performing loans in their portfolios, then strict bank closure rules requiring the closure of *any* insolvent bank, may be counterproductive. For such rules may simply induce bank managers to hide the true size of their loan losses for as long as they can. Such behaviour will in turn result in: (a) huge misallocations of investments: bank managers will typically roll over a positive fraction of bad loans in order to conceal the extent of their loan losses (thereby *softening* the firms' budget constraints!) and (b) a magnified banking crisis with massive banks' failures down the road. On the other hand, an unconditional soft bail-out policy would also be undesirable, first because it might lead bank managers to *under-invest ex ante* into evaluating and monitoring the financial

health of their debtor firms and into structuring their loan portfolios efficiently; second, because it would encourage bank managers to *exaggerate their recapitalisation requirements ex post*. The optimal bail-out policy will thus lie somewhere between no-bail-out and unconditional bail-out. It turns out that a conditional bail-out scheme can be designed, which can achieve the same *ex ante* incentives as a tough bail-out policy whilst minimising the scope for inefficient liquidations or bad-loan refinancing *ex post*: the scheme is one that involves *conditional* bail-out, with the carving out of bad loans by the government being made at a suitable *non-linear* transfer price. In particular, Aghion, Bolton and Fries (1998) suggest that the recapitalisation of insolvent banks should be performed by buying out non-performing loans rather than through capital injections by buying subordinated bonds. The key insight in that paper is that a *non-linear* transfer pricing mechanism for bad loans can be used to avoid over-reporting of non-performing loans by healthier banks at the time of bail-out.

23 This strategy of allowing only FDI at early stages of financial development is in fact what most developed countries have done, in particular in Europe where restrictions on cross-country capital movements were fully removed only in the late 1980s whereas FDI to – and between – European countries had been allowed since the late 1950s.

24 The less extreme case of a CES production technology is much harder to solve analytically, although it can be simulated; our simulations indicate that the main conclusions in this appendix carry over to the CES case whenever there is not too much substitutability between the two kinds of inputs.

25 This endowment is introduced for technical reasons so that wealth does not converge to zero if there is not production. This is due to our simplfying assumption that there no other source of income beside capital income. Since we can have z infinitely small, in the main text we set it to zero.

26 More precisely, one can compute:

$$\underline{W} = vay_N;\ \widehat{W} = \frac{(1-\alpha)(z+y_N)}{1+(1-\alpha)(\frac{1}{v}-1)r};\ \text{and}\ \overline{W} = \frac{vy_N}{r}.$$

27 The terms 'boom' and 'slump' are borrowed from Aghion, Banerjee and Picketty (1997) who analyse the closed-economy version of the model. It should be noticed, however, that in a closed economy 'boom' growth is usually smaller that in open-economy boom.

28 Indeed, during a boom:

$$\frac{1}{v}W_B^\tau > W_B^\tau + W_L^\tau,$$

which in turn can be re-expressed as:

$$\frac{1}{v}q^t > q^t + 1,$$

or equivalently: $\left(\frac{1}{v}-1\right)q^t = \left(\frac{1}{v}-1\right)q^0 > 1.$

REFERENCES

Aghion, P., B. Armendariz and H. Rey (1998). 'Preemption and Excessive Risk-Taking by Banks in Booming Economies', UCL, mimeo

Aghion, P., P. Bacchetta and A. Banerjee (1998). 'Capital Markets and the Instability of Open Economies', UCL, mimeo

Aghion, P., A. Banerjee and T. Piketty (1997). 'Dualism and Macroeconomic Volatility', UCL, mimeo

Aghion, P., P. Bolton and S. Fries (1998). 'Optimal Design of Bank Bailouts: The Case of Transition Economies', UCL, mimeo

Bacchetta, P and R. Caminal (1999). 'Do Capital Market Imperfections Exacerbate Output Fluctuations?', European Economic Review

Bacchetta, P. and E. van Wincoop (1998). 'Capital Flows to Emerging Markets: Liberalisation, Overshooting, and Volatility', NBER Working Paper, **6530**

Bernanke, B. and M. Gertler (1989). 'Agency Costs, Net Worth, and Business Fluctuations', American Economic Review, 79: 14–31

Bernanke, B., M. Gertler and S. Gilchrist (1997). 'The Financial Accelerator in a Quantitative Business Cycle Framework', NBER Working Paper, **6455**

Corbo, V., J. de Melo and J. Tybout (1986). 'What Went Wrong With Recent Reforms in the Southern Cone', Economic Development and Cultural Change, **34**: 607–40

Corsetti, G., P. Pesenti and N. Roubini (1998). 'What Caused the Asian Currency and Financial Crisis? Part I: A Macroeconomic Overview', NBER Working Paper, **6833**

Diamond, D. (1984). 'Financial Intermediation and Delegated Monitoring', Review of Economic Studies, **62**: 393–414

Edwards, S. (1997). 'The Mexican Peso Crisis: How Much Did We Know? When Did We Know It?', NBER Working Paper, **6334**

Galvez, J. and J. Tybout (1985). 'Microeconomic Adjustments in Chile during 1977–81: The Importance of Being a Grupo', World Development, **13**: 969–94

Gertler, M. and K. Rogoff (1990). 'North-South Lending and Endogenous Capital-Markets Inefficiencies', Journal of Monetary Economics, **26**: 245–66

Guerra de Luna, A. (1997). 'Residential Real Estate Booms, Financial Deregulation and Capital Inflows: An International Perpective', Banco de México, mimeo

Krugman, P. (1998). 'Whatever Happened to Asia?', http//web.mit.edu/krugman/www/DISINTER.html

Kyotaki, N. and J. Moore (1997). 'Credit Cycles', Journal of Political Economy, **105**: 211–48

de Melo, J., R. Pascale and J. Tybout (1985). 'Microeconomic Adjustments in Uruguay during 1973–81: The Interplay of Real and Financial Shocks', World Development, **13**: 995–1015

Milesi-Ferretti, G. M. and A. Rasin (1998). 'Current Account Reversals and Currency Crises: Empirical Regularities', NBER Working Paper, **6620**

Mishkin, F.S. (1996). 'Understanding Financial Crises: A Developing Country Perspective', Annual World Bank Conference on Development Economics: 29–62

Petrei, A.H. and J. Tybout (1985). 'Microeconomic Adjustments in Argentina during 1976–81: The Importance of Changing Levels of Financial Subsidies', *World Development*, **13**: 949–68

Razin, A., E. Sadka and C.-W. Yuen (1998). 'A Pecking Order of Capital Inflows and International Tax Principles', *Journal of International Economics*, **44**: 45–68

Radelet, S. and J. Sachs (1998). 'The Onset of the East Asian Financial Crisis', *NBER Working Paper*, **6680** (August)

World Bank (1997). '*Private Capital Flows to Developing Countries*', *Policy Research Report*, Oxford: Oxford University Press.

Discussion
Gianluca Femminis

Chapter 5 by Aghion, Bacchetta and Banerjee (hereafter ABB) sheds new light on the largely debated issue of the effects of financial liberalisation on output volatility. ABB support the view that relation is positive, as some other contributions do. For example, McKinnon and Pill (1996) suggest that the removal of constraints on international capital movement is at least partially responsible for the Mexico 1994 and the Southern Cone crises. Chang and Velasco (1998a, 1998b) take a similar position concerning the Asian currency and financial turmoils.

McKinnon and Pill blame the excessive optimism of the banking sector. According to their view, it favours a large capital inflow that finances an (unsustainable) increase in consumption and resolves into devaluation. Chang and Velasco remark that financial liberalisations often involve large capital inflows with short maturities. Hence, when short-term obligations in foreign currency exceed reserves and available credit, banks become vulnerable: a creditors' wave of panic may render possible a self-fulfilling bank run and therefore a financial crash with real consequences.

The channel highlighted by ABB is remarkably different: the driving force in their model is simply wealth accumulation and the possibility of output fluctuations is ascribed to the presence of capital market imperfections. Entrepreneurs, to produce, need to purchase a tradeable input (capital) and a non-tradeable one (skilled labour, real estates or land). Total investment is constrained by the presence of capital market imperfections and hence borrowers, when the country is open to international capital movements, enjoy a 'rent' as long as the marginal productivity of capital is higher than the world interest rate. The process of wealth accumulation raises the demand for, and hence the price of, the non-tradeable input. When the wealth accumulation process is 'fast enough', the economic system may experience an increase in the price of the non-tradeable factor so sharp that wealth accumulation is choked off and cycles may emerge.

International financial integration may well involve destabilising effects. Consider a country where the 'credit multiplier', being relatively high, allows for a level of borrowing which is, before the integration, higher than domestic lenders' wealth, so that entrepreneurs are not constrained by credit availability. In such a country, the process of wealth accumulation may continue slowly and smoothly until a steady state is reached. However, when the country opens to international capital movements, it experiences a boost in investment which can ultimately lead to the type of cyclical behaviour sketched above.

The *ex ante* policy prescriptions of this model are partly in line with those suggested by McKinnon and Pill: in an emerging economy, a complete international financial integration may be undesirable since it may increase output volatility (at least when the domestic financial sector is not sufficiently developed).

The *ex post* recipe involved in the model is less clear. According to ABB, a recession following a period of fast growth may be a natural feature of an emerging economy characterised by a high degree of international financial integration. Hence, one might even conclude that no active policy is desirable.

Since the policy prescriptions are so strong, one wonders whether they are robust to changes in the specification of the model.

ABB analyse at length the case of a 'Leontief' production function. However, they state that, as it is intuitive, their results remain effective when the elasticity of substitution between tradeable and non-tradeable goods is constant, as long as the two inputs are not too substitutable. It would be interesting to understand what would happen if the supply of non-tradeable inputs were not assumed to be fixed. In fact, if we allowed for the accumulation of real estate (or for some flexibility in the supply of skilled labour), the 'price effect' induced by the growth of wealth should be weakened.

The specification for the consumption function involves some relevant consequences, too. In particular, it may be related to the fact that, in ABB's model, when capital markets are fully liberalised and highly efficient ($\nu = 0$), borrowers/entrepreneurs possess no wealth in the steady state.[1] The shrinkage (until complete collapse) of the borrowers/entrepreneurs' wealth under financial liberalisation with 'perfectly efficient' capital markets seems to be an unpleasant and rather counterfactual characteristic of ABB's model.[2]

The reasons for the contraction of investors' wealth are clear. As ν tends to zero, borrowers are virtually unconstrained; therefore, investment may

Figure D5.1   *Dynamic behaviour of* W_B *when* $(1-\alpha)r$ *is about 1*

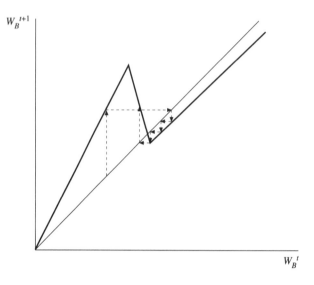

become so large, even when W_B^t is infinitesimal, that the price for non-tradeable goods reaches the level such that it is optimal for the investors not to borrow the full amount of resources they could.[3] Actually, entrepreneurs invest their wealth in production up to the point where manufacturing is as profitable as lending on the international capital markets, and loan the surplus. Hence, the whole of borrowers' wealth yields the interest factor r and, for *any* level of W_B^t, $W_B^{t+1} = (1 - \alpha)r W_B^t$, where α is the propensity to consume out of wealth. Clearly, if $(1 - \alpha)r < 1$, W_B tends to disappear. Actually, ABB drawing their (5.3), implicitly assume that $(1 - \alpha)r$ is much lower than unity (see figures 5.2–5.4).

It seems to me that this hypothesis is controversial. In fact, α is the propensity, identical for every agent, to consume out of the end-of-period wealth; hence the wealth accumulation equation implies that, for borrowers, $C^{t+1} = (1 - \alpha)r C^t$. If intertemporal preferences do not differ too much between this group of agents and the 'world average',[4] I am inclined to think that $(1 - \alpha)r$ should not be far from unity and might also be positive. In each case, investors' wealth decreases at a very low pace or does not shrink at all. However, if we accept that $(1 - \alpha)r$ is about one, we need to explore the consequences for ABB's instability results.

Consider figure D5.1, where the accumulation equation for borrowers' wealth has been drawn with a slope almost equal to unity: while cycles are still possible, under assumptions (i)–(ii) in ABB, their magnitude seem to be modest. Moreover, these fluctuations concern the distribution of income and wealth between borrowers and lenders. Although my criticism does not affect the desirability of FDI, which is one of ABB's major points,[5] when direct investments are insufficient the (limited) instability involved by financial liberalisation under imperfect capital markets may be a desirable price to pay for faster growth and for a more even income distribution.

While this criticism is 'internal' to the logic of ABB's model, I will now raise a more general point. The contribution by ABB overlooks the fact that many non-tradeable inputs, such as real estates or land, may be used as collateral. A relevant body of literature suggests that, even in advanced economies, the need of collateral to obtain credit is an important factor to explain the establishment of new firms and the growth of small business. If collateralisation is important, an increase in the price for the non-tradeable input may well have important *positive* consequences on aggregate investment. According to Ito and Iwaisako (1995), this is what happened in Japan after the mid 1980s: an initial expansion in investment raised the price of land and the boom in land prices, in its turn, increased collateral values, so that firms could borrow more and invest more.[6] While there is no clear evidence of the extent and of the relative importance of this phenomenon for the Asian Crisis, the 1998 BIS *Annual Report* clearly suggests that some variant of this mechanism was at work. According to that report, the use of equities and real estate as collateral not only provided a propellant to the asset-price bubble that probably affected those economies in the early 1990s, but also was an important stimulus for aggregate lending and investment.[7] Actually, BIS suggests that the use of collateral was so widespread that it contributed to dull the perception of risk of some financial institutions in the Far East.

A clue of the role played by real estate in the Asian crisis comes from the fact that commercial property prices peaked in most countries well before the beginning of the recession. In Korea the value of commercial estates reached its maximum in 1990:1, in Thailand during 1991:4, in Indonesia during 1992:3, and in Malaysia during 1995:2.[8] This behaviour is at least partly inconsistent with the one implied by the model proposed by ABB, where the slump in non-tradeable goods prices is the basis for the recovery,[9] and suggests that collateralised credit may be important to explain the asset-price level and/or the investment activity.

Obviously, the presence of credit contracts requiring collateral is not incompatible with the idea that a firm's creditworthiness depends on its current cash flow since they can both be grounded on the presence of moral hazard. In terms of ABB's model, investors could be allowed to own or acquire a fraction of the non-tradeable input, they might then use it as collateral, so that an increase in p would improve the borrowers' creditworthiness and hence negatively affect v.

I believe that the introduction of collateralised credit would represent a worthwhile extension of ABB's model, since it would display a richer dynamics and might fit a larger set of stylised facts.

NOTES

1 See ABB p. 181 and n. 26, considering z negligible.
2 Notice that the assumption concerning the production function does not drive this result: it may be easily replicated using a Cobb–Douglas technology.
3 For the Leontief technology studied in appendix 1 (ABB, p. 179), this is the case when $p = (1 - ar)/r$.
4 The propensity to consume out of income is low in some East Asian countries, so that α might even be under the world average.
5 But notice that, if $(1 - \alpha)r$ is close to unity, the condition for stable 'booms' introduced in appendix 2 (ABB, p. 182) – namely, $(1 - \alpha)1/a \leq 1$ – is likely not to be fulfilled.
6 Notice that these empirical findings provide some support for the story told by Kiyotaki and Moore (1997).
7 I thank Marco Lossani for a discussion on this point.
8 See Bank of International Settlements (1998), table VII.12.
9 However, in Hong Kong commercial property prices peaked in spring 1997. In the Philippines and in Singapore prices were at their top in 1996: Q1.

REFERENCES

Bank for International Settlements, (1998) 68th *Annual Report*, Basle: BIS.
Chang, R. and A. Velasco (1998a). 'Financial Fragility and the Exchange Rate Regime', C.V. Starr Center for Applied Economics, *Working Paper*, **98–05**
    (1998b), 'The Asian Liquidity Crisis', C.V. Starr Center for Applied Economics, *Working Paper*, **98–27**
Ito, T. and T. Iwaisako (1995). 'Explaining Asset Bubbles in Japan', *NBER Working Paper*, **5358**
Kiyotaki, N. and J. Moore (1997). 'Credit Cycles,' *Journal of Political Economy*, **105**: 211–48
McKinnon R. I. and H. Pill (1996). 'Credible Economic Liberalisations and International Capital Flows: The Overborrowing Syndrome', in T. Ito and A. Krueger (eds.), *Financial Deregulation and Integration in East Asia*, Chicago: Chicago University Press: 7–42

6 Volatility and the welfare costs of financial market integration

PIERRE-RICHARD AGÉNOR AND JOSHUA AIZENMAN

1 Introduction

The view that international financial market integration brings significant long-term benefits is hardly a controversial one among mainstream economists. Financial openness, for instance, increases opportunities for portfolio risk diversification and consumption smoothing through borrowing and lending; and producers who are able to diversify risks on world capital markets may invest in more risky (and higher-yield) projects, thereby raising the country's rate of economic growth (Obstfeld, 1994, 1998). Increased access to the domestic financial system by foreign banks is often viewed as raising the efficiency of the intermediation process between savers and borrowers, thereby lowering the cost of investment. Higher foreign direct investment flows (FDI) often have a direct, positive effect on productivity and the efficiency of domestic resource utilisation (through transfers of technology and other intangible assets), thereby raising the rate of economic growth.

But it is increasingly recognised that a high degree of financial openness may entail significant short-term costs as well. The magnitude of the capital flows recorded by some developing countries in recent years, and the abrupt reversals that such flows have displayed at times, have raised serious concerns among policy makers. The Mexican peso crisis of December 1994 led to financial instability throughout Latin America, particularly in Argentina. The collapse of the pegged exchange rate regime in Thailand on 2 July 1997 led to currency turmoil throughout Asia, particularly in Indonesia, Korea, Malaysia and the Philippines. Both events illustrated the growing tendency for a crisis in one country to have 'contagion' or 'spillover' effects on other countries where similar risk and vulnerability factors are perceived by financial markets as being present – notably real exchange rate appreciation and growing current account deficits, large stocks of short-term foreign currency-denominated liabilities, banking sector weaknesses, and rapid growth

Figure 6.1   *Secondary market yield spreads on US dollar-denominated euro bonds, September 1994–December 1997, percentage points*

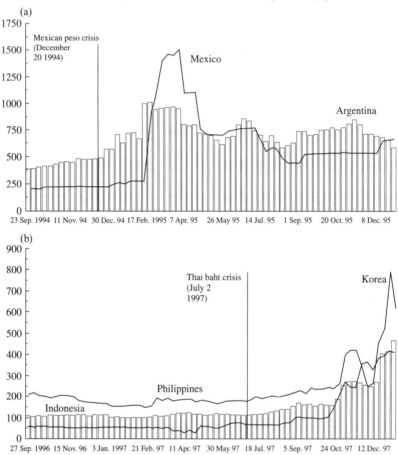

Source: Bloomberg.

in money and domestic credit.[1] As illustrated in figure 6.1, external interest rate spreads rose sharply after the collapse of the Mexican peso and the Thai baht.[2]

Several observers have noted that the magnitude and depth of the economic crisis that erupted in Argentina in the aftermath of the peso crisis, and in Asia after the collapse of the Thai baht, were compounded by domestic banking sector weaknesses. These weaknesses include inefficient intermediation, inadequate lending practices, large volumes of non-performing loans, excessive exposure to the property sector (as was the case in

Thailand), unhedged short-term liabilities in foreign currency, limited and inaccurate disclosure of financial statements by borrowers and ineffective supervision. In a previous paper (Agénor and Aizenman, 1998) we examined the implications of domestic capital market imperfections by considering an economy characterised by a direct link between bank credit and the supply side (through firms' working capital needs) and a two-level financial intermediation process: domestic banks were assumed to borrow at a premium on world capital markets, and domestic agents to borrow at a premium from domestic banks. We showed that both domestic and external financial intermediation spreads are related to default probabilities and underlying domestic shocks. We then defined 'contagion' as a mean-preserving increase in the volatility of aggregate shocks impinging on the domestic economy and argued that, to the extent that such an increase translates into a rise in the probability of default on existing loan commitments, domestic and foreign interest rate spreads will tend to rise, leading to a fall in output. Our analysis thus helped to identify a mechanism through which financial market imperfections may magnify an initial exogenous shock. It also helped to explain the effects of measures aimed at reducing inefficiencies in the intermediation process, such as a reduction in the cost of contract enforcement.

This chapter extends our previous work to examine the role played by volatility in assessing the costs and benefits of financial market integration. As in our earlier analysis, it combines the costly state-verification approach pioneered by Townsend (1979) and the model of limited enforceability of contracts used frequently in the external debt literature, as in Eaton, Gersovitz and Stiglitz (1986); Bulow and Rogoff (1989); Helpman (1989).[3] Section 2 presents the basic framework. Section 3 considers the case of autarky, in which domestic banks have access only to domestic savings as a source of loanable funds. Section 4 focuses on the case in which financial openness leads to free access to domestic capital markets by foreign banks and to lower costs of intermediation. Section 5 derives the welfare effects of capital market integration by comparing welfare under financial autarky and financial openness. Sections 6 and 7 extend the basic framework to consider the case of an upward-sloping domestic supply curve of funds. Section 8 summarises the main results of the analysis and offers some concluding remarks.

2 The basic framework

Our basic framework considers an economy in which risk-neutral banks provide intermediation services to domestic agents – producers which demand credit to finance their investment projects.[4] The project's future productivity is random. The realised productivity shock is revealed to banks only at a cost. If a producer chooses to default on its loan repayment obligations, the bank seizes any collateral set as part of the loan contract, *plus* a fraction κ, of the project's value. Seizing involves two types of costs. First, verifying the net worth of the project is costly; second, enforcing repayment requires costly recourse to the legal system.

We start with the simplest case, in which all projects are identical *ex ante*, and of the same scale. Investment H in project i yields (future) output of

$$y_i = M(1 + \epsilon_i), \ |\epsilon_i| \leq U < 1, \ i = 1, \ ...n \tag{6.1}$$

where ϵ_i is the realised productivity shock.[5] (6.1) can be viewed as a reduced form which relates a variable input, M, to output. For simplicity, we assume a Ricardian technology, and take the price of input M as constant and normalised to unity.

Again for simplicity, we assume that producers cannot issue claims on future output and cannot pledge collateral.[6] Let r_L^i be the contractual interest rate; producer i will default if repayment in the event of default, $\kappa M(1 + \epsilon_i)$, is less than contractual repayment, $(1 + r_L^i)H$:

$$\kappa M(1 + \epsilon_i) < (1 + r_L^i)H. \tag{6.2}$$

Let ϵ_i^* denote the highest value of the productivity shock leading to default, that is

$$\kappa M(1 + \epsilon_i^*) < (1 + r_L^i)H, \tag{6.3}$$

which implies that

$$\epsilon_i^* = (1 + r_L^i)H/\kappa M - 1. \tag{6.4}$$

This equation shows that, for ϵ_i^* to be negative, expected output, M, times κ, must exceed contractual repayment.

If default never occurs, ϵ_i^* is set at the lower end of the support ($\epsilon_i^* = -U$). In case of default, the bank's revenue on its loan to producer i, Π_i, is the producer's repayment *minus* the state-verification and contract enforcement cost, C_i,[7]

$$\Pi_i = \kappa M(1 + \epsilon_i) - C_i. \tag{6.5}$$

3 Financial autarky

Under financial autarky, domestic banks have access to only a given amount of domestic funds, S, at a real cost of r_A. More specifically, we assume that the domestic supply of funds is perfectly elastic up to a given ceiling. We are also assuming that the demand for credit is never constrained. These assumptions rule out the possibility of credit rationing due to supply shortage, a possibility modelled by Williamson (1986, 1987).[8] Banks are risk-neutral, and compete in a manner akin to monopolistic competition. This assumption about market structure is captured by postulating a mark-up pricing rule, whereby banks demand the expected yield on their loanable funds (net of enforcement costs) to be $\theta_A(1 + r_A)$, where $\theta_A \geq 1$.[9] The contractual interest rate is consequently determined by the break-even condition:

$$\theta_A(1 + r_A)H = \int_{\epsilon_i^*}^{U} [(1 + r_L^i)H]f(\epsilon)d\epsilon + \int_{-U}^{\epsilon_i^*} [\kappa M(1 + \epsilon_i) - C_i]f(\epsilon)d\epsilon \quad (6.6)$$

where $f(\epsilon)$ is the density function of ϵ. (6.6) can be rewritten as

$$\theta_A(1 + r_A)H = (1 + r_L^i)H - \int_{-U}^{\epsilon_i^*} [(1 + r_L^i)H - \kappa M(1 + \epsilon_i)]f(\epsilon)d\epsilon - C_i$$

$$\int_{-U}^{\epsilon_i^*} f(\epsilon)d\epsilon.$$

Substituting (6.3) for $(1 + r_L^i)H$ in the second term on the RHS of the above equation and rearranging yields the interest rate spread as

$$1 + r_L^i = \theta_A(1 + r_A) + \frac{\kappa M \int_{-U}^{\epsilon_i^*} (\epsilon_i^* - \epsilon)f(\epsilon)d\epsilon}{H} + \frac{C_i \int_{-U}^{\epsilon_i^*} f(\epsilon)d\epsilon}{H}. \quad (6.7)$$

(6.7) shows that the (gross) contractual interest rate is determined by a mark-up rule, which exceeds the bank's net return on its funds by the sum of two terms. The first term, $\kappa M \int_{-U}^{\epsilon_i^*} (\epsilon_i^* - \epsilon)f(\epsilon)d\epsilon/H$, is the expected revenue lost due to partial default in bad states of nature. The second term, $C_i \int_{-U}^{\epsilon_i^*} f(\epsilon)d\epsilon/H$, measures the expected state-verification and contract enforcement costs.

The producer's expected net income under autarky is equal to expected output, M, *minus* expected repayment in 'good' and 'bad' states of nature:

$$M - \int_{\epsilon_i^*}^{U} [(1 + r_L^i)H]f(\epsilon)d\epsilon - \kappa M \int_{-U}^{\epsilon_i^*} (1 + \epsilon_i)f(\epsilon)d\epsilon. \quad (6.8)$$

Applying (6.6), we can simplify (6.8) to

$$M - \theta_A(1 + r_A)H - C \int_{-U}^{\epsilon_i^*} f(\epsilon)d\epsilon. \quad (6.9)$$

Using (6.5), the domestic bank's expected net income is equal to expected repayment in 'good' and 'bad' states of nature, *minus* the cost of enforcement in bad states of nature and *minus* repayment of principal with interest at the rate r_A to lenders of funds:

$$(1 + r_L^i)H \int_{\epsilon_i^*}^{U} f(\epsilon)d\epsilon + \int_{-U}^{\epsilon_i^*} [\kappa M(1 + \epsilon_i) - C]f(\epsilon)d\epsilon -$$

$$(1 + r_A)H. \tag{6.10}$$

Using (6.6) and (6.10), the bank's expected net income can be written as

$$(1 + r_A)(\theta_A - 1)H. \tag{6.11}$$

4 Financial openness

Economists often claim that financial openness, by providing free access by foreign banks to domestic capital markets, leads to an increase in the degree of efficiency of the financial intermediation process (by lowering costs and 'excessive' profits) – thereby lowering the cost of investment and improving resource allocation. Levine (1996), for instance, has argued that foreign banks may

- improve the quality and availability of financial services in the domestic financial market by increasing bank competition, and enabling the application of more sophisticated banking techniques and technology

- serve to stimulate the development of the underlying bank supervisory and legal framework

- enhance a country's access to international capital

Surprisingly enough, there is relatively limited evidence supporting these claims. A study by Claessens, Demirgüç-Kunt and Huizinga (1998) provides the most systematic attempt to date to analyse empirically the cost and profitability effects of foreign banks, in both developed and developing countries. Some of the data used by Claessens, Demirgüç-Kunt and Huizinga is summarised in figures 6.2–6.5.[10] Figures 6.2, 6.3 and 6.4 suggest that in developed countries foreign banks have lower net interest margins – defined as net interest income divided by total assets – lower overhead costs and lower profitability than domestic banks. The evidence for Developing Countries, however, is somewhat mixed. Figure 6.5 suggests that increased penetration of foreign banks in the domestic banking system of DCs – as measured in terms of the importance of foreign banks in either numbers or assets – is associated with a reduction in both profitability and overhead

Figure 6.2   *Bank spreads: domestic vs. foreign banks, 1988–1995, per cent of total assets*

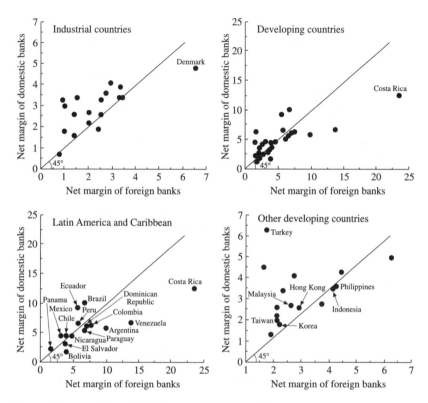

Source: Claessens, Demirgüç-Kunt and Huizinga (1998).

costs for domestic banks.[11] The econometric evidence provided by Claessens, Demirgüç-Kunt and Huizinga corroborate these last two findings in a more rigorous way.

To capture in a formal sense the evidence that foreign banks are more efficient than domestic banks (owing to either experience or scale effects) we assume that the loan enforcement and supervision costs faced by foreign banks, measured by C^*, may differ from the costs faced by domestic banks, C. Financial openness is also assumed to be associated with more intense competition, which leads to a drop in the mark-up from θ_A to $\theta_O < \theta_A$, and to a change in the supply cost of savings from r_A to r_O. Hence,[12]

$$\theta = \begin{cases} \theta_A \text{ in autarky} \\ \theta_O < \theta_A \text{ under openness} \end{cases}, r = \begin{cases} r_A \text{ in autarky} \\ r_O \text{ under openness} \end{cases}.$$

Figure 6.3   *Overhead costs: domestic vs. foreign banks, 1988–1995, per cent of total assets*

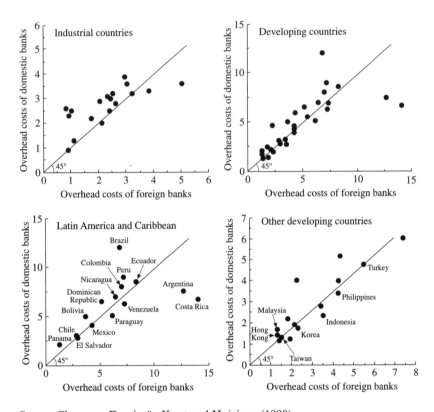

Source: Claessens, Demirgüç-Kunt and Huizinga (1998).

With financial openness, the break-even condition of foreign banks operating in the domestic economy is given by an equation analogous to (6.6):

$$\theta_O(1 + r_O)H = \int_{\epsilon_i^*}^{U} [(1 + r_L^i)H]f(\epsilon)d\epsilon + \int_{-U}^{\epsilon_i^*} [\kappa M(1 + \epsilon_i) - C^*]f(\epsilon)d\epsilon, \tag{6.12}$$

and the interest rate spread analogous to (6.7) is given by

$$1 + r_L^i = \theta_O(1 + r_O) + \frac{\kappa M \int_{-U}^{\epsilon_i^*} (\epsilon_i^* - \epsilon)f(\epsilon)d\epsilon}{H} + \frac{C^* \int_{-U}^{\epsilon_i^*} f(\epsilon)d\epsilon}{H}. \tag{6.13}$$

We assume that, in line with the literature on limit-pricing theory (see, for instance, Milgrom and Roberts, 1982), the threat of entry by foreign banks

Figure 6.4   *Net profits: domestic vs. foreign banks, 1988–1995, per cent of total assets*

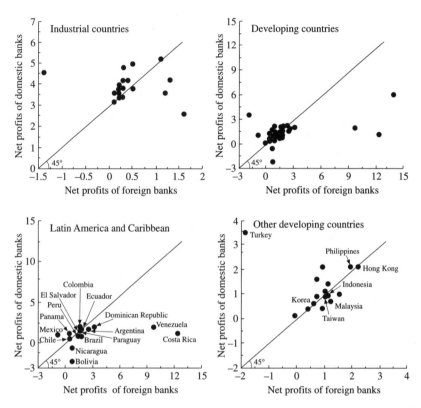

Source: Claessens, Demirgüç-Kunt and Huizinga (1998).

forces domestic banks to charge domestic borrowers the interest rate that foreign banks would potentially charge them. Hence, the contractual interest rate, r_L, is determined by (the threat of entry of) foreign banks. The domestic bank's expected net income is now

$$(1 + r_L^i)H \int_{\epsilon_i^*}^{U} f(\epsilon)d\epsilon + \int_{-U}^{\epsilon_i^*} [\kappa M(1 + \epsilon_i) - C]f(\epsilon)d\epsilon - (1 + r_O)H, \qquad (6.14)$$

with r_L determined by (6.13), instead of the break-even condition (6.6).

The producer's expected net income equals

$$M - \int_{\epsilon_i^*}^{U} [(1 + r_L^i)H]f(\epsilon)d\epsilon - \kappa M \int_{-U}^{\epsilon_i^*} (1 + \epsilon_i)f(\epsilon)d\epsilon. \qquad (6.15)$$

Figure 6.5   *Developing countries: foreign bank penetration vs. overhead costs and net profits, 1988–1995, per cent*

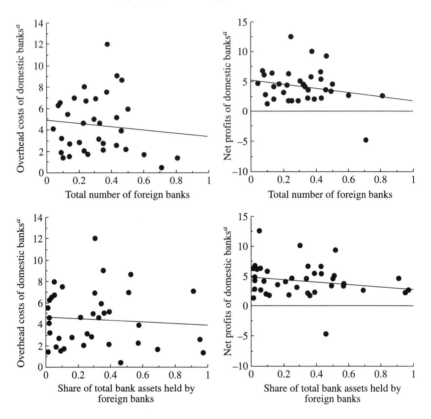

Note: [a] In per cent of total assets.
Source: Claessens, Demirgüç-Kunt and Huizinga (1998).

Applying (6.12), we can simplify (6.15) to

$$M - \theta_O(1 + r_O)H - C^* \int_{-U}^{\epsilon_i^*} f(\epsilon)d\epsilon. \qquad (6.16)$$

Suppose that the shock ϵ follows a uniform distribution, so that $-U \leq \epsilon \leq U$. The spread (6.13) is in this case characterised by a quadratic equation

$$1 + r_L^i = \theta_O(1 + r_O) + \frac{U\kappa M}{H}\Phi_i^2 + \frac{C^*}{H}\Phi_i \qquad (6.17)$$

where Φ_i, given by $\Phi_i = \int_{-U}^{\epsilon_i^*} f(\epsilon)d\epsilon = (U + \epsilon_i^*)/2U$, is the probability of default.

Figure 6.6   *Interest rate and expected repayment*

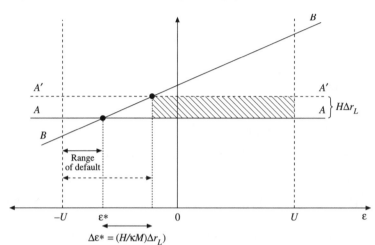

The second term of (6.17) is illustrative of how producers pay for the information asymmetry through the banks' mark-up rule. Combining equations (6.3), (6.15) and (6.17), the contractual interest rate can be solved for as a function of the banks' cost of funds. In general, this curve is non-linear, and in the case of a uniform distribution for ϵ it is quadratic:

$$\theta_O(1 + r_O) + \Psi g(r_L^i)^2 + \frac{C^*}{H} g(r_L^i) - (1 + r_L^i) = 0 \qquad (6.18)$$

where $\Psi = U \kappa M / H$ and

$$g(r_L^i) = \frac{1}{2} - \frac{1}{2U} + \frac{1 + r_L^i}{2\Psi}.$$

It can be inferred from (6.18) that

$$\frac{dr_L^i}{dr_O} = -\frac{\theta_O}{\Phi_i + (C^*/2H\Psi) - 1}. \qquad (6.19)$$

Further insight regarding (6.19) can be inferred from figure 6.6, which relates repayment to the value of the productivity shock, ϵ. Curve BB (respectively, AA) corresponds to the LHS (respectively, RHS) of (6.2). The intersection of these curves determines ϵ^*. The probability of repayment is determined by the length of the segment $U\epsilon^*$, normalised by $2U$. Curve $A'A'$ corresponds to a marginal increase in the contractual interest rate by Δr_L. A higher interest rate affects the bank's expected repayment in two opposite directions. On the one hand, expected repayment increases by the shaded area (which represents the increase in the value to be repaid in good states of nature, at a given level of the demand for loans) normalised by $2U$ – an area which is also equal to the probability of repayment, $1 - \Phi_i$, because Φ_i is the probability of default – times $H\Delta r_L$. On the other, expected repayment falls as a result of the increase in expected intermediation costs, which is equal to C^* times $[(d\epsilon^*/dr_L)/2U]\Delta r_L$.[13] The net increase in expected repayment is thus given by

$$\left\{(1 - \Phi_i)H - \frac{C^*}{2U}\frac{d\epsilon^*}{dr_L}\right\}\Delta r_L.$$

From (6.4), $d\epsilon^*/dr_L = H/\kappa M > 0$. Substituting this result in the above expression yields

$$\left\{(1 - \Phi_i) - \frac{C^*}{2U\kappa M}\right\}H\Delta r_L. \tag{6.20}$$

Hence, the condition for observing $\Delta r_L/\Delta r_O > 0$ is that, for $\Phi_i = 0$:

$$1 - \frac{C^*}{2U\kappa M} > 0,$$

or equivalently $C^*/2U < \kappa M$. Thus, if the foregoing condition is satisfied, we will observe an upward-sloping portion for the contractual interest rate/cost of loanable funds curve.

Suppose that this condition is met. If $\kappa M(1 - U) < H\theta_O(1 + r_O)$, then (given the definition of ϵ_i^* given above) $U + \epsilon_i^* > 0$ and the probability of default, Φ_i, will be positive. In these circumstances the interest rate/cost of credit curve is backward-bending, as shown in figure 6.7. In this figure, point M is reached when the term in brackets in (6.20) is zero.

With a low level of bank funding cost, if we also have $\kappa M(1 - U) > H\theta_O(1 + r_O)$, then Φ_i, the probability of default, will be zero – as is the case along portion KL in figure 6.7 where, as implied by the break-even condition (6.17) with $\Phi_i = 0$,

$$1 + r_L^i = \theta_O(1 + r_O).$$

At a high enough level of the banks' funding cost (and thus of the contractual lending rate), producers will default in the worst states of nature, as is the case if

$$r_O \geq \tilde{r}_O = \kappa M(1 - U)/\theta H - 1.$$

The point at which $r_O = \tilde{r}_O$ corresponds to point L in figure 6.7. Beyond $\tilde{r}_O$, a further increase in the banks' funding cost would increase the probability of default, leading to an increasing risk premium and a higher contractual

Figure 6.7   *Domestic interest rate – banks' cost-of-funds' curve*

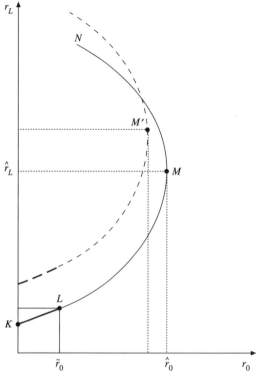

rate, moving along portion LM. (6.19) implies that, moving above point L, the slope of the curve increases as the probability of default rises. At a high enough cost of funding on world capital markets, the economy would reach point M (at which point $r_O = \hat{r}$), where further rises in the banks' funding cost would make the project unfeasible. This will happen because a higher contractual lending rate reduces the probability of repayment, and at point M further increases in this rate raises the probability of default at a rate that is high enough to reduce expected repayment. It can be verified that interest rates at point M are given by[14]

$$\hat{r}_L = \frac{\kappa M(1 + U) - C^*}{H} - 1, \; \hat{r}_O = \frac{(C^{*2}/4U\kappa M) + \kappa M - C^*}{\theta H} - 1. \qquad (6.21)$$

In general, given that changes in the cost of funds affects expected repayment in two opposite directions (as discussed earlier) there are two domestic contractual rates associated with each level of r_O. The high interest rate is also associated with a low probability of repayment. We will assume that competitive forces will prevent the inefficient equilibrium associated with operating on the backward-bending portion of the curve (segment MN). (6.21) implies that higher domestic volatility – an increase in U – would shift point M upward and to the left. This is confirmed by the dotted curve in figure 6.7, with point M shifting to point M'.[15]

5 Welfare effects of financial integration

We turn now to an evaluation of the dependency of domestic welfare on the foreign interest rate. Our welfare criterion is the sum of the expected net income of domestic producers and domestic banks, and the net surplus of domestic savers. We assume throughout this section that domestic saving is exogenously given at a level S, with $S \geq H$ with a reservation price of saving of $1 + r_A$. These assumptions imply that the supply of saving and the demand for credit have inverted L-shapes, elastic up to a ceiling. In the next section we focus on the more general case of upward-sloping supply and downward-sloping demand curves.

Consider first the case of financial autarky. Net expected income of domestic producers is given by (6.9) – that is, under the assumption of a uniform distribution, by

$$M - \theta_A(1 + r_A)H - C\Phi_A \tag{6.22}$$

where $\Phi_A = \int_{-U}^{\epsilon_i^*} d\epsilon/2U$ is the probability of default under autarky.

Using (6.10), expected net income of domestic banks under the assumption of a uniform distribution is given by

$$(1 - \Phi_A)(1 + r_L^i)H + \frac{1}{2U}\int_{-U}^{\epsilon_i^*}[\kappa M(1 + \epsilon_i) - C]d\epsilon - (1 + r_A)H$$

where $1 - \Phi_A = \int_{\epsilon_i^*}^{U} d\epsilon/2U$ is the probability of repayment under autarky.

As shown earlier (6.11), expected income of banks under autarky is given by $(1 + r_A)(\theta_A - 1)H$. Finally, the net surplus of domestic savers under autarky, given the assumption of a reservation gross rate of return of $1 + r_A$, is $(1 + r_A)H - (1 + r_A)H = 0$. Collecting terms, domestic welfare in autarky can be written as:

$$W_A = \begin{cases} M - \theta_A(1 + r_A)H - C\Phi_A \\ + (1 + r_A)(\theta_A - 1)H \\ + 0 \end{cases} = M - (1 + r_A)H - C\Phi_A. \tag{6.23}$$

Consider now the case of financial openness. As indicated earlier, we assume that, following financial integration, competitive forces bid up the interest rate facing domestic savers to the international level of r_O. Suppose first that following the liberalisation all projects are still financed domestically, at an interest rate that reflects the integrated equilibrium. Hence, the threat of foreign intermediation suffices to reduce the contractual interest rate that prevails in the financially closed economy to the level dictated by international market conditions.

Net expected income of domestic producers is now

$$M - \theta_O(1 + r_O)H - C^*\Phi_O$$

where Φ_O is the probability of default under openness. It is easy to verify that, as long as the assumption that $(1 + r_A)(1 + \theta_A) > (1 + r_O)(1 + \theta_O)$ holds initially, the incidence of default is lower under openness than under autarky ($\Phi_O < \Phi_A$).

To calculate the net expected income of domestic banks under openness proceed as follows. If all the effective financial intermediation is done by domestic banks, then the cost C is the effective cost of intermediation for welfare calculation (see (6.14)). As also noted above, under financial openness the cost of credit facing domestic borrowers is determined by the entry threat of foreign banks; as a result, domestic banks will charge the interest rate determined by (6.13). Using (6.13) and (6.14), we have

$$\{\theta_O(1 + r_O) - (1 + r_O)\}H - (C - C^*)\Phi_O.$$

Note that the threat of foreign competition induces banks to absorb the gap between their intermediation cost and that of foreign banks; this implies that their expected profits will be lower than that of foreign banks by the quantity $(C - C^*)\Phi_O$.

Finally, the net surplus of domestic savers is now

$$(1 + r_O)S - (1 + r_A)S = (r_O - r_A)S.$$

Collecting terms, domestic welfare under openness is thus

$$W_O = \begin{cases} \begin{aligned} &M - \theta_O(1 + r_O)H - C^*\Phi_O \\ &+ \{\theta_O(1 + r_O) - (1 + r_O)\}H - (C - C^*)\Phi_O \\ &+ (r_O - r_A)S \end{aligned} & \text{if } r_O < \hat{r}_O, \\[2ex] \begin{aligned} &0 \\ &+ 0 \\ &+ (r_O - r_A)S \end{aligned} & \text{if } r_O > \hat{r}_O \end{cases} \qquad (6.24)$$

or, after rearranging terms,

$$W_O = \begin{cases} M - (1 + r_O)H - C\Phi_O + (r_O - r_A)S & \text{if } r_O < \hat{r}_O, \\[2ex] (r_O - r_A)S & \text{if } r_O > \hat{r}_O. \end{cases} \qquad (6.25)$$

Figure 6.8   *Domestic welfare under openness*

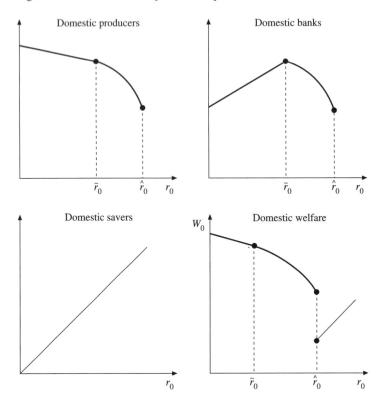

The first three panels in figure 6.8 depict the relationship between net expected income for each category of agents and the foreign interest rate, r_O.[16] The figures show that higher bank funding costs reduce the net expected income of domestic producers, as this implies both higher cost of credit and more frequent incidence of costly default. Banks' welfare has an inverted U-shape with a linear segment – higher interest rates raise net expected income for a given incidence of default, and increases the frequency of default. Savers are unambiguously better off.

The change in domestic welfare under openness resulting from an increase in the world interest rate is given, from (6.25), by:

$$\frac{\partial W_O}{\partial r_O} = \begin{cases} (S - H) - C(\partial \Phi_O / \partial r_O) & \text{if } r_O < \hat{r}_O, \\ S & \text{if } r_O > \hat{r}_O \end{cases}$$

where it can be verified that $\partial \Phi_O / \partial r_O > 0$. The lower panel on the right in figure 6.8 illustrates the relation between net welfare and the banks' funding cost, under the assumption that $(S - H) - C(\partial \Phi_O/\partial r_O) < 0$. The figure shows that welfare is concave in r_O for $r_O < \hat{r}_O$ and experiences a discrete downward jump for $r_O = \hat{r}_O$.

We infer the welfare effects of financial integration by comparing the welfare levels under financial autarky to those achieved under openness, as defined above. Applying (6.24) and (6.23) we infer that the welfare gain from financial integration, $\Delta W = W_O - W_A$, is

$$\Delta W = \begin{cases} C(\Phi_A - \Phi_O) + (r_O - r_A)(S - H) & \text{if } r_O < \hat{r}_O, \\ -(M - (1 + r_A)H - C\Phi_A) + (r_O - r_A)S & \text{if } r_O > \hat{r}_O. \end{cases} \tag{6.26}$$

The above expression shows that if the interest rate facing the country is sufficiently low, financial integration will be accompanied with a welfare gain due to the fall in (expected) intermediation costs associated with a lower probability of default, as well as the increase in the net surplus of domestic savers attributed to the higher interest rate on saving net of investment. However, if the interest rate facing the country is relatively high, projects will become unfeasible, leading to a loss of the entire expected net income of domestic producers in that state of nature. The limited ability of lenders to enforce the provisions of loan contracts prevents the financing of domestic projects, despite the fact that they may lead to a large expected net income.

To illustrate the impact of volatility on welfare, suppose that the only source of macroeconomic uncertainty is fluctuations in the world interest rate, r_O^*, whose degree of volatility may be affected by global conditions, as well as contagion effects induced by events occurring in, say, neighbouring countries. Specifically, suppose that the foreign interest rate fluctuates between $r_O^* + \delta$ and $r_O^* - \delta$, each state with probability one half, that is,

$$r_O = \begin{cases} r_O^* + \delta & \text{with prob. } 0.5 \\ r_O^* + \delta & \text{with prob. } 0.5. \end{cases}$$

This specification implies a monotonic relationship between changes in δ and increased volatility. Let $\Phi_O|_{r_O = r_O^* + \delta}$ (respectively $\Phi_O|_{r_O = r_O^* - \delta}$) denote the value of the probability of default when $r_O = r_O^* + \delta$ (respectively $r_O = r_O^* - \delta$). The expected value of Φ_O, $E\Phi_O$, is given by

$$E\Phi_O = 0.5(\Phi_O|_{r_O = r_O^* + \delta} + \Phi_O|_{r_O = r_O^* - \delta}).$$

Using (6.25), we have

$$W_O = \begin{cases} M - (1 + r_O^*)H - CE\Phi_O + (r_O^* - r_A)S & \text{if } \delta < \hat{r}_O - r_O^* \\ 0.5[M - (1 + r_O^* - \delta)H - C\Phi_O|_{r_O = r_O^* - \delta}] + (r_O^* - r_A)S \\ & \text{if } \delta > \hat{r}_O - r_O^*. \end{cases}$$

Figure 6.9   *Domestic welfare and volatility of banks' funding cost under openness*

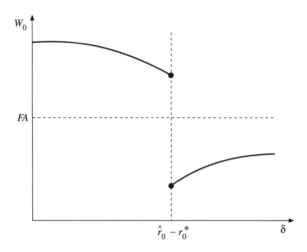

This equation implies that, at $\delta = \hat{r}_O - r_O^*$, welfare drops by

$$0.5[M - (1 + r_O^* - \delta)H - C\Phi_O|_{r_O = r_O' + \delta}].$$

Domestic welfare is plotted in figure 6.9. As shown in the figure, as long as $\delta < \hat{r}_O - r_O^*$, higher volatility reduces welfare by a second-order magnitude owing to the convexity of the welfare function. If $\delta > \hat{r}_O - r_O^*$, by contrast, volatility induces a potentially large welfare loss, as it leads to a fall in domestic investment in bad states of nature, when the foreign interest rate is high. This is because, as indicated earlier, projects become unfeasible in bad states of nature, leading to a loss of the entire expected net income of domestic producers. Figure 6.9 shows that if welfare under financial autarky is at level *FA*, financial openness is welfare-improving only if the volatility of the foreign interest rate is sufficiently low.

The foregoing discussion can thus be summarised by the following proposition:

Proposition 1 *Financial integration may be welfare-reducing if the foreign interest rate facing the economy under openness is more volatile than the interest rate that prevails under financial autarky.*

It is worth emphasising that the above results do not depend on C^* being either greater or lower than C, the enforcement and verification costs faced by domestic banks. For instance, the welfare gain from financial integration, as given by (6.26), does not depend on C^*. This is important because, in the present model – in which, despite the threat of entry by foreign banks, financial intermediation is actually conducted by domestic banks – whether C^* is greater or lower than C cannot be established *a priori*. It may be argued, in particular, that although foreign banks may face lower *monitoring* costs than domestic banks (as a result of, say, better screening technologies for loan applications), domestic banks may face lower *enforcement* costs as a result of a privileged relationship with domestic law-enforcement agencies.

6 Endogenous supply of funds

Our framework can be extended to allow for an upward-sloping domestic supply curve of saving, and by assuming *ex ante* heterogeneity of projects – which translates into heterogeneity of loan contracts as well. Specifically, suppose that the domestic saving function is given by

$$S = S(r), \ S' \geq 0. \tag{6.27}$$

The production function is now given by a modified version of (6.1). Specifically, we now assume that although projects continue to be of the same scale – requiring a lump-sum investment of H to be implemented – they are *ex ante* heterogeneous, and are ranked according to their productivity:

$$Y_i = M(i)(1 + \epsilon_i); \ M(i) \geq M(i+1) \tag{6.28}$$

where n is the total number of projects, which is determined endogenously below. We assume that, *ex ante*, banks do not observe the productivity of producer i, hence, banks cannot discriminate among producers and are offering the same interest rate. Consequently, the probability of default from the point of view of the various producers varies, being higher for higher i. To simplify notations, we will denote by $\Phi(i)$ the probability of default of producer i, and by Φ the average probability of default. This average probability of default is the one that determines the expected repayment from the point of view of domestic banks.

The closed-economy equilibrium is characterised by two conditions. First, the expected rent of the marginal producer (denoted by n_A) is dissipated. Second, the domestic supply of saving finances the investment. These two conditions are

$$M(n_A) = \theta_A(1 + r_A)H + C\Phi_A(n_A), \ S(r_A) = n_A H \tag{6.29}$$

or, alternatively,

$$\frac{M(n_A) - C\Phi_A(n_A)}{\theta_A H} = 1 + r_A, \ S(r_A) = n_A H \tag{6.30}$$

Figure 6.10   *Endogenous savings: welfare under autarky*

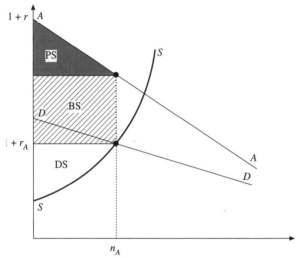

where $S(r_A)$ is the supply curve of domestic savings, denoted SS in what follows.

For simplicity of exposition, we normalise H to unity and ignore integer constraints implied by the ranking procedure used in (6.28). Figure 6.10 provides a diagrammatic analysis of welfare under financial autarky. Curve DD plots the combinations of $(n, 1 + r_A)$ that satisfy the LHS of the first equation in (6.30), the marginal producer's expected output net of enforcement costs, divided $(H = 1)$ by the mark-up – that is, $[M(n_A) - C\Phi_A(n_A)]/\theta_A$. It defines the demand for saving (or loanable funds) by domestic banks. Curve AA magnifies DD by the mark-up – that is, it is the marginal producer's expected output net of enforcement costs, $M(n_A) - C\Phi_A(n_A)$. The area BS corresponds to expected banks' rents, PS to the producers' surplus and DS to savers' surplus.

The scale of production, n_A, is determined by the intersection of the demand for saving, DD, with the supply curve, SS. Note that the expected producers' surplus is given by

$$\int_0^{n_A} M(i)di - n_A[C\Phi_A + \theta_A(1 + r_A)]. \tag{6.31}$$

Hence, the expected surplus of producer i is $M(i) - C\Phi_A(i) - \theta_A(1 + r_A)$.

Under financial openness, the equilibrium condition (6.29) becomes (again, with $H = 1$):

$$M(n_O) = \theta_O(1 + r_O) + C^*\Phi_O(n_O). \tag{6.32}$$

Figure 6.11   *Endogenous savings: welfare under openness*

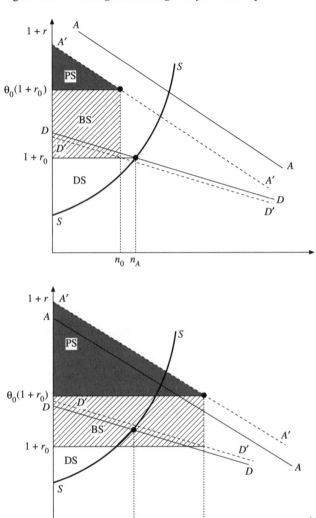

Figure 6.11, drawn for the case in which all domestic intermediation is actually done by domestic banks (as assumed earlier), evaluates domestic welfare in the open economy. The upper panel corresponds to the case in which the cost of credit is relatively high, whereas the lower panel depicts the case in which the cost of credit is relatively low. Opening the economy to financial flows has the effect of shifting both AA and DD to new positions,

which correspond to the dashed curves $A'A'$ and $D'D'$. The position of these curves relative to that in autarky is affected by the change in the probability of default. If the cost of foreign capital is relatively low, it will reduce the incidence of default, and will shift both curves upward. This is depicted in the lower panel. The availability of intermediation services at a lower monitoring cost shifts curve AA upward, to $A'A'$. The fall in the mark-up rate and the reduction in monitoring costs shifts curve DD also upward, to $D'D'$. Assuming that banks have access to capital at a cost of $1 + r_O$, the domestic interest rate facing savers drops from $r = r_A$ to $r = r_O$. In this particular case, the surplus of domestic savers drops, as the interest rate falls. The net outcome for domestic banks is ambiguous – the volume of intermediation has increased but the mark-up has declined; and banks are absorbing the domestic–foreign monitoring and enforcement cost gap. The net expected income of domestic producers unambiguously increases, as a result of the fall in the cost of financing and the rise in output.[17] Overall, domestic welfare will increase.

Formally, from (6.31) we infer that the net expected income of producers under financial openness is

$$\int_0^{n_O} M(i)di - n_O[C^*\Phi_O + \theta_O(1 + r_O)].$$

Assuming again that all intermediation is actually done by domestic banks, their net expected income is

$$n_O[C^*\Phi_O + \theta_O(1 + r_O)] - n_O[C\Phi_O + (1 + r_O)].$$

Adding the net expected income of producers and banks yields

$$\int_0^{n_O} M(i)di - n_O[C\Phi_O + (1 + r_O)].$$

Hence, the marginal social benefit of project n, obtained by deriving the above expression with respect to n, is

$$-nC\frac{\partial\Phi}{\partial n} + M(n) - [C\Phi_O + (1 + r_O)]. \tag{6.33}$$

The socially optimal number of projects, n_O, is thus determined by

$$M(n_O) - C\Phi_O - n_O C\frac{\partial\Phi}{\partial n} = 1 + r_O, \tag{6.34}$$

from which it can be shown that $n_O > n_A$ in the lower panel of figure 6.11.

By contrast, if financial integration increases the cost of funds to a high level, it would ultimately increase the probability of partial default, shifting both curves inward; this is the case depicted in the upper panel of figure 6.11. In this case, domestic welfare will unambiguously fall.

7 Congestion externalities

The foregoing discussion can be further extended to consider jointly the case of endogenous domestic savings and congestion externalities. In the presence of such externalities, output is now determined, instead of (6.28), by:

$$Y_i = M(i)^{n-\alpha}(1 + \epsilon_i); \quad M(i) \geq M(i+1) \tag{6.35}$$

where $\alpha > 0$ measures the intensity of congestion. The conditions that characterise the closed-economy equilibrium are now given by, with $H = 1$:

$$\frac{n_A^{-\alpha}M(n_A) - C\Phi_A(n_A)}{\theta_A} = 1 + r_A, \quad S(r_A) = n_A \tag{6.36}$$

where $S(r_A)$ is again the supply curve of domestic savings under autarky.

The upper panel in figure 6.12 provides a diagrammatic analysis of welfare in the closed economy. Curve DD plots, as before, the demand for saving by domestic banks, that is, the quantity $[n_A^{-\alpha}M(n_A) - C\Phi_A(n_A)]/\theta_A$. Curve AA magnifies DD by the mark-up, and is given by $n_A^{-\alpha}M(n_A) - C\Phi_A$. The scale of production, n_A, is again determined by the intersection of DD and SS.

The expected producers' surplus is now given by

$$n_A^{-\alpha} \int_0^{n_A} M(i)di - n_A[C\Phi_A + \theta_A(1 + r_A)]. \tag{6.37}$$

Hence, the expected surplus of producer i is $n_A^{-\alpha}M(i) - C\Phi_A(i) - \theta_A(1 + r_A)$, for $i = 1,...n_A$. Curve OO depicts producer i's expected output net of enforcement costs, plotted for the closed-economy equilibrium, where $n = n_A$ (it corresponds to $n_A^{-\alpha}M(n_A) - C\Phi_A(n_A) - \theta_A(1 + r_A)$). As before, area DS is the savers' (or depositors') surplus, BS is the banks' surplus, and PS is the expected producers' surplus.

Under financial openness, the equilibrium condition (6.29) becomes (again, with $H = 1$):

$$n_O^{-\alpha}M(n_O) = \theta_O(1 + r_O) + C^*\Phi_O(n_O). \tag{6.38}$$

The lower panel in figure 6.12 evaluates domestic welfare in the open economy, drawn for the case in which all domestic intermediation is done by domestic banks. The availability of intermediation services at a lower

Figure 6.12   *Congestion externalities: welfare under autarky and openness*

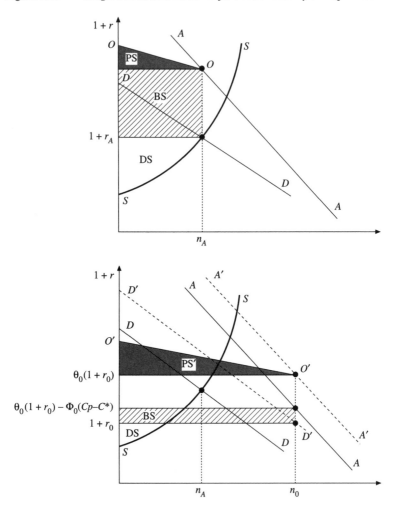

monitoring cost again shifts curve AA upward, to $A'A'$. The fall in the mark-up rate and the reduction in monitoring costs shifts curve DD also upward, to $D'D'$. With banks' cost of capital equal to $1 + r_0$, the domestic interest rate facing savers drops from $r = r_A$ to $r = r_0$. The surplus of domestic savers drops, as the interest rate goes down.

The position of domestic banks is ambiguous – the volume of intermediation has increased, but the mark-up has declined, and banks are absorbing the domestic–foreign monitoring and enforcement cost gap. The

Figure 6.13   *The effect of congestion externalities*

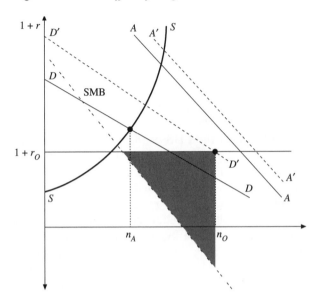

surplus of domestic producers is now affected in two opposite directions: on the one hand, greater congestion reduces the surplus; on the other, the fall in the cost of financing and the rise in output increase the surplus. In the absence of congestion effects, as shown earlier, the expected surplus would unambiguously increase; but in the presence of such effects, the overall impact is ambiguous.

Figure 6.13 focuses on the production inefficiency contributed by congestion externalities. From (6.37) we infer that the expected producers' surplus under financial openness is

$$n_O^{-\alpha} \int_0^{n_O} M(i)di - n_O[C^*\Phi_O + \theta_O(1 + r_O)].$$

Assuming that all intermediation is done by domestic banks, their expected surplus is

$$n_O[C^*\Phi_O + \theta_O(1 + r_O)] - n_O[C\Phi_O + (1 + r_O)].$$

Adding the producers' and banks' surpluses, we infer that the combined surplus is

$$n_O^{-\alpha} \int_0^{n_O} M(i)di - n_O[C\Phi_O + (1 + r_O)].$$

Hence, the marginal social benefit of project, n, obtained by deriving the above expression with respect to n, is

$$-\left[\alpha n^{-(1+\alpha)} \int_0^n M(i)di + nC\frac{\partial\Phi}{\partial n}\right] + n^{-\alpha} M(n) - [C\Phi_O + (1+r_O)]. \quad (6.39)$$

Thus, the socially optimal level of n is determined by

$$n_O^{-\alpha}M(n_O) - C\Phi_O - \alpha n_O^{-(1+\alpha)} \int_0^n M(i)di - n_O C\frac{\partial\Phi}{\partial n} = 1 + r_O. \quad (6.40)$$

Curve SMB in figure 6.13 traces the LHS of (6.34). In the financially open economy the optimal level of investment (that is, the optimal number of projects) is where the SMB curve equals the cost of funds, $1 + r_O$. Borrowing under financial openness is determined by the intersection of curve $D'D'$ with the banks' funding cost, $1 + r_O$, determining n_O. Hence, unregulated foreign borrowing results in a welfare cost given by the shaded triangle. Recall that under financial autarky, $n = n_A$ (determined by the intersection of SS and DD). This implies that opening domestic capital markets may lead to a fall in welfare relative to financial autarky if congestion effects are relatively large (that is, if α is large). The implied welfare loss tends to be larger when the supply curve of domestic savings is relatively inelastic, and when the country faces a relatively elastic supply of credit with integrated capital markets.

Figure 6.13 illustrates a more general principle of second-best theory, which can be summarised in the following proposition:

Proposition 2 *Increased financial integration may magnify the welfare cost of existing distortions.*

In autarky, the welfare cost of the distortion was, in a sense, 'contained' by the limited pool of domestic saving. In our example, the distortion is caused by congestion externalities, which are magnified by increased financial openness. A similar assessment would apply to other distortions, such as the implicit insurance (or bail-out guarantee) that regulatory authorities may provide to domestic banks.

8 Conclusions

The events that followed the Mexican peso crisis in December 1994 and those of the past year in Asia have prompted many economists to reconsider the costs, benefits, and sustainability of capital account liberalisation and financial integration with world capital markets. The contribution of this chapter – which draws on the analysis provided by Agénor and Aizenman (1998) – to this ongoing process has been to focus on the links between capital flows, the financial system and the supply side of the economy, using a model in which state-verification is costly and the enforcement of the provisions of loan contracts is limited. Section 2 presented the basic framework, which assumes that productivity shocks are random. We then considered in section 3 the case of financial autarky, in which domestic banks have access only to domestic savings as a source of loanable funds. Section 4 focused on the case of financial openness, defined as a situation in which foreign banks (with lower costs of intermediation and a lower mark-up) have unrestricted access to domestic capital markets. We then measured the net cost of capital market integration in section 5 by comparing welfare losses under financial autarky and financial openness. We showed that if the interest rate facing the country is not high, financial integration may lead to a welfare gain, as a result of the fall in expected intermediation costs as well as the increase in the net surplus of domestic savers attributed to the higher interest rate on saving. However, if the interest rate facing the country is high, it will render projects unfeasible, leading to a loss of the entire expected net income of domestic producers surplus in that state of nature. The limited enforcement of contracts prevents the financing of these projects, despite the fact that they may lead to a large expected net income. Financial integration may thus lower welfare if the foreign interest rate facing the economy under openness is more volatile relative to the degree of volatility of interest rates under financial autarky.

Sections 6 and 7 extended the basic framework to consider the case of an upward-sloping domestic supply curve of funds, and examined the case in which projects are *ex ante* heterogeneous, and congestion externalities prevail. Our analysis showed that opening the economy to unrestricted inflows of capital may magnify the welfare cost of existing distortions. In autarky, the welfare cost of the distortion (congestion externalities, in our example), is, in a sense, 'contained' by the limited pool of domestic saving. However, in a financially open economy, such distortions are magnified by the inflow of capital. A similar assessment applies to other distortions, such as the implicit insurance provided by domestic authorities, as shown by Aizenman (1998) in a related framework in which moral hazard is modelled explicitly.

The analysis developed here can be further extended in various directions. First, in both Asia and Latin America, financial volatility has prompted policy makers to take various measures to strengthen prudential supervision, such as imposing limits on the open foreign exchange position of commercial banks and preventing banks from making foreign currency-denominated loans.[18] Understanding the extent to which such measures may help reduce volatility and the cost of financial openness remains, however, to be explored. Second, extending the analysis to a multi-period model would allow us to consider the case where external shocks (such as, for instance, an increase in the cost of external funds, or a higher perceived volatility of shocks) would induce debt rescheduling. The presence of a backward-bending cost of the funds-borrowers' interest rate curve may imply multiple equilibria, where a given outstanding stock of debt is rescheduled at a relatively low or high interest rate. In these circumstances, coordination failures may lead the economy to the inefficient equilibrium, associated with the relatively high interest rate.

NOTES

We would like to thank, without implication, Stijn Claessens (who provided some of the data used in this study), David Vines, and participants at the CEPR–World Bank Conference on 'Financial Crises: Contagion and Market Volatility', (London) (8–9 May 1998) and seminars at the Universities of Miami and São Paolo, for helpful discussions and comments. The views expressed here do not necessarily represent those of the International Monetary Fund or the World Bank.

1. Although economic fundamentals in some of the Asian countries that suffered from contagion appeared stronger than in Thailand (notably in Korea, Malaysia, and the Philippines), banking sector weaknesses were a key characteristic of all of them.
2. Evidence that movements in external spreads depend mainly on shifts in market sentiment rather than shifts in fundamentals is provided by Eichengreen and Mody (1998), in an analysis of data on a large number of developing country (DC) bonds (public and private) launched during January 1991–December 1996.
3. Limitations in the ability of banks to enforce the provisions of loan contracts (including seizure of collateral) has been viewed by some observers as one of the key weaknesses of the legal infrastructure that characterises many of the Asian countries that suffered from contagion in the aftermath of the Thai baht crisis.
4. More specifically, only producers who lack access to the equity market rely on bank credit to finance their projects.
5. Note that there is no aggregate risk in our model. All firms are identical and the productivitiy shock, ϵ_i is uncorrelated among them.
6. We also ignore the possibility of randomised monitoring. The key results of our analysis would continue to hold in this case as long as implementation and enforcement of loan contracts involves real costs, as implied by the

results of Bernanke and Gertler (1989) and Boyd and Smith (1994). In the Bernanke–Gertler framework, for instance, loan contracts under random monitoring also involve a schedule specifying the probability of monitoring as a function of the output announced by the borrower. They show that the monitoring probability is positive for a low value of declared output, depending negatively on the announced output. Random monitoring thus does not negate the need to engage in costly verification of the realised state of nature.

7. C is a lump-sum cost paid by banks in order to identify the productivity shock, ϵ_i, and to enforce proper repayment. The analysis would be more involved if some costs were paid *after* obtaining the information about ϵ_i. In these circumstances, banks would refrain from forcing debt repayment when the realised productivity is below an 'enforcement threshold'. For simplicity of exposition, we refrain from modelling this possibility. We also ignore all other real costs associated with financial intermediation. Adding these considerations would not modify the key insight of our analysis.

8. The key results in Sections 3–5 can be shown to hold even if the supply of saving is upward-sloping, as long as it is sufficient to finance existing projects at an interest rate, r_A, that is not prohibitively high. Sections 6 and 7 extend our discussion to consider the case in which the supply curve of domestic funds is positively related to interest rates.

9. See Sussman (1993) for a model where the mark-up is derived endogenously for an economy where the cost of financial intermediation increases with the producer's distance from the bank.

10. The sample considered by Claessens, Demirgüç-Kunt and Huizinga in their study relates to bank-level data for 80 countries (developed and developing) covering the period 1988–95, with about 7,900 individual commercial bank observations. The source of the data is IBCA, Europe's largest credit-rating agency. The data shown in figures 6.2–6.5 exclude transition countries from the original sample. A bank is said to be foreign-owned if 50 per cent or more of its capital is owned by foreign residents.

11. The effect on net interest margins, by contrast, is not significant.

12. Note that we do not make any assumption regarding the value of C^* relative to the costs faced by domestic banks, C.

13. Recall from the previous discussion that $\Phi_i = (U + \epsilon_i^*)/2U$. Thus, $d\Phi_i/dr_L = (2U)^{-1}d\epsilon^*/dr_L$.

14. It can be inferred from (21) that

$$sg\left(\frac{d\hat{r}_O}{dC^*}\right) = sg\left(\frac{C^*}{2U\kappa M} - 1\right) < 0, \ sg\left(\frac{d\hat{r}_O}{d\kappa}\right) = -sg\left(\left[\frac{C^*}{2U\kappa M}\right]^2 U - 1\right) > 0,$$

given the condition derived earlier for generating an upward-sloping portion for the curve linking r_L and r_O. Higher enforcement and verification costs, for instance, lower the threshold level of the funding cost above which lending becomes unfeasible.

15. As noted earlier, banks are assumed to operate only (as a result of efficiency considerations) on the upward-sloping portion of this curve. It can be verified that if $C^*/2U < \kappa M$, a credit ceiling will be reached at the lowest level of loans associated with default. In these circumstances the supply curve has an inverted L shape. This would occur if verification costs are too large to be recovered, in which case banks would not supply credit levels that would lead to default in some states of nature.

16. In drawing figure 6.8 we assume that $r_A = 0$.

17. As discussed below, however, in the presence of congestion effects the surplus of domestic producers would be also affected in an opposite direction: greater congestion would tend to reduce net expected income. Figure 6.11 assumes that $C = C^*$

18. Of course, whether some of these measures can be viewed as distinct from capital controls may be a matter of semantics.

REFERENCES

Agénor, P.-R. and J. Aizenman (1998). 'Contagion and Volatility with Imperfect Credit Markets', *IMF Staff Papers*, **45**: 207–35

Aizenman, J. (1998). 'Capital Mobility in a Second-best World: Moral Hazard with Costly Financial Intermediation', *NBER Working Paper*, **6703**

Bernanke, B. S. and M. Gertler (1989). 'Agency Costs, Net Worth, and Business Fluctuations', *American Economic Review*, **79**: 14–31

Boyd, J. H. and B. D. Smith (1994). 'How Good are Standard Debt Contracts?', Stochastic versus Nonstochastic Monitoring in a Costly State Verification Environment', *Journal of Business*, **67**: 539–61

Bulow, J. I. and K. Rogoff (1989). 'A Constant Recontracting Model of Sovereign Debt', *Journal of Political Economy*, **97**: 155–78

Claessens, S., A. Demirgüç-Kunt and H. Huizinga (1998). 'How Does Foreign Entry Affect the Domestic Banking Market?', World Bank (February), unpublished

Demirgüç-Kunt, A. and H. Huizinga (1998). 'Determinants of Commercial Bank Interest Margins and Profitability: Some International Evidence', *Policy Research Working Paper*, **1913**, World Bank

Eaton, J., M. Gersovitz and J. Stiglitz (1986). 'The Pure Theory of Country Risk', *European Economic Review*, **30**: 481–513

Eichengreen, B. and A. Mody (1998). 'What Explains Changing Spreads on Emerging-Market Debt: Fundamentals or Market Sentiment?', *NBER Working Paper*, **6408**

Helpman, E. (1989). 'The Simple Analytics of Debt–Equity Swaps', *American Economic Review*, **79**: 440–51

Levine, R. (1996). 'Foreign Banks, Financial Development, and Economic Growth', in C. E. Barfield (ed.), *International Financial Markets*, Washington, DC: American Enterprise Institute Press

Milgrom, P. and D. J. Roberts (1982). 'Limit Pricing and Entry under Incomplete Information: An Equilibrium Analysis', *Econometrica*, **50**, 443–59

Obstfeld, M. (1994). 'Risk-taking, Global Diversification, and Growth', *American Economic Review*, **85**: 1310–29

(1998). 'The Global Capital Market: Benefactor or Hindrance?', *NBER Working Paper*, **6559**.

Sussman, O. (1993). 'A Theory of Financial Development', in A. Giovannini (ed.), *Finance and Development: Issues and Experience*, Cambridge: Cambridge University Press

Townsend, R. M. (1979). 'Optimal Contracts and Competitive Markets with Costly State Verification', *Journal of Economic Theory*, **21**: 265–93

Williamson, S. D. (1986). 'Costly Monitoring, Financial Intermediation, and Equilibrium Credit Rationing', *Journal of Monetary Economics*, **18**: 159–79.

(1987). 'Costly Monitoring, Loan Contracts, and Equilibrium Credit Rationing', *Quarterly Journal of Economics*, **102**: 135–45

Discussion
John Driffill

In their chapter 6, Agénor and Aizenmann develop a theoretical model of the effects of opening up the financial markets of a country. They explore the effects on the returns of domestic firms, banks and savers, and explore the amount of investment undertaken and the effects on welfare. The chapter begins with a model in which the domestic economy can provide a fixed supply of saving at a constant reservation price, which meets a fixed domestic demand for funds, well below domestic saving. This is the central case which occupies most of the exposition and provides most of the chapter's insights. The chapter goes on to consider two extensions. One allows for an upward-sloping supply curve of funds and heterogeneity of projects in terms of their expected returns, and the other allows additionally for congestion externalities. These two cases allow the opening up of financial markets to affect the amount of investment that takes place in the economy. Congestion externalities increase the likelihood that internationalisation will lead to excessive investment which reduces welfare.

The analysis assumes that there is asymmetric information between banks and the firms to which they lend, in that the firms alone discover costlessly the returns on their investments, which are random variables. While the banks can also discover the returns to investment projects, monitoring is costly, and is carried out only when firms default on loans. However, although asymmetric information and costly monitoring are assumed, there is no room for moral hazard or adverse selection in the model. These sources of inefficiency, widely discussed in the context of the

Asian crises are thus omitted from this analysis, which therefore offers a rather different perspective than the usual one.

In the base case dealt with in the chapter (in sections 2–5), that of an autarkic economy, a fixed supply (S) of saving (which has a reservation rate of return of r_A) is loaned to domestic banks, who lend it on to domestic firms. There is imperfect competition between the banks who expect to receive a return of $\theta_A(1 + r_A)$ on their loans, where $\theta_A > 1$ is a mark-up factor. Competition between the banks drives the rate of interest charged on loans to firms down to a level which leaves the banks just making their required rate of return $\theta_A(1 + r_A$, taking into account expected costs associated with partial default). The firms will undertake investment projects provided that their expected return after repaying bank loans, in so far as they are required to, is positive. Since it is assumed in the chapter that the supply of projects is fixed and does not exhaust the available savings, the surplus of the entrepreneurs is not driven to zero, while the persons who lend money only get their reservation rate of return (in the autarkic economy).

In the case of an economy opened up to international financial markets, the potential entry of foreign banks with lower required mark-ups (θ_O), forces domestic banks to offer lower rates for loans to domestic firms than they would be in the absence of such competition. The availability of funds to banks at the international interest rate (r_O) rather than the autarkic rate (r_A) also affect the costs of loans to firms, and may enable domestic savers to obtain a return higher than their reservation rate. Again, in the proposed equilibrium, the domestic producers are left making positive expected returns. There is an unlimited supply of funds at the international rate of interest (r_O), and a fixed demand for loans coming from the finite number of potential projects. Although ruled out by assumption in the chapter, if the reservation rate of return of r_A on domestic saving S were to exceed the open economy rate of return r_O, then presumably it would be natural to assume that domestic savers would not offer their funds to banks (which offer only r_O) but use them in some other way to collect the reservation return r_A. Consequently (6.24) would then under-state domestic welfare under openness by $(r_A - r_O)S$ for the case $r_O < r_A$.

The chapter argues that volatility of the world interest rate may have the adverse consequence for the domestic economy of causing all investment projects to become unprofitable (when world interest rates are particularly high), and thus cause investment to be volatile also. Of course, the extreme effect produced here, where a critical rise in the world interest rate can reduce domestic investment from the maximum level to zero is a consequence of the extreme assumption that all investment projects are identical *ex ante*. With projects of different expected productivity, this effect of volatile world interest rates would not be so extreme. The banks' inability to enforce loan contracts is important in arriving at the result (in proposition 1, p. 212) that high world interest rates can lead to lower welfare for the domestic economy. In the absence of inefficiency in financial markets, the increase in the returns to domestic savers on world markets would lead to an increase in welfare; and it would be inefficient to finance domestic investments which could not earn, on average, the high world rate of return.

The effect of a higher world interest rate on welfare (provided the world rate exceeds the autarkic rate) is to increase the returns to savers, whose return is presumably $S.\min(r_O, r_A)$, and to reduce the returns to the combination of banks and firms. Their combined return is given as $M - (1 + r_O)H - C\phi_O$, provided the project is undertaken and the domestic banks provide the intermediation. As the world interest rate rises, the repayments to world suppliers of savings, $(1 + r_O)H$, rises, and the default probability, ϕ_O, rises also, and with it the monitoring cost borne by domestic banks. When the world interest rate rises to a high enough level, the projects are not undertaken, because the banks cannot achieve a sufficiently high expected return at any lending rate. At this point, all the positive net gains to the banks and firms resulting from the project are lost. Whether rises in world interest rates make the domestic economy better or worse off would therefore seem to depend on the amount of domestic saving S relative to the size of the project H, the size of the banks' markup (ϕ_O) and the monitoring cost C. If S is large enough relative to H and C, then it would seem that higher world interest rates would make the economy better off, by raising the return to domestic saving, this factor outweighing the losses to firms and banks. If domestic saving, S, is only just enough to cover investment needs, H, then higher world rates diminish total returns (while the projects are undertaken), cause a step fall in welfare at the point at which the projects cease to be undertaken and, for higher world interest rates, raise domestic welfare. The overall effect of higher volatility of world interest rates on expected welfare is clearly complicated and could go different ways. That it reduces welfare overall is clearly one possibility, as is claimed, but it is only one of several possibilities.

It should be noted that the analysis of effects of volatility of world interest rates on welfare involves a comparison between a constant domestic rate and a volatile world rate. And since the chapter makes the assumption that the autarkic interest rate is always below the world rate, the comparison lies between a constant domestic rate and a world rate which is both more variable and higher on average. How valid is this? Arguably a potential benefit of access to international capital markets, at least in normal non-crisis times, is that it gives access to an effectively unlimited supply of funds or outlets for savings which can absorb fluctuations in a single country's balance between desired saving and investments without large fluctuations in interest rates that might emerge under autarky. In this respect the chapter stands the usual comparison between autarky and openness on its head. While recent financial crises in Asia have caused costs of, and access to, capital to vary dramatically in the countries involved, these fluctuations have arisen because of financial factors peculiar to those countries, rather than fluctuations in world (real) interest rates of the kind the chapter suggests. Implicitly, in the analysis here, it seems that the lower mark-ups imposed on banks by international competition, and the lower international level of monitoring costs that influences the loan rates charged to firms, are not enough to offset the effects of higher international interest rates.

In terms of the empirical relevance of this result that internationalism may reduce welfare, one may argue that in so far as the projects under discussion here are long-term investments, then the relevant interest rate is an appropriate long-term, rather than a short-term rate. Since long-term rates are much less variable than short-term rates, it is unlikely that exposure to world capital markets will have such pronounced effects on long-term investment. The argument in the chapter is most readily applicable to short-term investments, such as in working capital, which are more often financed by short-term bank finance, and are most susceptible to highly variable short-term interest rates.

In the analysis up to this point (the end of section 5) in the chapter, it is noticeable that there is no possibility for access to international financial markets to increase the amount of investment or economic activity in the economy. The benefits come from the reduction in the costs of intermediation. The model by assumption places rather tight limits on the potential benefits of internationalisation. While section 6 discusses the implications of an upward-sloping supply curve of funds and heterogeneous projects, when internationalisation might potentially increase investment, few clear conclusions are drawn from this section. Again, the effects on internationalisation can go either way.

If one were to attempt to draw from the analysis in this chapter a message for the current crisis or crises in Asia, it is broadly the idea that opening up local financial markets to international borrowing and lending may have negative effects, which come about by exposing domestic markets to volatility from which autarky would have protected them, or by magnifying the effects of other distortions in the economy, as in the case of congestion externalities. While the chapter does not allow for the most widely discussed sources of problems in Asia, which depend on moral hazard and adverse selection, it shows that problems may arise even in the absence of these issues. But it may be felt that the analysis here stacks the cards rather heavily against the possibility that internationalisation is beneficial, by ruling out of the base case the possibility that it increases investment. Nevertheless this is a thoughtful and lucid analysis of some of the possible effects of opening up financial markets which, as the authors suggest in their concluding comments, is capable of further development.

7 A theory of the onset of currency attacks

STEPHEN MORRIS AND HYUN SONG SHIN

1 Introduction

The swiftness and devastating effect of recent financial crises pose considerable challenges for economists seeking an explanation of their onset. It is easy
to give a narrative of the sequence of events leading up to the crisis with the
benefit of hindsight. However this falls short of an explanation, since it begs
the question of why the crisis occurred at that particular moment in time.
More importantly, it does not explain the *absence* of a crisis in apparently
similar countries, or in the same country at different moments in history. The
challenge is all the more acute in the light of evidence that the onset of the
Asian financial crisis of 1997 was largely unanticipated by market participants, as well as by the international agencies. Radelet and Sachs (1998) note
that credit-risk spreads for borrowers in the region increased only after the
crisis was in full swing, and the credit-rating agencies were largely reacting to
events rather than acting in advance. Nor was there much indication from
international agencies or the country analysts of normally canny investment
banks that a crisis of such magnitude was brewing.

Given the difficulties in coming up with a rigorous theory, it is tempting
to fall back on unexplained shifts of sentiment on the part of fickle
investors, or the unexplained onset of panic among creditors as an explanation. As a formal counterpart to such an approach, multiple equilibrium
models of currency attacks have gained acceptance among many commentators, and such acceptance owes a great deal to the difficulty in predicting
the exact timing of currency attacks, as well as the observation that they are
triggered without any apparent change in the underlying fundamentals of
the economy. Such models incorporate the self-fulfilling nature of the belief
in an imminent speculative attack. If speculators and exposed borrowers
believe that a currency will come under attack, their actions in anticipation
of this precipitate the crisis itself, while if they believe that a currency is not
in danger of imminent attack, their inaction spares the currency from

attack, thereby vindicating their initial beliefs. The onset of a currency attack is thus explained in terms of a shift from one equilibrium to another.

A large and growing literature has emerged developing this theme and formalising the intuition.[1] Obstfeld's work (1986, 1994, 1996) has been influential in this regard, and has served to draw a line between multiple-equilibrium models of currency attacks and the earlier generation of theories which rely on a secular deterioration of fundamentals (such as Krugman, 1979 and Flood and Garber, 1984a, 1984b), and whose argument builds on insights from models of price-fixing in exhaustible goods markets (Salant and Henderson, 1978).

However, the multiple-equilibrium approach is open to the charge that it does not fully explain a currency attack, since the shift in beliefs which leads to the movement from one equilibrium to another is left unexplained. In short, there is an indeterminacy in the theory. The beliefs of the economic actors are seen as being autonomous from the economic fundamentals, and liable to unexplained coordinated shifts. Such a view not only runs counter to our theoretical scruples against indeterminacy but, more importantly, runs counter to our intuition that bad fundamentals are somehow 'more likely' to trigger a crisis. Indeed, a growing empirical literature has examined the relationship between the incidence of currency attacks and the underlying economic fundamentals.[2] A satisfactory theory of the onset of crisis must explain the shift in beliefs which trigger the attack.

In this chapter, we attempt to construct such a theory of the onset of currency attacks. The theory builds on two main features.

- The actions of diverse economic actors which exacerbate a currency crisis are *mutually reinforcing*. For instance, a hedge fund will find it profitable to attack a currency if it can rely on borrowers with unhedged dollar liabilities to scramble to cover their positions, and thereby exacerbate the crisis. Conversely, the borrower will find it more attractive to hedge if the currency is under attack from speculators.

- Market participants have access to a large mass of information concerning the economic fundamentals, and hence are often well informed of the underlying state of the economy. However, perhaps because of the sheer volume of information, there are *small disparities in the information* at the disposal of each economic actor.

The first of these features is standard in multiple-equilibrium accounts, and we adopt this basic starting point. Our innovation comes with the second feature. When there are small disparities in the information of the market participants, the indeterminacy of beliefs inherent in the multiple-equilibrium story is largely removed. Instead, it is possible to track the shifts in beliefs as we track the shifts in the economic fundamentals. This is so since uncertainty about others' beliefs now takes on a critical role, and such uncertainty often dictates a particular course of action as being the uniquely optimal one. Even vanishingly small differences in information suffice to generate such uncertainty about others' beliefs. When we consider the sheer quantity of information available to market participants – the news wire services, in-house research, leaks from official sources, as well as the press and broadcasters, exact uniformity of information is the last thing we can expect.

Indeed, the fragmentation of the media in modern times has generated the paradoxical situation in which ever-greater quantities of information is generated and disseminated, but comes at the expense of the shared knowledge of its recipients. Apart from totalitarian regimes in which there is a single source of information (or perhaps in the heyday of the BBC Home Service), the receipt of information is rarely accompanied by the knowledge that everyone else is also receiving precisely this information at that time. Even among financial markets, the foreign exchange market is especially fragmented. Its market microstructure is characterised by the decentralised nature of the trade necessitated by round-the-clock trading and the geographical spread which goes with it. At its most basic, a speculative attack is a resolution of a coordination problem among the diverse interested parties – both foreign and domestic. Small disparities of information determine the outcome of such coordination problems.

In earlier work (Morris and Shin, 1998), we have illustrated this point in the context of a simple static model where speculators observe accurate, but idiosyncratic, signals concerning the fundamentals, and they hold uniform prior beliefs about the fundamentals. In this case, the multiplicity of equilibrium is completely eliminated, and a unique outcome emerges in equilibrium.

Here, we develop this line of inquiry further, and clarify the role of differential information in currency attacks. The static framework and the strong distributional assumptions in our earlier work did not allow us to distinguish between the issue of the uniqueness of equilibrium from the more general issue of how the set of equilibria of the imperfect information game is affected by the departures from common knowledge. Although changes in the equilibrium set to shifts in the nature of differential information is to be expected, uniqueness of equilibrium requires additional pieces of the jigsaw to be in place. Also, the static nature of the model in our earlier work detracted from the goal of serving as a theory of the *onset* of currency attacks. Any such theory must take into account the evolution of the fundamentals over time, and incorporate differential information in this dynamic context.

In what follows, the fundamentals evolve according to a Brownian motion process, and market participants monitor the fundamentals accurately, but with small differences in their information. We demonstrate the existence of an accompanying stochastic process – called the 'hurdle process' – whereby, as long as the fundamentals lie above the realisation of the hurdle process, there is no currency attack. However, as soon as the fundamental process falls below the hurdle process, an attack inevitably follows. The imagery is intended to be suggestive. As long as fundamentals can negotiate the hurdle, there is no attack. However, as soon as it 'trips over' the hurdle, an attack is triggered. This hurdle process also has the feature that it moves in the opposite direction to the fundamentals. Thus, when fundamentals deteriorate, the hurdle shifts upwards, making it more difficult to clear the hurdle.

We readily acknowledge that such a model is still too rudimentary to yield detailed policy implications. However, it makes a small step in the direction of giving us the framework in which such questions can be addressed *within* the theory, rather than appealing to forces outside it.

2 Elements of a theory

Defending a currency peg in adverse circumstances entails large costs for the government or monetary authorities. The costs bear many depressingly familiar symptoms – collapsing asset values, rising bankruptcies, the loss of foreign exchange reserves, high interest rates and the resulting reduction in demand leading to increases in unemployment and slower growth. Whatever the perceived benefits of maintaining a currency peg, and whatever their official pronouncements, all monetary authorities have a pain threshold at which the costs of defending the peg outweighs the benefits of doing so. Understanding the source and the severity of this pain is a key to understanding the onset of currency attacks.

Facing the monetary authority is an array of diverse private sector actors, both domestic and foreign, whose interests are affected by the actions of the other members of this group, and by the actions of the monetary authority. The main actors are domestic corporations, domestic banks and their depositors, foreign creditor banks, and outright speculators – whether in the form of hedge funds or the proprietary trading desks of the international financial houses. Two features stand out, and deserve emphasis.:

- Each actor faces a choice between actions which exacerbate the pain of maintaining the peg and actions which are more benign.

- The more prevalent are the actions which increase the pain of holding the peg, the greater is the incentive for an individual actor to adopt the action which increases the pain. In other words, the actions which tend to undermine the currency peg are mutually reinforcing.

For domestic corporations with unhedged foreign currency liabilities, they can either attempt to hedge their positions or not. The action to hedge their exposure – of selling baht to buy dollars in forward contracts, for example – is identical in its mechanics (if not in its intention) to the action of a hedge fund which takes a net short position in baht. For domestic banks and finance houses which have facilitated such dollar loans to local firms, they can either attempt to hedge their dollar exposure on their balance sheets or not. Again, the former action is identical in its consequence to a hedge fund short-selling baht. As a greater proportion of these actors adopt the action of selling the domestic currency, the greater is the pain to the monetary authorities, and hence the greater is the likelihood of abandonment of the peg. This increases the attractiveness of selling baht. In this sense, the actions which undermine the currency peg are mutually reinforcing. They are 'strategic complements', in the sense used in game theory.

Indeed, the strategic effects run deeper. As domestic firms with dollar liabilities experience difficulties in servicing their debt, the banks which have facilitated such dollar loans attempt to cover their foreign currency losses and improve their balance sheet by a contraction of credit. This in turn is accompanied by a rise in interest rates, fall in profit and a further increase in corporate distress. For foreign creditor banks with short-term exposure, this is normally a cue to cut off credit lines, or to refuse to roll over short-term debt. Even for firms with no foreign currency exposure, the general contraction of credit increases corporate distress. Such deterioration in the domestic economic environment exacerbates the pain of maintaining the peg, thereby serving to reinforce the actions which tend to undermine it. To make matters worse still, the belated hedging activity by banks is usually accompanied by a run on their deposits, as depositors scramble to withdraw their money.

Table 7.1 contains a (somewhat simplistic) taxonomy of the various actors and their actions which undermine the peg. The feature to be emphasised is the increased pain of maintaining the peg in the face of widespread adoption of such actions, and hence the *mutually reinforcing* nature of the action which undermines the peg. The greater is the prevalence of such actions, the more attractive such actions become to the individual actor.

To be sure, the actual *motives* behind these actions are as diverse as the actors themselves. A currency speculator rubbing his hands and looking on in glee as his target country descends into economic chaos has very different

Table 7.1   *Undermining the peg*

Actor	Action(s) undermining peg
Speculators	Short sell Baht
Domestic firms	Sell Baht for hedging purposes
Domestic banks	{ Sell Baht for hedging purposes
	Reduce credit to domestic firms
Foreign banks	Refuse to roll over debt
Depositors	Withdraw deposits

motives from a desperate owner of a firm in that country trying frantically to salvage what he can, or a depositor queueing to salvage her meagre life savings. However, whatever the motives underlying these actions, they are similar in their consequences. They all lead to greater pains of holding to the peg, and hence hasten its demise.

For the purposes of the formal development of the theory, we will abstract from the diverse motives of the private sector actors, and simply treat everyone as being a potential 'speculator' against the currency. Hence, in what follows, the label of 'speculator' should be taken to apply to the array of economic actors discussed above.

We summarise by θ the overall perception of the monetary authorities concerning the robustness of the underlying economy and, by implication, the ease with which the monetary authorities can withstand speculative selling of the currency. When θ is low, the economy is in bad shape and the costs of defending the currency peg is high. When θ is high, the reverse is true and the cost of defending the peg is low. When θ is sufficiently low, the monetary authorities abandon the peg irrespective of the actions of the speculators. Conversely, when θ is sufficiently high, the government maintains the peg irrespective of the actions of speculators. However, the cost of defending the peg depends on the extent to which the peg comes under concerted attack. For intermediate values of θ, the cost of maintaining the peg is pivotal in the government's decision on whether to abandon it.

Let $a(\theta)$ be the degree of ferocity of the attack on the currency which is just sufficient to induce the monetary authorities to abandon the peg, as measured by the proportion of speculators who sell the currency (we assume that each speculator has the binary choice of whether to attack the currency, or not to do so). In other words, if proportion $a(\theta)$ or greater attack the currency at state θ, the monetary authorities abandon the peg, while if the proportion attacking the currency is less than $a(\theta)$, the government maintains the peg. We further assume that

• There is $\underline{\theta}$ such that $a(\theta) = 0$ for $\theta \leq \underline{\theta}$

- There is $\bar{\theta}$ such that $a(\theta)$ is undefined for $\theta \leq \bar{\theta}$
- $a(\theta)$ is strictly increasing in θ when $0 < a(\theta) < 1$, and there is a bound b on the slope of $a(\cdot)$, so that $0 < b \leq a'(\theta)$.

2.1 Evolution of θ

Time is discrete, and advances in increments of $\Delta > 0$. The value of θ at time t is denoted by $\theta(t)$. Conditional on $\theta(t)$, the value of θ at time $t + \Delta$ is distributed normally with mean $\theta(t)$ and variance Δ. Such a feature would result if observations of θ are snapshots of a process which evolved according to the Brownian motion process

$$d\theta = z\sqrt{\Delta}dt \qquad (7.1)$$

where z is the standard normal random variable.

The monetary authorities observe θ perfectly (after all, θ is the *perception* of the monetary authorities). However, other parties do not observe θ perfectly. In particular, the speculators are able to observe θ only after a delay of Δ. Thus, at time $t + \Delta$, they observe $\theta(t)$.

However, although the speculators do not observe the current value of θ, they do have a noisy signal of the current θ. Speculator i observes at time t the random variable

$$x_i(t) = \theta(t) + \eta_i \qquad (7.2)$$

where η_i is a normal random variable with mean zero, and variance $\epsilon\Delta$, where ϵ is a small positive number. So, the variance of the noise term is ϵ times the one-period-ahead variance of θ itself. Furthermore, each η_i is independent of θ, and of η_j for all $j \neq i$.

To summarise, at time t, the information at the disposal of the monetary authorities and the speculators are as follows.

- Monetary authorities: $\{\theta(t)\}$
- Speculator i: $\{\theta(t - \Delta), x_i(t)\}$.

2.2 Payoffs

In each period, the speculators decide whether to attack the currency or not, based on their information. There is a cost of attacking the currency,

Table 7.2   Matrix of payoffs

	Peg maintained	Peg abandoned
Attack	$-c$	$1 - c$
Refrain	0	0

given by a constant $c > 0$. As well as the transaction costs associated with attacking a currency, c incorporates any differences in the interest rates between the target currency and the dollar. For a speculator who borrows the target currency and sells it for dollars, the higher interest cost of the borrowing can sometimes be substantial. Our model does not address the determination of this cost. We assume it to be a known parameter.

The monetary authorities observe the aggregate short-selling of the speculators and maintains the peg at θ if and only if the proportion of speculators who attack the currency does not exceed the threshold level $a(\theta)$. When the currency peg is removed, the currency depreciates by a known amount $D > 0$, and remains at this lower level forever. We normalise payoffs and assume from now on that $D = 1$. We thus have the matrix of payoffs to a particular speculator shown in table 7.2.

If θ were common knowledge among the speculators, there is the familiar multiplicity of equilibria in the range $(\underline{\theta}, \bar{\theta})$. If speculators believe that the peg will be maintained, they refrain from attacking the currency, which leads to the peg being maintained. If, however, they believe that the peg will be abandoned, they attack the currency, leading to its downfall.

However, common knowledge of fundamentals would be an inappropriate assumption in the context of financial markets, as we shall argue below.

2.3 Joint distributions

In thinking about the joint distributions generated by our model, recall that if (X, Y) has a bivariate normal distribution, then the conditional distribution of X given $Y = y$ is normal with mean

$$\mu_x + (\rho \sigma_X / \sigma_Y)(y - \mu_Y)$$

and variance

$$\sigma_X^2 (1 - \rho^2)$$

where μ denotes the mean of the subscripted random variable, σ^2 denotes its variance and ρ is the correlation coefficient between X and Y.

In our case, we will be interested in the one-step-ahead covariances conditional on θ at time $t - \Delta$. From our assumptions,

$$
\begin{aligned}
\text{cov}\,(x_i(t), x_j(t)\,|\,\theta(t-\Delta)) &= \text{cov}\,(x_i(t), \theta(t)\,|\,\theta(t-\Delta)) \\
&= \text{var}\,(\theta(t)\,|\,\theta(t-\Delta)) \\
&= \Delta.
\end{aligned}
$$

Similarly,

$$
\begin{aligned}
\text{var}\,(x_i(t)\,|\,\theta(t-\Delta)) &= \text{var}\,(\theta(t)\,|\,\theta(t-\Delta)) + \text{var}\,(\eta_i) \\
&= \Delta\,(1 + \epsilon).
\end{aligned}
$$

When no confusion is possible, we will economise on notation, and drop the time argument. Unless otherwise stated, all covariances are conditional on the realisation of θ in the previous period. Hence, we write $\text{cov}(x_i, x_j)$ and $\text{var}(x_i)$ for the expressions above.

The one-step-ahead correlation coefficients between x_i and x_j and between x_i and θ are given by

$$
\begin{aligned}
\rho(x_i, x_j) &= \frac{\text{cov}\,(x_i, x_j)}{\sqrt{\text{var}\,(x_i)\,\text{var}\,(x_j)}} \\
&= \frac{\text{var}\,(\theta)}{\text{var}\,(\theta) + \text{var}\,(\eta_i)} \\
&= \frac{1}{1 + \epsilon}
\end{aligned}
$$

and

$$
\begin{aligned}
\rho(x_i, \theta) &= \frac{\text{cov}\,(x_i, \theta)}{\sqrt{\text{var}\,(x_i)\,\text{var}\,(\theta)}} \\
&= \frac{\text{var}\,(\theta)}{\sqrt{[\text{var}\,(\theta) + \text{var}\,(\eta_i)]\,\text{var}\,(\theta)}} \\
&= \frac{\Delta}{\sqrt{\Delta(1 + \epsilon)\Delta}} \\
&= \frac{1}{\sqrt{1 + \epsilon}}.
\end{aligned}
$$

In both cases, the correlation is high when ϵ is small, and the speculators have good information concerning θ and the signals of others. In terms of the inference problem, the distributions of interest are, first, the conditional distribution of $\theta(t)$ on $x_i(t)$ and the previous realisation of θ denoted by

$$
f(\theta\,|\,x_i, \theta_{-\Delta}) \tag{7.3}
$$

and the conditional distribution of $x_i(t)$ on $\theta(t)$, denoted by $f(x_i|\theta)$. The former summarises the beliefs of speculator i concerning the fundamentals, while the latter gives the distribution of signals for a given state of fundamentals. We know that

$$f(x_i|\theta) = \eta_i \qquad (7.4)$$

so that it is normal with mean zero and variance $\epsilon\Delta$. As for $f(\theta|x_i,\theta_{-\Delta})$, normality of the underlying random variables implies that $f(\theta|x_i,\theta_{-\Delta})$ is also normal whose mean is given by

$$E(\theta) + \frac{\text{cov}(x_i,\theta)}{\text{var}(x_i)}(x_i - E(x_i))$$

$$= \theta_{-\Delta} + \frac{\text{var}(\theta)}{\text{var}(\theta) + \text{var}(x_i)}(x_i - \theta_{-\Delta})$$

$$= \left(\frac{\epsilon}{1+\epsilon}\right)\theta_{-\Delta} + \left(\frac{1}{1+\epsilon}\right)x_i.$$

In other words, when trader i observes signal x_i, she forms her beliefs on the current value of θ by taking a convex combination of her current signal x_i and the previous realisation of θ. As the signal gets more accurate (i.e. as ϵ becomes small), the trader puts more weight on her signal, and less on the prior realisation. The variance of $f(\theta|x_i)$ is given by $\text{var}(\theta)(1-\rho^2)$, or

$$\frac{\epsilon\Delta}{1+\epsilon}.$$

To summarise,

- $f(x_i|\theta)$ is normal with mean zero and variance $\epsilon\Delta$.
- $f(\theta|x_i,\theta_{-\Delta})$ is normal with mean $\left(\frac{\epsilon}{1+\epsilon}\right)\theta_{-\Delta} + \left(\frac{1}{1+\epsilon}\right)x_i$, and variance $\frac{\epsilon\Delta}{1+\epsilon}$.
- The correlation between x_i and x_j is $1/(1+\epsilon)$.

2.4 Failure of common belief

Although the signals of the speculators are highly correlated when ϵ is small, there is a qualitative difference between the case when ϵ is small but positive and when ϵ is precisely zero for the degree of common knowledge. In the former, there is common knowledge of the fundamentals, but in the latter even *approximate* common knowledge fails, as we shall demonstrate.

The fact that an individual believes some feature of the economy to be this or that way is as much a description of the world as any statement about the fundamentals of the economy. For event E, we can associate those states of the world at which some group of individuals hold certain beliefs concerning E. Define the operator $B_q(.)$ as:

$$B_q(E) \equiv \left\{ \theta \mid \begin{array}{l} \text{proportion } q \text{ or higher of speculators} \\ \text{believe } E \text{ with probability } q \text{ or higher} \end{array} \right\}.$$

When θ belongs to $B_q(E)$, proportion q or higher of speculators believe event E with probability q or higher at θ. Consider the event $E = [\theta,\infty)$ – i.e. the event that the fundamentals are consistent with the peg. When $\epsilon = 0$, we have $B_1(E) = E$, and hence

$$E = B_1(E) = B_1(B_1(E)) = B_1(B_1(B_1(E))) = \ldots$$

for any number of iterations of the operator $B_1(.)$, so that whenever fundamentals are consistent with the peg (i.e. when $\theta \in E$), everyone believes this with probability 1, everyone believes that everyone believes it, everyone believes that everyone believes that everyone believes it, and so on, without bound.

Contrast this with the case when ϵ is small, but positive. Consider when at least 90 per cent or speculators believe E with probability at least 0.9 (see figure 7.1). Graph 7.1a illustrates the density $f(\theta|x,\theta_{-\Delta})$ – the posterior density over θ given the information $(x,\theta_{-\Delta})$. In order for a speculator to place belief 0.9 or greater on the event E, the signal x must be at least as high as x_*. Graph 7.1b illustrates the density of the signals generated by the noise. In order for 90 per cent of speculators to receive a signal greater than x_*, the value of θ must be at least θ_*. Thus, the event in which at least 90 per cent of speculators believe E with probability at least 0.9 is given by the interval $[\theta_*,\infty)$. In other words,

$$B_{0.9}(E) = [\theta_*,\infty) \subsetneq E.$$

Indeed, for $q > 1/2$, we have

$$\theta \notin B_q(\ldots (B_q(B_q(E))) \ldots)$$

for some finite number of iterations. In other words, when ϵ is small but positive, even *approximate* common knowledge of fundamentals fails.

We should think of common belief not in terms of the mental gymnastics of higher-order beliefs, but in terms of the 'transparency' of the situation. When two individuals are seated across the same table in a well-lit room, we can reasonably claim that there is common knowledge of this fact, given its transparency to both individuals. The fundamentals, in this case,

Figure 7.1 ϵ *small but positive*

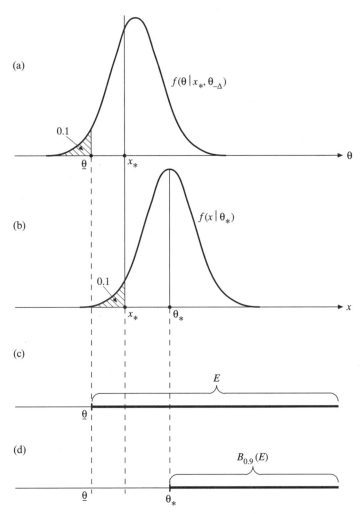

satisfy a fixed-point property in that this situation obtains if both individuals know that this is so.[3]

Away from such special circumstances, common knowledge, and even approximate common knowledge is very rarely in place in the real world. For financial markets, common knowledge of fundamentals is a singularly inappropriate assumption. In what follows, therefore, the results which stand in contrast to the benchmark case should be attributed to the failure of common knowledge. We build on the work of game theorists who have investigated the effects of higher order uncertainty (Rubinstein, 1989; Monderer and Samet, 1989; Carlsson and Van Damme, 1993a, 1993b; Morris, Rob and Shin, 1995; Kajii and Morris, 1997). Morris and Shin (1997) is a survey of some of the main results to date.

3 The incomplete information game

At date t, if the currency peg is still intact, each speculator decides whether or not to attack the currency based on her information. A strategy for speculator i is a function

$$(x, \theta_{-\Delta}) \mapsto \{\text{Attack, Refrain}\}. \tag{7.5}$$

In principle, a speculator can choose an action conditional on the whole history of θ, but since history reveals no more information than the previous realisation, we restrict attention to Markov strategies of the above form.

The monetary authority observes θ and the proportion, s, of speculators who attack. It abandons the peg if and only if

$$s \geq a(\theta).$$

If the peg is abandoned, it is never reinstated. In effect, the game ends when the peg is abandoned. The payoffs of the game are given in table 7.2.

We can now state the main result of the chapter. We shall do it in terms of the following pair of theorems.[4]

Theorem 1 For ϵ sufficiently small, there is a stochastic process $\{h(t)\}$ such that the currency peg is maintained as long as $\theta > h$, but the peg is abandoned as soon as $\theta \leq h$.

Theorem 2 $h(t) \geq h(t - \Delta)$ if $\theta(t - \Delta) \leq \theta(t - 2\Delta)$.

Theorem 1 states that when market participants have sufficiently accurate information concerning the fundamentals, we can construct a stochastic process – an accompanying 'hurdle process' – such that the onset of a speculative attack can be characterised in terms of the fundamentals 'tripping over' the hurdle.

Theorem 2 states that the hurdle moves in the opposite direction to the fundamentals. So, when economic fundamentals deteriorate, the hurdle becomes higher than before. Conversely, when fundamentals improve, the hurdle falls further away. This implies that when the fundamentals deteriorate, the prospect of a currency attack increases *more than proportionately* to the deterioration of the fundamentals.

The model and conclusions presented here may be contrasted with our earlier work, Morris and Shin (1998). The economic model in this chapter is more reduced-form; but it captures the same essential features. Our earlier work made distributional assumptions that guaranteed uniqueness of equilibrium; the normal processes assumed in this chapter do not guarantee uniqueness, but uniqueness is guaranteed for sufficiently small noise and, as we discuss below, this noise does not need to be too small. Finally, by explicitly modelling a dynamic process, we are able to see how the hurdle changes through time. Previous period fundamentals influence the threshold at which an attack occurs because they influence speculators' beliefs about other speculators' beliefs.

3.1 Overview of the argument

Before giving the detailed proofs for theorems 1 and 2, we give an outline of the shape of our argument. The first step in our analysis is to identify bounds on equilibrium actions. For any given profile of strategies by the speculators, denote by

$$\pi(x,\theta_{-\Delta}) \tag{7.6}$$

the proportion of traders who attack the currency given $(x,\theta_{-\Delta})$.

Define the set $\mathscr{E}$ as the set of all π which may arise in an equilibrium of the game. In other words, $\pi \in \mathscr{E}$ if and only if there is some equilibrium in which the proportion of speculators who attack given $(x,\theta_{-\Delta})$ is given by $\pi(x,\theta_{-\Delta})$. Define

$$\underline{x}(\theta_{-\Delta}) = \inf\{x \,|\, \pi(x,\theta_{-\Delta}) < 1 \text{ and } \pi \in \mathscr{E}\} \tag{7.7}$$
$$\bar{x}(\theta_{-\Delta}) = \inf\{x \,|\, \pi(x,\theta_{-\Delta}) > 0 \text{ and } \pi \in \mathscr{E}\}. \tag{7.8}$$

Thus, $\underline{x}(\theta_{-\Delta})$ is the greatest lower bound on the signal at which at least some of the traders do *not* attack the currency. Thus, if $x < \underline{x}(\theta_{-\Delta})$, we can be sure that every speculator attacks given $(x,\theta_{-\Delta})$ in *every* equilibrium, while if $x > \bar{x}(\theta_{-\Delta})$, every speculator refrains given $(x,\theta_{-\Delta})$ in every equilibrium.

We will show that the bounds $\underline{x}(\theta_{-\Delta})$ and $\bar{x}(\theta_{-\Delta})$ can be identified by constructing a continuous function $U(x,\theta_{-\Delta})$ which has four features.

- $U \to 1-c$ as $x \to -\infty$, and $U \to -c$ as $x \to -\infty$

- $\underline{x}(\theta_{-\Delta}) = \min \{x \mid U(x,\theta_{-\Delta}) = 0\}$
- $\bar{x}(\theta_{-\Delta}) = \max \{x \mid U(x,\theta_{-\Delta}) = 0\}$
- $U(x,\theta_{-\Delta})$ is decreasing in $\theta_{-\Delta}$.

The function U is positive for small values of x, and is negative for large values. It is continuous, and so must cut the horizontal axis at least once. The smallest value of x at which U cuts the horizontal axis is shown to be $\underline{x}(\theta_{-\Delta})$, while the largest value at which U cuts the horizontal axis is shown to be $\bar{x}(\theta_{-\Delta})$. Thus, once this function has been identified, the characterisation of equilibrium actions can be reduced to the simple task of checking where it cuts the horizontal axis.

Moreover, this function is also shown to have the feature that, for sufficiently small ϵ,

$$\frac{\partial U}{\partial x} < 0, \tag{7.9}$$

so that U cuts the horizontal axis precisely once. This implies that $\underline{x}(\theta_{-\Delta}) = \bar{x}(\theta_{-\Delta})$, so that we can tie down equilibrium actions precisely. For sufficiently small ϵ, there is a unique θ^* for each $\theta_{-\Delta}$ such that, in *any* equilibrium, the government abandons the currency peg if

$$\theta \leq \theta^*. \tag{7.10}$$

The hurdle process $\{h(t)\}$ can then be constructed by defining the realisation of $h(.)$ at time t to be the value of θ^* associated with the realisation $\theta(t - \Delta)$. Theorem 1 follows from this definition and (7.10).

We now present the proofs of theorems 1 and 2, as well as illustrating the argument with a number of simulations.

4 The argument

4.1 Conditional expected payoff

Denote by $s(\theta,\pi)$ the proportion of speculators who end up attacking the currency when the state of fundamentals is θ, given the aggregate selling strategy π. It is given by

$$s(\theta,\pi) \equiv \int_{-\infty}^{\infty} \pi(x,\theta_{-\Delta})f(x \mid \theta)dx. \tag{7.11}$$

Denote by $A(\theta_{-\Delta},\pi)$ the event in which the monetary authority abandons the currency peg when the speculators' aggregate short selling is π. In other words,

$$A(\theta_{-\Delta},\pi) = \{\theta \mid s(\theta,\pi) \geq a(\theta)\}. \tag{7.12}$$

When the government abandons the peg, there is a devaluation in the currency of $D=1$. Since a speculator does not observe θ directly, the optimal decision rests on the expected payoff from attacking the currency conditional on the signal x received. We denote by $u(x,\theta_{-\Delta},\pi)$ the expected payoff from attacking the currency conditional on $(x,\theta_{-\Delta})$ when the aggregate short selling is given by π. Then,

$$u(x,\theta_{-\Delta},\pi) = \int_{A(\theta_{-\Delta},\pi)} f(\theta \mid x,\theta_{-\Delta}) \, d\theta - c. \tag{7.13}$$

4.2 Defining $U(x,\theta_{-\Delta})$

The function $U(x,\theta_{-\Delta})$ is defined to be the expected payoff conditional on $(x,\theta_{-\Delta})$ when speculators follow the strategy of attacking the currency if the realisation of the signal is x or lower. In other words,

$$U(x,\theta_{-\Delta}) \equiv u(x,\theta_{-\Delta},I_x)$$

$$= \int_{A(\theta_{-\Delta},Ix)} f(\theta \mid x) \, d\theta - c \tag{7.14}$$

where $I_x(y)$ is the indicator function which takes the value 1 when $y \leq x$, and takes value 0 when $y > x$. That is

$$I_x(y) = \begin{cases} 1 & \text{if } y \leq x \\ 0 & \text{if } y > x. \end{cases} \tag{7.15}$$

In order to express U more succinctly, we characterise the event $A(\theta_{-\Delta},I_x)$ – i.e. the event in which the peg is abandoned when the speculators' aggregate sales of the currency given by I_x.

The distribution of x given θ is normal with mean θ and standard deviation $\sqrt{\epsilon\Delta}$. Denoting by $\Phi(\kappa,\mu,\sigma)$ the cumulative normal distribution at k when the mean is μ and the standard deviation is σ, we have

$$s(\theta,I_x) = \Phi\left(x,\theta,\sqrt{\epsilon\Delta}\right)$$

$$= 1 - \Phi\left(\theta,x,\sqrt{\epsilon\Delta}\right).$$

So, $A(I_x, \theta_{-\Delta}) = (-\infty, \psi(x)]$ is the unique θ which solves

$$1 - \Phi\left(\theta, x, \sqrt{\epsilon\Delta}\right) = a(\theta). \tag{7.16}$$

The solution is unique, since a is increasing, while $1 - \Phi\left(\theta, x, \sqrt{\epsilon\Delta}\right)$ is decreasing. Figure 7.2 illustrates $\psi(x)$

Hence,

$$U(x, \theta_{-\Delta}) = \int_{-\infty}^{\psi(x)} f(\theta \mid x, \theta_{-\Delta}) \, d\theta - c$$

$$= \Phi\left(\psi(x), \frac{x + \epsilon\theta_{-\Delta}}{1 + \epsilon}, \sqrt{\frac{\epsilon\Delta}{1 + \epsilon}}\right) - c. \tag{7.17}$$

We note the following properties of this function:

- $\underline{\theta} < \psi(x) < \bar{\theta}$
- U is positive for small x (tends to $1 - c$)
- U negative for large x (tends to $-c$)
- U is continuous in x.

We can conclude therefore, that U is positive for small values of x, negative for large values of x, and that it crosses the horizontal axis at least once. Consider the smallest and largest values of x for which $U = 0$. We can prove:

Lemma 1

$$\underline{x}(\theta_{-\Delta}) = \min \{x \mid U(x, \theta_{-\Delta}) = 0\}$$

$$\bar{x}(\theta_{-\Delta}) = \max \{x \mid U(x, \theta_{-\Delta}) = 0\}.$$

In our argument for this result, we will need the following preliminary result.

Lemma 2   If $\pi \geq \pi'$, then $u(x, \theta_{-\Delta}, \pi) \geq u(x, \theta_{-\Delta}, \pi')$.

Lemma 2 states that the payoff to attacking the currency is higher when the attack on the currency is stronger. In other words, speculators' decisions to attack are strategic complements. To prove lemma 2, note that if $\pi(x, \theta_{-\Delta}) \geq \pi'(x, \theta_{-\Delta})$, we have $s(\theta, \pi) \geq s(\theta, \pi')$ for every θ, so that

$$A(\pi, \theta_{-\Delta}) \supseteq A(\pi', \theta_{-\Delta}).$$

Figure 7.2  $\psi(x)$

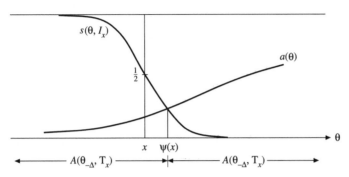

In other words, the event in which the currency peg is abandoned is strictly larger under π. Thus,

$$u(x,\theta_{-\Delta},\pi) = \int_{A(\theta_{-\Delta},\pi)} f(\theta|x)\, d\theta - c$$

$$\geq \int_{A(\theta_{-\Delta},\pi')} f(\theta|x)\, d\theta - c$$

$$= u(x,\theta_{-\Delta},\pi').$$

To prove lemma 1, note that

$$\underline{x}(\theta_{-\Delta}) \leq \inf\{x \mid 0 < \pi(x,\theta_{-\Delta}) < 1 \text{ and } \pi \in \mathscr{E}\}$$
$$\leq \sup\{x \mid 0 < \pi(x,\theta_{-\Delta}) < 1 \text{ and } \pi \in \mathscr{E}\}$$
$$\leq \bar{x}(\theta_{-\Delta}).$$

Now, if $\pi < 1$, then some speculators do not attack. This is consistent with equilibrium only if the payoff from not attacking is at least as high as attacking. By continuity, the same is true at $\underline{x}(\theta_{-\Delta})$. Hence,

$$u(\underline{x}(\theta_{-\Delta}),\theta_{-\Delta},\pi) \leq 0. \tag{7.18}$$

By strategic complementarity of actions (lemma 2),

$$U(\underline{x}(\theta_{-\Delta}),\theta_{-\Delta}) \leq u(\underline{x}(\theta_{-\Delta}),\theta_{-\Delta},\pi) \leq 0 \tag{7.19}$$

implying that

$$\min\{x \mid U(x,\theta_{-\Delta}) = 0\} \leq \underline{x}(\theta_{-\Delta}). \tag{7.20}$$

Meanwhile, we can construct a symmetric equilibrium in switching strategies at $\min\{x \mid U(x,\theta_{-\Delta}) = 0\}$. In other words, there is an equilibrium in which every speculator attacks if and only if

$$x \leq \min\{x \mid U(x,\theta_{-\Delta}) = 0\}.$$

To see this, suppose that every speculator follows this strategy. Then, by construction, the speculator who receives the marginal message min $\{x \,|\, U(x,\theta_{-\Delta}) = 0\}$ is indifferent between attacking the currency and not. But from (7.17) the expected payoff from attacking the currency is decreasing in the message x. Thus, any speculator who receives a message greater than the marginal one prefers to refrain, while a speculator who receives a message lower than the marginal one prefers to attack. Thus, we have an equilibrium. The fact that there is a symmetric equilibrium in switching strategies at min $\{x \,|\, U(x,\theta_{-\Delta}) = 0\}$ implies

$$\min \{x \,|\, U(x,\theta_{-\Delta}) = 0\} \geq \underline{x}(\theta_{-\Delta}), \tag{7.21}$$

so that together with (7.20),

$$\min \{x \,|\, U(x,\theta_{-\Delta}) = 0\} = \underline{x}(\theta_{-\Delta}). \tag{7.22}$$

There is an analogous argument for

$$\min \{x \,|\, U(x,\theta_{-\Delta}) = 0\} = \bar{x}(\theta_{-\Delta}). \tag{7.23}$$

This completes the proof of lemma 1.

The shape of the U function determines the equilibrium set, and when ϵ is small, U is a monotonic function of x.

Lemma 3 $\partial U/\partial x < 0$ if ϵ is sufficiently small.

Proof   From

$$s(\psi(x),I_x) = \Phi\left(x,\psi(x),\sqrt{\epsilon\Delta}\right),$$

and denoting by Φ_n the partial derivative of Φ with respect to its nth argument, total differentiation with respect to x yields

$$\Phi_1 + \Phi_2 \psi'(x) = a'(\psi(x))\psi'(x).$$

Rearranging,

$$\psi'(x) = \frac{\Phi_1}{a'(\psi(x)) - \Phi_2}.$$

However, Φ_1 is the value of the normal density at x, so that $\Phi_1 = \phi\left(x,\psi(x),\sqrt{\epsilon\Delta}\right)$, where ϕ is the density corresponding to Φ. The partial derivative Φ_2 is the negative of Φ_1. Thus,

$$\psi'(x) = \frac{\phi(x,\psi(x),\sqrt{\epsilon\Delta})}{a'(\psi(x)) + \phi(x,\psi(x),\sqrt{\epsilon\Delta})}. \tag{7.24}$$

Consider $\Phi(k,\mu,\sigma)$. If both k and μ are differentiable functions of x while the variance is constant, then $\Phi(k,\mu,\sigma)$ is decreasing in x if $k' < \mu'$. Hence,

$$\partial U/\partial x < 0 \Leftrightarrow \psi'(x) < \frac{1}{1+\epsilon}. \tag{7.25}$$

We know that

$$\psi'(x) = \frac{\phi(x,\psi(x),\epsilon\Delta)}{a'(\psi(x)) + \phi(x,\psi(x),\epsilon\Delta)}$$

$$= \frac{1}{\frac{a'}{\phi} + 1}.$$

Thus, $\psi'(x) < \frac{1}{1+\epsilon}$ if $a'/\phi > \epsilon$, or

$$a' > \epsilon\phi. \tag{7.26}$$

Any normal density attains its maximum value at its mean and this is

$$\frac{1}{\sigma\sqrt{2\pi}}$$

where σ is its standard deviation and π is the number pi (not to be confused with the use we have made of it so far). In our case, $\sigma = \sqrt{\epsilon\Delta}$. Thus,

$$\epsilon\phi \le \sqrt{\frac{\epsilon}{2\Delta\pi}}. \tag{7.27}$$

Hence $\epsilon\phi \to 0$ as $\epsilon \to 0$. Thus, for sufficiently small ϵ the inequality (7.26) holds. This is sufficient for U to be decreasing in x. This proves lemma 3.

Figure 7.3 illustrates the point.

The horizontal axis measures x, the vertical axis measures θ. For any given realisation of θ in the previous period, the mean of the conditional distribution $f(\theta|x,\theta_{-\Delta})$ is a linear function of x, with slope $1/(1 + \epsilon)$. The smaller is ϵ, the greater is the weight placed on the noisy signal and smaller is the weight placed on the previous realisation of θ. The whole distribution $f(\theta|x,\theta_{-\Delta})$ is depicted above. The function $\psi(\cdot)$ maps x into the value of θ at which the government switches from maintaining the peg to abandoning the peg. $\psi(x)$ takes values in the open interval $(\underline{\theta},\bar{\theta})$, and is increasing.

From the diagram, we can see that $U(x,\theta_{-\Delta}) + c$ is given by the area under $f(\theta|x,\theta_{-\Delta})$ to the left of the point $\psi(x)$. This is what (7.17) says. Moreover, we can see that the question of whether $U(x,\theta_{-\Delta})$ is decreasing or not

Figure 7.3   *Proof of lemma 3*

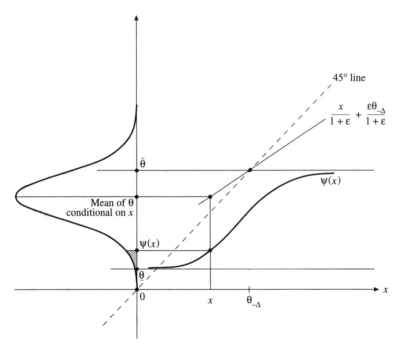

depends on the 'race' between the mean of $f(\theta \mid x, \theta_{-\Delta})$ and the point $\psi(x)$ as x increases. If the mean is increasing faster than the point $\psi(x)$, then we indeed have decreasing U. In general, this cannot be guaranteed. However, we saw above that when ϵ is sufficiently small, it can be.

4.3 Example

We illustrate the effect of shifts in ϵ by means of a numerical example. Let $\Delta = 1$, $\underline{\theta} = 0$, $\bar{\theta} = 1$, and $\theta_{-\Delta} = 0.5$. We plot the function $\psi(x)$ and the posterior mean $(x + \epsilon \theta_{-\Delta})/(1 + \epsilon)$ for four values of ϵ. In figure 7.4a–d, the horizontal axis measures x, while the vertical axis measures θ. The posterior mean is the straight line, while $\psi(x)$ is the curve.

As is clear from these plots, even for moderately large values of ϵ, the slope of the posterior mean is steeper than the slope of ψ, so that U is monotonic. Only when ϵ is very large (certainly larger than 5) do we have the possibility of ψ being steeper than the posterior mean. These simulations

Figure 7.4   *Effect of shifts in ε: case 1–4*

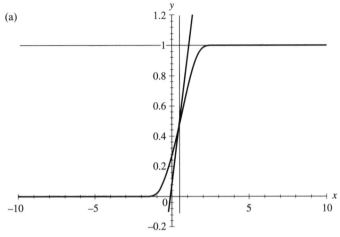

(a)

Case 1: ε = 0.2

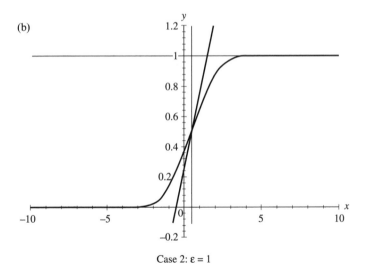

(b)

Case 2: ε = 1

suggest that the possible multiple equilibria resulting from a non-monoto-nic U function may not be important in practice.

From lemmas 1 and 3, theorem 1 follows from the following argument. For sufficiently small ϵ, we have a unique point $x^*(\theta_{-\Delta})$ at which $U(x,\theta_{-\Delta})$ cuts the horizontal axis. Hence, in every equilibrium, every speculator attacks given $(x,\theta_{-\Delta})$ if $x \leq x^*(\theta_{-\Delta})$. Then, consider the value of θ given by

Figure 7.4 (*cont.*)

(c)

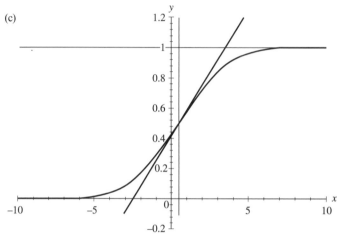

Case 3: ε = 5

(d)

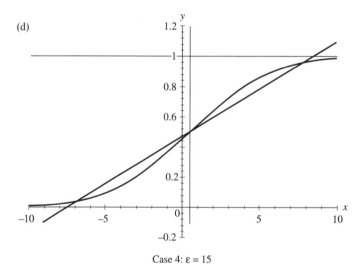

Case 4: ε = 15

$\psi(x^*(\theta_{-\Delta}))$, where ψ is the function defined in (7.16). The *hurdle process* $\{h(t)\}$ is defined to be the stochastic process such that

$$h(t) \equiv \psi(x^*(\theta(t - \Delta))). \tag{7.28}$$

To prove theorem 2, note from (7.17) that $U(x, \theta_{-\Delta})$ is decreasing in $\theta_{-\Delta}$ since an increase in $\theta_{-\Delta}$ induces a rightward shift in the posterior density f

$(\cdot \mid x, \theta_{-\Delta})$. This, in turn implies a lower value of $x^*(\theta_{-\Delta})$, and hence a lower value of $\psi(x^*(\theta_{-\Delta}))$. This completes the proof. ∎

5 The limiting case

A case of particular interest to us is the limiting case when the noise ϵ tends to zero. This serves as a benchmark in several respects. Since we envisage ϵ as being very small, the limit gives us an indication of the likely shape of the various quantities we have been working with, in particular the function U. Indeed, the U function has a particularly simple characterisation in terms of the pain threshold function $a(.)$.

Theorem 3 $\lim_{\varepsilon \to 0} \partial U / \partial x = -a'$.

Since U lies between $1 - c$ and $-c$, theorem 3 determines the U function uniquely as the 'upside-down' version of the function $a(.)$, where its level is fixed to lie between $1 - c$ and c. To prove this result, let us use the short-hand of

$$\phi = \phi\left(x, \psi(x), \sqrt{\epsilon \Delta}\right), \text{ and } \hat{\phi} = \phi\left(\psi(x), \frac{x + \epsilon \theta_{-\Delta}}{1 + \epsilon}, \sqrt{\frac{\epsilon \Delta}{1 + \epsilon}}\right),$$

then we have

$$\frac{\partial U}{\partial x} = \hat{\phi}\left[\frac{\phi}{a' + \phi} - \frac{1}{1 + \epsilon}\right]$$

$$= \left[\frac{\hat{\phi}}{(1 + \epsilon)(a' + \phi)}\right](\epsilon \phi - a').$$

In the interval $(\underline{\theta}, \bar{\theta})$, these densities become degenerate as ϵ becomes small, so that the expression in square brackets tends to 1, while $\epsilon \phi \to 0$. Hence,

$$\frac{\partial U}{\partial x} \to -a'. \tag{7.29}$$

This is a very appealing result, in that it gives a simple characterisation of the U function in terms of the fundamentals of the problem. The shape of the U function in the limit is the mirror image of the 'pain threshold' function a. This puts the focus squarely on the factors which determine the a function.

For instance, if the interval $(\underline{\theta}, \bar{\theta})$ is wide, then the slope of a is shallow, and a small increase in cost has large impact on the cutoff θ^*. In terms of the economic interpretation, a wide interval $(\underline{\theta}, \bar{\theta})$ translates into the statement that speculators' actions are more influential/decisive in dictating the exchange rate. A variety of factors will influence such decisiveness. The size of a country relative to the pool of 'hot' money will certainly be a factor, as well as the composition of financial flows and the maturity structure of debt. A shallow $a(.)$ function can also be seen reflecting the strength of the mutually reinforcing nature of the actions undermining the peg.

6 Concluding remarks

While the theory advanced in this chapter is too rudimentary to serve as a tool for assessing practical policy alternatives, it does set out the considerations which could guide our thinking. We regard the contribution here very much as a conceptual one. We believe that our approach provides a handle on the evolution of beliefs which trigger the change of sentiment, which in turn precipitates the attack. In this sense, we propose our theory as one of the *onset* of currency attacks. Developments of this framework may shed further light on the problem.

NOTES
We are grateful to Manmohan Kumar, Marcus Miller, Jonathan Thomas, Harald Uhlig, David Vines and Paolo Vitale for their comments on an earlier draft of the chapter. Shin acknowledges support from the TMR Network in Financial Markets.
1. An excellent bibliography on the Asian financial crisis is maintained by Nouriel Roubini on http://www.stern.nyu.edu/~nroubini/asia/AsiaHomepage.html

    Corsetti, Pesenti and Roubini (1998) is a recent survey fo the debate, as is Corbett and Vines (1998). Edison, Luangaram and Miller (1998) offer a perspective on the Thai financial crisis based on the role of assets as collateral.
2. The Roubini bibliography cited earlier contains a comprehensive list. A paper with suggestive results is Kumar, Moorthy and Perraudin (1998).
3. This fixed-point characterisation of common knowledge was first given formal treatment by Aumann (1976), and emphasised in Barwise (1988), Shin (1993) and others. Monderer and Samet (1989) discuss the analogous fixed-point characterisation of common p-belief.
4. We are grateful for Jonathan Thomas for suggesting this particular formulation of our results.

REFERENCES
Aumann, R. (1976). 'Agreeing to Disagree', *Annals of Statistics*, **4**: 1236–9
Barwise, J. (1988). 'Three Views of Common Knowledge' in M. Vardi (ed.), *Proceedings of the Second Conference on Theoretical Aspects of Reasoning about Knowledge*, San Francisco: Morgan Kaufmann: 365–79

Carlsson, H. and E. van Damme (1993a). 'Global Games and Equilibrium Selection', *Econometrica*, **61**: 989–1018

(1993b). 'Equilibrium Selection in Stag Hunt Games', in K. Binmore, A. Kirman and P. Tani (eds), *Frontiers of Game Theory*, Cambridge, Mass: MIT Press

Corbett, J. and D. Vines (1998). 'Lessons from Vulnerability, Crisis and Collapse' *Working Paper*, Balliol College, Oxford

Corsetti, G., P. Pesenti and N. Roubini (1998). 'Paper Tigers? A Preliminary Assessment of the Asian Crisis', *Working Paper*, Yale University; see also chapter 4 in this volume

Edison, H., P. Luangaram and M. Miller (1998). 'Asset Bubbles, Domino Effects and "Lifeboats": Elements of the East Asian Crisis', *Working Paper*, Warwick University

Flood, R. and P. Garber (1984a). 'Collapsing Exchange Rate Regimes: Some Linear Examples', *Journal of International Economics*, **17**, 1–13

(1984b). 'Gold Monetisation and Gold Discipline', *Journal of Political Economy*, **92**: 90–107

A. Kajii and S. Morris (1997). 'The Robustness of Equilibria to Incomplete Information', *Econometrica*, **65**: 1283–1309

Krugman, P. (1979). 'A Model of Balance-of-Payments Crises', *Journal of Money, Credit, and Banking*, **11**: 311–25

Kumar, M., U. Moorthy and W. Perraudin (1998). 'Predicting Emerging Market Currency Crises', *Working Paper*, Credit Suisse First Boston and Birkbeck College, London

Monderer, D. and D. Samet (1989). 'Approximating Common Knowledge with Common Beliefs', *Games and Economic Behavior*, **1**: 170–90

Morris, S. and H. S. Shin (1997). 'Approximate Common Knowledge and Coordination: Recent Lessons from Game Theory', *Journal of Logic, Language and Information*, **6**: 171–90

(1998). 'Unique Equilibrium in a Model of Self-fulfilling Currency Attacks', *American Economic Review*, **88**: 587–97

Morris, S., R. Rob and H. S. Shin (1995). '*p*-Dominance and Belief Potential', *Econometrica*, **63**: 145–57

Obstfeld, M. (1986). 'Rational and Self-fulfilling Balance-of-payments Crises', *American Economic Review*, **76**: 72–81

(1994). 'The Logic of Currency Crises', *Cahiers économiques et monétaires* (Banque de France), **43**: 189–213

(1996). 'Models of Currency Crises with Self-fulfilling Features', *European Economic Review*, **40**: 1037–48

Radelet, S. and J. Sachs (1998). 'The Onset of the East Asian Financial Crisis', *Working Paper*, Harvard Institute for International Development

Rubinstein, A. (1989). 'The Electronic Mail Game: Strategic Behavior under almost Common Knowledge', *American Economic Review*, **79**: 385–91

Salant, S. and D. Henderson (1978). 'Market Anticipations of Government Policies and the Price of Gold', *Journal of Political Economy*, **86**: 627–48

Shin, H. S. (1993). 'Logical Structure of Common Knowledge', *Journal of Economic Theory*, **60**: 1–13

Discussion
Jonathan P. Thomas

Chapter 7 takes further the ideas of Morris and Shin (1998) in that it allows for more natural Brownian-motion representation of fundamentals. In addition the chapter assumes that the information of market participants about the true value of the fundamental is distributed according to a normal distribution about the true value, as opposed to a uniform distribution in the earlier paper. This allows the authors to tell a dynamic story about when a currency attack might occur, and also to examine what happens when the nature of the differential private information is varied. The results remain startling: a tiny departure from common knowledge entirely eliminates the multiplicity of equilibria. This work represents a major challenge to the traditional multiple-equilibrium models of currency attacks, most notably associated with Obstfeld (1986, for example). Of course the insights here are also applicable to other market situations with similar multiple-equilibrium properties, such as bank-run models.

The arguments of the chapter, however, are technical and it is difficult to get a clear idea of why a small departure from common knowledge about the fundamental can lead to such a radical change in the set of equilibria. So I will start by attempting an overview of the argument, before discussing the extent to which I think these insights are important.

Rather than arguing that it is possible to rule out all but one arbitrary equilibria, I shall present their argument in terms of a single but natural class of equilibria. Recall some of the essential ingredients of the model: the lagged value of the fundmental θ is known to be $\theta_{-\Delta}$, and the typical speculator receives an idiosyncratic signal about the current value of θ equal to x. She then has to decide whether to attack the currency (sell short) or not. The attack succeeds only if the proportion of speculators attacking exceeds $a(\theta)$, where $a(\theta)$ is an increasing function. In what follows $\theta_{-\Delta}$ should be regarded as being fixed. Consider then equilibria of the following form, which we shall call 'cutoff speculation rules': 'attack the currency if the signal received (x) is no greater than a critical $\hat{x}$.' While there are many other types of conceivable equilibria, this is the most natural class and we shall see that the argument extends easily to all other putative equilibria.[1]

First, assume that there is no differential information so that it is common knowledge that each speculator knows θ (i.e. $x \equiv \theta$). Then the multiplicity of equilibria within this class is demonstrated by the fact that any $\hat{x}$ between $\underline{\theta}$ and $\bar{\theta}$ will do for an equilibrium cutoff speculation rule. That is, under complete information, all speculators can coordinate their decisions perfectly and provided everyone else is attacking, it is optimal for each individual to attack since for $\theta \in (\underline{\theta}, \bar{\theta})$, the monetary authority will not defend the peg if everyone attacks, while if no one else is attacking it is optimal not to attack since the authority will defend. Clearly, then, this is an equilibrium if $\hat{x} \in (\underline{\theta}, \bar{\theta})$. It is important, for the line of thinking used by Morris and Shin, to think of the multiplicity of equilibria in this model not in terms of there being multiple equilibria once θ is known (which, of course, there are) but, as above, in terms of there being a continuum of *ex ante* equilibrium speculation rules, parametrised by $\hat{x}$.

Now introduce the noise, so that x is a noisy signal of θ. We ask the same question: which cutoff speculation rules are consistent with equilibrium? Naturally the problem is now much more complicated for the individual speculator: knowing only her own signal x, she cannot know whether other speculators' signals are above or below $\hat{x}$, nor can she know the true value of θ and hence the critical size of attack needed to bring down the peg. Fortunately to check whether a particular $\hat{x}$ works, it is necessary only to analyse the problem faced by the 'critical speculator' who receives the signal $\hat{x}$. This speculator must be indifferent about attacking or not. This is clear: if she strictly preferred to attack, then by continuity a speculator with x slightly above $\hat{x}$ would also want to attack, which is inconsistent with the putative equilibrium which says that the latter speculator should not attack. A similar argument establishes that the critical speculator cannot strictly prefer not to attack. So the critical speculator must be indifferent, and a speculator with $x < \hat{x}$ will have a higher conditional utility from attacking as she believes that it is more likely that θ is lower, which both implies that the authority is less willing to defend, and implies that more speculators will atack (since the distribution of signals is shifted to the left, while $\hat{x}$ remains constant). So all those who are supposed to attack according to the speculation rule will want to. Likewise, those receiving signals above $\hat{x}$ will strictly not want to attack. So the indifference of the critical speculator is necessary and *sufficient* for a particular $\hat{x}$ to be an equilibrium.[2]

It should be intuitively clear that the continuum of equilibrium cutoff rules in the complete information environment will not survive the introduction of noise: an equilibrium now depends on finding an $\hat{x}$ for which the indifference condition exactly holds. Since it involves a calculation of a nontrivial conditional expectation, there is absolutely no reason why it should not hold at any particular value of x. (By contrast, with complete information, perfect coordination was possible and there was no such condition that needed to be checked.) This does not establish uniqueness, however. To do that, it is necessary to show that there is a single $\hat{x}$ for which the indifference condition holds. It seems quite intuitive that there should be only a single indifference point. If there were two such values – say, $\hat{x}_1$ and $\hat{x}_2$ with $\hat{x}_1 < \hat{x}_2$ – then the critical speculator under the rule associated with

$\hat{x}_1$ would be receiving a lower signal ($\hat{x}_1$) than the critical speculator under the $\hat{x}_2$ rule, and would consequently expect θ to be lower (i.e. the mean of $f(\theta|\hat{x},\theta_{-\Delta})$ would be lower). This conditional expectation will not be lower by as much as $\hat{x}_2 - \hat{x}_1$, however, as it is a weighted average of x and $\theta_{-\Delta}$, and will not fully respond to the change in the signal. Now for each point in the conditional density $f(\theta|\hat{x},\theta_{-\Delta})$, for $\hat{x}_1$ this corresponds to a lower value of θ which implies that the monetary authority is less resistant to attack, but at the same time because the density has shifted to the left by less than $\hat{x}_2 - \hat{x}_1$, that part of the signal density falling below $\hat{x}_1$ will be smaller – i.e. the size of the attack will be lower. As long as the latter effect is smaller than the former, then there will be more points in the density corresponding to successful attacks. In other words, the probability of a successful attack would increase as $\hat{x}$ falls. Since the utility of attacking is just this probability *less* c, this would imply that the critical speculator cannot be indifferent at both $\hat{x}_1$ and $\hat{x}_2$. Morris and Shin show that as ϵ becomes small, the latter effect becomes insignificant and there will be a unique equilibrium.

The reason for this seems to be as follows[3]: Δ (the unit of time) is held constant, so the variance of the signal, $\epsilon\Delta$, decreases, and the speculator will put less weight on the lagged value of the fundamental $\theta_{-\Delta}$, and more on the signal x itself. Consider, again, for a fixed cutoff rule associated with $\hat{x}$, the marginal speculator who receives the signal $\hat{x}$. While the conditional mean of θ, $E[\theta|\hat{x},\theta_{-\Delta}]$, will become very close to $\hat{x}$, as $\epsilon \to 0$, the variance of both the conditional distribution of θ and of the signal distribution for each possible value of θ declines, and it is not obvious how this affects the probability that there will be sufficient signals falling below $\hat{x}$ to bring down the peg. Suppose that $\hat{x} < \theta_{-\Delta}$. Note that the speculator receiving this signal $\hat{x}$ must believe that it is more likely that θ lies above than below $\hat{x}$. From the expression below (7.4) in the chapter (p. 239), for ϵ small

$$E[\theta|\hat{x},\theta_{-\Delta}] - \hat{x} \simeq \epsilon(\theta_{-\Delta} - \hat{x})$$

and consider the distance d such that a fraction $k < 0.5$ of the conditional density lies below $E[\theta|\hat{x},\theta_{-\Delta}] - d$; this is proportional to the standard deviation of this distribution

$$\sqrt{\epsilon\Delta/(1 + \epsilon)}$$

i.e. $d \simeq K(k)\sqrt{\epsilon\Delta}$ for ϵ small. As

$$\epsilon \to 0, \quad \epsilon(\theta_{-\Delta} - \hat{x}) < K(k)\sqrt{\epsilon\Delta},$$

so that for any $k < 0.5$, there is a small enough ϵ such that the critical speculator believes that the probability that $\theta < \hat{x}$ is greater than k. Consequently, as the precision of the signal becomes very large, the speculator receiving the signal $\hat{x}$ (or indeed any signal) will reckon that it is equally likely that the *true value of the fundamental, θ lies below or above $\hat{x}$.* The crucial point, though, is that the lagged value of θ does not matter in the calculations of the critical speculator – that is, her beliefs about the signal distribution relative to $\hat{x}$ do not depend on where $\hat{x}$ happens to be; since, however, at lower values of $\hat{x}$, θ and hence the proportion of speculators needed to successfully attack is likely to be smaller, the anticipated payoff of the critical speculator must be higher than at a putative equilibrium with a higher $\hat{x}$.[4] The indifference condition cannot be satisfied at more than one $\hat{x}$.

In some ways, the importance of the result is not so much the uniqueness result *per se*, although of course it is very striking, but the fact that even a small departure from common knowledge destroys the coordination amongst speculators and requires a completely different analysis.[5] And their story for the lack of common knowledge in terms of fragmentation of information is surely very compelling.

It is important, though, to realise the way of looking at the problem that Morris and Shin adopt. One might think about a possible multiple-equilibrium story as follows: the economy is currently sitting in some good equilbrium when a piece of unexpected bad news turns up which might precipitate a shift to a bad equilibrium. In the Morris–Shin version of this, speculators have already thought about all the possible pieces of bad news that could possibly turn up and have a clear idea of what the critical piece of bad news would be that would induce them to assume that the bad equilibrium is appropriate. This does require a great deal of rationality and contingent planning on the part of speculators.

The model, while rudimentary, also seems to have quite strong empirical implications. In the first place, as they point out, it at least *has* empirical implications, whereas this is debatable in the case of multiple equilibrium models in the absence of any compelling account of equilibrium selection. Secondly, if the continuous-time approximation is taken seriously (Δ very small) it implies that provided that θ is not close to the 'hurdle' process, the probability of the peg collapsing in the next period is very close to zero. As θ gets very close to the hurdle, this probability will suddenly become very large. It may be possible to see from estimates of risk premia whether this sharp spike in the probability away from zero is reasonable. Devaluation probabilities which were small but positive and reasonably constant over time would seem to be *prima facie* evidence against at least the simple Shin–Morris model. Indeed, Sutherland (1997) shows how the term structure of interest rates can be used to differentiate between multiple-equilibrium-[6] and fundamentals-based crisis models. The latter will lead to very similar implications as the Morris–Shin model.

The model is very stylised. As a dynamic model it may be somewhat inconsistent. For example, each period there will be some speculators who unsuccessfully speculate, and who thus lose c, but the model assumes their continued participation. It is difficult to think of a more fully specified model in which each speculator can sell short at most one unit of currency per period (credit-constrained?), and in addition this is independent of how many times in the past the speculator has been unsuccessful. Likewise, the monetary authority is assumed to defend the peg whenever the size of attack is insufficiently large. This means that each period it will have to defend against some attack; yet $a(\theta)$ is assumed to be independent of the past history of attacks. Again, this assumption appears to be rather strong; it would be interesting to know to what extent such features of the model are critical to the conclusions.

Nevertheless, the chapter represents a fundamental challenge to the way we think about multiple-equilibrium models, not just of currency attacks, but in a wide range of situations.

NOTES

1. See n. 3 below. Although Morris and Shin do not present the argument explicitly in this way, their argument essentially says that one can restrict attention *without loss of generality* to this class of strategies.
2. The indifference condition is just the condition $U(\hat{x}, \theta_{-\Delta}) = 0$ of the chapter, as $U(\hat{x}, \theta_{-\Delta})$ is defined to be the utility from attacking for a critical speculator in the cutoff speculation rule associated with $\hat{x}$.
3. Again we are restricting attention to cutoff rule equilibria. However this is without loss of generality: suppose it is true that there is a unique cutoff rule equilibrium at $\hat{x}$. If there were some other type of equilibrium, consider the lowest (infimum) x' (say, x') such that speculators do not attack with probability one; if this was below $\hat{x}$ then a speculator receiving the signal x' would be in a better position than the critical speculator in a cutoff rule at x' because of the fact that there are now additional speculators (by virtue of the fact that this is not a cutoff rule equilibrium), with higher signals than x' who attack, and this can only help the attack ('strategic complementarity', lemma 2, p. 246). Since the critical speculator in a cutoff rule at x' will be shown to have a positive utility from attacking, this is true *a fortiori* for the x' speculator in this other equilibrium, contradicting the fact that this speculator does not attack (or at least must be indifferent). So $x' \geq \hat{x}$. A symmetric argument establishes the highest x such that an attack takes place with positive probability is $\hat{x}$. Hence there can be no other equilibrium (this is just lemma 3, p. 248).
4. To be rather more precise, the standard deviation of the signal distribution, given θ, is $\sqrt{\epsilon\Delta}$, and so the speculator knows for ϵ small that the variance of the signal about θ is the same as the variance of θ about $\hat{x}$. Hence a successful attack, which requires roughly a fraction $a(\hat{x})$ of speculators to attack (i.e. a fraction $a(\hat{x})$ of signals to be below $\hat{x}$), will happen with probability $1 - a(\hat{x})$ – this simply follows from the symmetry of the normal distribution. Since the indifference condition

requires that this probability equal c (the cost of attacking), and $a' > 0$, the condition can be satisfied only at a single point. In fact this is what lemma ? states: the utility for the critical speculator from attacking as $\hat{x}$ is varied as slope $-a'(\hat{x})$.

5. Thus introducing further sources of non-uniqueness into the model may alter the conclusions substantially. Boonprakaikawe (1998) shows that in a formally similar model of bank runs with a monopoly bank, an analogous argument for uniqueness holds in the absence of common knowledge of the fundamental. With two banks competing for deposits, however, there may still be multiple equilibria. The cause is an externality operating between the banks: each bank's failure probability is increasing in the number of depositors attracted by the other bank. The lack of common knowledge of the fundamental does not remove the non-uniqueness owing to this externality.

6. A switch in equilibrium to a coordinated attack is modelled by a Poisson process.

REFERENCES

Boonprakaikawe, J. (1998). 'Unique Equilibrium Model of Bank Runs', MSc. dissertation, University of Warwick

Morris, S. and H. S. Shin (1998). 'Unique Equilibrium in a Model of Self-fulfilling Currency Attacks', *American Economic Review*, **88**: 587–97

Obstfeld, M. (1986). 'Rational and Self-fulfilling Balance of Payments Crises', *American Economic Review*, **76**: 72–81

Sutherland, A. (1997). 'Currency Crises and the Term Structure of Interest Rates', University of York, mimeo

Part Three

Contagion

8 Contagion: monsoonal effects, spillovers and jumps between multiple equilibria

PAUL MASSON

1 Introduction

Since the crisis in Mexico in late 1994 and early 1995, which was accompanied by speculative pressures in other countries of Latin America and elsewhere, there has been much discussion of contagion effects. Studies by Gerlach and Smets (1995); Sachs, Tornell, and Velasco (1996a); Valdés (1996); and Agénor and Aizenman (1997) present explanations of why a crisis in one country might trigger a crisis in another. Eichengreen, Rose and Wyplosz (1996), using data for 20 industrial countries from 1959–93, show that the occurrence of crises elsewhere increases the probability of a crisis occurring in a given country, after allowing for the standard set of macroeconomic fundamentals. They also attempt to identify what features of countries explain such contagion effects, finding that it is trade linkages, rather than similarity of macroeconomic fundamentals, that have the greatest explanatory power. We will follow them in defining 'exchange rate crises' broadly, to include not only devaluations but also successful defence of a peg that involves substantial increases in interest rates and losses of reserves.

The crisis in Thailand and other emerging market economies has once again raised the question of contagion effects. The Thai economy had for several years experienced a period of strong domestic demand associated with an appreciating real exchange rate and large current account deficits, as well as financial sector problems linked to over-exposure to a property market whose prices had fallen sharply. After long resisting pressures on the baht through measures that included capital controls and massive forward intervention, the Thai authorities were eventually forced to abandon the dollar exchange rate peg in July 1997. The depreciation (and the lead-up to it) were associated with pressures on the currencies of neighbouring countries (especially Indonesia, Malaysia and the Philippines) which also attempted to keep their exchange rates against the dollar in a narrow range.

265

These countries shared some features (including current account deficits) with Thailand and were quickly forced to accept more exchange rate flexibility, their currencies depreciating by about the same amount as the Thai baht. More curiously, Hong Kong and Singapore, with strong current account and fiscal positions, were also briefly exposed to downward pressure on their currencies, and Korea, which was spared for several months, succumbed to contagion effects in November. More generally, the currency turmoil seems to have triggered plunges in stock markets of the region and elsewhere.

Clearly there may be many reasons for expecting crises to be contemporaneous in time. First, they may be due to a common cause – for instance, policies undertaken by industrial countries which have similar effects on emerging markets. Second, a crisis in one emerging market may affect the macroeconomic fundamentals in other emerging markets – for instance, because a devaluation reduces the price competitiveness of other countries, or because lack of liquidity in one market leads financial intermediaries to liquidate other emerging market assets (Valdés, 1996). Third, a crisis in one country may conceivably trigger a crisis elsewhere for reasons unexplained by macroeconomic fundamentals, perhaps because it leads to shifts in market sentiment or changes the interpretation given to existing information (Banerjee, 1992; Bikchandani, Hirschleifer and Welch, 1992; Lee, 1997). For instance, a crisis might lead investors to reassess the fundamentals of other countries, even if they had not changed, or lead to a change in the risk-tolerance of investors.

In this chapter, we attempt to distinguish between these various reasons and to apply the term 'contagion' only to the third category, those that cannot be identified with observed changes in macroeconomic fundamentals. In contrast, the first category will be called 'monsoonal effects' (see Masson and Mussa, 1995), defined as major economic shifts in industrial countries that trigger crises in emerging markets. Though not primarily the fault of those countries' policies, the extent of their vulnerability will importantly be affected by their previous exposure to foreign currency borrowing, the size of government debt and problems in their banking system. The debt crisis in the early 1980s was to a substantial extent a common response to the sharp increase in interest rates in the USA relative to their very low levels (in real terms) of the late 1970s.[1] The appreciation of the US dollar against the yen in 1995–6 was an important factor contributing to the recent weakening of net exports of Southeast Asian countries. The second category is termed 'spillovers', rather than 'contagion', because it results from interdependence among developing countries themselves. A crisis in one country may have a substantial effect on the macroeconomic fundamentals of its neighbours. An example from advanced countries illustrates this point: the devaluations of several EMS currencies in 1992–3 made the parities of the remaining ones more fragile, since those countries' real effective exchange rates had appreciated.[2]

As defined here, pure contagion involves changes in expectations that are not related to changes in a country s macroeconomic fundamentals. It is most natural to think of this in a context where financial markets are subject to multiple equilibria, or self-fulfilling expectations. There is an extensive literature on exchange rate crises which involve multiple equilibria, but these models have so far been developed only for countries considered in isolation – for example, Obstfeld (1986, 1994); Cole and Kehoe (1996); Sachs, Tornell and Velasco (1996b); Jeanne (1997); Jeanne and Masson (1996).[3] However, by analogy to the literature on bank runs (Diamond and Dybvig, 1983), attacks on countries which involve a simultaneous move from a non-run to a run equilibrium seem to be relevant for recent experience in emerging market countries. It is argued here that our macro models need to be specified such that the relationship between fundamentals and currency crises allows for the possibility of multiple equilibria, as well as the monsoonal and spillover channels.

While such a model may not explain the timing of jumps between equilibria or of contagion, it could be consistent with various micro theories that explain how expectations are formed in a context of imperfect and asymmetric information (Banerjee, 1992; Bikchandani, Hirschleifer and Welch 1992; Lee, 1997). For instance, one view concerning contagion operating through changes in expectations for unchanged values of a country's fundamentals is that a crisis in another country constituted a 'wake-up call' (Goldstein, 1998). In this view, the true fundamentals were really poor, but investors did not realise this until problems elsewhere made it manifest – for instance, banking sector problems were quickly seen to be pervasive in East Asia after the devaluation of the Thai baht. It could further be argued that there was just a single (bad) equilibrium, but that the true fundamentals were at first incorrectly perceived to be good. However, the fact that an optimistic view about East Asian economies prevailed for so long (in the face of some reports of banking sector problems), the rapidity of the change in view and the suddenness and severity of the resulting crisis, all argue in favour of the multiple-equilibrium story (even if the appeal to unobservable fundamentals could conceivably make the two explanations observationally equivalent). It is also hard to explain without appeal to arbitrary shifts in sentiment why the lessons learned in Mexico in 1994–5 were so quickly forgotten.

A criticism of models with multiple equilibria or 'sunspots' is that they seem to disculpate policy makers from any blame for the speculative crises (Garber, 1996). However, this is not really the case. A clear implication of most such models is that multiple equilibria are possible only in a certain range for the fundamentals (Jeanne, 1997). An implication is that policy makers should try to ensure that they avoid that range – for instance, by reducing their exposure to short-maturity, foreign currency debt (Kehoe, 1997). Models with multiple equilibria, however, typically produce predictions concerning the vulnerability to contagion: only in certain ranges of the fundamentals and for certain parameter values are multiple equilibria possible.

The chapter then looks at some of the symptoms of monsoonal effects, spillovers and contagion. At least on the face of it, the first two factors do not seem to explain the coincidence of speculative pressures felt by a number of emerging market economies in two periods: end-1994–early 1995 (associated with the Mexican crisis), and the second half of 1997 and early 1998 (associated, at least initially, with a crisis in Thailand). It is therefore argued that contagion was, at least in part, the result of self-fulfilling shifts in sentiment.

2 Empirical Evidence

The phenomenon of the coincidence of speculative crises in a number of emerging markets is striking, and has been extensively discussed elsewhere so that no chronology or detailed analysis of the various crises will be presented here.[4] Suffice it to say that the exchange rate devaluation in Mexico in December 1994 and the pressures on and eventual depreciation of the Thai baht in 1997 quickly led to speculative pressures on other currencies. For instance, there is high correlation between the spike upward in December 1994 of Mexican Brady bond spreads with those of Argentina, Brazil, and the Philippines (figure 8.1).

As for Asian currency crises, it is harder to discern the coincidence of pressures in interest rates, since few have issued Brady bonds and domestic rates are subject to institutional differences and are hard to compare. However, the effect of the crises shows up in a striking co-movement of the US dollar exchange rates of Indonesia, Malaysia, the Philippines and Thailand after a long period of relative stability (figure 8.2). In this crisis, unlike the Mexican one where the effects of contagion (for example, on Argentina and Brazil) were successfully resisted, all the currencies affected experienced large devaluations. As a result, the spillover effects were compounded.

Figure 8.1   *Stripped yield spreads, selected Brady bonds, January*
1994–January 1998, basis points

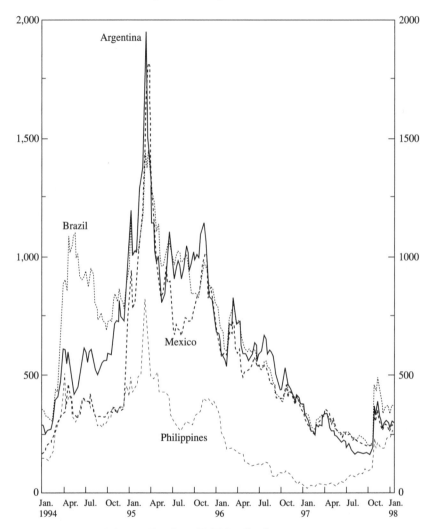

Sources: Reuters; Salomon Brothers, IMF Staff estimates.

This coincidence of speculative crises may have been caused by developments in industrial economies through monsoonal effects that involve
interest rates (and capital flows) and trade flows. For instance, the Mexican
crisis was preceded by an increase in US short-term rates beginning in
March 1994 (figure 8.3). Though this was a contributory factor to the

Figure 8.2   *US dollar per domestic currency unit, January 1994–January 1998[a]*
Indices: 1995 end-week 1 = 100

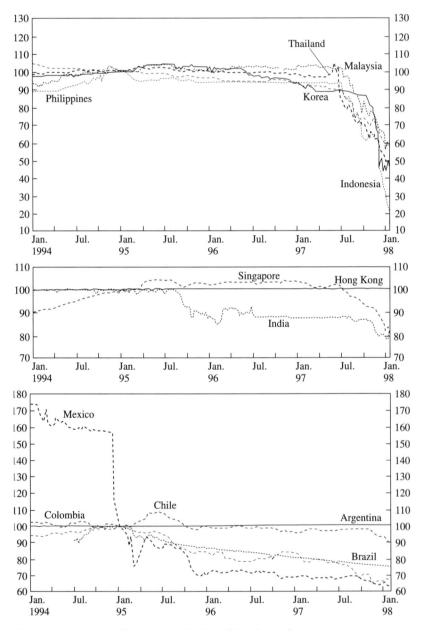

Note: [a] An increase indicates appreciation of the domestic currency.

Figure 8.3   *Mexican interest rates and foreign reserves and US interest rates,*
              January–December 1994

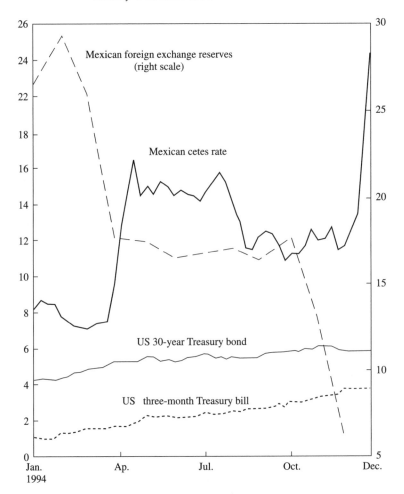

Sources: Bloomberg; IMF, *International Financial Statistics*.

crisis in Mexico, it does not seem likely that it can explain its timing, nor
the coincidence of crises elsewhere, which occurred not when the USA
raised interest rates, but shortly after Mexico devalued some nine months
later.

Similarly, trade linkages with industrial countries could contribute to
the existence of monsoonal effects on emerging markets. It is interesting in
that regard to examine the trade patterns of these economies. The recent

Table 8.1   *Selected Southeast Asia countries: exports to various country groups, 1996, mn US Dollars*

(Per cent of total exports within parenthesis)

| | | | Destination of exports | | |
| | | | Other Southeast Asia[a] | | |
Country	USA	Japan		Of which: Thailand	All countries
Indonesia	7,948	13,839	5,539[b]	854	48,059
	(16.5)	(28.8)	(11.5)	(1.8)	(100)
Malaysia	14,245	10,484	21,377	3,207	78,246
	(18.2)	(13.4)	(27.3)	(4.1)	(100)
Philippines	6,966	3,668	3,971[b]	780	20,543
	(33.9)	(17.9)	(13.6)	(3.8)	(100)
Singapore	23,062	10,254	31,908[c]	7,096	125,118[c]
	(18.4)	(8.2)	(25.5)	(5.7)	(100)
Thailand	10,026	9,373	10,240	—	55,789
	(18.0)	(16.8)	(18.4)		(100)

Notes: [a] Indonesia, Malaysia, the Philippines, Singapore, Thailand.
     [b] Exports to some countries estimated on the basis of previous year's figures.
     [c] Excluding Indonesia.
     — = Not available.
Source: IMF (1997c).

crises affecting Southeast Asian countries do seem consistent with some impact of the fluctuations of the yen/dollar rate, given the large extent of their trade with both the USA and Japan (table 8.1). Hence, pegging to a basket giving a dominant weight to the dollar led to a strong nominal (and real) effective appreciation when the dollar appreciated against the yen, which occurred over the period April 1995–July 1997 (figure 8.4). However, the timing of the major appreciation of the dollar against the yen predates the Southeast Asian exchange rate crisis by at least a year, and it also needs to be recognised that trade patterns differ substantially across countries in the region.

Spillover effects are another possible explanation for the coincidence of speculative attacks. However, table 8.1 shows that exports to Thailand constitute a very small proportion of exports from the other countries in the region, suggesting only a modest scope for spillover effects. Table 8.2 shows that the importance of Mexico for the other two largest Latin American economies is even smaller. Of course, as the Asian crisis spread the regional competitiveness effects became amplified. Nevertheless, an estimate of the

Figure 8.4   *Effective exchange rates and the Japanese yen per US dollar rate,*
              January 1992–January 1998
              Indices: January 1992 = 100

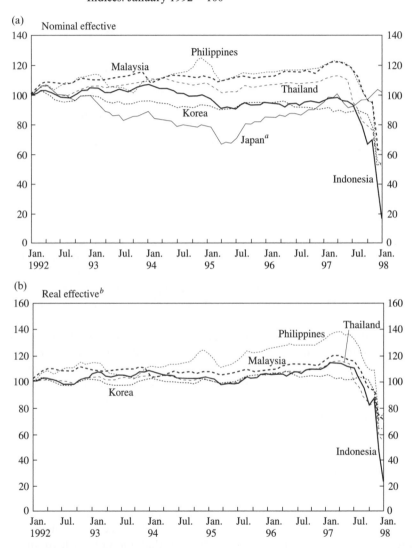

Notes: [a] Japanese yen per US dollar.
          [b] Based on relative consumer price indices.
Sources: IMF, *Information Notice System, International Financial Statistics*; IMF
           Staff calculations.

Table 8.2   *Selected Latin American countries: exports to various country groups, 1996, US dollars mn*

(Per cent of total exports within parenthesis)

	Destination of exports			
Country	USA	Japan	Mexico	All countries
Argentina	1,974	513	248	23,794
	(8.3)	(2.2)	(1.0)	(100)
Brazil	9,312	3,047	679	47,747
	(19.5)	(6.4)	(1.4)	(100)
Mexico	80,663	1,363	—	95,991
	(84.0)	(14)		(100)

Note: — = Not available.
Source: IMF (1997c).

loss of competitiveness, in each of the five Asian countries principally affected by the crisis is given in table 8.3, and this shows that until November, when the won started to depreciate significantly (relative to its modest rate of crawl), regional competitiveness spillovers were small. Furthermore, there was no reason to expect a crisis in Korea to be triggered through this channel.

This rough quantification therefore suggests that there may have been a role for pure contagion effects – that is, the simultaneous occurrence of crises which is not linked to changes in observed macroeconomic fundamentals. Section 3 therefore considers the ingredients of macro models that could produce multiple equilibria, jumps between which could be triggered by a crisis elsewhere.

3 Models with multiple equilibrium

In a companion study (Masson, 1998) a simple balance of payments model is developed which, for fundamentals in a certain range, can produce multiple equilibria. The mechanism that allows for self-fulfilling crises is a simple one: the cost of external borrowing depends on investors' assessments of the probability of devaluation or default, and the higher are those borrowing costs, the greater is the likelihood that a further negative shock (for example, to net exports) will push reserves below a threshold level, triggering a crisis. This model implies that such

Table 8.3   Selected Asian economies: real effective exchange rates[a], January 1997–March 1998

(January 1997 = 100)

	Korea		Indonesia		Malaysia		Philippines		Thailand	
	Actual	Adjusted[b]	Actual	Adjusted[b]	Actual	Adjusted[b]	Actual	Adjusted[b]	Actual	Adjusted[b]
1997 Jan.	100.0	100.0	100.0	100.0	100.0	100.0	100.0	100.0	100.0	100.0
Feb.	100.2	100.2	102.5	102.5	102.2	102.2	101.8	101.8	101.6	101.6
Mar.	97.1	97.1	102.8	102.8	103.3	103.3	103.0	103.0	102.6	102.6
Apr.	98.0	98.0	102.9	102.9	102.6	102.6	103.4	103.4	101.9	102.6
May	96.8	96.8	101.1	101.1	101.2	101.2	102.0	102.0	101.9	101.9
Jun.	96.8	96.8	100.1	100.1	99.8	99.8	101.7	101.7	101.3	101.3
Jul.	97.9	97.9	98.8	101.3	99.0	101.3	98.6	102.8	87.5	102.5
Aug.	99.5	99.5	91.4	103.2	95.0	103.5	93.8	104.6	85.1	105.0
Sep.	99.4	99.4	85.7	104.1	87.5	104.6	85.7	105.8	77.1	106.4
Oct.	99.2	100.0	74.1	104.5	81.0	105.5	81.4	106.6	75.8	107.6
Nov.	90.5	101.0	79.7	106.7	80.2	107.4	83.6	108.9	74.1	109.7
Dec.	66.0	104.2	60.7	112.2	75.6	112.4	81.0	113.4	67.4	114.5
1998 Jan.	60.6	108.0	33.5	115.4	67.7	116.9	72.6	116.3	59.1	118.7
Feb.	63.6	105.6	39.6	112.7	77.1	113.1	75.3	113.8	68.1	115.4
Mar.	71.3	106.7	38.1	113.2	77.5	112.8	80.0	114.2	75.7	116.2

Notes: [a]Partner country weights based on bilateral trade data for 1994–6
[b] Assumes constant bilateral US dollar exchange rate in the case of Indonesia, the Philippines and Thailand, a constant real bilateral exchange rate in the case of Korea and a constant rate of nominal depreciation against the US dollar (based on the average rate over the preceeding 12 months) in the case of Malaysia.

Source: IMF. *International Financial Statistics* and author's calculations.

multiple equilibria cannot occur if the 'fundamentals' of the economy are especially favourable, because even sharply higher interest rates cannot sufficiently worsen the balance of payments to produce a crisis. Conversely, for fundamentals that are sufficiently bad a crisis is virtually inevitable. Only for a middle range is there the possibility of multiple equilibria: a crisis may or may not be triggered, depending on investor sentiment. There are six key factors that influence the possibility of multiple equilibria in this model:

(1) a country's external debt/GDP ratio

(2) the variance of shocks to the trade balance

(3) the level of world interest rates

(4) the expected value of the trade balance

(5) foreign exchange reserves/GDP

(6) expected devaluation size.

Factors (3), (4), and (6) incorporate monsoonal and spillover channels, through the usual competitiveness effects and the cost of servicing debt.

Back-of-the-envelope calculations reported in Masson (1998) suggest that many emerging market countries had fundamentals that put them in the multiple-equilibria region where self-fulfilling crises, perhaps triggered by contagion, were possible. However, the model calculations do not seem to have much discriminatory power with respect to identifying those countries that experienced crises from those that did not – especially as the crises in emerging markets became more and more generalised. It is therefore important to consider more complicated models with a richer set of channels through which expectations of a crisis can be self-fulfilling, or can have reinforced feedback effects. These include rollover risk, banking sector problems and the existence of risk-averse investors.

In particular, the fear of non-rollover next period could trigger higher interest rates today, and even the refusal to roll over debt today (Sachs, 1984). With heterogeneous agents, the probability that other agents will not roll over debt will influence any given agent's decision. As in bank runs, the expectation of what others will do is crucial to the possibility of self-fulfilling balance of payments crises, and shifts in investors' assessments of 'market' sentiment could trigger movements between equilibria. These factors may expand the region in which multiple equilibria were possible, and also amplify the potential effect of crises on other countries.

A weak banking system may also contribute to vulnerability to balance of payments crises (Kaminsky and Reinhart, 1996). Banks are typically exposed to interest rate risk and currency risk: if the central bank resists a depreciation by raising interest rates, banks suffer because their liabilities are of shorter maturity than their assets, while devaluation hurts them if they have net foreign currency exposure. The first factor may make crises more likely because speculators will know that central banks will be less likely to defend the currency, while the second may make the severity of the crisis greater.

The simple model described above assumed risk-neutral investors. However, this is unrealistic, and a more satisfactory approach would allow for the fact that they need to be compensated for greater riskiness in emerging markets than in advanced economies. Moreover, the degree of perceived riskiness may also vary over time, as well as the degree of aversion to risk. Flood and Marion (1996) show that changes in views on riskiness can be self-fulfilling, that is, an increase in expected risk can raise the actual variability of asset prices, the exchange rate in particular. Such riskiness effects could be the result of contagion if they were triggered by crises in other countries.

4 Conclusions

This chapter has attempted first to sort through various explanations for what has been called 'contagion', while retaining that term for only a narrow set of effects. In particular, pure contagion is associated here with multiple equilibria, and it is suggested that multiple equilibria are possible in simple balance of payments models where borrowing costs depend on investors' expectations of a crisis. Some back-of-the-envelope calculations suggest that spillover and monsoonal effects are insufficient to explain the coincidence of crises at the time of attacks on Mexico in 1994–5 and Thailand in 1997–8. However, no actual tests for contagion itself are presented here.

With refinements, such a model may have some use in constructing early-warning indicators of balance of payments crises (see, for instance, Kaminsky, Lizondo, and Reinhart, 1997). The value for the composite fundamental can be used to identify countries that may be vulnerable to multiple equilibria. It needs to be recognised, however, that the existence of contagion as defined here implies that early warning of crises may be difficult, since they are triggered by stochastic events that are inherently unpredictable.

Actually estimating the models with multiple equilibria would also need to consider the probability structure of jumps between equilibria (as in Jeanne and Masson, 1998), and whether there was evidence that the probability of jumps was related to crises, or at least speculative pressures, in other countries. This would constitute a test for the existence of contagion, and may be the subject of another study.

NOTES

This chapter is an abridged version of Masson (1998). The subject of the original paper was inspired by conversations with Michael Mussa, who coined the term 'monsoonal effects', and has benefited from comments by Mario Bléjer, Eduardo Borensztein, Barry Eichengreen, Matthew Fisher, Bob Flood, Peter Isard, Olivier Jeanne, Tom Krueger, Marcus Miller and Charles Wyplosz. I am grateful to Matthew Olson for research assistance. The views expressed are those of the author and do not represent those of the IMF or other official institutions.

1. However, over-borrowing for non-productive uses was also a large contributor to the debt crisis in many developing countries.
2. The crisis itself had an important monsoonal component owing to German unification, however, as the high interest rates in Germany and the tendency for the Deutsche mark to appreciate put pressures on the ERM parities of many European currencies. Drazen (1998) points to other spillovers among these countries, which he calls 'political contagion'.
3. Eaton and Gersovitz (1988) show that the existence of public debt (which needs to be serviced through taxation) and of decentralised private investment decisions can lead to an equilibrium with no investment as well as the social optimum, with positive investment.
4. See, for instance, IMF (1997a, 1997b) and Corsetti, Pesenti and Roubini (1998).

REFERENCES

Agénor, P.R., and J. Aizenman (1997). 'Contagion and Volatility with Imperfect Credit Markets', *NBER Working Paper*, **6080**

Banerjee, A. (1992). 'A Simple Model of Herd Behavior', *Quarterly Journal of Economics*, **107**

Bikchandani, S., D. Hirshleifer and I. Welch (1992). 'A Theory of Fads, Fashion, Custom, and Cultural Change as Informational Cascades', *Journal of Political Economy*, **100 (5)**

Cole, H., and T. J. Kehoe (1996). 'A Self-fulfilling Model of Mexico's 1994–5 Debt Crisis', *Journal of International Economics*, **41**

Corsetti, G., P. Pesenti and N. Roubini (1998). 'What Caused the Asian Currency Crisis?', paper presented to a CEPR/World Bank Conference, 'Financial Crises: Contagion and Market Volatility' (London) (8–9 May)

Diamond, D., and P. Dybvig (1983). 'Bank Runs, Deposit Insurance, and Liquidity', *Journal of Political Economy*, **91**: 401–19

Drazen, A. (1998) 'Political Contagion in Currency Crises', University of Maryland, mimeo

Eaton, J., and M. Gersovitz (1988). 'Country Risk and the Organization of International Capital Transfer', in J.B. de Macedo and R. Findlay (eds.), *Debt, Growth and Stabilization. Essays in Memory of Carlos F. Diaz-Alejandro,* Oxford: Basil Blackwell

Eichengreen, B., A. Rose and C. Wyplosz (1996). 'Contagious Currency Crises', *NBER Working Paper,* **5681**

Flood, R. and N. Marion (1996). 'Speculative Attacks: Fundamentals and Self-fulfilling Prophecies', *NBER Working Paper,* **5789**

Garber, P. (1996). 'Comment on Krugman', *NBER Macroeconomics Annual 1996,* Cambridge, Mass.: MIT Press

Gerlach, S., and F. Smets (1995). 'Contagious Speculative Attacks', *European Journal of Political Economy,* **11**: 1–13

Goldstein, M. (1998). 'The Asian Financial Crises: Causes, Cures, and Systemic Implications', *Policy Analyses in International Economics,* **55**, Washington, DC: Institute for International Economics

IMF (1997a). *International Capital Markets: Developments, Prospects, and Key Policy Issues,* Washington, DC: International Monetary Fund

(1997b). *World Economic Outlook: Interim Assessment,* Washington, DC: International Monetary Fund

(1997c). *Direction of Trade Statistics Yearbook: 1990–96,* Washington, DC: International Monetary Fund

Jeanne, O. (1997). 'Are Currency Crises Self-fulfilling? A Test', *Journal of International Economics,* **43**

Jeanne, O. and P. Masson (1996). 'Was the French Franc Crisis a Sunspot Equilibrium?', Washington, DC: International Monetary Fund, mimeo

(1998). 'Currency Crises, Sunspots and Markov-switching Regimes', Washington, DC: International Monetary Fund, mimeo

Kaminsky, G. and C. Reinhart (1996). 'The Twin Crises: The Causes of Banking and Balance-of-payments Problems', Washington, DC: International Monetary Fund, mimeo

Kaminsky, G., S. Lizondo and C. Reinhart (1997). 'Leading Indicators of Currency Crises', *IMF Working Paper* **WP/97/79**

Kehoe, T. (1997). 'Modeling Mexico's 1994–95 Debt Crisis', paper presented at a CEPR/ESRC/GEI conference on 'The Origins and Management of Financial Crises' (Cambridge, UK) (11–12 July)

Lee, I. H. (1997). 'Market Crashes and Informational Avalanches', paper presented at a CEPR/ESRC/GEI conference on The Origins and Management of Financial Crises' (Cambridge, UK) (11–12 July)

Masson, P. (1998). 'Contagion: Macro Models with Multiple Equilibria', Washington, DC: International Monetary Fund, mimeo

Masson, P. and M. Mussa (1995). 'The Role of the Fund: Financing and its Interactions with Adjustment and Surveillance', *Pamphlet Series,* **50**, Washington, DC: International Monetary Fund

Obstfeld, M. (1986). 'Rational and Self-fulfilling Balance-of-payments Crises', *American Economic Review,* **76**: 72–81

(1994). 'The Logic of Currency Crises', *Cahiers économiques et monétaires* (Banque de France), **43**: 189–213

Sachs, J. (1984). 'Theoretical Issues in International Borrowing', *Princeton Studies in International Finance*, **54**

Sachs, J., A. Tornell and A. Velasco (1996a). 'Financial Crises in Emerging Markets: The Lessons from 1995', *NBER Working Paper*, **5576**

(1996b). 'The Mexican Peso Crisis: Sudden Death or Death Foretold?', *Journal of International Economics*, **41**

Valdés, R. (1996). 'Emerging Market Contagion: Evidence and Theory', MIT, mimeo

Discussion
Axel A. Weber

I enjoyed reading chapter 8 because it presents a systematic and straightforward approach to modelling contagion in a currency crisis. The chapter stands in the tradition of the so-called 'second-generation' currency-crisis models, which originate in the work of Flood and Garber (1984) and Obstfeld (1986). In these models a self-propagating and potentially self-fulfilling speculative attack may occur even if economic fundamentals are consistent with the maintenance of a given exchange rate peg. The outbreak of the speculative attack typically involves multiple equilibria and the jump between a non-attack equilibrium and an attack equilibrium is driven by market sentiment rather than economic fundamentals. It has been stressed that such self-fulfilling speculative attacks may also have contagious effects on other currencies; for the precise modelling of these international spillovers through trade links or foreign debt accumulation, see Gerlach and Smets (1995), Buiter, Corsetti and Pesenti (1995, 1996), or Eichengreen, Rose and Wyplosz (1995).

Like the papers mentioned above, the present chapter views contagion models as a specific variant of the model of purely speculative currency crises. The key point about contagious currency crises is that the sudden swings in market expectations about future exchange rate movements are driven by the occurrence of a speculative attack in another emerging market economy. For contagion effects to work, both economies must have close economic links and/or similar economic structures. But the chapter rightly stresses that such interdependencies exist irrespective of speculative attacks, and it is important to distinguish between contagion and the other forms of interdependence. For example, in Masson's terminology 'monsoonal effects' characterise the exchange rate consequences of economic disturbances in industrialised economies for emerging markets, and these may be transmitted through capital flows and/or trade flows. Other forms of fundamental interdependencies are 'regional spillovers', which refer to the exchange rate effects of events in other emerging market economies, again transmitted through direct trade links or via trade competition on third markets. Finally, purely speculative exchange rate movements are viewed as a 'residual' and contagion effects are given if these residuals are causally related across emerging market economies.

How may this concept of contagion be implemented empirically? The chapter uses the term 'contagion' if the probability of an exchange rate change in one country is a (positive) function of the probability of an exchange rate change in another. Given the focus on devaluation probabilities it is obvious that a natural framework for testing this specific concept of contagion is Bayesian econometrics. In addition, given the multi-country aspect of contagion it is clear that such interdependencies can only be captured in a cross-country framework. However, the residual nature of contagion makes it very difficult – if not impossible – to empirically test for its existence.

Whilst the chapter presents no formal contagion tests, section 2 (p. 268) nevertheless presents an empirical assessment of the Asian currency crisis by displaying some graphs and tables. Figure 8.2 shows the striking co-movement between the Asian exchange rates. It is argued that these parallel exchange rate movements cannot be the result of strong monsoonal effects through either trade or capital flows, since both factors were of minor importance during the Asian crisis. The chapter also rules out regional spillovers through direct trade interaction or trade competitiveness on third markets as an important contributing factor. Consequently, this leaves contagion as the only possible explanation for the Asian currency crisis. Whilst I may agree with this general judgement, I think that the informal evidence provided is not sufficiently convincing to justify this statement.

Section 3 of the chapter provides useful insights about the potential contribution of a broad set of economic fundamentals and pure speculation to a currency crisis in the context of a model with multiple equilibria. To understand these links, let me briefly review the formal model is now part of a companion paper (Masson, 1998). At the core of that model which are two key assumptions, which generate multiple equilibria and the possibility of sudden jumps between them.

First, Masson explicitly models interest rate risks. The domestic interest rate (r_t) is linked to the exogenous foreign interest rate (r^*) through uncovered interest rate parity (UIP). Exchange rate expectations are formed under two potential policy scenarios: with probability π_t the monetary authority is expected to realign the exchange rate (S_t) to a new

$S_{t+1}^d \equiv S_t(1 + \delta)$ level and with probability $1 - \pi_t$ to peg it at the current level S_t. Formally this implies:

$$r^* = r_t - \pi_t \ln(S_{t+1}^d/S_t) - (1 - \pi_t)\ln(S_t/S_t) = r_t - \pi_t \ln(1 + \delta)$$
$$\cong r_t - \pi_t \delta \qquad (D8.1)$$

where $\pi_t \delta$ is the probability of a devaluation multiplied by the expected devaluation size. Secondly, Masson (1998) endogenises the probability of a crisis by linking it to the probability that future foreign exchange reserves (R_{t+1}) will fall below a positive critical threshold $(\bar{R})$, which formally implies

$$\pi_t = \text{Prob}_t[(R_{t+1} - \bar{R}) < 0].$$

Combined with a financing constraint through the current account equation

$$R_{t+1} - R_t = T_{t+1} - (r^* + \pi_t \delta)D$$

where T_t is the trade balance and D_t is the accummulated external indebtedness incurred in domestic currency, an expression for the probability of a crisis is obtained such that:

$$\pi_t = \text{Prob}_t[T_{t+1} - r^*D + (R_{t+1} - \bar{R}) < \pi_t \delta D]. \qquad (D8.2)$$

In this simple model an increase in the probability of a speculative attack results from:

• increasing trade deficits (or decreasing trade surpluses)

• increasing world interest rates

• increasing foreign debt

• an increase in the expected devaluation size

• a decrease in international reserves.

The first two of these effects incorporate monsoonal and spillover channels through the usual competitiveness effects and the costs of saving debt. Purely speculative effects become obvious when considering the possibility of multiple equilibria, which may arise because the RHS and LHS of (D8.2) depend on π_t.[1]

Secondly, in order to come to grips with contagion effects, Masson (1998) proposes a simple extension of the above single-country model to a multi-country setting. By endogenising the trade balance and assuming that future trade depends on the expected trade-weighted real exchange rate it is possible to show that a change in the probability of a devaluation in the country under study depends, among other things, on the potential occurrence of a devaluation in any of the remaining countries. The nice feature of this extended model is that although contagion still triggers a crisis through its capital account effects, these can be traced back to a mechanism which works through trade channels. Bilateral trade weights thus matter for the strength of the contagion effects between the emerging market economies. This straightforward approach to modelling the typical 'contagion-through-trade' story provides a nice basis for empirical work on the role of economic interdependence during currency crises, and empirical papers such as Rose and Glick in chapter 9 in this volume present compelling evidence on the relevance of this interdependence for the Asian currency crisis.

NOTE
1. More formally, what is required for multiple equilibria is that the dependence of Prob($\bullet$) on π be non-linear, which it will be if the shocks to the trade balance are assumed to have a bell-shaped function. In this case the cumulative probability function has an S-shape. Alternatively one could make Prob($\bullet$) a rectangular distribution and allow δ to depend in a non-linear manner on the shocks to the system.

REFERENCES
Buiter, W., G. Corsetti and P. Pesenti (1995). 'Interpreting the ERM Crisis: Country-specific and Systemic Issues', mimeo

(1996). 'A Centre–Periphery Model of Monetary Coordination and Exchange Rate Crisis', mimeo

Eichengreen, B., A. Rose and C. Wyplosz (1995). 'Contagious Speculative Attacks', *CEPR Discussion Paper*, **1453**

Flood, R. P. and P. Garber (1984). 'Gold Monetization and Gold Discipline', *Journal of Political Economy* **92**: 90–107

Gerlach, S. and F. Smets (1995). 'Contagious Speculative Attacks', *European Journal of Political Economy* **11**: 1–13

Glick, R. and A. Rose (1999). 'Contagion and Trade: Why are currency crises regional?', chapter 9 in this volume

Masson, P. (1998). 'Monsoon Effects, Spillovers, and Contagion', IMF Working Paper, *WP/98/142* (September)

Obstfeld, M. (1986). 'Rational and Self-fulfilling Balance-of-payments Crises', *American Economic Review* **76**: 72–81

9 Contagion and trade: why are currency crises regional?

REUVEN GLICK AND ANDREW K. ROSE

1 Introduction

The 'Asian flu' of 1997–8, the Mexican meltdown and 'Tequila hangover' of 1994–5, and the European Monetary System (EMS) crisis of 1992–3 are three samples of speculative attacks on fixed exchange rate regimes. These currency crises generally involved countries in the same region. Once a country had suffered a speculative attack – Thailand in 1997, Mexico in 1994, Finland in 1992 – other countries in the same region were disproportionately likely to be attacked themselves.

Why? One explanation is that currency crises tend to spread through a region because countries are linked by trade, and trade tends to be regional.[1] Once Thailand floated the baht, its main trade competitors (for example, Malaysia and Indonesia) were suddenly at a competitive disadvantage, and so were themselves likely to be attacked. The spread of currency crises thus reflects international trade patterns: countries that trade and compete with the targets of speculative attacks are themselves likely to be attacked.

Prima facie, then, trade linkages seem like an obvious place to look for a regional explanation of currency crises. But most economists think about currency crises using variants of two standard models of speculative attacks. The 'first-generation' models of, for example, Krugman (1979) direct attention to inconsistencies between an exchange rate commitment and domestic economic fundamentals such as an underlying excess creation of domestic credit, typically prompted by a fiscal imbalance. The 'second-generation' models of, for example, Obstfeld (1986) view currency crises as shifts between different monetary policy equilibria in response to self-fulfilling speculative attacks. What is common to both classes of models is their emphasis on macroeconomic and financial fundamentals as determinants of currency crises. But macroeconomic phenomena do not tend to be regional – that is, countries in the same region do not necessarily exhibit similar macroeconomic features. Thus, from the perspective of most speculative-attack models, it is hard to understand why currency crises tend to be regionally clustered, at least without an extra ingredient explaining why the relevant macro fundamentals are intra-regionally correlated.[2]

In this chapter we argue that trade is indeed an important channel for contagion empirically, above and beyond macroeconomic and financial influences. Most importantly, it demonstrates that trade links help explain the intensity as well as the incidence of currency crises as captured by measures of exchange rate pressure. We focus on explaining the pattern of contagion across countries for five different currency crisis episodes: the breakdown of the Bretton Woods system in 1971, the collapse of the Smithsonian Agreement in 1973, the EMS crisis of 1992–3, the Mexican meltdown and the 'Tequila effect' of 1994–5, and the 'Asian flu' of 1997–8. We ask why some countries were hit during each of these episodes of currency instability, while others were not.

Our analysis ignores a number of related issues. For instance, in trying to model 'contagion' in currency crises, we do not rule out the possibility of (regional) shocks common to a number of countries, nor the possibility of contagion spreading through non-trade-related channels.[3] Moreover, we do not attempt to study the timing of currency crises. We *do* show that, given the occurrence of a currency crisis, the incidence and intensity of speculative attacks across countries is linked to the importance of international trade linkages. That is, currency crises spread along the lines of trade linkages, after accounting for the effects of macroeconomic and financial factors. This linkage is intuitive, economically significant, statistically robust, and important in understanding the regional nature of speculative attacks.

Section 2 motivates the analysis by discussing the regional nature of three recent waves of speculative attacks. This is followed by section 3, considering the possible channels of contagion that provide a framework for our analysis. Our methodology and data are discussed in section 4. Section 5 presents empirical results on the incidence of currency attacks; results concerning the intensity of attacks follow in section 6. The chapter ends with a brief conclusion.

2 The regional nature of currency crises

The last decade has witnessed three important currency crises. In the autumn of 1992, a wave of speculative attacks hit the EMS and its periphery. Before the end of the year, five countries (Finland, the UK, Italy, Sweden and Norway) had floated their currencies. Despite attempts by a number of countries to remain in the EMS with the assistance of devaluations (by Spain, Portugal and Ireland), the system was unsalvageable. The bands of the EMS were widened to ±15 per cent in August 1993. Eichengreen and Wyplosz (1993) provide a well known review of the EMS crisis.

The Mexican peso was attacked in late 1994 and floated shortly after an unsuccessful devaluation. Speculative attacks on other Latin American countries occurred immediately. The most prominent targets of the 'Tequila hangover' were Latin American countries, especially Argentina and Brazil, but also including Peru and Venezuela. Not all Latin countries were attacked – Chile being the most visible exception – and not all economies attacked were in Latin America (Thailand, Hong Kong, the Philippines and Hungary also suffered speculative attacks). While there were few devaluations, the attacks were not without effect. Argentine macroeconomic policy, in particular, tightened dramatically, precipitating a sharp recession. Sachs, Tornell and Velasco (1996) provide one of many summaries of the Mexican crisis and its aftermath.

The 'Asian flu' began with continued attacks on Thailand in the late spring of 1997 and continued with flotation of the baht in early July 1997. Within days, speculators had attacked Malaysia, the Philippines and Indonesia. Hong Kong and Korea were attacked somewhat later on; the crisis then spread across the Pacific to Chile and Brazil. The effects of 'Bahtulism' linger on as this chapter is being written; Alba et al. (chapter 1 in this volume) and Corsetti, Pesenti and Roubini (chapter 4 in this volume) provide exhaustive surveys.

All three waves of attacks were largely regional phenomena.[4] Once a country had suffered a speculative attack – Thailand in 1997, Mexico in 1994, Finland in 1992 – other countries in the same region were disproportionately likely to be attacked themselves.

3 Channels of contagion

For the purposes of this study, we think of a currency crisis as being 'contagious' if it spreads from the initial target(s), for whatever reason. There are three different types of explanation for why contagion spreads:[5]

- The first relies on *macroeconomic or financial similarity*. A crisis may spread from the initial target to another if the two countries share various economic features, making them equally vulnerable to attack. The work of Sachs, Tornell and Velasco (1996) can be viewed in this light. Sachs *et al.* show that three intuitively reasonable fundamentals – real exchange rate over-valuation, weakness in the banking system and low international reserves (relative to broad money) – can explain half the cross-country variation in a crisis index, itself a weighted average of exchange rate depreciation and reserve losses. They use data for 20 developing countries (DCs) in late 1994 and early 1995. Tornell (1998) extends this analysis to include the Asia crisis.[6] Currency crises may be regional if macroeconomic features of economies tend to be regional.

• A second view is that crises spread *via trade links across countries.* For example, a devaluation in one country adversely affects the international competitiveness of other countries, in the presence of short-run nominal rigidities. Those trade competitors most adversely affected by the devaluation are likely to be attacked next. Gerlach and Smets (1994) and Corsetti *et al.* (1998) formalise this reasoning; Huh and Kasa (1997) provide related analysis. In this way, a currency crisis that hits one country (for whatever reason) may be expected to spread to its trading partners.[7] Since trade patterns are strongly negatively affected by distance, currency crises will tend to be regional.

• A third explanation of contagion focuses on *cross-country financial links.* For example, financial problems and illiquidity in one market may force financial intermediaries to liquidate assets in other markets. Goldfajn and Valdés (1997) analyse the interaction of banking and currency crises via this channel. In this view, currency crises will be regional if the pattern of cross-border asset holdings are concentrated regionally.[8]

These different explanations are not mutually exclusive. Major trading partners are not always attacked during currency crises. Macroeconomic and financial influences are certainly not irrelevant. Ultimately determining the relative roles of the different channels of contagion is an empirical exercise.

The limited availability of data on bilateral cross-country asset holdings, particularly bank claims, precludes testing the role of financial market links. However, Eichengreen and Rose (1998) found both 'macroeconomic' and 'trade' channels of transmission to be empirically relevant in a large quarterly panel of post–1959 industrial country data: trade effects dominated. It is not clear *a priori* which of these mechanisms for contagion, if any, might be present in the data we examine. For this reason, we try to account for both in our empirical work.

4 Methodology

Our objective in this chapter is to demonstrate that trade provides an important channel for contagion above and beyond macroeconomic and financial similarities. As a result, we focus on the incidence and intensity of currency crises *across countries*. We ask why some countries are hit during certain episodes of currency instability, while others are not.

4.1 Empirical strategy

Our strategy keys off the 'first victim' in a given currency crisis episode. A country is attacked for some reason. We do not take a stance one way or another on whether this initial attack is warranted by bad fundamentals (as would be true in a first-generation model) or is the result of a self-fulfilling attack (consistent with a second-generation model). Instead, given the incidence of the initial attack (for example, Mexico in 1994, Thailand in 1997), we ask how the crisis spreads from 'ground zero'. Were the subsequent targets closely linked by international trade to the first victim? Do they share macroeconomic similarities? We answer this by estimating a crosscountry relationship for each crisis episode which compares the incidence of crises across countries with a measure of each other country's trade linkage with the first crisis victim as well as relevant macroeconomic variables. We interpret evidence in favour of the first hypothesis as indicating the importance of the trade channel of contagion.

Clearly we do not deal with a number of related and important issues. We assume that there is contagion, and do not test for its presence. We do not attempt to explain the timing of currency crises.[9] Finally, we do not ask why some crises become contagious and spread while others do not.

Our estimation framework is of the form:

$$Crisis_i = \varphi Trade_i + \lambda M_i + \epsilon_i$$

where $Crisis_i$ is an indicator variable of crisis victims which is initially defined as unity if country i was attacked in a given episode, and zero if the country was not attacked; $Trade_i$ is a measure of trade linkage between country i and ground zero; M_i is a set of macroeconomic control regressors; λ is the corresponding vector of nuisance coefficients; and ϵ is a normally distributed disturbance representing a host of omitted influences which affect the probability of a currency crisis.

We estimate this binary Probit equation across countries via maximum likelihood. The null hypothesis of interest is H_0: $\varphi = 0$. We interpret evidence against the null as being consistent with a trade-contagion effect.

We also use a different set of regressands, involving more quantitative crisis indicators, to measure exchange market intensity. When the regressand is a continuous indicator of exchange market intensity, we estimate this cross-country equation by OLS.

4.2 Data set

We use cross-sectional data from five different episodes of important and widespread currency instability. These are: (1) the breakdown of the Bretton Woods system in the spring of 1971; (2) the collapse of the Smithsonian Agreement in the late winter of 1973; (3) the EMS Crisis of 1992–3; (4) the Mexican meltdown and the 'Tequila effect' of 1994–5; and (5) the 'Asian flu' of 1997–8. Our data set includes data from 161 countries, many of which were directly involved in *none* of the five episodes.[10]

Making our work operational entails: (a) measuring currency crises; (b) measuring the importance of trade between the 'first victim' and country i; and (c) measuring the relevant macroeconomic and financial control variables. We now deal with these tasks in order.

4.3 Currency crises

To construct our simple binary indicator regressand, it is relatively easy to determine crisis victims from journalistic and academic histories of the various episodes (we rely on *The Financial Times*, in particular). Our list of crisis countries attacked during each episode is included in appendix table 9A.1 (p. 301).[11]

Table 9A.1 also lists the 'ground-zero' countries first attacked. For some periods 'ground zero' is relatively straightforward (Mexico in 1994, Thailand in 1997). For others, it is more arguable. In 1971 and 1973 we consider Germany to be ground zero. A case can be made that the USA should be ground zero for the 1971 and 1973 episodes. However, since the US dollar was the key currency of the international monetary system, the change in the value of the dollar during these periods can be interpreted more as a common shock. *A priori*, we choose to rule out such a common shock when testing for contagion effects transmitted through the trade channel. The 1992 crisis is more complex still. We think of the Finnish flotation as being the first important incident (making Finland 'ground zero'), but one can make a case for Italy (which began to depreciate immediately following the Danish referendum) or Germany because of the

Table 9.1   *Regional distribution of currency crises, 1971–1997*

		Americas	Europe	Asia	Africa	Total
1971	No crisis	27	8	31	41	107
	Crisis	1	16	2	0	19
	Total	28	24	33	41	126
	Test for independence $\chi^2(3) = 62$.					
1973	No crisis	27	9	32	41	109
	Crisis	1	15	3	0	19
	Total	28	24	35	42	128
	Test for independence $\chi^2(3) = 54$.					
1992	No crisis	28	15	37	41	121
	Crisis	0	10	0	0	10
	Total	31	25	37	41	131
	Test for independence $\chi^2(3) = 46$.					
1994	No crisis	22	30	39	40	131
	Crisis	6	1	4	0	11
	Total	28	31	43	40	142
	Test for independence $\chi^2(3) = 12$.					
1997	No crisis	25	29	35	38	127
	Crisis	3	3	9	1	16
	Total	28	32	44	39	143
	Test for independence $\chi^2(3) = 7$.					

aftermath of Unification (though as the centre of the EMS, German shocks are common).[12]

The five waves of currency crises we examine all appear to have a strongly regional nature. Table 9.1 is a series of cross-tabulations of crisis and non-crisis countries in our five episodes grouped into four regions. The chi-squared tests of independence confirm that currency crises appear to be regional.

4.4 Trade linkages

Once our 'ground-zero' country has been designated, we need to be able to quantify the importance of international trade links between it and other countries. We focus on the degree to which ground zero competes with each other country in foreign export markets. Our default measure of trade competition between country 0 and each country i in all foreign (third-country) export markets k is

$$Trade_i \equiv \Sigma_k \{[(x_{0k} + x_{ik})/(x_{0.} + x_{i.})] \cdot [1 - |(x_{ik} - x_{0k})|/(x_{ik} + x_{0k})]\}$$

where x_{ik} denotes aggregate bilateral exports from country i to k ($k \neq i$, 0) and $x_{i.}$ denotes aggregate bilateral exports from country i (i.e. $\Sigma_k x_{ik}$). This index is a weighted average of the mutual importance of exports from countries 0 and i to each country k. The mutual importance of exports to country k is defined to be greatest when it is an export market of equal importance to both 0 and i, as measured by bilateral export levels. The weights are proportional to the importance of bilateral exports of countries 0 and i to country k relative to their combined aggregate trade. Higher values of $Trade_i$ denote greater trade competition between 0 and i in foreign export markets.[13]

This is clearly an imperfect measure of the importance of trade linkages between country i and 'ground zero'. It relies on actual rather than potential trade, and aggregate data. It ignores direct trade between the two countries; imports are also ignored. Countries of vastly different size are a potential problem, and cascading effects are ignored.[14]

We have computed a number of different perturbations to our benchmark measure, and found that our trade measures are relatively insensitive to the exact way we measure the trade linkage. For example, we have calculated a measure of trade linkages which uses trade shares as our measure of competition in foreign export markets, so as to adjust for the varying size of countries:

$$Tradeshare_i \equiv \Sigma_k \{[(x_{0k} + x_{ik})/(x_{0.} + x_{i.})] \cdot$$
$$[1 - |\{(x_{0k}/x_{0.}) - (x_{ik}/x_{i.})\}|/\{(x_{0k}/x_{0.}) + (x_{ik}/x_{i.})\}]\}.$$

We check extensively for the sensitivity our results to ensure that our results do not depend on the exact measure of trade linkage.[15]

We computed our trade measures for our different episodes using annual data for the relevant crisis year taken from the IMF's *Direction of Trade* data set.[16] The rankings of the top 20 trade competitors of 'ground zero', – i.e. the 'first victim', for each episode are tabulated (by ranking of '$Trade_i$') in table 9A.2 (p. 302), and seem sensible. For instance, the most important export competitors for Finland in 1992 are Norway and Denmark; in 1997 all of Thailand's top 10 trade competitors and 16 of its top 20 trade competitors were located in Asia.[17] But some of the competitors are not intuitive. For instance, some countries enter the rankings that are probably not direct trade competitors (for example, OPEC countries); this is an artifact of the aggregate nature of our data.

4.5 Macroeconomic controls

Our objective is to use a variety of different macroeconomic controls to account for the standard determinants of currency crises dictated by first- and second-generation models. We do this so that our trade linkage variable picks up the effects of currency crises abroad that spill over because of trade – that is, *after* taking account of macroeconomic and financial imbalances that might lead to a currency crisis.

Our controls include the annual growth rate of domestic credit (*IFS* line 32); the government budget as a percentage of GDP (a surplus being positive, *IFS* line 80 over line 99b); the current account as a percentage of GDP (*IFS* line 78ald multiplied by line rf in the numerator); the growth rate of real GDP (*IFS* line 99b.r); the ratio of M2 to international reserves (*IFS* lines 34 + 35 multiplied by line rf over line11.d) and domestic CPI inflation (*IFS* line 64); and the degree of currency under-valuation.[18] These variables are suggested by a variety of different models of speculative attacks (as discussed in Eichengreen, Rose and Wyplosz, 1995) which can be viewed as primitive determinants of vulnerability to speculative pressure.

Our data are annual, and were extracted from the IMF's *International Financial Statistics*.[19] They have been checked for outliers via both visual and statistical filters.

5 Results: explaining the incidence of currency crises

5.1 Univariate evidence on trade and macroeconomic linkages

Table 9.2 is a series of *t*-tests that test for equality of cross-country means for countries affected and unaffected during each currency crisis episode. These are computed under the null hypothesis of equality of means between crisis and non-crisis countries (assuming equal but unknown variances). Thus, a significant difference in the behaviour of the variable across crisis and non-crisis countries – for instance, consistently higher money growth for crisis countries – would show up as a large (positive) *t*-statistic.

There are two important messages from table 9.2. First, for all five episodes, the strength of trade linkage to the 'first victim' is systematically higher for crisis countries at all reasonable levels of statistical significance – i.e. countries that become 'infected' by the crisis have closer trade linkages to the 'first victim' than countries that escape the disease. In contrast,

Table 9.2   *T-tests for equality, by crisis incidence,*
              1971–1997[a]

	1971	1973	1992	1994	1997
Trade	9.5	10.9	4.7	6.9	7.5
%ΔM1	−0.8	−1.1	−1.2	0.9	0.1
%ΔM2	−1.6	−0.8	−1.1	0.6	−0.0
%ΔCredit	−0.8	−1.3	−0.4	0.2	0.4
%ΔPrivate credit	−1.2	−0.1	−0.7	0.5	−0.3
M2/Reserves	3.5	2.6	−0.3	−0.5	0.3
%ΔReserves	1.8	−0.7	−1.3	−1.4	−2.1
%ΔExports	1.0	0.9	−0.1	0.5	−0.1
%ΔImports	1.5	1.1	−0.8	1.1	0.6
Current account/GDP	2.0	2.1	0.8	−0.2	0.8
Budget/GDP	1.6	1.9	−1.4	0.9	0.4
Real growth	−0.7	−0.5	−1.1	1.6	2.7
Investment/GDP	3.2	2.8	−1.0	0.2	2.7
Inflation	0.3	−0.7	−1.5	1.0	−0.6
Under-valuation	0.5	0.9	−0.6	−1.5	0.6

Notes: [a] Values tabulated are *t*-statistics, calculated under the null
       hypothesis of equal means and variances. A significant
       positive statistic indicates that the variable was significantly
       higher for crisis countries than for non-crisis countries.

none of the macroeconomic variables typically varies systematically across
crisis and non-crisis countries. While some variables sometimes have
significantly different means, these results are not consistent across episodes. And they are never as striking as the trade results. These findings are
consistent with the importance of the trade channel in contagion.

5.2 Multivariate probit results for crisis incidence

The top panel of table 9.3 is a multivariate equivalent of table 9.2, including our macroeconomic variables simultaneously with the trade variable.
It reports Probit estimates of cross-country crisis incidence on trade
linkage and macroeconomic controls for each episode. Table 9.3b uses a
wider range of countries (since many macroeconomic observations are
missing in our sample) but restricts attention to the degree of currency

Table 9.3   *Probit estimates of cross-country crisis incidence on trade linkages and macroeconomic controls, 1971–1997*

a Multivariate Probit results with macro controls[a]

	1971	1973	1992	1994	1997
Trade	2.09	3.18	0.003	0.50	0.68
	(2.7)	(2.7)	(2.1)	(2.9)	(2.6)
%ΔCredit	−0.01	−0.01	0.00	0.00	N/A.
	(1.2)	(0.4)	(1.1)	(0.0)	
Budget/GDP	0.01	0.04	−0.00	0.00	N/A.
	(0.3)	(1.2)	(0.8)	(0.9)	
Current account/GDP	0.00	0.03	0.00	−0.00	0.00
	(0.2)	(1.0)	(0.1)	(1.7)	(0.0)
Real growth	−0.00	0.04	−0.00	0.00	0.04
	(0.2)	(1.2)	(1.6)	(0.1)	(2.2)
M2/Reserves	0.00	0.01	0.00	−0.00	0.00
	(0.2)	(0.4)	(1.0)	(0.5)	(0.8)
Inflation	0.01	0.01	−0.00	0.00	0.00
	(0.4)	(0.5)	(1.3)	(0.7)	(0.3)
Observations	53	60	67	67	50
Slopes (7)	26	36	24	16	17 (5df)
McFadden's R^2	0.38	0.49	0.50	0.36	0.38
P-value: Macro = 0	0.89	0.64	0.59	0.68	0.26

Note: [a] Absolute value of z-statistics in parentheses; Probit estimated with maximum likelihood.

b Probit results with currency misalignment[a]

	1971	1973	1992	1994	1997
Trade	2.25	2.88	0.31	0.45	0.54
	(4.5)	(4.2)	(3.2)	(3.8)	(4.5)
Under-valuation	0.00	0.00	−0.00	−0.00	0.00
	(1.3)	(1.8)	(0.5)	(1.4)	(1.1)
Observations	80	85	111	109	107
McFadden's R^2	0.38	0.48	0.21	0.34	0.36

Note: [a] Absolute value of z-statistics in parentheses; Probit estimated with maximum likelihood.

under- or over-valuation. This is viewed by some as a summary statistic for macroeconomic misalignment. Table 9.3c pools the data for all five episodes.

Since Probit coefficients are not easily interpretable, we report the effects of one-unit (i.e. 1-percentage point) changes in the regressors on the

Table 9.3   (*cont.*)

c Pooled Probit results with macro controls[a]

Trade	0.73	0.69
	(4.8)	(5.5)
%ΔCredit	0.00	N/A.
	(1.0)	
Budget/GDP	0.01	N/A.
	(1.0)	
Current account/GDP	0.00	0.00
	(0.5)	(0.4)
Real growth	0.00	−0.01
	(0.1)	(1.1)
M2/Reserves	−0.00	−0.00
	(2.0)	(2.1)
Inflation	−0.00	−0.00
	(1.3)	(0.0)
Observations	189	274
Slopes (df)	53.4 (7df)	59.0 (5df)
McFadden's R^2	0.30	0.24

Note: [a] Absolute value of z-statistics in parentheses; Probit estimated with maximum likelihood.
Data pooled by weighting episode cross-sections by corresponding pseudo-R^2.

probability of a crisis (also expressed in probability values so that 0.01 = 1 per cent), evaluated at the mean of the data. We include the associated z-statistics in parentheses; these test the 'null of no effect' variable by variable. Diagnostics are reported at the foot of the table. These include a test for the joint significance of all the coefficients ('slopes') which is distributed as chi-squared with seven degrees of freedom under the null hypothesis of no effect. We also include a p-value for the hypothesis that none of the macro effects is jointly significant (i.e. all the coefficients except the trade effect).

The results are striking. The trade channel for contagion seems consistently important in both statistical and economic terms. While the economic size of the effect varies significantly across episodes it is consistently different from zero at conventional levels of statistical significance. Its consistently positive sign indicates that a stronger trade linkage is associated with a higher incidence of a currency crisis.

On the other hand, the macroeconomic controls are small economically and rarely of statistical importance. This is true both of individual variables, of all seven macroeconomic factors taken simultaneously, and of currency under-valuation. Succinctly, the hypothesis of no significant trade channel for contagion seems wildly inconsistent with the data, while macro-economic controls do not explain the cross-country incidence of currency crises.

We have checked for the sensitivity of our probit results with respect to a number of perturbations to our basic methodology. Our trade-linkage variable remains positive and statistically significant despite these changes.[20]

We have also explored the impact of our trade variable on the results of other recent studies of contagion. Corsetti, Pesenti and Roubini (1998) and Tornell (1998) use cross-sectional techniques and data similar to ours to examine the incidence of the Asian crisis; Tornell also considers the 1994–5 'Tequila' attacks. We have reproduced the results of both studies, using their own data. When we added our trade variable to the default Tornell regression (which explains crisis severity with a pooled data set from 1994 and 1997), it is correctly signed and significant at the 0.02 level. When we added our trade variable to the default Corsetti *et al.* regression, our benchmark trade variable is again correctly signed and significant at better than the 0.01 level. The robustness of our key result – the important role played by trade linkages even after taking into account macroeconomic effects – is quite reassuring.

6 Results: explaining the intensity of currency crises

In section 5 we showed that our measure of trade competition worked well in explaining the incidence of currency crises defined in terms of a simple binary indicator. In this section we seek to explain both the direction and intensity of crises, using a quantitative index of exchange market pressure during crisis episodes.[21]

We employ two continuous measures of exchange market intensity. The first measure is the cumulative percentage change in the nominal devaluation rate with respect to the ground-zero currency for six months following the occurrence of a crisis.[22] The second measure is a weighted average of the devaluation rate and the percentage decline in international reserves for six months following the crises. (We check for robustness by also examining three- and nine-month horizons.) Following others (Eichengreen, Rose and Wyplosz, 1995, 1996; Frankel and Rose, 1996; and Sachs, Tornell and Velasco, 1996), we weight the components so as to equalise their volatilities – that is, we weight each component by the inverse of its variance over the sum of inverses of the variances, where the variances are calculated using three years of monthly data prior to each episode. This weighting scheme gives a larger weight to the component with a smaller variance.

Our measures of exchange rate crisis intensity are not without their limitations. First, countries that successfully defend themselves against speculative attacks may show no sign of attack by experiencing either an exchange rate depreciation or reserve losses. A somewhat broader measure of possible responses to speculative attacks would include the interest rate; however, the lack of such data for many of the countries in our sample precluded this. Second, threatened or actual changes to capital controls are difficult to measure quantitatively, but may influence results. The same is true of international rescue packages organised by, for example, the IMF. We proceed bearing these limitations in mind.

Our null hypothesis is that in episodes in which the ground-zero country depreciates (e.g. 1992, 1994, 1997) other countries will depreciate and/or lose reserves the more they compete in world export markets with country 0: i.e. Ho: $\varphi > 0$. Conversely, when the ground-zero currency appreciates (e.g. 1971, 1973) other countries should appreciate more (or depreciate less) the more they compete with ground zero in export markets: i.e., Ho: $\varphi < 0$.

We test these hypotheses by regressing our measures of exchange rate intensity on our basic trade competition variable, $Trade_i$, as well as on the same set of macroeconomic control variables as in table 9.3a. Table 9.4a presents the coefficients on the trade variable from regressions of (three-, six- and nine-month) depreciation rates. The analogue for exchange market pressure measured as a weighted average of reserve losses and depreciation is presented in table 9.4b. For the sake of brevity, coefficients on the macro controls are not reported. For the sake of variety we use our trade share measure of trade linkages.[23]

When we use depreciation as the regressand, the sign of the trade coefficient is sensible (at all horizons) for all five episodes.[24] For 1992, 1994 and 1997, the coefficient is positive; countries that compete more intensely with 'ground zero' (Finland in 1992, Mexico in 1994, Thailand in 1997) tend to depreciate more, after accounting for macroeconomic factors. The sign is negative for the 1971 and 1973 episodes, implying that countries which competed more with Germany tended to appreciate more (along with Germany) following the appreciation of the Deutsche mark. These results are generally significant at standard levels, particularly at the longer horizons. When we consider exchange market pressure – the weighted average of depreciation and reserve losses – as the crisis measure, the overall results for the six- and nine-month horizons are similar, though the significance level generally declines.[25]

Table 9.5 reports the complete results for the six-month horizon for depreciation and exchange market pressure, respectively. Only inflation

Table 9.4   *Multivariate OLS results for exchange rate pressure, 1971–1997*

Coefficient on trade share variable; macro controls not reported

	1971	1973	1992	1994	1997
a Depreciation					
3 months	−4.24	−10.68	24.00	5.8	4.99
	(2.4)[a]	(2.6)	(3.8)	(2.9)	(1.6)
6 months	−6.81	−21.78	32.92	10.06	56.69
	(2.1)	(3.4)	(4.0)	(3.1)	(3.4)
9 months	−7.60	−24.60	31.76	6.38	—
	(0.7)	(3.8)	(3.0)	(1.9)	—
b Exchange market pressure					
3 months	−4.36	−10.30	22.40	4.91	6.60
	(1.3)[a]	(2.1)	(3.2)	(2.4)	(1.6)
6 months	(0.9)	(2.8)	(2.4)	(1.8)	(2.8)
	(0.9)	(2.8)	(2.4)	(1.8)	(2.8)
9 months	−8.60	−27.55	32.40	6.01	—
	(0.6)	(3.2)	(2.6)	(1.6)	—

Notes: [a] Absolute value of *t*-statistics in parentheses; regressand is weighted average of depreciation and reserve losses.
— = Not available.

is generally significant across all episodes. In contrast, as noted above with our cumulative depreciation measure as the regressand, the trade variable appears to provide consistent explanatory power for all crisis episodes.[26]

We conclude that our continuous quantitative indicators, particularly the cumulative depreciation rate, provide support for the hypothesis that trade contributes significant power in explaining the intensity as well as incidence of currency crises.

7 Conclusions

We have found strong evidence that currency crises tend to spread along regional lines using both binary and more continuous measures of crises. This is true of five recent waves of speculative attacks (in 1971, 1973, 1992, 1994–5 and 1997). Accounting for a variety of different macroeconomic

Table 9.5   *Multivariate OLS results for exchange rate pressure:
six-month horizon, 1971–1997*

	1971	1973	1992	1994	1997
a Depreciation					
Trade share	−6.81	−21.78	32.92	10.06	56.69
	(2.1)[a]	(3.4)	(4.0)	(3.1)	(3.4)
%ΔCredit	0.02	−0.01	0.01	0.05	−0.09
	(0.3)	(0.1)	(1.1)	(2.0)	(0.7)
Budget/GDP	−0.42	−0.68	−0.24	−0.04	−1.63
	(2.7)	(2.3)	(0.7)	(0.6)	(1.3)
Current account/GDP	−0.12	−0.13	0.07	−0.22	−0.39
	(1.5)	(0.43)	(0.8)	(2.0)	(0.8)
Real growth	0.26	0.46	0.06	0.61	1.57
	(2.3)	(1.5)	(0.2)	(2.8)	(1.2)
M2/Reserves	0.02	0.04	−0.2	0.12	−0.20
	(0.8)	(1.7)	(1.5)	(1.7)	(1.3)
Inflation					
	0.39	0.60	0.42	0.23	0.29
	(2.5)	(3.1)	(9.9)	(4.6)	(1.3)
Observations	53	59	66	67	25
R^2	0.48	0.40	0.75	0.49	0.48
P-value: Macro = 0	0.00	0.00	0.00	0.00	0.41
b Exchange market pressure					
Trade share	−4.96	−22.22	23.65	6.46	66.72
	(0.9)	(2.8)	(2.4)	(1.8)	(2.8)
%ΔCredit	0.04	−0.08	0.23	0.05	−0.13
	(0.4)	(0.5)	(4.2)	(2.2)	(0.8)
Budget/GDP	−0.53	−0.55	0.28	0.01	−3.28
	(2.4)	(1.8)	(0.6)	(0.2)	(1.3)
Current account/GDP	−0.16	−0.17	−0.14	−0.26	−0.21
	(1.2)	(0.5)	(1.2)	(2.2)	(0.2)
Real growth	0.14	0.82	−0.64	0.41	2.60
	(0.7)	(2.4)	(1.8)	(1.7)	(1.6)
M2/Reserves	0.04	0.25	−0.11	0.10	−0.34
	(0.6)	(1.5)	(0.8)	(0.9)	(1.2)
Inflation	0.24	0.75	−0.06	0.14	0.51
	(1.0)	(3.5)	(0.8)	(2.7)	(0.7)
Observations	36	47	62	64	17
R^2	0.45	0.46	0.43	0.37	0.58
P-value: Macro = 0	0.01	0.00	0.00	0.00	0.45

Note: [a]Absolute value of *t*-statistics in parentheses; regressand is a weighted
average of depreciation and reserve losses.

effects does not change this result. Indeed, macroeconomic factors do not consistently help much in explaining the cross-country incidence or intensity of speculative attacks.

Our evidence is consistent with the hypothesis that the regional spread of currency crises occurs through trade linkages. This evidence of contagion through trade links does not negate the importance of identifying economic and financial fundamentals that affect the relative vulnerability of individual countries to currency crises. Indeed, recent speculative-attack episodes have spurred greater research into finding early-warning signals or macroeconomic and financial indicators that tend to have predictive power for such crises.

However, the finding that crises may spill over contagiously through trade links, over and above the effects of fundamentals, suggests the importance of recognising this externality associated with such crises. Countries may be attacked because of the actions (or inaction) of their neighbours, who tend to be trading partners merely because of geographic proximity. During the Asian crisis, although some individual country problems – notably Thailand and Korea – were foreseen by at least some analysts, the eventual regional spread of the downturn throughout Asia was less widely perceived.

If a country's risk of speculative attack depends not just on its own economic conditions but also on its trade (and possibly financial) links with other countries, these links must be taken into account when properly assessing the risks. This suggests the importance of enhanced international monitoring on a regional basis, with particular attention to regional economic linkages. In addition, a lower threshold for international and/or regional assistance also may be warranted in order to limit the spread of speculative attacks beyond their initial victim(s). Moral hazard issues aside, the externalities associated with contagious crises provide a justification for timely multilateral assistance beyond what would be forthcoming if speculative attacks were solely the result of domestic factors.

APPENDIX

Table 9A.1 *Countries affected by speculative*
attacks, 1971–1997[a]

Country	1971	1973	1992	1994	1997
USA	1	1			
UK	1	1	1		
Austria	1	1			
Belgium	1	1	1		
Denmark	1	1	1		
France	1	1	1		
Germany	0	0			
Italy	1	1	1		
Netherlands	1	1			
Norway	1	1			
Sweden	1	1	1		
Switzerland	1	1			
Canada				1	
Japan		1			
Finland	1	1	0		
Greece	1	1			
Iceland		1			
Ireland	1		1		
Portugal	1	1	1		
Spain	1		1		
Australia	1	1			
New Zealand	1	1			
South Africa					1
Argentina				1	1
Brazil				1	1
Mexico				0	1
Peru				1	
Venezuela				1	
Taiwan					1
Hong Kong				1	1
Indonesia				1	1
Korea					1
Malaysia					1
Pakistan					1
Philippines				1	1
Singapore					1
Thailand				1	0
Vietnam					1
Czech Republic					1
Hungary				1	1
Poland					1

Note: [a] '0' denotes 'first victim'/'ground zero'; '1' denotes target
of speculative attack.

Table 9A.2 *Default measure of trade linkage, Trade$_i$, 1974–1997*[a]

Rank	1971	1973	1992	1994	1997
0	Germany	Germany	Finland	Mexico	Thailand
1	UK	France	Norway	Canada	Malaysia
2	France	UK	Denmark	Taiwan	Indonesia
3	Italy	USA	Portugal	Hong Kong	Saudi Arabia
4	USA	Belgium	Ireland	Korea	Australia
5	Japan	Italy	Turkey	Venezuela	India
6	Belgium	Japan	Poland	China	Korea
7	Netherlands	Netherlands	Russia	Singapore	Brazil
8	Canada	Canada	Austria	Brazil	Taiwan
9	Sweden	Sweden	Sweden	Malaysia	Philippines
10	Switzerland	Switzerland	India	Thailand	Singapore
11	Australia	Saudi Arabia	South Africa	UK	Israel
12	Denmark	Australia	Yugoslavia	Japan	Switzerland
13	Saudi Arabia	Brazil	Algeria	Israel	China
14	Brazil	Denmark	Israel	Saudi Arabia	South Africa
15	Hong Kong	Spain	Greece	Philippines	Un. Arab Emirates
16	Spain	Hong Kong	Hungary	Indonesia	Sweden
17	Austria	Norway	Iran	Nigeria	Finland
18	Norway	Taiwan	Brazil	India	Ireland
19	Libya	Austria	Switzerland	Switzerland	Hong Kong
20	Finland	Venezuela	Spain	Colombia	Denmark

Note: [a] Countries listed in order of decreasing degree of trade linkage with 'ground zero' for each crisis episode.

NOTES

We thank Priya Ghosh and Laura Haworth for research assistance. For comments, we thank the participants of the CEPR/World Bank Conference, 'Financial Crises: Contagion and Market Volatility' (London) (8–9 May 1998), Joshua Aizenman, Gabriele Galati, Marcus Miller, Richard Portes, Javier Suárez, Mark Taylor and especially David Vines. The views expressed below do not represent those of the Federal Reserve Bank of San Francisco or the Board of Governors of the Federal Reserve System, or their staffs. This is a revised version of a paper entitled 'Contagion and Trade: Why are Currency Crises Regional?', which is available as *NBER Working Paper*, **6806** and *CEPR Discussion Paper*, **1947**. The (Excel 97 spreadsheet) data set used in the paper is available at http://haas.berkeley.edu/~arose

1. The evidence for the regional nature of trade is overwhelming; Leamer and Levinsohn (1995) provide a survey.
2. Rigobon (1998) provides an alternate theoretical framework that argues that the regional nature of currency crises is caused by investors learning about a given model of development (assuming that such models tend to be regional).
3. Of course, currency crises may spread through other channels as well, such as international asset and debt relationships. However, these non-trade linkages tend to be correlated with trade flows. Data constraints prevent us from explicitly comparing these channels to our trade and macro channels for contagion.

4. Trade patterns have had important effects in spreading currency crises before the 1990s, as we document below.
5. Eichengreen, Rose and Wyplosz (1996) provide a critical survey and some early evidence. Masson (chapter 8 in this volume) also distinguishes among different concepts of contagion.
6. Similarity in terms of structural characteristics of the economy is analysed in Rigobon (1998).
7. This reasoning is strengthened if devaluing countries tend to experience contractions, as seems to the historic norm. For instance, if devaluing countries tend to have unhedged external liabilities, devaluation may cause bankruptcies in the financial sector, a domestic credit crunch and hence a recession. Since imports are highly cyclic, this puts even more pressure on neighbouring countries.
8. Another view is that a crisis in one country triggers a crisis elsewhere because it leads to shifts in market sentiments or to changes in the evaluation of existing information (Calvo and Mendoza, 1998).
9. For a summary of various indicators employed to predict currency crises, see Kaminsky, Lizondo and Reinhart (1998) and Kumar, Moorthy and Perraudin (1999).
10. The exact list (in order of *IFS* country code) is: USA; UK; Austria; Belgium; Denmark; France; Germany; Italy; Netherlands; Norway; Sweden; Switzerland; Canada; Japan; Finland; Greece; Iceland; Ireland; Malta; Portugal; Spain; Turkey; Yugoslavia; Australia; New Zealand; South Africa; Argentina; Bolivia; Brazil; Chile; Colombia; Costa Rica; Dominican Republic; Ecuador; El Salvador; Guatemala; Haiti; Honduras; Mexico; Nicaragua; Panama; Paraguay; Peru; Uruguay; Venezuela; Bahamas; Barbados; Greenland; Guadeloupe; Guinea, French; Guyana; Belize; Jamaica; Martinique; Suriname; Trinidad; Bahrain; Cyprus; Iran; Iraq; Israel; Jordan; Kuwait; Lebanon; Oman; Qatar; Saudi Arabia; Syria; United Arab Emirates; Egypt; Yemen; Afghanistan; Bangladesh; Myanmar; Cambodia; Sri Lanka; Taiwan; Hong Kong; India; Indonesia; Korea; Laos; Macao; Malaysia; Pakistan; Philippines; Singapore; Thailand; Vietnam; Algeria; Angola; Botswana; Cameroon; Central Africa Republic; Congo; Zaire; Benin; Ethiopia; Gabon; Gambia; Ghana; Guinea–Bissau; Guinea; Ivory Coast; Kenya; Lesotho; Liberia; Libya; Madagascar; Malawi; Mali; Mauritania; Mauritius; Morocco; Mozambique; Niger; Nigeria; Réunion; Zimbabwe; Rwanda; Senegal; Sierra Leone; Sudan; Swaziland; Tanzania; Togo; Tunisia; Uganda; Burkina Faso; Zambia; Fiji; New Caledonia; Papua New Guinea; Armenia; Azerbaijan; Belarus; Georgia; Kazakhstan; Kyrgz Republic; Bulgaria; Moldova; Russia; Tajikistan; China; Turkmenistan; Ukraine; Uzbekistan; Czech Republic; Slovak Republic; Estonia; Latvia; Hungary; Lithuania; Mongolia; Croatia; Slovenia; Macedonia; Bosnia; Poland; Yugoslavia/Macedonia; and Romania. This set of countries was determined by economies with bilateral exports of $5 million or more to at least one trade partner in 1971. Not all countries exist for all episodes, and not all countries with trade relations have currencies.

11. Countries that were not attacked during any of our five episodes are not included in table 9A.1, though they are included in our empirical analysis depending on trade and macroeconomic data availability.

12. In Glick and Rose (1998), we show that our results do not appear to be very sensitive to the exact choice of the 'first-victim' country.

13. This measure has an obvious similarity to the Grubel–Lloyd measure (1971) of cross-country intra-industry trade.

14. After Finland floated the marka in 1992, Sweden was immediately attacked. One might then ask how the crisis could spill over from both Finland and Sweden.

15. Results of using a 'direct' and 'total' measure of trade are reported in Glick and Rose (1998).

16. The timing of our data is as follows: the 1971 episode uses control data for both macroeconomic and trade linkages from 1970; the 1973 episode uses 1972 data; 1992 uses 1992; 1994 uses 1994; and 1997 uses 1996.

    This data set was supplemented with Taiwan trade data from *Monthly Statistics of Exports and Imports, Taiwan Area*, Department of Statistics, Ministry of Finance, Taiwan, and macro data from *Financial Statistics, Taiwan District*, Central Bank of China, Taiwan (various issues).

17. The analysis of Diwan and Hoekman (chapter 10 in this volume) also provides evidence of strong trade links among Asian countries.

18. We measure currency under-valuation by constructing an annual real exchange rate index as a weighted sum of bilateral real exchange rates (using domestic and real CPIs) in relation to the currencies of all trading partners with available data. The weights sum to one and are proportional to the bilateral export shares with each partner. The degree of currency under-valuation is defined as the percentage change in the real exchange rate index between the average of the three prior years and the episode year. A positive value indicates that the real exchange rate is depreciated relative to the average of the three previous years.

19. Limited availability of macroeconomic data generally reduces the number of usable observations in our regression analysis far below the set of 161 countries for which we have trade data.

20. In Glick and Rose (1998) we show that these results are robust to the inclusion of other macro and financial variable regressors, different measures of trade linkages and alternative designations of ground zero for particular episodes. Our results are also unaffected by the occurrence of bank crises or the existence of capital controls.

21. It would be interesting to extend this analysis by using financial measures (for example, equity prices or interest rate spreads) as regressands.

22. For the 1971 episode, the exchange rate change is measured from the end of April; for the 1973 episode the change is measured from the end of December 1972; for 1992, from the end of August; for 1994, from the end of November; for 1997, from the end of June.

23. We have omitted Chile from the samples for 1971 and 1973 because during both episodes it experienced depreciation rates of over 100 per cent; Chile was an outlier in many respects during these periods.

24. Using our default measure of trade reduces significance levels slightly, and reverses the coefficient on the trade measure for the 1994 episode, though it is not significant.
25. For the 1971 and 1973 episodes the trade effect sign at three months is now positive, although these effects are not significant at standard levels.
26. We get the same qualitative results using $Trade_i$ as the trade-share measure.

REFERENCES

Alba, P., A. Bhattacharya, S. Claessens, S. Ghosh and L. Hernandez (1999). 'The Role of Macroeconomic and Financial Sector Linkages in East Asia's Financial Crisis', chapter 1 in this volume

Calvo, G. and E. Mendoza (1998). 'Rational Herd Behavior and the Globalization of Securities Markets', University of Maryland, unpublished ms

Corsetti, G., P. Pesenti and N. Roubini (1998). 'Paper Tigers': A Model of the Asian Crisis', *NBER Working Paper* **6783** (November)

    (1999). 'The Asian Crisis: An Overview of the Empirical Evidence and Policy Rebate', chapter 4 in this volume

Corsetti, G., P. Pesenti, N. Roubini and C. Tille (1998). 'Trade and Contagious Devaluations: A Welfare-based Approach', paper written for the conference 'Perspectives on the Financial Crisis in Asia' (Fordham University) (October)

Diwan, I. and B. Hoekman (1999). 'Competition, Complementarity and Contagion in East Asia', chapter 10 in this volume

Eichengreen, B. and A. K. Rose (1998). 'Contagious Currency Crises: Channels of Conveyance', in T. Ito and A. Krueger (eds.), *Changes in Exchange Rates in Rapidly Developing Countries*, Chicago: Chicago University Press

Eichengreen, B. and C. Wyplosz (1993). 'The Unstable EMS', *Brookings Papers on Economic Activity*, **1**: 51–143

Eichengreen, B., A. K. Rose and C. Wyplosz (1995). 'Exchange Market Mayhem: The Antecedents and Aftermath of Speculative Attacks', *Economic Policy*, **21**: 249–96

    (1996) 'Contagious Currency Crises: First Tests', *Scandinavian Journal of Economics,* **98**: 463–84

Frankel, J. and A. K. Rose (1996). 'Currency Crashes in Emerging Markets', *Journal of International Economics,* **41**: 351–66

Gerlach, S. and F. Smets (1994). 'Contagious Speculative Attacks', *CEPR Discussion Paper,* **1055**

Glick, R. and A. Rose (1998). 'Contagion and Trade: Why are Currency Crises Regional? *NBER Working Paper,* **6806**; *CEPR Discussion Paper,* **1947**

Goldfajn, I. and R. Valdés (1997). 'Capital Flows and the Twin Crises: The Role of Liquidity', *IMF Working Paper,* **97/87**

Grubel, H. and P. Lloyd (1971). 'The Empirical Measurement of Intra-industry Trade', *Economic Record,* **47**: 494–517

Huh, C. and K. Kasa (1997). 'A Dynamic Model of Export Competition, Policy Coordination and Simultaneous Currency Collapse', Federal Reserve Bank of San Francisco Center for Pacific Basin Studies, *Working Paper,* **PB97-08**

Kaminsky, G., S. Lizondo and C. Reinhart (1998). 'Leading Indicators of Currency Crises', *IMF Staff Papers*, **45**: 1–48

Krugman, P. (1979). 'A Model of Balance-of Payments Crises', *Journal of Money, Credit, and Banking*, **11**: 311–25

Kumar, M., U. Moorthy and W. Perraudin (1999). 'Predicting Emerging Market Currency Crises', paper presented at conference on World Capital Markets and Financial Crisis, Warwick University, 24–25 July 1998

Leamer, E. E. and J. Levinsohn (1995). 'International Trade Theory: The Evidence', chapter 26 in G. Grossman and K. Rogoff (eds.), *Handbook of International Economics*, III, New York: Elsevier

Masson, P. (1999). 'Contagion: Monsoonal Effects, Spillovers and Jumps between Multiple Equilibria', chapter 8 in this volume

Obstfeld, M. (1986). 'Rational and Self-fulfilling Balance-of-payments Crises', *American Economic Review*, **76**: 72–81

Rigobon, R. (1998). 'Informational Speculative Attacks: Good News is no News', MIT, unpublished ms

Sachs, J., A. Tornell and A. Velasco (1996). 'Financial Crises in Emerging Markets: The Lessons from 1995', *Brookings Papers on Economic Activity*, **1**, 147–217

Tornell, A. (1998). 'Common Fundamentals in the Tequila and Asian Crises', Harvard University, unpublished ms

Discussion
Mark P. Taylor

The analogy between economics and medicine is sometimes a useful one. In medicine, progress is often made first through an improvement in understanding of a certain disease and then by improvements in treatment of the underlying causes of the disease and through preventive measures such as improvements in standards of hygiene. Similarly in economics, many 'diseases' which were apparently poorly understood by policy makers in the past – such as the hyperinflation which results from persistent recourse to the inflation tax through strong expansion of the money supply – have now been largely eradicated in industrialised countries; the IMF Mission Chief knows how to treat the hyperinflation of a programme country, and the Central Bank Governor knows how to avoid one. On the other hand, the medical profession has found it difficult to find a means of preventing or curing some diseases, and economists, too, have found certain economic diseases – in particular speculative attacks on exchange rates – hard to find a panacea for. In the interesting chapter 9 by Glick and Rose, the authors seek to improve our understanding not of the underlying causes of the speculative-attack disease, but of the way in which the disease is transmitted from one victim to another, in other words the contagion of speculative attacks.

Standard speculative-attack models have tended to emphasise macroeconomic and financial factors. The 'first-generation' models – designed to aid our understanding of crises affecting developing countries such as Mexico and Argentina in the 1970s and early 1980s – show how excessively expansionary macroeconomic fundamentals combined with a fixed exchange rate will trigger a crisis as the markets seek to profit from the inconsistency. The 'second-generation' models – designed to capture features of the 1992 ERM crisis and the 1994 Mexican crisis – show how, while there may be no initial inconsistency between the exchange rate and the macroeconomic fundamentals, the expectation of the attack itself may alter the behaviour of agents in the economy and thereby trigger the attack in a self-fulfilling way. More recent models – designed to capture features of the recent East Asian crisis – have stressed macro and financial issues such as the link between moral hazard issues in financial markets arising from misperceived financial guarantees, asset-market bubbles, capital flight and exchange rate collapse.[1]

In all of these models, trade does not explicitly feature as an important factor. But this is because they are models of speculative attack, not of contagion. The authors argue that where there are strong trade linkages between two countries then, if there is a speculative attack leading to the devaluation of the currency of one country, this will – with short-run nominal rigidities – affect the international competitiveness of the second country. Since competitiveness is itself an element of the overall macroeconomic fundamentals of an economy, this may then trigger a speculative attack on the currency of the second country. This link between trade and exchange rate crisis epidemics has in fact previously been formalised by Gerlach and Smets (1994), Huh and Kasa (1997) and Corsetti et al. (1998) and bears the hallmark of good economics in that it is at once intuitively plausible and technically sound. On this reasoning, currency-crisis epidemics will be correlated with trade flows. Moreover, since we know that the gravity model of trade fits the data well – i.e. trade flows are negatively related to distance – exchange rate crisis epidemics will tend to be regional. A stylised fact concerning exchange rate crisis epidemics is that they do indeed tend to be largely regional. The trade model of contagion is thus consistent with the facts.

As Glick and Rose note, however, there are other types of explanations of the contagion of exchange rate crises, such as macroeconomic or financial similarity or cross-country financial linkages. The degree of macroeconomic similarity between economies and the degree of financial linkage between them are also, however, likely to be a function of geographical proximity, so that there is a need to distinguish between these alternative explanations of regional contagion and the trade-contagion model. Glick and Rose attempt to do this by controlling for macroeconomic influences by including a set of macroeconomic variables in their regressions, while acknowledging that these other channels of contagion are not necessarily mutually exclusive with the trade channel.

Glick and Rose examine five currency-crisis epidemics: the collapse of the Bretton Woods system in 1971, the collapse of the Smithsonian Agreement in 1973, the collapse of the ERM in 1992, the Mexican peso crisis of 1994 and the East Asian currency crisis. For each episode they identify an initial 'carrier' (Germany, Finland, Mexico and Thailand respectively) and, through a battery of econometric analyses, find that the degree to which a country competes in trade in third markets with the initial carrier is a significant predictor both of the likelihood of infection and of the intensity of the attack, controlling for macroeconomic effects. Macroeconomic effects tend, in fact, to be insignificant. Glick and Rose conclude from their study that surveillance should incorporate a regional factor classified by trade linkages. Since currency crises may be caused by 'trade externalities', a lower threshold for international and regional assistance is warranted than might be indicated by domestic macro and financial fundamentals.

The econometric analysis is clearly well executed – the statistical significance of the trade variable in the contagion of currency crises is clearly demonstrated. Impressively, the authors also find that their trade variable significantly improves the fit of other regressions used to study contagion by Corsetti, Pesenti and Roubini (1998) and Tornell (1998).

While this contribution is certainly to be welcomed as a thorough study of the importance of trade linkages in currency crisis epidemics, a number of issues are implicitly raised in the chapter which may be addressed in future work. First, there are a number of issues which Glick and Rose explicitly do not attempt to address within their framework, such as the timing of attacks and whether or not an attack will become contagious. In general, however, the issues that I have in mind relate to identification of the trade effect. Since the gravity model of trade fits so well, the Glick and Rose trade variable will itself be a good proxy for regional proximity. The question is, do trade linkages provide a significant explanation of crisis contagion, over and above other potential explanators which may themselves have a regional bias?

Further work might, for example, control for and test for the significance of other financial variables. One has to have some sympathy with the authors' claim that certain relevant financial variables may not be available for all of the countries under investigation, but relevant financial variables may be available for a subset of the episodes considered.[2] The 'moral hazard' view of the East Asian crisis, for example, suggests that asset prices such as stock prices played an important role. This would suggest that contagion between stock markets might generate contagion of the ensuing exchange rate crisis. Inclusion of stock prices would thus seem an obvious candidate.

A number of authors have also stressed the influence of capital flows from developed to emerging capital markets – and their potential reversal – as important factors in currency crises (for example, Alba *et al.*, chapter 1 in this volume; Sarno and Taylor, 1998) and, as Ghosh and Wolf (1998) have demonstrated, these capital flows also tend to have a strong regional bias. Ghosh and Wolf show that a gravity model is highly successful in explaining capital flows to emerging markets. Controlling for these effects would be necessary in order to determine the degree to which trade linkages were proxying for financial linkages through their common correlation with geographical proximity[3].

Solving this identification problem may, however, prove to be extremely difficult or even impossible. For some purposes, however, its solution may be unimportant.

Econometrically, the identification problem will never be fully soluble because of the problem of multicollinearity. Any variables or set of variables that explain crisis contagion and which have a regional bias will be more or less collinear with a measure of trade linkages. Apart from exercising one's priors concerning which of a set of collinear variables are the more important variables to include in a regression equation – in a formal or informal Bayesian fashion – the collinearity problem is insoluble.[4]

One way, however, of seeing that trade linkages do not tell the whole of the contagion story – although they may tell a great deal – is to examine the nature of outliers in the Glick–Rose analysis. Table 9A.2, for example, reveals that Australia ranks fourth in its degree of trade linkage with Thailand on the Glick–Rose measure. Yet the Australian dollar escaped relatively unscathed in the East Asian crisis. It seems plausible here that, notwithstanding the high degree of trade linkage of Australia with the initial carrier, this effect was outweighed by the degree of *dissimilarity* – in particular, financial dissimilarity – between Australia and the other East Asian crisis economies. Sarno and Taylor (1998), for example, demonstrate that, in contrast to the other East Asian crisis economies, the Australian economy was not characterised by stock market bubbles in the run-up to the East Asian crisis and that equity and bond flows to Australia showed a much lower degree of potential reversibility than did comparable flows to other East Asian economies. Further, it seems reasonable to conjecture that weaknesses in corporate governance and financial transparency, which some authors (notably Alba *et al.* in chaper 1, pp. 54, 55) have emphasised as important in the East Asian crisis, were not as extreme in the relatively more mature economy of Australia.

To conclude, I am convinced that the statistical importance of trade linkages in explaining contagion – as demonstrated by Glick and Rose – does indeed largely represent the economic importance of those linkages. As Glick and Rose acknowledge, however, there are other channels of contagion that are likely to be working alongside the trade channel. It seems likely, therefore, that trade linkages will also to some extent proxy for a range of other important effects on contagion – in particular financial linkages, which also have a regional bias. Sorting out definitively which effects are relatively more important is, in my view, likely to be extremely difficult econometrically.

To the extent that we are interested in the underlying economic determinants of contagion, this means that we will – as always – have to rely on a combination of our economic priors and the empirical evidence. To the extent that we are interested in drawing policy implications, however, the implications of the Glick and Rose analysis are clear: when a currency crisis becomes contagious, it is extremely likely that both the pattern and the intensity of the ensuing epidemic will follow along the lines of trade linkages. To that extent, Glick and Rose's results clearly support their central policy prescription – a call for enhanced international monitoring on a regional basis and for timely multilateral assistance beyond that which might be justified on purely domestic factors.

NOTES

1. See Flood and Marion (1999) for a discussion of the currency-crisis literature.
2. Fratzscher (1998), for example, analyses the relative statistical importance of a range of influences on contagion – including trade and financial linkages – during the early 1990s Mexican crisis and the East Asian crisis. Interestingly, Fratzscher finds that both financial and trade linkages are important factors in explaining crisis contagion.
3. Ghosh and Wolf (1998) conclude:

   The results also have immediate implications for regional contagion effects: the strong dependence of flows on distance implies that changes in the capital account of major creditors will have similar effects on all recipient countries in the neighbourhood, leading to regionally correlated inflow and outflow episodes.

4. Glick and Rose (n. 3) acknowledge the collinearity problem:

   Of course, currency crises may spread through other channels as well, such as international asset and debt relationships. However, these non-trade linkages tend to be correlated with trade flows. Data constraints prevent us from explicitly comparing these channels to our trade and macro channels for contagion.

   Our view, however, is slightly stronger in the sense that, even if the relevant data were available, we believe it would be largely uninformative to the extent that they are correlated with the trade variable.

REFERENCES

Alba, P., A. Bhattacharya, S. Claessens, S. Ghosh and L. Hernandez (1999). 'The Role of Macroeconomic and Financial Sector Linkages in East Asia's Financial Crisis', chapter 1 in this volume

Corsetti, G., P. Pesenti and N. Roubini (1998). 'Paper Tigers: A Model of the Asian Crisis', *NBER Working Paper*, **6783** (November)

Corsetti, G., P. Pesenti, N. Roubini and C. Tille (1998). 'Trade and Contagious Devaluations: A Welfare-based Approach', paper presented at the *Journal of International Money and Finance* conference 'Perspectives on the Financial Crisis in Asia (New York) (October)

Flood, R. and N. P. Marion (1999). 'Perspectives on the Recent Currency Crisis Literature', *International Journal of Finance and Economics*, **4**: 1–26

Fratzscher, M. (1998). 'Why are Currency Crises Contagious? A Comparison of the Latin American Crisis of 1994–1995 and the Asian Crisis of 1997–1998', *Review of World Economics*, **134**: 664–91.

Gerlach, S. and F. Smets (1994). 'Contagious Speculative Attacks', *CEPR Discussion Paper*, **1055**

Ghosh, S. and H. Wolf (1998). 'The Spatial Properties of Capital Flows: Is Location Destiny?', Georgetown University, unpublished manuscript

Huh, C. and K. Kasa (1997). 'A Dynamic Model of Export Competition, Policy Coordination and Simultaneous Currency Collapse', Federal Reserve Bank of San Francisco Center for Pacific Basin Studies, *Working Paper*, **PB97-08**

Sarno, L. and M. P. Taylor (1998). 'Moral Hazard, Asset Price Bubbles, Capital Flows, and the East Asian Crisis: The First Tests', paper presented at the *Journal of International Money and Finance* conference 'Perspectives on the Financial Crisis in Asia (New York) (October)

Tornell, A. (1998). 'Common Fundamentals in the Tequila and Asian Crises', Harvard University, unpublished ms

10 Competition, complementarity and contagion in East Asia

ISHAC DIWAN AND BERNARD HOEKMAN

1 Introduction

The magnitude and speed of the contagion effects that materialised in East Asia in the second half of 1997 has attracted much attention. This chapter asks to what extent the observed contagion may have had 'real' under-pinnings, in the sense that the pattern of production, consumption and trade increased the vulnerability of East Asian countries to external shocks. In particular, we explore two major possibilities that are relevant in this connection: the 'competition-cum-export similarity' story or the 'flying-geese-cum-Asia Inc.' story which puts greater emphasis on regional integration and specialisation in complementary production structures.

The competition story posits that Asian economies have specialised in similar export bundles. In a longer-term perspective, the competition story hinges importantly on the emergence of China as a major exporter to world markets. An implication is that given a major devaluation by one country, others are forced to follow in order not to lose export market share. The complementarity story is based on the recent experience of Asianwide growth based on intra-regional trade and geographically cascading invest-ments. In the past two decades, labour-intensive production gradually moved down from Japan, first to the Tigers – the 'newly industrialised economies'(NIEs) of Taiwan, Singapore, Hong Kong and Korea – then on to the Dragons (Thailand, Indonesia, Malaysia and the Philippines) and then to China and Vietnam. As a result East Asia became more integrated, its growth path generated by a constant process of industrial upgrading, in turn driven by a rapidly expanding stock of skills and real assets. In the process, the region also became more interdependent. A key role in this story is played by Japan, as an important source of technology, financial capital, capital goods and a large market for East Asian output (both tradeables and 'non-tradeables' such as tourism or real estate). Here, contagion could also occur, but it is driven by the interdependence of East Asian economies.

In reality, both competition and complementarity are likely to operate simultaneously. In particular, while the emergence of China and other labour-intensive producers is likely to hurt producers of relatively unskilled products in the region, it also offers huge potential for mutual gains from trade with the recently industrialised countries, which are already rich in skills and capital, but where labour costs have been rising. In the longer run, the emergence of China on world markets pushes up the return to education and creates incentives for other East Asian countries to move up the quality ladder faster. Indeed, in the absence of new entrants from below, the process of growth convergence – very rapid in this region – would soon exhaust gains from trade caused by dissimilarities; further trade growth would increasingly have to be based on product differentiation and intra-industry trade. As long as complementarities dominate, the region remains vulnerable to risks of failures in its higher rungs – in particular, a serious slowdown in Japan would have strong ripple effects on the whole group of countries, encroaching on production capacity already in place in the rungs directly below and, ultimately, destroying growth opportunities all the way to the poorest country of the formation.

The premise of this chapter is that the strong financial regional contagion in East Asia must have been due, at least in part, to a complex set of real-side links between the various countries of the regions. Strong regional competition and/or complementarities would both transmit shocks and lead to regional contagion. But the ripple effects would be of a different nature, and the policy instruments needed for stabilisation would be different. A better understanding of the prevailing production/ investment/ consumption/ finance relationships could help us gauge the 'fundamentals' behind the financial veil of the crisis.[1]

The objective of the chapter is to make an initial attempt to explore what the available data reveal regarding the relative importance of competition vs. complementarity. It is structured as follows. In section 2 we first lay out the two main real-side 'stories.' In section 3, we attempt to obtain a better understanding of the changing pattern of trade and investment in Asia by looking at the cross-country co-variation in the various aggregates. In section 4, we explore the structure of Asian trade and in section 5, that of the investment flows. Section 6 presents our conclusions about the relative importance of the various contagion channels.

2 Real-side stories

Several real-side stories focusing on the 'fundamentals' can be proposed in an attempt to understand developments in East Asia. These stories attempt either to explain the genesis of the crisis (a common cause would explain the similarities in countries' performances), or to propose reasons why the crisis has created contagion effects in the rest of the region once it started. Many of these stories can be collapsed into two archetypes, one that emphasises competition between Asian countries, and the other that emphasises their complementarity. The first model posits that the various Asian economies are fierce competitors in world markets, and that none can afford to let the others get a lead through devaluation. The second model, the 'flying-geese formation', posits instead a strong form of complementarity.[2] This model would lead to a different interpretation of the crisis, one where the internal weaknesses experienced by Japan played a key role. In contrast, with global competition for investment flows and market share rising, the first model questions the competitiveness of many countries of the region. Different stories emphasise different types of competition:

- The *rise of low-wage producers* – China, India, and Vietnam – must have hurt mainly Asian low-wage producers (mainly the ASEAN countries) in world export markets. Here, there is a particular emphasis given to the 1994 (alleged) devaluation of the yuan (Bergsten, 1998). To be relevant from a policy and contagion perspective, it is necessary that emerging competitors are large enough to pose a credible threat to 'traditional' East Asian suppliers. In principle, China is a big enough player to be a threat; whether its rapid export growth has in fact come at the detriment of East Asian Dragons is an empirical question.

- *Medium-skill countries* are often mentioned as victims of the revival of major Latin American economies, trade diversion resulting from NAFTA and the emergence of former COMECON nations as exporters. At the higher end of this range, medium-skill industries in the NIEs (and to a lesser extent the ASEAN countries) must have been badly hurt after 1995 by the sharp devaluation of the yen, which reduced their competitiveness relative to producers of similar goods in Japan.

The competition story is supported by the observed deterioration of the terms of trade of some Asian economies in 1996 (especially Korea) which was caused in large part by a decline in world prices for major export commodities. Seemingly, this was driven by excess capacity and over-investment in particular sectors – for example, prices of semiconductors and computer components fell dramatically in 1996 (Dasgupta and Imai, 1997). A particular variant of these types of arguments is that competition in the region is very fierce in that East Asian countries have tended to specialise in very similar output bundles (DeRosa, 1995; Muscatelli, Stevenson and Montagna 1994). This in turn might help explain possible contagion effects arising from a financial crisis and associated exchange rate depreciation in any given Asian country.

Stories emphasising complementarity are more complex to trace out precisely. In the past, and under Japan's leadership, the region integrated rapidly through strong intra-regional trade growth and large movements of capital. In the standard 'flying-geese' model, industries that first emerged in the leading country make their way over time into countries with lower levels of skills (from textiles to chemicals, iron and steel, electrical products, electronics and automobiles). Both the labour and capital markets play an important role in this. As the labour markets tighten and wages rise, it becomes tempting to move labour-intensive industries to a neighbouring country with cheaper labour, and to upgrade production by moving up the quality ladder. Rapid gains in education also played a key role in allowing this model to operate for two decades. In addition to well functioning labour markets and a strong emphasis on education, the conditions that have facilitated this pattern of division of labour include short distances, openness to trade and investment and large disparities in incomes (Kwan, 1997).

From a 'flying-geese' perspective, the countries of the region should be sensitive to the ripple effects emanating from the recent recession in Japan. Japan is the largest economy in Asia, an important market, and the main source of foreign investment and finance. Since 1995, the yen has been falling in the context of weak aggregate demand and a banking crisis. As a result, Japanese demand has fallen, and so have its investments in the region. The real effects of this add up to a large negative shock, and one that is especially devastating, coming on the heels of a decade-long strong yen (from the Plaza Agreements in 1985 to 1995). The strong yen, in contrast had accelerated deindustrialisation in Japan and led to a rapid rise in Japanese direct investments in the region (first in the NIEs, then in the ASEAN countries and more recently, in China, India and Vietnam).[3]

Putting the competition and complementarity stories back to back, it appears that the combined effects of the long-term rise of China in international markets and the weaknesses in the Japanese economy may have added up to a strong pincer effect on the 'flying-geese' formation. Starting in the mid-1980s, several Asian countries must have had strong incentives to expand their production structure and exports up the quality ladder (in some cases prematurely), under the dual pressure of rising low-skill production in China, and deindustrialisation in Japan. This movement was facilitated by the availability of large capital flows, including from Japan itself, which were partly invested in this industrial upgrading. In many countries, the rapid growth of industry led to the emergence of domestic supply constraints in the early 1990s, such as inadequate skilled labour to move products upmarket, or excessive wage growth. It is in this context that the recession in Japan emerged. By creating strong competitive pressures from above, the resulting slowdown throughout the region must have squeezed the profitability of the new investments in manufacturing (and perhaps exposed their fragility), pushing all the NIEs into a scramble for the lower end of medium-skill industries, a market segment already heavily invested by the emerging economies of Latin America and Europe.[4]

Both competitive and complementary forces therefore operated simultaneously in transmitting the effects of a devaluation of one East Asian country to the rest of the region. It is useful to think of three channels of regional transmission: a price effect, an income effect and an investment effect:

- *Price effects*   A devaluation in one country of the region can affect the other countries in several ways. Lower prices are good for consumers, but their effect on local producers will depend on whether competition or complementarity dominates in production:

  - If the two countries produce similar goods, competition will dominate, and there will be pressure on the domestic economy to devalue as well: the 'price effect' is negative, and will be larger the more similar are export bundles.

  - If the production structures are different and complementary, a devaluation by a partner can be good for the domestic economy because it enhances the competitiveness of their 'joint' output. This will be especially the case if the domestic economy imports capital goods or intermediary goods from the devaluing economy. In this case, we expect price effects to be positive and to be a function of the relative importance of intra-regional trade in intermediates and capital equipment. Complementarities will dominate trade relations when intra-regional trade is intra-industry, which is expected to be the case for rich–rich and rich–poor pairs of countries (because assembly work using sophisticated parts is usually done in the poorer countries). Complementarities in production are likely to be low in the relation between poor–rich and or poor–poor.[5]

- *Income effects*   A recession in one country reduces aggregate demand, and thus for final goods imports, and also affects over time demand for intermediate and capital goods. These effects will be larger the greater is the share of intra-regional trade in total trade – i.e. the larger are complementarities in consumption.

- *Investment effects*   If the affected country is rich (e.g. Japan), currency depreciation and slow or negative growth reduces FDI outflows towards the poorer countries and exports of complementary intermediate goods. Moreover, if the exchange rate remains at a significantly lower level or continues to fall for a protracted period, the country will become a more important competitor for richer economies on export markets (e.g. Korea). If the country is poor (e.g. Thailand) a devaluation makes it more competitive in attracting investments, especially for tradeables, and consequently creates pressures on countries lower on the quality ladder to follow. The trade and investment relationship between rich–poor country pairs will often be complementary; those between poor–poor pairs competitive; while in rich–poor cases the net effect is ambiguous In a 'flying-geese' context complementary effects operate through FDI outflows from richer to poorer countries, with FDI being a channel for trade in goods and the transfer of technology.

The net effect of these effects therefore depends in part on how deeply regional economies are integrated on the consumption side (negative income effect) and on the production side (ambiguous 'price' effect). With several countries of the region experiencing devaluation and recession, we would expect contagion to spread rapidly through the combined channels of increased competition, lower demand for imports and less FDI. On the other hand, complementarity in production will provide a positive countervailing effect: regional devaluations make the regional product more competitive in the rest of the world, and therefore reduce the pressure on the home economy to devalue. However, these complementarities in production are unlikely to be effective in the short run in reducing the severity of the regional shock given the weak balance sheets in the financial sector (limiting financing for new growth opportunities) and the fall in FDI from Japan.

In what follows, we use the available data to explore the relative importance of the various effects at play.

3 Linkages between East Asian economies

Correlations between macro aggregates can inform us regarding the relationships between China, Japan and the rest of Asia. If China is a major source of competition for East Asia, this should be reflected in negative correlations between Chinese and other East Asian exports and high levels of export similarity. The same variables can also give a sense of the relative importance of the complementarity story. As Japan plays a central role in this connection, both as a source of demand and as a source of investment and technology, we also report measures of co-variation between Japan and the rest of East Asia.

In what follows, we focus on growth rates rather than levels. The reason is that the levels of the main aggregates move very much in parallel and are not very informative about differences among the countries. On the other

Table 10.1. *Regressions on macro aggregates, 1970–1995*

	ALL	HKG	KOR	SGP	MYS	THA	PHL	IND
1 GDP growth								
Constant	–	5.9	9.1	6.4	6.8	4.7	6.1	7.9
GDP growth rate: Japan	0.2^a	1.3^c	–	0.6^c	0.7^c	0.3^a	–	–
Japan 1980–9	–	−1.6^c	–	–	–	1.5^c	1.0^b	–
1990–5	–	−1.7^c	–	–	–	0.5^a	−0.9^c	–
GDP growth rate: China	–	−0.4^c	–	–	−0.3^c	–	−0.2^a	–
China 1980–9	−0.2^b	0.7^c	–	–	–	−0.5^c	−0.7^a	−0.2^a
1990–9	–	0.4^b	–	–	0.5^c	–	–	–
$R^2 = 0.51$								
2 Investment growth:								
Constant	–	12.1	8.2	9.7	12.7	2.9	13.5	19.4
Japan	–	0.6^a	–	–	–	–	–	–
1980–9	–	–	–	–	–	–	1.6^b	–
1990–5	–	–	1.4^a	1.3^a	–	2.1^b	–	–
China	–	–	0.5^c	–	–	0.5^c	–	–
1980–9	−0.8^c	−0.5^a	−0.7^b	–	0.6^a	−0.7^b	−0.6^c	−1.6^c
1990–5	–	–	−0.6^a	–	–	–	−0.5^a	–
$R^2 = 0.37$								
3 Exports growth								
Japan exports	–	–	–	–	–	–	–	0.5^b
1980–9	−0.36^a	–	−1.2^b	–	–	–	−0.7^a	−1.7^c
1990–5	−1.14^a	–	–	–	–	–	−2.3^a	–
Japan consumption	1.4^c	1.6^b	5.4^c	–	–	–	–	2.6^c
1980–9	–	–	−5.6^c	–	1.6^a	–	–	–
1990–5	–	–	−7.3^c	–	–	–	–	–
China exports	–	–	–	0.2^a	–	–	–	–
1980–9	0.17^a	–	–	–	–	–	0.7^b	–
1990–5	0.51^c	–	–	–	0.5^a	–	0.9^b	–
China consumption	−1.1^b	−1.0^a	−3.7^c	–	–	–	–	−1.3^a
1980–9	0.8^b	1.5^c	3.5^c	–	–	–	–	1.1^a
1990–5	1.1^c	1.6^c	3.9^c	–	–	–	–	1.9^c
$R^2 = 0.37$								

Notes: ^{a} Significant at 5 per cent level.
^{b} Significant at 10 per cent level.
^{c} Significant at 20 per cent level.
– = Not available.

hand, we suspect that structures have a more marked effects on new activity. We look at the growth in GDP, consumption, investment and exports. The results are displayed in table 10.1 and figures 10.1–10.4.

In table 10.1, we report results from regressions of various variables in seven East–Asian economies on similar variables in Japan and China, over the period 1970–95. No lags are used, but we have added time dummies to test for structural shifts in the elasticities (for the period 1980–9 and 1990–5). The graphs attempt to look in more detail – admittedly, in a quite

Figure 10.1 Significant beta ($R^2 > 0.1$) of GDP growth with respect to GDP growth of China (BGGC_nnn) or Japan (BGGJ_nnn), 1980–1994

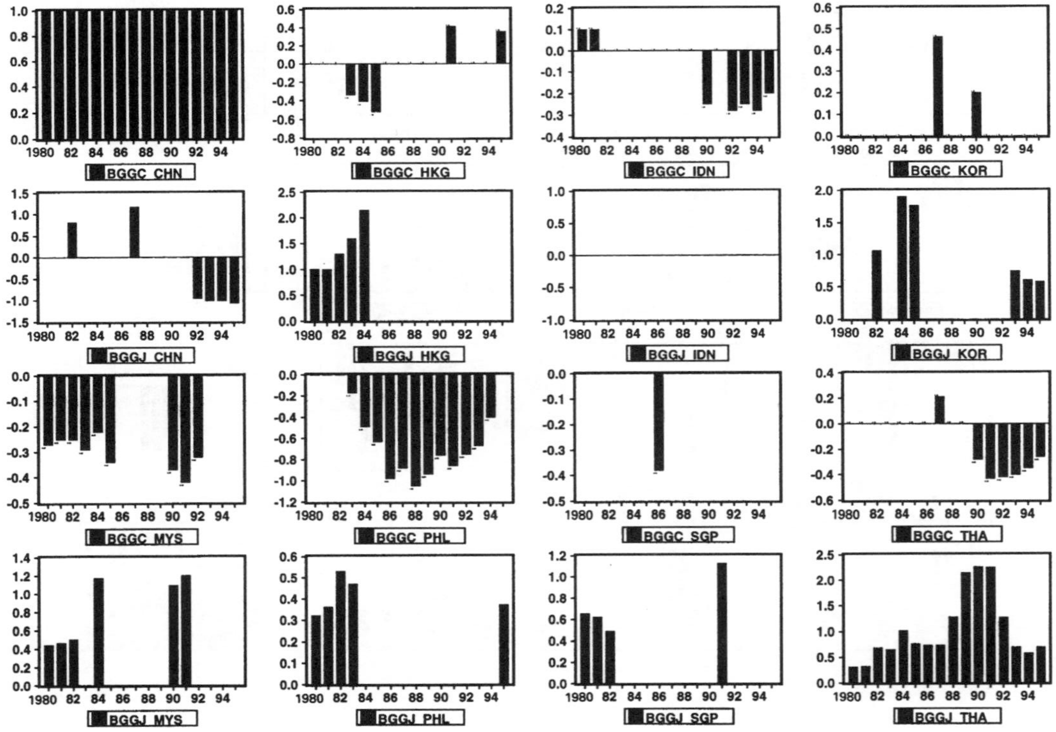

Figure 10.2   Significant beta ($R^2 > 0.1$) of investment growth with respect to investment growth of China (BIIC_nnn) or Japan
(BIIJ_nnn), 1980–1995

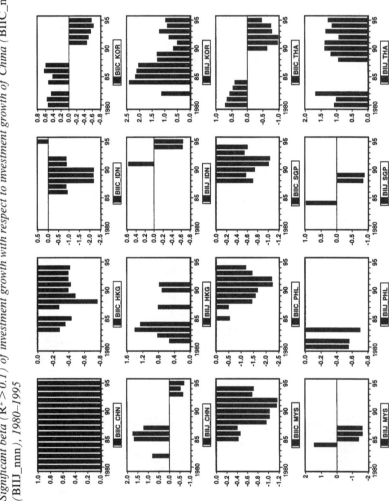

Figure 10.3   *Significant beta ($R^2 > 0.1$) of GDP growth with respect to GDP growth of China (BGGC_nnn) or Japan (BGGJ_nnn), 1980–1994*

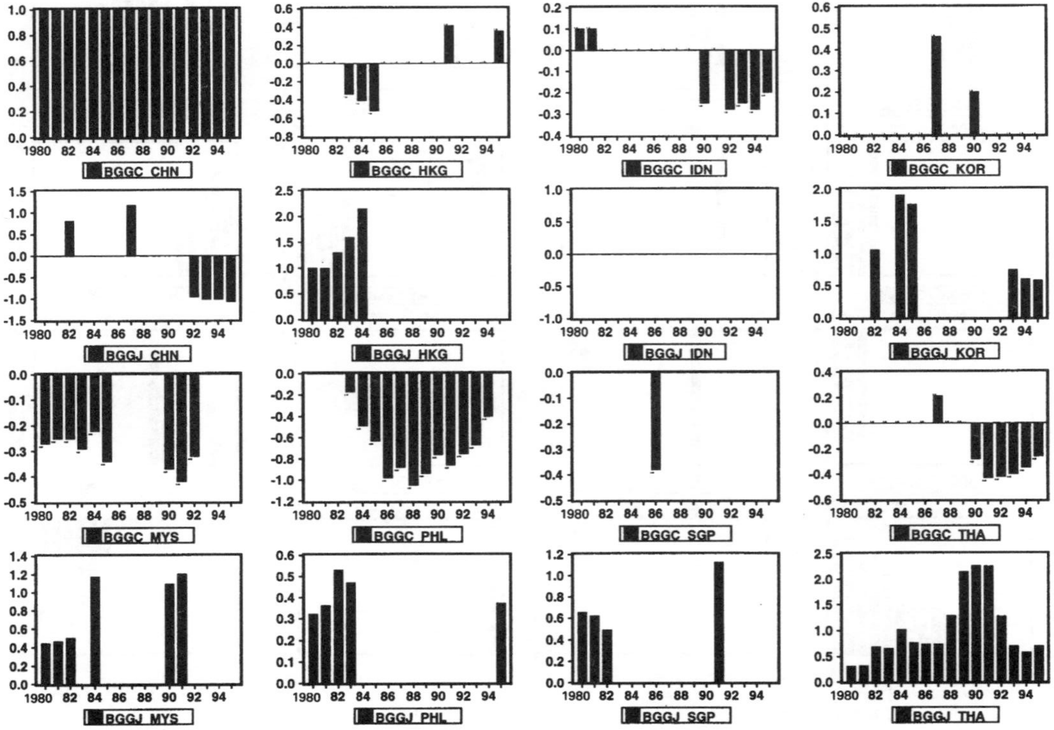

Figure 10.4   *Significant beta (R²>0.1) of export growth with respect to consumption growth of China (BXCC_nnn) or Japan (BXCJ_nnn), 1980–1995*

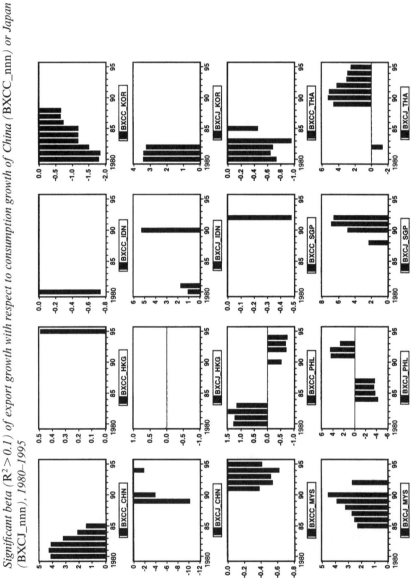

cavalier way – at the change in these elasticities through time.[6] For ease of comparison, for each East Asian nation we stack correlations with Japan on top of those with China.

The results paint a complex picture with some strong characteristics. In the first panel of table 10.1 and figure 10.1, we have regressed the growth rates of the NIEs and the ASEAN countries on output growth in Japan and China. Remarkably, growth in Japan and China 'explain' 50 per cent of the variability of growth in the rest of Asia. Two patterns appear clearly. Generally, Japan's growth is associated positively with growth elsewhere in Asia. The effect appears to weaken over time (except in the case of Thailand where the elasticity rises to 2.3), and to turn negative in the cases of China and Hong Kong in the 1990s. In contrast, China's growth is associated negatively – albeit weakly – with growth in most of Asia, and especially with the poorer and more labour-intensive countries. The correlation is positive for Hong Kong only. These results are consistent with a picture of an expanding 'flying-geese' formation in the process of integrating China into the group, with strong growth in all countries, but negative correlations in the variations of these rates of their trends, reflecting competition by China at the lower end followed by (ultimately creative) destruction in the leading countries.

In the second panel of table 10.1 and figure 10.2, we look at the structure of co-variations in investment growth rates among the countries of the region. China co-varies negatively with most countries of the region, including Hong Kong. These effects have risen sharply since the 1980s. With low-wage countries (the Philippines, Indonesia), the effects are now very large (elasticities close to 2). Conversely, Japan co-varies positively with most of the region. This suggests that China has increasingly become a competitor for investment in the region. In contrast Japan's investments growth moves generally with that of the other countries, as would be predicted by the 'flying-geese' model for the formation's leader.

Finally, we look at covariations in export growth (table 10.1, panel 3, figures 10.3 and 10.4). These are regressed on two variables: (1) consumption growth in Japan and China, to measure aggregate demand effects, if any; and (2) export growth in Japan and China, to measure the competitiveness vs. complementarity of exports. As expected, increased consumption growth in Japan pulls up exports from most of the region, and especially the poorer countries, but since the 1980s Japan has a large negative effect on Korea. China's consumption growth, too, is associated in several cases with rising export growth, but here the effect seems stronger with the more advanced countries. Japanese export growth tends to be negatively related to export growth in the rest of Asia. Competition between Japan and Korea seems particularly strong (with an elasticity of − 1.2). These effects increased a bit in the 1980s, and a lot in the 1990s. In contrast, the relation tends to be positive and larger over time between China and the rest of Asia.

This means that aggregate demand effects are likely to be large (at least in the short term), as would be expected among economies that are close together and open to each other. More important, the results corroborate the hypothesis of rising competition between Japan and the higher-end producers in the region, especially in recent years. At the same time, and somewhat surprisingly, the results also suggest that in the relation with China, complementarity in trade dominates. Although China competes in the same range of products as some of the poor countries of the region, its large needs for imports makes complementarity a dominant force.

To summarise, then, Korea appears to be competitive with Japan on the trade front, but its growth and investment rates are in sync with Japan and it is highly dependent on Japan as a market – a worst-case scenario given Japanese conditions. Thailand and Malaysia also appear highly dependent on Japan as a market and a source of capital. There are indications of increased competition with Japan, and decreased competition with China, presumably in parallel with an upgrading of production towards higher-value-added products. Finally, the labour-intensive Philippines and especially Indonesia compete with China in attempting to attract investment flows. They also depend on Japan as a market and investor. In what follows we explore to what extent data on the composition and pattern of trade and investment flows in the East Asia region shed light on the factors that may underpin the conclusions suggested by the co-variation measures.

4 Patterns of trade

Three factors should be looked at to gauge the relative importance of competition and complementarity in trade relations: (1) aggregate demand – the extent to which East Asia is a destination for Asian-produced output; (2) complementarities in production – the share of imported inputs that originates within the Asian region; and (3) competition – the extent to which the composition of the export mix of East Asian countries is similar and there are incentives for countries (markets) to emulate a depreciation by one country in order to maintain relative market shares in export markets.

4.1 Demand linkages

Intra-regional trade in East Asia is very substantial. If Japan is included, East Asia comes second after the EU in terms of the share of intra-regional in total trade. Intra-regional exports among East Asian countries

Table 10.2. *East Asia: Intra-and extra-regional*
trade, 1990–1997: 2 (percentage
share of total merchandise exports)

	1990	1996	1997:2
Intra-Asia-9[a]	31.7	38.5	39.4
Asia-9-Japan	14.5	13.1	11.8
Extra-regional	53.8	48.4	48.8

Note: [a] Asia-9 is China, Hong Kong, Indonesia, Korea,
Malaysia, the Philippines, Singapore, Taiwan,
Thailand.
Source: IMF, *Direction of Trade.*

accounted for almost 40 per cent of total exports in 1996, up from 31.7 per cent in 1990. If Japan is included the share of intra-regional trade rises to 51 per cent (table 10.2). These high levels of intra-regional trade reflect an ongoing process of specialisation between countries in the region, but has always been a distinct feature of East Asia. The intra-regional trade share was around 40 per cent in the 1930s through the 1950s (Anderson and Francois, 1997, p. 18).

The country with the lowest 'dependence' on other Asia-9 as an export destination is the Philippines (25 per cent of total exports); Singapore, Hong Kong and Malaysia have the greatest dependence (40 to 45 per cent) (table 10.3). China, Hong Kong, Malaysia, the Philippines, Singapore and Thailand source more than 50 per cent of their imports from East Asia, reflecting intense trade relations among pairs of countries. Abstracting from Hong Kong–China and Malaysia–Singapore – where geography and history explain the very intense trade relations that prevail, Japan–China is an important bilateral pair: 22 (11) per cent of Chinese (Japanese) imports originate in Japan (China). Taiwan is also an important source of imports for China (13 per cent of the total). Japan is particularly important as a source of products for Korea, Malaysia, Thailand and Taiwan. Some indicative comparisons: Hong Kong is as important as an export destination for Taiwan as the USA; Singapore ships as much to Malaysia as it does to the USA; Thailand exports almost as much to Singapore as it does to Japan; China–Hong Kong is as important for Korea as the US market is; and Korea and Taiwan together buy almost as much from Japan as the EU-15 member countries. Japan is a major market for most of the East Asian economies, the exceptions being Hong Kong and Singapore. China and Hong Kong are major export markets for Taiwan. With Japan, UN statistics suggest that these three countries absorbed half of Taiwan's exports in 1995.

All in all, the statistics clearly reveal a more complex pattern of trade than would be expected if the simple competitive model were to hold. Korea

Table 10.3. *Intra-regional exports, by country, 1995 (percentage share of total exports)*

	China	Hong Kong	Indonesia	Korea	Malaysia	Philippines	Singapore	Thailand	Taiwan	Japan	East Asia
China	0.00	0.24	0.01	0.04	0.01	0.01	0.02	0.01	0.02	0.19	0.56
Hong Kong	0.27	0.00	0.01	0.01	0.01	0.01	0.05	0.01	0.03	0.05	0.47
Indonesia	0.04	0.04	0.00	0.06	0.02	0.01	0.08	0.02	0.04	0.27	0.58
Korea	0.07	0.08	0.02	0.00	0.02	0.01	0.05	0.02	0.03	0.14	0.45
Malaysia	0.03	0.05	0.01	0.03	0.00	0.01	0.20	0.04	0.03	0.13	0.53
Philippines	0.01	0.05	0.01	0.02	0.02	0.00	0.05	0.05	0.03	0.16	0.40
Singapore	0.02	0.09	0.01	0.03	0.19	0.02	0.00	0.06	0.04	0.08	0.53
Thailand	0.03	0.05	0.01	0.01	0.03	0.01	0.14	0.00	0.02	0.17	0.48
Taiwan	0.13	0.23	0.02	0.02	0.03	0.01	0.04	0.03	0.00	0.12	0.63
Japan	0.05	0.06	0.02	0.07	0.04	0.02	0.05	0.04	0.07	0.00	0.42
East Asia	0.05	0.10	0.02	0.04	0.04	0.01	0.06	0.03	0.04	0.09	0.49

Source: UN, Comtrade data base.

provides an illustration of how some countries in the region have come to rely more on East Asia as a market. Korean exports have grown at double-digit rates for over two decades. Over time, Korea's trade has been re-orientated away from exporting to the rest of the world (especially the USA) towards other East Asian countries. As of the mid-1990s, the share of OECD countries in total Korean exports stood at around 50 per cent, down from 80 per cent as recently as 1987. Exports to developing East Asia had expanded from 12 to almost 40 per cent over the same period. Giorgianni and Milesi-Ferretti (1997) document that this is not simply a reflection of slower growth or a decline in demand for Korean products. They conclude that Korea lost market share in OECD markets during 1987–97 to other East Asian economies including China, Hong Kong, Malaysia and Thailand. However, this was more than offset by booming exports to East Asia, which increasingly took the form of capital goods. As of 1995, Japan and Hong Kong–China figured among Korea's largest trading partners. Consequently, Korea became much more dependent on the economic health of the region.

The foregoing focuses on regional shares in total trade, which does not take into account the size of partner-country markets. Controlling for the size of import markets absorbing exports is important in determining whether trade flows are more concentrated within the region that would be 'normal' given the region's share of the world economy. One way to do this is to use export intensities as a measure of trade patterns. This is defined as $XI = (Xij \mid Xi) \mid (Mj \mid (Mw - Mi))$ where M and X are imports and exports of goods respectively, i is a reporting (or source) country, j a partner (importing) country; and w is the world. If this measure is greater than 1, trade is more 'intense' than would be expected. Export intensities of trade within the region are often significantly greater than 1 (table 10.4). For Japan and Korea, intensities for exports are above 1 for all East Asian partners. The same is true for the poorer countries, although with less uniformity. Japan and Korea are large markets for China, but the poorer East Asian economies are not. On average, export intensities within the region are about 2, and are particularly high for trade between Hong Kong and China, Hong Kong and Taiwan and Malaysia–Singapore.

4.2 Complementarity

Most of this intra-regional trade is in intermediates. These account for 65–75 per cent of total imports of East Asian countries from the world (table 10.5).[7] Between 60 and 80 per cent of total imports from East Asia by East Asian countries consist of intermediate inputs and parts (table 10.6). The

Table 10.4. Export intensity of total trade, 1996

Reporter	JPN	CHN	HKG	TAI	IDN	KOR	MYS	PHL	THA	SGP	EAS	NAM	EU	WLD
JPN	–	1.82	1.47	2.95	2.44	2.34	2.32	2.80	2.94	1.81	1.58	1.39	0.37	0.93
CHN	2.92	–	5.44	0.91	1.09	1.70	0.59	0.96	0.57	0.94	2.15	0.94	0.33	0.97
HKG	0.75	10.2	–	1.53	0.84	0.42	0.76	1.70	0.83	1.76	1.86	1.36	0.44	0.96
TAI	1.69	0.19	5.80	–	1.96	0.79	1.67	2.40	1.67	1.50	1.99	1.24	0.35	0.98
IDN	3.77	1.51	0.83	1.63	–	2.30	1.48	2.02	1.16	3.48	2.29	0.74	0.40	0.99
KOR	1.77	3.26	1.95	1.37	2.96	–	1.87	2.17	1.47	1.41	1.78	0.93	0.31	0.97
MYS	1.94	0.87	1.49	2.03	1.82	1.06	–	1.73	2.86	7.84	2.21	0.96	0.35	0.99
PHL	2.62	0.59	1.09	1.62	0.83	0.64	2.25	–	2.70	2.32	1.71	1.83	0.43	0.99
THA	2.43	1.05	1.31	1.19	1.68	0.49	1.82	1.06	–	5.38	1.94	0.97	0.39	0.99
SGP	1.17	0.97	2.23	1.91	–	1.04	11.70	2.61	3.92	–	2.09	0.95	0.33	0.97
EA	0.98	1.23	1.96	1.48	1.38	1.18	2.16	1.74	2.72	0.98	1.45	0.90	0.28	0.75
NA	1.09	0.53	0.35	0.94	0.56	0.99	0.58	0.92	1.11	0.30	0.76	1.52	0.35	0.81
EU	0.19	0.20	0.17	0.18	0.31	0.19	0.19	0.18	0.33	0.12	0.19	0.24	0.98	0.61

Note: – = Not available
Source: UN Comtrade data base.

import composition from East Asia is not much different from that from the rest of the world (e.g. North America and the EU), where intermediates are also the dominant type of product. What stands out, however, is that imports of intermediates from other East Asian countries represent 35–40 per cent of global imports of East Asian economies. East Asia accounts for 55–60 per cent of total imports of intermediates for China, Malaysia, the Philippines and Thailand, rising to 70 per cent for Hong Kong (table 10.5, last column). Japan plays a major role in this connection: between 10 and 20 per cent of global East Asian imports comprise intermediate inputs from Japan. East Asia accounts for fully one-third of Japan's total exports of intermediates to the world. Japan is much less important as a market for intermediates than it is a source of such products, but it is nonetheless quite significant for some countries (Indonesia, the Philippines, Thailand – around 10 per cent of their global exports) (appendix Table 10A.1, p. 341). The share of intermediates in total exports to individual countries and regions indicates that intermediates are less important in exports to North America and the EU than to East Asia (appendix table 10A.2, p. 341). These markets absorb a greater proportion of final goods (consumer products).

Export-intensity numbers confirm the importance of trade in intermediates, using the same definition of intensity as before, but limiting the trade flows to intermediate products (table 10.7). The intensity of Japan's exports to East Asian economies is above 1 in all cases. China is less 'dependent' on exports of intermediates to the region, having intensities above 1 primarily in richer-country markets (Japan, Taiwan and Korea), and not being an intensive importer itself for most East Asian partners. Korea has high intensities of exports to the region, but the converse is not true – except for China and Japan, Korea is not an important market for intermediate exports from other countries. Other NIEs and ASEAN countries all have intensities above 1 as import markets for regional exports of intermediates. In general, the figures closely mirror those for total trade reported in table 10.4, although on average they are somewhat higher, reflecting the importance of intermediates in total intra-regional trade. The data suggest there are strong complementarities between rich–poor pairs (cf. Japan's and Singapore's intensities with ASEAN countries), but that this is less so for poor–poor-country pairs.

4.3 Competition?

The foregoing suggests there are significant complementarities in trade in the region. They also illustrate that trade dependence is high, so that the vulnerability to demand shocks and what we earlier called 'income effects' will be

Table 10.5. *Share of intermediates in global imports of East Asian countries, 1995*

	JPN	CHN	HK	TAI	IDN	KOR	MYS	PHL	THA	SGP	EAS	NA	EU	World	EAS/world
JPN	–	3.6	0.4	2.2	1.5	2.5	1.7	0.7	1.5	0.8	15.2	15.7	7.3	46.3	32.8
CHN	17.4	–	4.5	9.7	0.8	7.2	1.4	0.2	1.0	1.3	43.6	9.8	11.5	76.6	56.9
HK	10.3	15.8	–	7.2	0.6	4.0	1.6	0.4	1.2	2.7	43.7	5.9	8.0	63.0	69.4
TAI	24.6	2.3	1.0	–	0.9	3.5	2.9	0.7	1.1	1.8	39.2	14.6	9.8	72.6	53.9
IDN	17.7	2.5	0.5	3.2	–	4.9	1.4	0.1	1.2	3.1	34.8	10.5	18.7	75.3	46.2
KOR	18.4	3.8	0.6	1.6	1.0	–	1.3	0.3	0.4	0.9	28.6	18.0	11.0	66.1	43.3
MYS	20.2	1.8	1.8	4.2	1.2	4.3	–	1.0	2.5	9.9	47.0	12.8	11.5	77.4	60.7
PHL	17.5	1.6	3.5	4.3	1.4	4.3	1.9	–	1.1	3.9	39.9	15.5	9.3	72.5	55.0
THA	24.7	2.2	1.1	3.5	0.6	2.7	3.4	0.7	–	3.7	42.9	10.0	11.8	75.5	56.8
SGP	14.2	1.9	2.1	3.3	–	2.5	10.1	1.0	2.9	–	38.2	12.4	10.4	65.4	58.4

Note: – = Not available.

Table 10.6. *Share of intermediates in total imports from East Asia, North America and the EU, 1995*

	JPN	CHN	HK	TAI	IDN	KOR	MYS	PHL	THA	SGP	EA	NA	EU
JPN	–	31.3	54.2	51.2	33.7	55.8	49.4	56.7	49.6	39.4	42.0	60.9	51.5
CHN	82.8	–	80.2	82.9	49.8	79.6	86.9	56.4	73.4	50.9	79.0	73.0	80.6
HK	75.9	42.4	–	89.2	71.9	84.3	71.6	73.0	75.3	51.0	59.0	69.8	72.2
TAI	91.0	77.2	64.4	–	49.6	88.9	81.8	87.4	65.7	67.4	84.0	69.8	60.1
IDN	89.4	67.6	77.7	83.4	–	87.0	74.8	69.9	45.9	46.9	76.4	77.0	87.2
KOR	84.9	63.8	83.7	86.0	36.3	–	63.8	72.0	52.1	53.0	74.5	73.8	77.0
MYS	80.2	72.9	76.1	81.3	66.2	89.5	–	93.8	74.4	75.0	78.7	77.6	77.6
PHL	80.2	71.3	83.2	86.5	70.0	83.4	77.7	–	58.1	74.9	78.5	76.1	83.1
THA	86.7	81.1	92.5	80.8	49.4	73.2	67.9	84.9	–	67.8	80.3	75.1	78.3
SGP	78.8	57.1	67.5	83.2	–	74.4	67.3	89.6	52.4	–	70.8	73.5	71.4

Note: – = Not available.

Table 10.7. *Intensity of intermediate goods exports, 1996*

Reporter	JPN	CHN	HKG	TAI	IDN	KOR	MYS	PHL	THA	SGP	EA	NAM	EU	WLD
JPN	–	1.64	1.49	3.08	2.52	2.62	2.22	2.65	2.76	1.81	1.75	1.41	0.35	0.95
CHN	2.84	–	5.64	1.13	1.30	1.89	0.75	0.95	0.79	0.94	2.08	0.91	0.35	0.96
HKG	0.89	11.6	–	1.27	1.01	0.41	0.82	2.17	1.06	2.50	2.39	0.79	0.27	0.96
TAI	1.61	0.19	6.76	–	1.86	0.85	1.50	2.51	1.53	1.61	2.06	1.15	0.29	0.98
IDN	3.67	1.04	1.19	1.32	–	1.68	1.64	2.73	0.86	3.50	2.03	0.65	0.49	0.99
KOR	1.97	3.28	2.45	1.51	3.12	–	2.05	2.22	1.31	1.57	1.98	1.00	0.26	0.97
MYS	2.17	0.93	1.57	2.18	1.45	0.87	–	1.71	2.20	7.89	2.19	0.93	0.34	0.98
PHL	3.19	0.36	1.07	1.52	0.85	0.62	2.47	–	3.10	2.76	1.78	1.77	0.46	0.99
THA	3.22	0.58	1.93	1.24	1.25	0.49	1.9	1.09	–	5.63	2.07	0.85	0.36	0.98
SGP	1.19	0.81	1.84	1.87	–	0.92	12.6	2.85	3.76	–	2.19	0.85	0.30	0.97
EA	0.89	1.15	1.99	1.54	1.45	1.23	2.14	1.75	2.41	1.07	1.47	0.88	0.25	0.73
NA	1.31	0.45	0.35	0.83	0.51	1.01	0.57	0.92	1.02	0.29	0.75	1.62	0.38	0.82
EU	0.21	0.20	0.19	0.17	0.29	0.20	0.17	0.19	0.30	0.14	0.20	0.29	0.97	0.62

Note: – = Not available.
Source: UN Comtrade data base.

high. To what extent do the data support the hypothesis that East Asian countries are competing with each other for external markets? It has often been noted in this connection that countries in the region tend to have similar export structures. With the exception of Indonesia (which is an outlier because it is an important exporter of natural resource-based products), for each of the East Asian countries two of the three countries with the most similar export structures in the mid-1980s were other East Asian countries (Noland 1997).[8] Export similarity rankings for 1995 are reported in table 10.8 for extra- and intra-regional trade. Japan, a high-income industrialised nation not surprisingly, has exports that are most similar to those of other OECD countries. Noteworthy, however, is that in intra-regional trade Singapore and Korea come in third place in terms of similarity. China's exports are more similar to those of Portugal and Italy than of other East Asian economies, while Hong Kong is most similar to Tunisia. These rankings clearly are driven by the importance of clothing exports for all these countries.

Correlations between export structures of East Asian countries in 1995 also reveal there is significant similarity for some country pairs, although correlations for many country pairs are relatively low (table 10.9). For some East Asian countries (Japan, China, Hong Kong, Indonesia) countries with the highest correlation ratios are outside the region (appendix table 10A.3, p. 342). The correlations and similarity indices do not suggest that China is a major source of 'competition' for East Asian countries – abstracting from Hong Kong, Chinese exports are highly correlated only with Indonesia (0.53) and the Philippines (0.54), and in extra-regional trade only (table 10.9). Indonesia, too, has very low correlations with the exports of other East Asian countries. For the other countries, exports tend to be more similar, especially for intra-regional trade. In general, correlations are significantly higher for trade within the region than in rest-of-the-world markets. While for some country pairs (e.g. Malaysia–Singapore) this is likely to reflect intra-industry trade (complementarity), for many there is certainly a strong competitive dimension as well. Countries such as Laos, Vietnam, and Taiwan clearly devalued for competitive reasons.

Another way of investigating the competition hypothesis is to determine whether East Asian nations have been losing market share to each other in major markets. With the exception of Korea and Singapore, East Asian countries expanded their shares of world markets in 1995 and 1996. Greater international competition did emerge in major markets such as the USA and EU, but this did not come at the 'expense' of East Asia. For example, despite the fact that Central and Eastern European (CEE) countries doubled or tripled their share of the EU market in products where East Asian economies were major suppliers (e.g. electrical equipment) from the 1–2 per cent range to 6 or 7 per cent, with the exception of Korea, East

Table 10.8. *Export similarity, 1995*

	Extra-regional trade			Intra-regional trade		
	Most similar	2nd most similar	3rd most similar	Most similar	2nd most similar	3rd most similar
Japan	Germany	USA	UK	Germany	USA	Singapore/Korea
China	Portugal	Taiwan	Italy	Hong Kong	Taiwan	Italy
Hong Kong	Tunisia	China	Philippines	China	Taiwan	Japan
Singapore	Malaysia	Korea	Ireland	Malaysia	Japan	USA
Taiwan	Singapore	Korea	Malaysia	Korea	Japan	Hong Kong
Korea	Japan	Philippines	UK	Taiwan	Singapore	Japan
Malaysia	Singapore	Philippines	Japan	Singapore	Philippines	Japan
Philippines	Malaysia	Korea	China	Malaysia	Singapore	Portugal
Indonesia	China	Portugal	Malaysia	Malaysia	Korea	Canada
Thailand	–	–	–	–	–	–

Note: – = Not available.
Source: UN Comtrade, 3-digit SITC (174 product categories).

Table 10.9. *Export share correlations in intra-regional and extra-regional trade, 1996[a]*

	JPN	CHN	HKG	IDN	KOR	MYS	PHL	SGP	TWN
JPN	1	0.15	0.06	0.01	0.78	0.43	0.38	0.44	0.48
CHN	0.29	1	0.85	0.53	0.35	0.40	0.54	0.26	0.41
HKG	0.63	0.81	1	0.72	0.23	0.31	0.58	0.16	0.25
IDN	0.17	0.20	0.34	1	0.18	0.34	0.31	0.10	0.16
KOR	0.80	0.35	0.69	0.28	1	0.67	0.72	0.50	0.55
MYS	0.77	0.36	0.69	0.37	0.78	1	0.82	0.76	0.74
PHL	0.73	0.32	0.64	0.14	0.76	0.92	1	0.64	0.65
SGP	0.79	0.36	0.66	0.32	0.79	0.91	0.88	1	0.94
TWN	0.81	0.43	0.70	0.32	0.90	0.77	0.72	0.76	1

Note: [a] *Above* the diagonal: correlations in world market; *below* the diagonal: correlations in regional market.
Source: UN Comtrade, 3-digit SITC (174 product categories).

Asian market shares continued to rise in 1995–6.[9] This is not to say greater competitive pressure from new sources of supply did not affect East Asian producers: maintaining market share could clearly be a motivation underlying the competitive devaluations that were observed in 1997. Enterprises located in Poland, Hungary, the Czech Republic and Mexico are also vigorous competitors; these countries have export structures that are very similar to those of higher-income East Asian countries (correlation coefficients are in the 0.8 range – not reported). Others such as Romania, Turkey and India are competing in sectors such as footwear and clothing.

5 Direct investment flows

Investment flows have played an important role in the region during the 1990s. Led by private investors, capital flows to Asia expanded from $20 bn to $110 bn between 1990 and 1996: the extra flows accruing to the region represent nearly half of the increase in capital flows to all developing regions. The second closest receiving region was Latin America, where the flows grew more slowly, from $12bn to $74bn over the same period. Europe and Central Asia came third, with flows rising from $10 to $31bn (table 10.10).

Intra-regional FDI flows have been a significant part of these flows. About half of the stock of FDI in East Asia is of East Asian origin – Japan and Hong Kong being the major outward investors (Anderson and Francois, 1997, p. 22). Frankel and Wei (1996) note that FDI into East Asian developing countries has doubled every two years since 1987. Up to the mid-1980s, the USA was the main investor in East Asia. Thereafter it was supplanted by Japan. Initially Japanese FDI was concentrated in Korea and Indonesia, mostly in activities such as clothing and electronics. In some cases (e.g. semiconductor investment in Malaysia), much of the output was exported to other East Asian nations (Encarnation, 1992). Starting in the second half of the 1980s, following the appreciation of the yen, Japanese FDI outflows accelerated, with an increasing share of the total in manufacturing going to East Asia (Kawai and Urata, 1998). As of 1990, Japan accounted for about one-third of the flow of FDI in Malaysia, the Philippines, Indonesia, Korea, Taiwan and Singapore (Rao, 1995). This was driven by production-cost considerations, and exporting back to Japan was an important motive for many investors. These investments, coupled with increased competition in low-skill products encouraged an upgrading of industries.

Malaysia vividly illustrates this. Since the mid-1980s when FDI took off, Malaysia has transformed itself from an economy heavily dependent on exports of primary commodities to a NIE highly competitive in manufacturing. Primary commodities dropped from 70 to 30 per cent of exports, while the share of manufacturing goods rose from 30 to 70 per cent. Similar, but less spectacular, patterns are also observed in Thailand and to a lesser extent, in the Philippines and Indonesia.

As of the late 1980s, enterprises located in other rich Asian economies such as Taiwan, Hong Kong and Singapore also began to engage in outward FDI, driven in part by real exchange rate appreciation. Over the 1985–91 period, FDI inflows from Taiwan into ASEAN were roughly equal to those of Japan. Total East Asian (including Japan) FDI into ASEAN countries accounted for well over half of all inflows. Much of this went into electrical machinery, including electronics (Kawai and Urata, 1998). In the period leading up to the crisis, intra-regional FDI flows shifted to China and Indochina, and ASEAN countries became sources of FDI. By 1996, China was attracting over $50bn, seven times more than in 1990, and more than half of the total capital inflows to the region for the fifth year in a row. Since the early 1990s, two-thirds of all FDI into China came from the NIEs; add a rising flow from Japan (which grew to $5bn in 1995), and the total rises to over 75 per cent. It is reported that about 10–15 per cent of FDI into China in the mid-1990s originated in ASEAN (Frankel and Wei, 1996, p. 31). To a large extent, these inflows represent investments for the production of local consumption goods, especially durables, and have been encouraged by China's preference for markets against technology-type deals. But a large fraction has also been in export sectors, increasingly competing with ASEAN countries' products such as textiles and toys.

As in the case of trade flows there is a strong intra-regional bias in FDI

Table 10.10. Net private long-term capital flows[a] to developing countries, by country group, 1990–96 (US$ bn)

Country group[b] or country	1990	1991	1992	1993	1994	1995	1996[c]
All developing countries	44.4	56.9	90.6	157.1	161.3	184.2	243.8
Sub-Saharan Africa	0.3	0.8	-0.3	-0.5	5.2	9.1	11.8
East Asia and the Pacific	19.3	20.8	36.9	62.4	71.0	84.1	108.7
South Asia	2.2	1.9	2.9	6.0	8.5	5.2	10.7
Europe and Central Asia	9.5	7.9	21.8	25.6	17.2	30.1	31.2
Latin America and the Caribbean	12.5	22.9	28.7	59.8	53.6	54.3	74.3
Middle East and North Africa	0.6	2.2	0.5	3.9	5.8	1.4	6.9
Top country destination[d]							
China	8.1	7.5	21.3	39.6	44.4	44.3	52.0
Mexico	8.2	12.0	9.2	21.2	20.7	13.1	28.1
Brazil	0.5	3.6	9.8	16.1	12.2	19.1	14.7
Malaysia	1.8	4.2	6.0	11.3	8.9	11.9	16.0
Indonesia	3.2	3.4	4.6	1.1	7.7	11.6	17.9
Thailand	4.5	5.0	4.3	6.8	4.8	9.1	13.3
Argentina	-0.2	2.9	4.2	13.8	7.6	7.2	11.3
India	1.9	1.6	1.7	4.6	6.4	3.6	8.0
Russia	5.6	0.2	10.8	3.1	0.3	1.1	3.6
Turkey	1.7	1.1	4.5	7.6	1.6	2.0	4.7
Chile	2.1	1.2	1.6	2.2	4.3	4.2	4.6
Hungary	-0.3	1.0	1.2	4.7	2.8	7.8	2.5

Notes: [a] Country groups are classified according to the World Bank's 'Debt Reporting System'.
[b] 'Private flows' include commercial bank lending guaranteed by export credit agencies.
[c] Preliminary.
[d] Country ranking is based on cumulative 1990–5 private capital flows received. 'Private flows' include commercial bank loans guaranteed by export credit agencies.
Source: World Bank (1997).

flows. The intra-regional FDI intensity index for East Asia as a region (defined analogously to the trade-intensity index) rose during the 1980s (Primo Braga and Bannister, 1994). There is a strong link between FDI and trade – both in components (inputs) and outputs (Urata, 1993). Frankel and Wei (1996) and Kawai and Urata (1998) fit gravity model-type regressions including FDI as a regressor and conclude that FDI helps expand exports from the source country to the destination country. Kawai and Urata (1998) note that 40 per cent of total procurement of foreign affiliates from Japan are intermediates. In the electrical equipment and electronics sectors the share is higher, averaging 50 per cent. However, Rao (1995) also notes that 40–50 per cent of components used by Japanese affiliates in East Asia are sourced from Japan, and that at least 25 per cent of output was exported to regional destinations. Controlling for distance and *per capita* income differences, Primo Braga and Bannister (1994) regress measures of East Asian intra-industry trade on lagged Japanese FDI inflows, and find that such FDI has a statistically significant positive association with the level of intra-industry trade. They also find that intra-firm trade involving Japanese parent firms and affiliates in East Asia is much more oriented towards 'upstream' than 'downstream' activities (trade flows from the affiliate to the parent are triple those going the other way).

Kimura (1997), using more recent and disaggregated data on Japanese FDI, argues that the role of Japan as a market for affiliate output is smaller than is often assumed. He concludes that much of the output of affiliates in East Asia is for the local market and for export to other Asian countries. In value added terms, almost 50 per cent of affiliate output is for local consumption; about 40 per cent or so is for East Asian consumption (including Japan). Kawai and Urata (1998) note that Japan accounts for a significantly larger share of sales of affiliates located in East Asia than those located elsewhere (16 per cent instead of 1–3 per cent). For precision and electrical machinery the ratios are much larger: 50 and 25 per cent, respectively.

All of this is suggestive of relatively strong processing-type relationships between FDI into East Asia from other East Asian countries, in particular Japan: part of the complementary, intra-regional trade is connected to FDI. But it also reveals that much of the output of foreign affiliates in East Asia is oriented towards domestic and regional markets, increasing the sensitivity to macro-economic developments in partner countries and at home. Over time, large shifts in the pattern and composition of FDI flows could have had significant implications for some East Asian countries. Unfortunately we do not have access to FDI data on a bilateral origin–destination basis analogous to trade. Aggregate Japanese data for East Asia as a destination reveal that FDI in manufacturing grew substantially in absolute terms between 1993 and 1995, but fell in 1996. FDI in services, in contrast, continued to expand through 1996, reflecting real estate-related investment (appendix table 10A.5, p. 344). No equivalent fall in manufacturing FDI outflows to the world is observed in 1996 (appendix table 10A.4). This suggests that macro conditions in East Asia were playing a role in inducing a shift towards non-tradeables and away from trade-ables.[10] (Data for 1997 were not yet available at the time of writing.)

A noteworthy feature of the region's trade with Japan during 1995–6 was a substantial decline in Japan's imports from Korea (down 9 per cent in 1996) and a large drop in East Asia's imports from Japan (down 18 per cent). Total imports by Japan from Asia grew in 1996 by 6 per cent, making Korea's weak export performance stand out even more.[11] This could reflect the increasing competition in the high-end markets, as hypothesized above. More surprisingly, total Asian imports fell by only 3.5 per cent in 1996, much less than the 18 per cent decline in imports from Japan. Given the depreciating yen/appreciating dollar, this is difficult to understand. One possibility is that the decline in Japanese exports to East Asia in 1996 reflected the domestic slowdown in Japan, reducing demand for 'processing services' in East Asia, which is reflected in a fall in components and materials shipped there. Another possibility is that the decline reflects the slowdown in direct investment in machinery and capital good sectors in East Asia.

6 Conclusions

Between June 1997 and the time of writing the currencies of the countries of the region have fallen by 30–35 per cent in the case of Korea, the Philippines, Thailand and Malaysia, and by 70 per cent in Indonesia (but remained stable in China, Singapore and Hong Kong). Real-side factors were an important factor in both the emergence and rapid spread of the crisis across East Asia. The evidence reviewed in this chapter tends to assign a large role to Japan and China for the genesis of the crisis, and to the extent of intra-regional integration in its spread. A number of channels were identified as having a cumulative negative impact: competition for markets, demand effects and investment (FDI) effects.

Rising competition from below (China, India, Vietnam) and from above (Japan), on both trade and investment, put pressures on many of the East Asian economies. China's entry into global markets marked a major change in the 'flying-geese' formation. Increased competition on lower-end producers affected mostly the poorer countries (Indonesia, Thailand, Malaysia). This pushed them all to move (in some cases prematurely) up the technology ladder, resulting in high demands for investment, including FDI. Competition for capital therefore became fiercer. The depreciation of the yen then increased competition for higher-end products, pushing many East

Asian countries to scramble back towards medium-skills products. The continuing slow-growth macro environment in Japan reduced demand for Asian output, putting further pressure on producers. These developments have extended the 'flying-geese' formation to lower-wage countries, but they have also reduced growth opportunities for countries in the middle range.

It is difficult to argue that increased competition by China could have come as a surprise to the 1997 market. Some have argued that the shock was related to a devaluation in China. But available data suggests that China's effective devaluation in 1994 was relatively small; this was because it involved devaluing an official rate whose relevance was limited. Effective export prices increased by only one-fifth of the nominal devaluation (or 10 per cent), while leaving import prices unchanged. Since the unification, the real exchange rate has appreciated against the US dollar by some 20 per cent.[12] The more recent entry by countries such as Vietnam and Laos may have had a greater impact in terms of competition for the poorer East Asian countries.

Pressure from Japan is likely to be a major real-side factor underlying the Asian crisis. The yen depreciated by 35 per cent between its peak in 1995 and mid-1997. This adds up to a serious competitive shock, especially for the NIEs. It is also of the same order of magnitude as the subsequent depreciations of Korea, the Philippines, Malaysia and Thailand and suggests that the genesis of the crisis may be closely tied up with the realisation of what the Japan crisis means for the rest of Asia in terms of what we have called price, income and investment effects. The depreciation of the yen will have been good for users of Japanese-produced inputs, but will reduce the incentive for outward FDI, reduce Japanese demand for imports and increase the export competitiveness of Japanese firms that produce similar goods to those of East Asian firms.

Complementarity of trade flows in the region is significant. In principle, this should act as a stabiliser in the medium term, as the competitiveness of the Asia Inc. 'joint product' on world markets is enhanced following the depreciation of national exchange rates. In the short run, this positive effect was swamped by aggregate demand effects, and will not operate unless credit constraints diminish. However, export volumes from the region expanded substantially in 1998, rising by over 20 per cent, suggesting that this effect may be beginning to operate. Most of this flow is going to the rest of the world, not East Asia, where aggregate imports are expected to decline by some 5 per cent in 1998 (World Bank, 1998). Given the historical importance of intra-regional trade, the concern then is about the health of the Korean and Japanese economies. Without a resumption in growth and continued movement towards an information and service-based economy in the richer economies in the region, the adjustment process will be severely impeded.

APPENDIX

Table 10A.1.   Share of intermediates in global exports of East Asian countries, by destination, 1995

	JPN	CHN	HK	TAI	IDN	KOR	MYS	PHL	THA	SGP	EA	NA	EU	World
JPN	–	4.2	4.5	5.4	2.0	6.0	3.1	1.6	3.6	3.7	34.3	17.9	9.6	68.3
CHN	7.0	–	10.8	1.3	0.6	2.8	0.7	0.4	0.7	1.2	26.0	7.4	6.0	44.4
HK	2.6	22.1	–	1.7	0.6	0.7	0.9	1.0	1.0	3.8	35.0	7.5	5.6	51.6
TAI	6.2	0.5	20.2	–	1.4	2.0	2.1	1.5	2.0	3.3	40.2	14.5	7.9	70.1
IDN	9.1	1.7	2.3	1.5	–	2.5	1.5	1.1	0.7	4.6	25.7	5.3	8.6	46.0
KOR	6.7	7.4	6.5	2.4	2.1	–	2.6	1.2	1.5	2.9	34.4	11.2	6.2	62.0
MYS	7.4	2.1	4.2	3.4	1.0	1.8	–	0.9	2.5	14.4	38.1	10.4	8.1	62.7
PHL	11.4	0.8	3.0	2.5	0.6	1.3	3.2	–	3.7	5.2	32.3	20.7	11.5	66.2
THA	9.1	1.1	4.2	1.6	0.7	0.8	2.0	0.5	–	8.5	29.8	7.9	7.3	52.1
SGP	3.6	1.7	4.4	2.6	–	1.7	14.1	1.4	3.9	–	34.2	8.5	6.5	55.8

Note: – = Not available.

Table 10A.2   Share of intermediates in total exports to East Asia, North America and the EU, 1995

	JPN	CHN	HK	TAI	IDN	KOR	MYS	PHL	THA	SGP	EA	NA	EU
JPN	–	78.6	72.6	86.0	88.6	84.1	84.4	78.1	80.7	74.3	80.2	62.1	62.4
CHN	34.2	–	49.6	68.8	67.8	55.8	74.6	54.4	79.2	49.7	46.6	39.3	45.7
HK	48.2	76.2	–	53.0	79.9	56.8	73.4	80.8	84.6	81.2	71.5	27.4	32.0
TAI	52.5	89.0	87.4	–	85.0	85.0	83.0	90.2	82.1	83.5	78.3	59.1	58.1
IDN	35.2	41.2	70.5	45.8	–	37.7	67.1	76.5	43.8	51.4	44.1	36.7	55.4
KOR	54.2	81.0	83.3	84.7	83.5	–	89.7	77.7	70.8	76.4	74.1	60.4	50.3
MYS	55.4	86.9	71.1	82.9	63.8	58.1	–	76.4	62.1	70.2	67.2	55.0	59.2
PHL	63.2	52.3	69.8	76.1	86.7	72.2	95.4	–	97.2	87.1	74.2	58.1	69.0
THA	54.3	37.5	82.3	67.0	49.3	57.9	72.8	65.8	–	60.6	59.9	41.8	48.4
SGP	44.4	60.8	49.2	67.4	–	55.2	78.8	74.9	68.9	–	63.1	45.3	49.9

Note: – = Not available.

Table 10A.3.   Correlations of export vectors, top nine countries, 1995 ($N = 48$)

JPN		CHN		HKG		IDN		KOR		MYS		PHL[a]		SGP		TAI		THA	
GER	0.798	HKG	0.793	CHN	0.793	NOR	0.656	JPN	0.786	SGP	0.786	MYS	0.762	TWN	0.872	SGP	0.846	TWN	0.664
USA	0.793	TUN	0.767	TUR	0.768	HKG	0.558	MYS	0.752	KOR	0.752	SGP	0.752	MYS	0.777	MYS	0.762	SGP	0.630
KOR	0.786	ROM	0.699	TUN	0.763	EGY	0.540	SGP	0.691	TWN	0.691	KOR	0.694	KOR	0.771	KOR	0.691	HKG	0.606
GBR	0.780	PRT	0.694	PRT	0.683	CHN	0.390	TWN	0.669	JPN	0.669	TWN	0.605	IRL	0.739	USA	0.690	CHN	0.587
MEX	0.721	TUR	0.660	GRC	0.643	ROM	0.382	PHL	0.665	THA	0.665	HKG	0.550	USA	0.580	THA	0.660	MYS	0.550
FRA	0.710	THA	0.587	ROM	0.636	MEX	0.380	USA	0.598	USA	0.598	USA	0.532	JPN	0.550	GBR	0.645	KOR	0.491
ESP	0.661	POL	0.558	THA	0.606	TUN	0.371	GBR	0.583	GBR	0.583	JPN	0.489	THA	0.548	JPN	0.630	USA	0.467
CAN	0.654	ITA	0.539	IDN	0.558	PRT	0.369	THA	0.491	HKG	0.491	GBR	0.397	GBR	0.513	IRL	0.625	ITA	0.463
SGP	0.645	HUN	0.521	POL	0.551	ARG	0.351	FRA	0.468	NLD	0.468	NLD	0.376	NLD	0.498	NLD	0.596	GBR	0.462

Note: [a] Philippines is based on SITC–3 digit export shares, 1995.
Source: Based on UN Comtrade data-base SITC–4 digit exports (Rev. 1), 1995.

Table 10A.4. *Japanese FDI to the world, 1989–1996 (mn yen)*[a]

	1989	1990	1991	1992	1993	1994	1995	1996
Manufacturing								
Food products	177,843	121,121	87,187	67,060	97,273	133,418	81,102	82,161
Textiles	71,238	116,208	84,508	55,686	57,728	67,386	100,804	68,236
Wood/pulp	72,446	45,408	42,972	55,856	40,564	14,817	35,095	69,768
Chemical	280,425	336,346	220,212	258,389	204,236	271,526	207,921	231,991
Basic metal	209,843	153,251	123,855	107,241	88,501	107,110	149,809	275,573
General machinery	235,852	213,715	175,320	142,800	136,348	169,652	180,987	161,982
Electric machinery	600,062	835,828	314,654	235,690	313,250	273,421	518,999	733,740
Transport equipment	273,788	274,064	271,329	155,815	109,772	213,637	193,930	436,279
Others	255,796	175,861	371,825	225,245	228,903	191,612	354,917	222,362
Total	2,177,293	2,271,802	1,691,866	1,303,786	1,276,578	1,442,583	1,823,568	2,282,095
Non-manufacturing								
Agriculture/forestry	20,047	22,383	38,304	18,269	8,540	15,767	13,352	15,659
Fishery	6,175	8,725	9,854	11,702	6,524	21,421	5,390	11,009
Mining	168,285	195,844	136,498	162,512	109,319	49,288	103,401	176,848
Construction	84,767	43,675	58,725	69,906	31,574	36,656	38,464	36,140
Commercial	684,601	903,468	715,028	478,758	593,407	458,001	514,852	538,698
Finance	2,042,419	1,180,119	681,339	596,192	726,473	687,194	527,224	875,960
Service	1,441,931	1,671,605	737,011	853,467	410,830	718,080	1,034,950	455,803
Transportation	389,204	316,207	338,892	222,502	251,598	272,176	220,552	202,702
Real estate services	1,894,204	1,620,987	1,213,662	667,655	705,488	539,258	581,284	699,587
Others	24,861	1,115	1,390	0	1,164	0	0	0
Total	6,756,494	5,964,128	3,930,706	3,080,967	2,844,922	2,797,846	3,039,472	3,012,410
Branches	100,081	116,668	63,590	46,511	29,864	40,394	93,760	114,878
Real estate	0	0	0	0	0	0	0	0
Grand total	9,033,879	8,352,686	5,686,163	4,431,265	4,151,365	4,280,824	4,956,800	5,409,383

Note: [a] Data are for fiscal years (March–April).
Source: Ministry of Finance of Japan, *Monthly Statistics*, **548** (December 1997).

Table 10A.5. Japanese FDI to East Asia, 1989–1996 (mn yen)[a]

	1989	1990	1991	1992	1993	1994	1995	1996
Manufacturing								
Food products	75,181	17,297	21,609	9,102	16,019	25,657	27,009	31,393
Textiles	26,026	43,268	29,723	29,324	34,729	51,931	72,807	40,256
Wood/pulp	8,120	10,919	4,823	6,593	9,506	6,480	10,143	25,812
Chemical	38,976	81,659	79,157	134,504	46,435	96,307	61,488	100,378
Basic metal	41,270	33,201	33,464	34,259	39,380	51,042	91,833	106,836
General machinery	46,779	38,672	34,828	27,875	50,293	41,007	77,057	62,483
Electric machinery	124,296	121,881	119,677	70,220	101,835	143,850	238,775	205,907
Transport equipment	18,998	55,142	25,958	22,068	30,406	41,605	82,175	89,654
Others	54,770	47,540	51,607	65,558	89,194	81,744	120,077	83,910
Total	434,420	449,582	400,850	399,506	417,800	539,626	781,363	746,634
Non-manufacturing								
Agriculture/forestry	2,640	4,984	3,683	1,866	2,327	1,947	4,653	889
Fishery	3,049	2,751	3,137	8,694	2,593	16,844	2,993	9,275
Mining	28,459	34,147	35,440	47,476	30,842	18,747	25,656	52,188
Construction	38,110	14,057	13,047	21,418	4,949	17,587	16,037	17,417
Commercial	87,931	178,240	96,950	99,362	82,343	62,978	78,706	89,443
Finance	142,138	94,319	108,829	88,664	79,606	121,112	73,819	89,126
Service	147,902	130,446	70,696	65,656	58,365	113,153	58,534	86,237
Transportation	52,116	16,591	13,168	43,201	32,881	33,995	31,398	30,233
Real estate services	148,600	94,413	48,829	33,751	41,796	52,603	65,643	100,684
Others	1,146	890	40	0	0	0	0	0
Total	652,096	570,843	393,823	410,093	335,706	438,970	357,444	475,495
Branches	13,745	13,867	16,036	22,031	13,712	29,770	53,327	861,213
Real estate	0	0	0	0	0	0	0	0
Grand total	1,100,262	1,034,293	810,711	831,631	767,219	1,008,374	1,192,136	1,308,344

Source: Ministry of Finance of Japan, Monthly Statistics, **548** (December 1997).

NOTES

An early version of this chapter was presented at the CEPR/WBI conference Financial Crises: Contagion and Market Volatility (London) (8–9 May). We are grateful to Jenny Corbett, Reuven Glick, Will Martin, Tony Venables, David Vines and conference participants for constructive suggestions and discussions, to Fukunari Kimura and Sandy Yeats for sharing data and Francis Ng, Ying Lin and Xibo Fan for outstanding research assistance. The views expressed are those of the authors and should not be attributed to the World Bank.

1. Much of the analysis that has emerged addressing the causes of the financial and currency crisis in East Asia has focused on domestic variables, in particular the mismatch between liberalisation of short-term capital flows in the absence of solid regulatory supervision of domestic banks and presence of a peg to an appreciating US dollar. Given perceptions that financial systems would be bailed out (moral hazard), this induced large-scale unhedged borrowing in foreign currency. Once the domestic currency began to depreciate significantly, fears of sovereign financial insolvency led to a complete collapse. See Corbett and Vines (1998) for a detailed discussion and references to the literature. We abstract from financial dimensions of the crisis and contagion.

2. The term 'flying geese' is due to Akamatsu (1962). It originally referred to graphs representing the share of a particular industry in national product as it evolved over time in a particular country. These graphs exhibit a series of inverse-U curves associated with industries of increased sophistication. For example, Japan started with textiles, which rose and then fell, being replaced by chemicals, which also rose and fell, and so on (Kwan, 1997).

3. Note that these countries had from the mid-1980s to the mid-1990s pursued policies of partially pegging their nominal exchange rates to the US dollar. As the dollar appreciated, and new competition came on stream, a serious competitiveness problem may have emerged for some countries. However, this seems to have been compensated by a boom in regional exports to Japan. In addition, and especially in high-skill economies such as Korea, exports to third markets became more competitive relative to Japan. McKibbin and Martin (1998) argue that real effective exchange rates of the countries most severely affected by the crisis did not appreciate significantly during the 1990–7 period.

4. See Hoekman and Djankov (1997) on Eastern Europe; Primo Braga and Yeats (1994) on Latin America.

5. The impacts of devaluation mentioned here operate through the trade account. McKibbin and Martin (1998) note that the devaluations in East Asia occurred after the countries floated (or at the same time) and must be seen as endogenous. The impact on other countries' exchange rates will then depend on the source of the exchange rate shocks. McKibbin and Martin argue that the devaluations were primarily the result of falls in investment demand in the countries, so that there is a capital account linkage to take into account as well. When investment demand falls in one group of countries, the exchange rate devaluation of the affected countries tends to put downward pressure on competitors' exchange rates. However, the fall in world investment demand also pulls down world interest rates, tending

to cause an appreciation of exchange rates in countries not experiencing investment demand shocks. When fed through a global CGE model, McKibbin and
Martin find that the two factors were almost completely offsetting.

6. The bars are drawn only when the respective R2 of these regressions are larger
   than 0.1.
7. 'Intermediate goods' include raw and processed materials, chemicals, leather,
   fabric and textiles, parts and accessories. Consumer goods comprise processed
   foods, clothing, household durables, electronic equipment (VCRs, cameras, CD
   players, etc.) and cars, motorcycles and bicycles. 'Capital goods' include
   machine tools, power-generation equipment, transport equipment, etc. A
   detailed concordance mapping the HS classification into the Basic Economic
   Classification of the UN is available on request from the authors.
8. The export similarity index is defined as $XS(a, b) = SUMi\,[\min(Xia, Xib)]*100$,
   where Xia and Xib are the industry i export share in country a's and b's exports,
   respectively, which were calculated at the 4-digit SITC level for 10 East Asian
   countries and a sample of other 40 countries. The index ranges between 0 and
   100, with 0 indicating complete dissimilarity and 100 indicating identical export
   composition. This measure was first proposed by Finger and Kreinin (1979).
9. In general, there is a pattern of shifting specialisation among East Asian countries, with lower-income countries expanding exports of labour-intensive goods
   such as clothing and footwear and higher-income Asian countries greatly
   expanding their exports of machinery and electronic products. But this is a
   longer-term phenomenon that has been under way for many years.
10. We are indebted to Professor Fukunari Kimura for providing data on Japanese
    FDI.
11. Japanese imports from China, the Philippines, and Thailand all increased in
    1996 in the 10 per cent range.
12. On this point see Hoekman and Martin (1998), and Liu et al. (1998).

REFERENCES

Akamatsu, K. (1962). 'An Historical Pattern of Economic Growth in Developing
    Countries,' *The Developing Economies*, 1:17–31
Anderson, K. and J. Francois (1997). 'Commercial Links Between Western Europe
    and East Asia: Retrospect and Prospects,' *CEPR Discussion Paper*, **1760**.
Bayoumi, T. (1997). *Financial Integration and Real Activity*, Ann Arbor: University
    of Michigan Press
Bayoumi, T. and B. Eichengreen (1994). 'One Money or Many? On Analyzing the
    Prospects for Monetary Unification in Various Parts of the World,' *Princeton
    Essays in International Finance*, **76**
Bergsten, C. F. (1998). 'Why the Asian Monetary Crisis?' *EDI Forum*, **2(4)**,
    Economic Development Institute, World Bank
Corbett, J. and D. Vines (1998). 'Asian Currency and Financial Crises: Lessons from
    Vulnerability, Crisis and Collapse', Oxford University, mimeo
Dasgupta, D. and K. Imai (1997). 'What Caused the 1996 Slowdown in East Asian
    Export Growth?', World Bank, mimeo

DeRosa, D. 1995. 'Regional Trading Arrangements Among Developing Economies: The ASEAN Example', Washington, DC: IFPRI

Encarnation, D. (1992). *Rivals Beyond Trade: America versus Japan in Global Competition*, Ithaca: Cornell University Press

Finger, J. M. and M. Kreinin (1979). 'A Measure of Export Similarity and Its Possible Uses', *Economic Journal*, **89**.

Frankel, J. and S. J. Wei (1996). 'ASEAN in Regional Perspective', mimeo

Hoekman, B. and S. Djankov (1997). 'Determinants of the Export Structure of Countries in Central and Eastern Europe', *World Bank Economic Review*, **11**:471–90

Hoekman, B. and W. Martin (1998). 'Trade Dimensions of East Asia's Financial Crisis', *PREM Notes (Economic Policy)*, 3, Washington, DC: World Bank

Giorgianni, L. and G. M. Milesi-Ferretti (1997). 'Determinants of Korean Trade Flows and their Geographical Destination,' *CEPR Discussion Paper*, **1703**

Kawai, M. and S. Urata (1998). 'Are Trade and Direct Investment Substitutes or Complements? An Empirical Analysis of Japanese Manufacturing Industries', in H. Lee and D. Roland-Holst (eds.), *Economic Development and Cooperation in the Pacific Basin*, Cambridge: Cambridge University Press

Kimura, F. (1997). 'East Asian Multinationals and Regional Integration in Asia', Keio University, mimeo.

Kwan, C. H. (1997). 'How the Yen's Appreciation has Deepened Economic Interdependence Between Asia and Japan'. World Bank, mimeo

Liu, L.-G., M. Noland, S. Robinson and Z. Wang (1998). 'Asian Competitive Devaluations', *Institute for International Economics Working Paper*, **98–2**

McKibbin, W. and W. Martin (1998). 'The East Asian Crisis: Investigating Causes and Policy Responses', mimeo

Muscatelli, V., A. Stevenson and C. Montaga (1994). 'Intra-NIE Competition in Exports of Manufactures', *Journal of International Economics*, **37**:29–47

Noland, M. (1997). 'Has Asian Export Performance Been Unique?,' *Journal of International Economics*, **43**:79–101

Primo Braga, C. and G. Bannister (1994). 'East Asian Investment and Trade: Prospects for Growing Regionalization in the 1990s', *Transnational Corporations*, **3**:97–136

Primo Braga, C. and A. Yeats (1994). 'Regional Integration in the Western Hemisphere: Déjà Vu all Over Again?', *World Economy* (July)

Rao, N. (1995). 'Intra-Asian Trade: Trends and Prospects,' in K. Fukusaka (ed.), *Regional Cooperation and Integration in Asia*, Paris: OECD

Urata, S. 1993. 'Japanese Foreign Direct Investment and its Effects on Foreign Trade in Asia', in T. Ito and A. Krueger (eds.), *Trade and Protectionism*. Chicago: University of Chicago Press

World Bank (1997). *Global Development Finance*, Washington, DC: World Bank
(1998). *Global Economic Prospects and the Developing Economies*, Washington DC: World Bank

Discussion
Jenny Corbett and David Vines

Chapter 10 is about the role of trade linkages in the Asian crisis. The authors argue that a proper understanding of these linkages is essential for an adequate understanding of the crisis. In doing so, they draw attention to the importance of differences between countries, and they note that much existing analysis of the crisis is unsatisfactory in that it has treated countries as if they were essentially similar. Their central idea is that the impact of events in one country on outcomes in an another will differ, depending on whether the countries in question have complementary or competitive trade structures.

The chapter deals with two distinct aspects of the Asian crisis. First it describes the way in which the *onset* of the crisis would be expected to be different for competitors and complementary countries. It then goes on to examine how *contagion* might have occurred between the different groups. Our comments are addressed mainly to the first issue. At the end of our comments we offer some rather brief remarks on the second.

In describing the onset of the crisis, and ascribing causes, the chapter first sets out a trade-competition story which describes the situation for countries producing in the same market segments, with high export concentration and similar export share structures. In such a story, an external shock, such as China's devaluation in 1994, affects all such countries similarly. A higher rate of Chinese growth would also increase competition in export markets and so would also have negative effects on them. For such trade-competitor countries competitive devaluations would be damaging; if one country began by devaluing, then the others would have to follow downward.

The authors contrast this story with one focusing on a story of complementarity. This would apply when countries were not all selling into the same markets and when their exports were not concentrated on the same goods. If such a story were to apply to the effects of China on other East Asian countries, then the expectation would be that an increase in Chinese exports would not damage their export revenue (i.e. it would not affect either their export volume or their export prices). Also, by contrast with the competitive story, an increase in Chinese growth would have a positive effect because it would absorb imports from the area. The same would be true of an increase in Japanese growth. In such a story Japan's slowdown would be bad news because of its demand effects. Because of the resulting depreciation of the yen it would also reduce the need to shift production offshore and so would slow down Japan's FDI into the region.

This analysis points to the possibility of important effects on the region of events in both China and Japan, coming via a number of effects. Both countries could have (in the chapter's terminology) either complementary or competitive effects (or a combination) on each of the different countries of the region. Competition from China would be expected to be important for poorer countries at the low end of the product ladder (Indonesia, Thailand, Malaysia). Note that most of what happened along these lines during the 1990s should not have been a surprise to the market because the process was so slow. However, on this analysis, the effect of the Chinese depreciation might well have come as a shock and been important. Competition from Japan would also, on this story, be likely to be particularly important for richer countries producing higher value-added products (Korea, Taiwan, Singapore, Hong Kong). For these countries we could argue too that the effect of the actual yen depreciation might well have been both sudden and large. Complementarity effects from Japan would have mattered for all countries as import demand dropped and FDI outflows were reduced.

We propose a simple model to clarify these various channels of effects, which we believe captures the spirit of the chapter. It relates trade and investment to GDP for a group of Asian countries (A), *plus* China (C), Japan (J), and the Rest of the World (R). For the Asian countries output is determined by exports:

$$Y_A = f(X_A). \tag{D10.1}$$

Total demand for the good which these countries export is determined by income in the rest of the world, Japan, and China, and by price[1]:

$$X_D = f(Y_R^+, Y_J^+, Y_C^+, P_X^-). \tag{D10.2}$$

Export supply from these countries is determined by price and investment (both domestic and foreign) in the export sector:

$$X_A = g(P_X^+, I_X^+). \tag{D10.3}$$

Equilibrium in the market for this export good implies:

$$X_D = X_A + X_C + X_J \tag{D10.4}$$

where X_C, X_J is export supply from China or Japan.

Substituting (D10.2) and (D10.3) into (D10.4) and solving gives a general expression for the export good which shows a mixture of demand (complementary) and trade (competitive) effects as well as an investment effect:

$$X = h(Y_R^+, Y_J^+, Y_C^+, X_J^-, X_C^-, I_X^+). \tag{D10.5}$$

At the same time export supply in Japan and China is related to each country's own output:

$$X_C = \alpha_1(Y_C^+)$$ (D10.6a)

$$X_J = \alpha_2(Y_J^+)$$ (D10.6b)

while foreign investment into the Asian countries is also determined by Chinese and Japanese output:

$$I_X = v_1(Y_J^+) + v_2(Y_C^-).$$ (D10.7)

Note that the sign of the Japanese effect, a supplier of investment, might be expected to be positive, while the sign of the Chinese effect, a competitor for FDI, might be expected to be negative.

This allows a derivation of the impacts of changes in either Chinese or Japanese output on exports by Asian countries. These are shown in (D10.8a) and (D10.8b):

$$\frac{dX}{dY_C} = \frac{\delta X}{\delta Y_C} + \frac{\delta X}{\delta X_c}\frac{\delta X_c}{\delta Y_C} + \frac{\delta X}{\delta I_X}\frac{\delta I_x}{\delta Y_C}.$$ (D10.8a)

$$\frac{dX}{dY_J} = \frac{\delta X}{\delta Y_J} + \frac{\delta X}{\delta X_j}\frac{\delta X_j}{\delta Y_J} + \frac{\delta X}{\delta I_K}\frac{\delta I_x}{\delta Y_J}.$$ (D10.8b)

These clearly show that the coefficient in a regression of Asian exports on Chinese or Japanese output is a combination of direct demand (complementarity) effects

$$\left(\frac{\delta X}{\delta Y_C} \text{ and } \frac{\delta X}{\delta Y_J}\right),$$

competitive export effects

$$\left(\frac{\delta X}{\delta X_C}\frac{\delta X_C}{\delta Y_C} \text{ or } \frac{\delta X}{\delta X_J}\frac{\delta X_J}{\delta Y_J}\right)$$

and investment effects

$$\left(\frac{\delta X}{\delta I_X}\frac{\delta I_X}{\delta Y_C}\right).$$

Our interpretation of the complementarity effect is that it reflects the impact of Japanese or Chinese demand increases resulting from increases in their income. The chapter, however, considers, in addition, the possibility of 'trade complementarity' – effects causing a rise in Asian exports when another country's exports increase, via trade in intermediate goods. In our stylised model (with only one export good) the effect of an increase in one country's exports on another country's exports is necessarily a a competitive one. The question of whether complementarity or competitive effects are larger then comes down, in our model, to the question of whether or not demand effects outweigh price-competition effects. We return to the connection between this stylised model and the chapter's empirical results below, but note here that the multi-faceted use of the term 'complementarity' sometimes makes the chapter's argument hard to follow.

Does the empirical work enable us to determine, for particular countries, whether complementarity effects or competitiveness effects were the most significant? Can we, as a result, thus determine whether, ultimately, Japan or China was the most important external shock? The chapter presents much interesting information relevant to these questions, but its attempt to answer them is only partly successful.

The chapter initially presents some descriptive data in order to make its first set of claims. Using regional trade intensities, shares of intermediate products in regional imports and indices of export similarity, the authors conclude that the degree of competitiveness is less than expected and that there is a surprising degree of trade complementarity even between China and the countries of the region both in inter- and extra-regional trade. Clear cases of devaluation resulting from competitive pressure are limited to Laos, Vietnam and Taiwan. However, these data are not fully exploited and therefore we do not get as clear a picture as possible of which countries were more affected by competitive pressure and which by complementarity. Trade-intensity indices (table 10.4) could be broken down into measures of trade 'bias' and measures of trade 'complementarity' (cf. Anderson and Francois 1997) in order to bolster the rather speculative descriptions such as that on the changed direction of Korean trade. Some further information is available from table 10.9 on intensity of intermediate-goods trade, but what is needed is a further table which clearly ranks countries according to the degree of trade complementarity or competitiveness. This should be done either pairwise with Japan and China, or with the entire region. (Alternatively, more use should be made of appendix table 10A.3.)

Adding this analysis to the results of a regression linking macro variables of each country to those in China and Japan presented in table 10.1 takes the analysis a little further. But again the piecemeal approach means that less useful information results than it might have. Table 10.1 suggests that GDP growth in most countries in the region is positively affected by Japan's GDP growth and negatively by China's (implying 'complementarity' relationships, in a broad sense, with Japan and broadly 'competitive' ones with China). Export growth, however, is positively linked with Japan's consumption growth (demand effects) but negatively with Japan's own export growth (competitive trade effects). Curiously Chinese consumption growth has either no effect (low significance) or a perverse[2] effect. while its export growth effect is positive (i.e. complementary, in the terminology of the chapter, *not* competitive).

These apparently contradictory results may stem from the rather crude nature of these regressions. As our model indicates, the impact of changes in Chinese or Japanese GDP on Asian countries' exports (or their GDP at one step further back in the analysis)[3] works through several channels. These are combined in the coefficient in the first single variable regression of table 10.1. But this total coefficient will be a mixture of positive and negative effects coming from the partial derivatives showing the size of each channel of effect. One (somewhat crude) mechanism for recovering the size and sign of these partial derivatives is to do single-variable regressions (as in panels 2 and 3, p. 318) on the different channels. But that is no substitute for doing a multiple regression on all the channels combined (i.e. estimating (D10.5) in our model directly) since the single-variable equations are obviously misspecified. Indeed, in this case, where there is interest in both changes over time and in the differing impact of China and Japan on different countries, panel-data methods would also be appropriate and informative.

We now comment briefly on what the chapter has to say about *contagion* (as distinct from its explanations of the *onset* of the crisis). The chapter proposes three channels of effect: a price effect, an income effect and an investment effect. Each of these effects operates differently, as between competitors and complementary trade partners. The price effect works via the impact of the initial devaluations on customers, competitors and producers of complementary goods. Price reductions will be good for the first and last, but bad for the second. The income effect results from the demand reductions within the region and is higher the greater the regional intensity of trade. Its impact will be greater, the chapter claims, the greater are complementarities in trade. (But see our comment on terminology above.) The investment effect is a mixture of a positive factor (the attraction of inward investment into the crisis-hit countries because of reduced costs after devaluation) and a negative effect of reduced Japanese outflow as its own domestic costs, and activity, are reduced. This investment effect will vary for different pairs of countries: for rich–poor country pairs the rich country's devaluation will reduce investment flows to the poor, while for poor–poor pairs devaluation in one will attract FDI away from similar countries, increasing pressure on them. One would have liked the empirical part of the chapter to have gone further here and to have identified whether direct trade (price) effects or demand (income) or investment effects were the most important source of contagion, and whether this differed for different types (competitors or complementary pairs) of countries. It is in this part of the chapter where the confusion, engendered by using the term complementarity to refer both to demand (income) effects (as in our stylised model) and to trade effects deriving from intermediate goods trade, is greatest.

There are two important final questions which should be asked of chapter 10. Does the authors' trade story about the onset of the crisis capture the main causal factors? Is trade contagion the most important contagion channel, out of several alternatives?

The authors conclude that the kinds of factors which they analyse *were* important in both the emergence and rapid spread of the crisis. They assign a large role to Japan and (smaller) to China in the genesis of the crisis. And they believe that intra-regional trade integration was important in its spread. But these explanations say nothing of other factors – such as deteriorating real exchange rate positions, inappropriate domestic macroeconomic policies, disturbances to international capital flows (apart from FDI) and faulty domestic financial systems. There is no discussion of panic, bubbles or excessive volatility of capital flow.

This may be refreshing but it probably exaggerates the role of slow-acting trade effects and it certainly under-rates the importance of the various contagion channels outlined in other chapters in this volume. Despite a lot of careful empirical work it is disappointingly difficult to glean a sense of the *relative* importance of trade, compared to other, effects.

Our own view on this issue will be apparent from our own chapter 2 in this volume (p. 67). It shares much with the argument put forward by Masson in chapter 8, and well summarised by Axel Weber in his discussion (p. 280). Trade shocks of the kind discussed in chapter 10 are an important component of the shocks to fundamentals which can lead to crises. We might call these shocks the 'first stage' of a crisis. It is clear that these shocks can be passed from country to country in the manner discussed here. There may thus be an important source of contagion in this 'first stage' of a crisis, as claimed here. But the 'mechanism' of crisis (the word used by Shin and Morris in chapter 7 in this volume, p. 230) has an important capital account component. This is because speculators need to decide whether, in the light of these 'first-stage' shocks, the economy is vulnerable to a crisis. What we might call the 'second stage' of a crisis sets in once speculators answer 'Yes' to that question. This then makes the country a risky place to invest, and triggers a risk premium on its assets and/or a withdrawal of funds. In turn, it is this capital account event which actually triggers the crisis. As Masson and Weber make abundantly clear, contagion can also take place at the 'second stage' as well as the 'first stage'. Absent *any* change in fundamentals, speculators can take fright about one country *simply because they believe that a crisis in another country makes crisis in the first country more likely*. That can of itself trigger the crisis.

To investigate the capital account route for contagion requires more factors to be in play than are found in this chapter. But the analysis which it provides almost certainly contains an important part of such more complete account.

NOTES
1. We insert signs of effects above the argument of functions where this helps to clarify the discussion.
2. We say this despite the interpretation given in the text.
3. Since

$$\frac{dY_A}{dY_C} = \frac{\delta Y_A}{\delta X_A} \frac{\delta X_A}{\delta Y_C}.$$

REFERENCE
Anderson, K. and J. Francois (1997). 'Commercial Links Between Western Europe and East Asia: Retrospect and Prospects', *CEPR Discussion Paper*, **1760**

Part Four

Policy Responses

11 Coping with crises: is there a 'silver bullet'?

AMAR BHATTACHARYA AND MARCUS MILLER

1 Introduction: globalisation challenged

Rome was not built in a day: nor can global capital markets be created over-night. The smooth functioning of a market economy needs more than freedom to buy and sell: institutions matter too, and creating them can take time. Accounting, banking and legal practices developed in Renaissance Italy, for example, played a central role in expanding mercantile trade from Venice and its sister states to the world at large (Jardine, 1996). The institu-tional framework is even more important when the items traded are promises to pay – as the history of financial crises testifies. Nineteenth-century London capital markets were plagued by recurrent liquidity crises until the Bank of England learned to act as a lender-of-last-resort (LOLR): and it was the catastrophic bank runs of the early 1930s that led the fledgling Fed to implement a policy of deposit insurance.

Now, at the end of the twentieth century, the need for institutions to underpin emerging markets has been dramatically demonstrated yet again. First in the traumatic experience of economies in transition from commu-nism, where the lack of adequate legal and accounting systems and the per-vasive presence of corruption and crime (to say nothing of political failure) has so threatened enterprise and stunted development in Russia, for example, that some no longer consider it an emerging market. Second in the financial crises that have racked the newly liberalised capital markets in East Asia and drained the funds of the institutions set up after the Second World War to manage the international financial system. Why is it that rapid liberalisation of financial markets seems to court crisis? What can be done about it? This is what we study here.

Even today, in many countries capital markets operate without adequate supervision and regulation; and at the global level there is, for sovereign debtors, no proper LOLR in a liquidity crisis, nor is there any mechanism to offer them bankruptcy protection. For George Soros (1998, pp. xxviii–xxix) global capitalism is in crisis because financial markets have outgrown the regulatory framework needed to stabilise them: 'financial markets are inherently unstable,' he says, yet 'there are practically no institutions for rule-making on an international scale. We have a global economy without a global society.' His is by no means a lone voice. In speculating on whether financial crises need be this frequent and this painful, Joseph Stiglitz (1998b, reprinted as chapter 12 in this volume) expresses much the same sentiments; and the reform of global financial institutions was a key item of debate at the Fund/Bank meetings in 1998 and at Davos in 1999.

Some observers, following a 'top-down' approach, have proposed the creation of a troika to replace the IMF: a global financial regulator to ensure banking standards; a LOLR to supply liquidity when appropriate; and a global bankruptcy court to oversee debt restructuring (see Edwards, 1998). Others, dismissing such plans as politically impossible, recommend incremental solutions. Eichengreen (1999), for example, looks to improved financial regulation and the redesign of private debt contracts as the key elements. Cline (1998), on the other hand, expresses broad agreement with the strategies used to handle the East Asian crises, but stresses the need for prompter action with more adequate funding to maintain creditor confidence. Incentive effects can pose problems for this piecemeal approach, however. Simply enlarging funding for bail-outs will have adverse incentive effects ('moral hazard'), for example; and it may take threats of something worse to persuade creditors to offer new contracts. Where should one begin?

We start with the observation that it is those emerging market economies which have rapidly liberalised their capital markets that have suffered the worst crises, in 1994–5, 1997 and 1998. One does not have to subscribe to the Polanyi-like perspective that the domain of political control must march in step with market size to concede that capital inflows can have undesirable welfare consequences in the presence of domestic distortions. Generous capital flows to emerging markets can greatly increase the vulnerability of poorly regulated financial systems, and the downside risks they face. (With unregulated but insured institutions attracting funds from global markets, Krugman, 1998a, shows how asset prices can be driven to untenably high levels – Pangloss values – with widespread insolvency inevitable in all but the best of all possible worlds.)

History has shown that financial institutions involved in liquidity transformation are particularly vulnerable to creditor panic, which is why domestic distortions matter. At the very least this implies that capital market integration is an exercise in the economics of 'second best', with the losses of increased distortions being set against the gains of increased market access. After surveying the Asian crisis, indeed, Morris Goldstein (1998, p. 66) concludes bluntly 'Efforts to promote financial and capital account liberalisation without first strengthening the prudential framework are a recipe for disaster.' The added prospect of financial contagion means that premature liberalisation may involve globalising market failure.

If not *laissez-faire*, then what? We start in section 2 with a *tour d'horizon* encompassing the principal ideas for reform that have been put forward as panaceas for the problems of globalisation – each promising in its own way. In section 3 we review key features of the recent East Asian crisis which need to be taken into account in redesigning the system. Designing a 'second-best' system is complicated by the role of expectations as crisis measures implemented *ex post* can change things *ex ante*: if you are fully insured, why take precautions? These issues are taken up in section 4 which presents the 'time-consistency' problem facing the current system in game-theoretic terms and puts the strategic case for intitutional change. In section 5, we spell out the elements of an integrated approach, considering both measures of crisis prevention and those for crisis resolution. Section 6 concludes.

2 Six key ideas in the debate

Is there a 'silver bullet' that can rid the system of crisis? Maybe not. But even so, it is well worth examining those that have been proposed to see what to include in a more integrated approach[1].

2.1 More transparency and disclosure

Many have found fault with the lack of auditing and disclosure in East Asian banks, and have blamed it for creditor panic: hence the cry for greater monitoring and transparency. With the UK holding the chairmanship of the G-7, it was reported that Chancellor Gordon Brown was pushing for

the establishment of a new global regulator . . . which would bring together central bankers, stock market authorities and the IMF in an effort to coordinate action and prevent the spread of global financial contagion. Among the other proposals he has tabled are codes of conduct imposing new rules on accountability and transparency, which will force individual nations to open their books to IMF scrutiny.

(*Guardian*, 7 January, 1999, p.21)

It is difficult to reject the call for more accurate information, and greater transparency is surely part of the solution. It will, in particular, help to identify those debtor countries for whom ready official liquidity may be available in a crisis, as opposed to those with potential problems calling for a debt work-out. But the notion that more transparency can be relied on to avert crisis flies in the face of both theory and practical experience. The incidence of bank runs and boom–bust cycles involving property prices in banking systems all over the world (including, of late, both the USA and Scandinavia, for example) is a sobering, practical challenge to the idea. More fundamentally, as Eichengreen (1999, pp. 80–2) points out, it

underestimates the extent to which information asymmetries are intrinsic to financial markets … It is unavoidable that borrowers should know more than lenders about how they plan to use borrowed funds. This reality is a key reason why banks exist in market economies . . . [And] if asymmetric information is why most economies continue to rely on banks for intermediation services, bank fragility is unavoidable. The advocates of information-related initiatives mislead when they assume the problem away.

2.2 More money – and more quickly

The proximate cause of all financial crises is the inability of the debtor to provide creditors with the cash they demand. Bagehot's (1873) solution to this liquidity problem is for the central bank to act as LOLR. (Another is for a bankruptcy court to authorise a standstill, as discussed below.) The IMF has tried to act as an international LOLR – to act as the central banker for central banks. But it has been criticised, on the one hand, for not providing money quickly enough – nor in sufficient quantity – to give confidence to private investors, Radelet and Sachs (1998); and, on the other, for creating moral hazard by lending without the regulatory authority that usually accompanies domestic liquidity provision. One response is to strengthen the Fund's capacity to act as LOLR, so that more money could be disbursed more quickly. This was the approach taken by Stanley Fischer (1999) in his address at the AEA Meetings where he pointed out that 'At the end of 1997, the IMF introduced the Supplemental Reserve Facility [SRF], which can make short-term loans in large amounts at penalty rates to countries in crisis.' He also noted (p. 11) that

the Executive Board of the IMF is considering the possibility of introducing a contingency or precautionary facility, to supplement the reserves of countries threatened by a crisis but not yet in one.

This would doubtless find favour among creditors: but routine rescues without regulatory control could be a recipe for escalating bail-outs and moral hazard (as is argued in more detail in section 4, below).

One way of limiting moral hazard might be to restrict the list of countries to whom support is available by severe preconditions in terms of domestic financial regulation. This is the route taken by Charles Calomiris (1998). It has been compared to the 'narrow banking' solution for containing moral hazard at the domestic level – and faulted for the same reason: the restriction of support to the selected group is not credible given the systemic risks posed by the collapse of those outside it, Eichengreen (1999, pp. 101–2).

In his address, Fischer (1999, p. 12) emphasised the role of transparency and bail-ins for reducing moral hazard. He argued that

improvements in transparency and the provision of information by the public sector and improved regulation, together with bail-in procedures that set the right incentives, would encourage better monitoring and self-regulation by the private sector. The charging of a penalty rate would discourage borrower moral hazard and the new procedures to bail in the private sector would greatly reduce investor moral hazard.

Likewise, the proposals of George Soros (1999), are a mix of *ex ante* conditionality for countries known to possess strong fundamentals who can be promised financial support and the prospect of standstills and workouts – creditor bail-ins instead of bail-outs – for the others. It is to these we now turn.

2.3 More 'haircuts': strategic standstills and bankruptcy protection

If solvent debtors in a liquidity squeeze cannot find cash, they can nevertheless seek legal protection against creditors' demands. These facets of life in the 'economic emergency room' were eloquently described by Jeffrey Sachs (1993, p. 511) in his famous contrast of the options available to Macy's department store and to the Russian economy.

Consider the case of an overly indebted corporation in the United States that is unable to service its debt in the short run. Under chapter 11 of the US Bankruptcy Code, the debtor enterprise can file for bankruptcy to obtain a 'standstill' on debt servicing. Under a standstill, creditors must refrain from attempting to collect the debt, pending a collective solution to the indebtedness problem. Moreover, the law provides for the enterprise to borrow new working-capital funds even after filing for bankruptcy, in order to ensure the continued efficient operation of the firm.

No such procedures operate with heavily indebted countries in the grip of a balance of payments crisis. A country cannot file for an immediate standstill in an international bankruptcy court. Perhaps it can achieve one, following months of laborious negotiations with creditors, but usually only after tremendous damage has been done by capital flight, a withdrawal of trade credits, and other hostile creditor actions. Moreover, there is no routine way to obtain the working capital vitally needed to keep the economy functioning. It is literally the case that Macy's had an easier time raising $600 million in emergency working capital loans after filing for bankruptcy than did Russia (trying to raise the same amount) in 1992.

Such considerations have led several observers to propose that there should be an International Bankruptcy Agency to afford sovereign debtors some protection from short-term lenders and bond-holders. (Longer-term intergovernmental lending can already be restructured by the Paris Club, and the London Club covers bank lending.) Williamson (1985, quoted in Cline, 1995, p. 484) for example proposed that such an agency

might be able to act as arbiter on past loans . . . and suggested that criteria for determining whether and to what extent forgiveness was appropriate would incorporate some broad assessment of insolvency versus liquidity, as well as other factors.

In fact, for Latin American bank debt in the 1980s, the Brady Plan acted as the mechanism for financial reconstruction and debt write-downs; but that solution took several years to emerge. Governments can always declare a unilateral moratorium, of course, with the dire consequences we can see in Russia today.

Is there any other feasible mechanism? Both Soros and Fischer are looking for private sector bail-ins. The IMF can provide 'debtor-in-possession' finance by lending into arrears, as it did in Latin America in respect of arrears to banks in the 1980s, for example; and the IMF could choose to authorise a 90-day standstill on all cross-border and cross-currency debt contracts.[2] These would provide a breathing space for the borrower and an incentive for the lender to come to the bargaining table to discuss financial reconstruction. Miller and Zhang (1998) suggest that such procedures might be developed into those of a 'Basle Club' to act as a forum for work-outs.

2.4 Better state contingent contracts

There is no International Bankruptcy Court for sovereign debtors in existence, and it may be politically impossible to set one up. Is there a substitute? In theory, there is. As Cornelli and Felli (1995, p. 71) put it:

In a world in which contracting parties are fully rational and can forecast every future contingency and specify them without any significant cost in a comprehensive contract, no purpose is served by bankruptcy law . . . In general, provided the contract is enforceable and binding, there is no need for a law to tell the parties what to do, but simply an authority which guarantees the enforcement of their preferred contract.

Because of the many practical problems of writing and enforcing such contracts, bankruptcy is a superior option at the domestic level. But if this option is not available at the global level, would state contingent contracts not make a good 'second best'. That is the thinking behind proposals by Eichengreen and Portes (1995) for changing the contractual provisions governing sovereign debt so as to allow for (1) collective representation of bondholders, (2) qualified majority voting on changing the terms and conditions of the debt contract and (3) sharing of proceeds among creditors.

Despite strong endorsement of such ideas in both the G-10 (1996) and G-22 (1998) Reports, however, no such bond holders' committee has been established; nor are the recommended clauses included in sovereign debt instruments. Eichengreen (1999) explains that this is because of signalling problems: who wants to be the first to say they may write down their obligations? It may be that there are incentive problems, too. Why would creditors want to take the risk of write-downs if the option of bail-outs is available? But creditors threatened with rough justice in some broad negotiation might prefer the outcomes of prepositioned contracts (i.e. the threat of 'haircuts' may induce improved contracts).

2.5 More insurance

The Brady Plan involved a considerable write-down of bank loans to Latin American debtors and its replacement with sovereign bonds, so it was widely assumed that the next crisis would be in the bond market. So as to widen market participation and improve prudential discretion in this market, observers such as Cline (1995, pp. 482–3) proposed the creation of an International Bondholders' Corporation (IBC) 'to provide insurance of international bonds issued by developing countries, in return for premiums paid by bond purchasers . . . [and] to do for bonds what the Multilateral Investment Guarantee Agency does for direct investment'. The corporation would monitor potential borrowers and its terms of access would send a powerful signal about the creditworthiness of a country. 'The IBC would provide an alternative opinion to the private rating agencies. This function could be important, as there is always some risk that the rating agencies become influenced by the rated countries that pay their fees.'

Contrary to the expectations of Cline and others, however, the East Asian crisis once again centred on bank lending and not on bonds. Nevertheless, at the end of 1997, when the crisis was at its peak, George Soros recommended just such an agency as the means of avoiding a breakdown of international finance. His proposal is roundly criticised by Eichengreen (1999, chapter 5), who specifically focuses on the restrictions that

> to ensure that the scheme was actuarially sound, each country's access would be limited to a ceiling set by the IMF on the basis of its assessment of the country's macroeconomic and financial condition . . . Loans in excess of the ceiling would be uninsured. Moreover, the IMF would make clear that it was not prepared to aid countries having difficulty servicing uninsured loans.

Using the same logic as in section 2.2, Eichengreen (1999, p. 86) suggests that these restrictions are not credible:

> to assert that the international community would be able to stand aside in the event of default on uninsured loans, in disregard of the systemic consequences, is to assume a solution to the problem.

(When Soros next proposed a solution for the problems of the system in the *Financial Times* in 1998 a year later, it involved two of the other ideas mentioned above – LOLR and 'haircuts' for creditors.)

2.6 Capital controls

To discourage short-term, in-and-out capital flows, and increase the autonomy of monetary policy after the breakdown of Bretton Woods, James Tobin (1974, pp. 88–9) proposed an internationally agreed uniform *transactions tax* on all spot conversions of one currency into another. The idea did not attract much attention until after the 1994–5 Mexican crisis, leading Tobin (1996, p. xi) to complain that his critics were missing

> the essential property of the transactions tax – the beauty part – that this simple, one-parameter tax would automatically penalise short-horizon round trips, while negligibly affecting the incentives for commodity trade and long-term capital investments. A 0.2% tax on a round trip costs 48% a year if transacted every business day, 10% if every week, 2.4% if every month. But this is a trivial charge on commodity trade or long-term foreign investments.

In support of Tobin's position, Jeffrey Frankel (1996) noted that if – as survey data suggest – expectations of exchange rate movements over short horizons are extrapolative, but mean-reverting over longer horizons, then such a tax would help to reduce the volatility of exchange rates by driving short-term extrapolative speculators from the market – reducing the influence of Chartists in favour of Fundamentalists. But even its supporters acknowledge that, in crises such as those engulfing the ERM in 1992–3 and East Asia of late, the exit of investors fearing imminent devaluations of 15 per cent or more is unlikely to be deterred by such a tax. Likewise, given the euphoria prevailing before 1997, it would hardly have checked the inflows to East Asia.

A much stronger case can be made for *inflow controls*, not least because they can be implemented unilaterally. Thus, in the 1990s, Chile adopted a battery of policies to discourage short-term inflows while still encouraging FDI. In June 1991 a 20 per cent non-interest-bearing reserve requirement (*'encaje'*) was imposed on external credits, and in May 1992 this was raised to 30 per cent; later, this 'tax' was extended to time deposits in foreign currency and, in 1995, to foreign financial investments, particularly in the Chilean stock market. With Chilean interest rates of around 10 per cent in 1994 attracting gross portfolio inflows of about 3.5 per cent of GDP, Agosin and Ffrench-Davis (1996, pp. 173–4) describe the extension of reserve requirements to these inflows as a pre-emptive strike to deal with an incipient problem (and show that the implicit taxes added 4 per cent to the cost of foreign borrowing on a 12-month basis and over 16 per cent on a 3-month basis). As a result of these inflow controls, Chile avoided a build-up of short-term debt. Recently, with no problem of excess inflows, the Chilean *encaje* has been reduced to zero; proving not that it has failed but that

variations in the *encaje* can be used as a flexible instrument of short-run macro policy to help insulate a country against the vagaries of boom and bust in the international capital market.   (Williamson, 1999, p.9)

Just how successful the Chilean controls have proved may be a matter of debate; but as *ex ante* measures to limit vulnerability, the implicit taxation of 'excessive' capital inflows has much to commend it. What of the drastic *outflow controls* used by Malaysia, which effectively ban the repatriation of all funds till further notice? Like a tourniquet, this can be used as a crisis measure to stop the haemorrhage of funds when all else fails: and, as Krugman (1998b) pointed out, it gives the country involved the freedom to cut interest rates to promote economic recovery. But measures which unilaterally cut the country off from capital markets involve a major interference with the conduct of business in an open economy, and are quite likely to spread contagion as investors expect 'copy-cat' controls in neighbouring economies. It is very difficult to recommend them as the 'magic bullet' to solve financial crisis. As the last resort of policy makers trapped by the vagaries of unregulated capital markets, such desperate remedies are incentives to find better solutions.

3 Elements of the East Asia crisis: creditor panic, asset bubbles and sharks

To redesign the system requires diagnosis of the problems that plague it; in particular the roots of the recent crises in East Asia. But different observers see things differently. To some it was reminiscent of a nineteenth-century British bank panic, and called for prompt intervention by a lender of last resort. It put others in mind of Japan in 1990, when an asset bubble burst and left most banks broke, calling for wholesale financial reconstruction (and the attendant bill for local taxpayers). To one of those intimately involved, Prime Minister Mahathir of Malaysia, the crisis seemed to be the fiendish creation of large speculators and hedge funds who can profit from disruption ('sharks').

Radelet and Sachs (1998, p.4) have endorsed the first view – that the crises were essentially 'failures of collective action' on the part of creditors. 'Our preferred explanation' they say,

turns on the critical distinction between illiquidity and insolvency . . . A liquidity crisis occurs if a solvent, but illiquid, borrower is unable to borrow fresh funds from the capital market in order to make current debt servicing obligations. The inability of the capital market to provide fresh loans to the illiquid borrower is the nub of the matter.

Chang and Velasco (1998) take much the same approach (and add that under fixed exchange rates, a run on banks becomes a run on the currency if the central bank attempts to act as lender of last resort). To make their point they use the model of bank runs developed by Diamond and Dybvig (1983), who formally derive the two expectations-dependent equilibria for a bank (in business, or bust), and show how deposit insurance can help to coordinate expectations on the good one.

The idea that economies in East Asia were buoyed by a bubble was expressed most persuasively by Michael Dooley (1998) and Paul Krugman (1998a), who noted that, without prudential control, deposit guarantees were a recipe for misdirected lending, insolvency and ultimate financial collapse. The combination of weak regulation and implicit deposit guarantees meant that local bankers were free to gamble with the money that global capital markets poured into their parlours: they reckoned that they could gain on the upside and leave the government to cover the downside, and that international depositors would not mind so long as the guarantee lasted. This set the scene for a bubble economy, with assets priced on the Panglossian assumption that all would be for the best in the best of all possible worlds.

These interpretations are illustrated diagramatically[3] by the two circles in figure 11.1. On the left is Sachs' view – that the problem was like a

Figure 11.1   *Elements of the East Asian crisis*

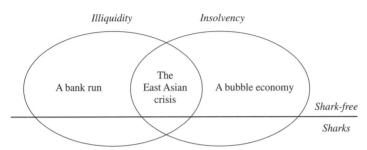

bank run, with creditor panic leading to financial collapse of illiquid busi-nesses. On the right is Krugman's view – that the problem was one of insolvency, with misdirected investment and mispriced assets, a bubble economy.

To force a choice between them is to pose a false dichotomy, however, as the two views are not incompatible: and the truth probably lies in the inter-action of both factors – domestic distortions and creditor panic, as indi-cated by the overlap in figure 11.1.[4] Indeed, recent work on multiple equilibria suggests an interesting interaction between the state of funda-mentals and multiple equilibria: if fundamentals are very strong there is a unique good equilibrium, if they are very weak a unique bad equilibrium, but multiple equilibria are possible for intermediate values of funda-mentals.[5]

The liberalisation of capital movements undoubtedly amplified the size of the domestic bubble and the severity of the subsequent collapse. Capital surged in when global capital gained unfettered access to new markets, with implicit guarantees on downside risks. But foreign funds were pulled out in panic when creditors suspected that not all was well (that much of the money pouring into Thailand was ending up in empty office blocks, for example, or that funds funnelled through Korean banks were feeding the many-headed hydra of the *chaebol* conglomerates) and that there were not enough dollar reserves for the guarantee to be credible. Surging inflows could explain how initial bank problems of non-performing loans worth, say, 5–10 per cent of GDP were amplified to, say, 20–25 per cent of GDP, and creditor panic and the collapse of exchange rates could have doubled this figure to the 40–50 per cent now seen in Thailand, for example. This underlines the 'second-best' case for caution in liberalising capital move-ments (Flemming, 1999).

Evidently, in models of multiple equilibria, large traders may play a crucial role in coordinating expectations. But large-scale, short-term investors who can place bets and then make them come true could make even more money catching the markets by surprise: that is where the sharks come in. Where forward rates are set on the basis of the prevailing pegged rate equilibrium, for example, then big players should be able to make money by shorting the currency and pulling out the reserves so the currency collapses. Is there any evidence of this?

In their IMF report on hedge funds Eichengreen and Mathieson (1998, p. 24) observe that so-called 'second-generation' models of currency crisis, which emphasise the possibility of multiple equilibria,[6] leave a potential role for large traders who

can precipitate a crisis in two ways. First, they can themselves undertake a [sufficient] volume of sales . . . Second, they can serve as the leaders who other small traders will follow . . . In this case it will be unnecessary for large traders to actually take large positions, only to signal their intention of doing so. This mechanism is consistent with models of herding in foreign exchange markets.[7]

Reassuringly, there is, according to the IMF report, no evidence that this was the case in East Asia, at least not on the part of hedge funds.

The [Thai] baht was the only currency for which the hedge funds collectively took short positions, in the view of market participants

they report, and in Thailand

hedge funds were at the rear, not the front of the herd, which appears to have been led by domestic corporates, domestic banks, and international commercial and investment banks.   (Eichengreen and Mathieson, 1998, p.18)

It was, however, the subsequent attack on the Hong Kong dollar[8] – which, along with the Singapore dollar, had the most pukka fundamentals East of Suez – that has given credence to the view that big players could be playing a specific role in triggering crises. The possibility that large players could be responsible for deliberately triggering or spreading crisis is indicated by the area under the horizontal line in the figure 11.1: above the line is 'shark-free'.

It is fascinating to observe that there is a close resemblance between recent academic analysis of financial crisis and that espoused by George Soros in his book on *The Crisis in Global Capitalism* (1998). His view that global financial markets have multiple equilibria, for example, is mirrored by the Diamond and Dybvig model of bank runs – and by the history of the nineteenth-century City of London before institutional innovations to stabilise markets. And the concept of 'reflexivity' Soros appeals to corresponds almost exactly with the expectations – induced shifts of equilibria described by Obstfeld and others in the 'second-generation' models of currency crisis discussed above. (While Soros may agree with Mahathir that the current financial system is badly accident-prone, he would presumably not agree that big players deliberately make mayhem to make money.)

4 The strategic case for changing the rules of the game[9]

A salient feature of current financial crises is that in almost all cases the IMF has been forced to provide bail-outs and this has effectively guaranteed the creditor's investment in sovereign debt. The Russian default is an exception: but the dire state into which this plunged the economy serves to underline the pressures on the IMF to intervene. What can be done to prevent the IMF being manoeuvred into supplying emergency financing in this way? It can hardly say that it will not assist members in distress: that is not credible.[10] What is needed, we believe, are rules or procedures that can protect the debtor from litigation, allow for some financial restructuring – – including possibly debt write-down – – and impose some conditionality to ensure appropriate effort on the part of the debtor.

The logic of this situation may be clarified by treating it as a strategic game between two players, namely a creditor and the IMF representing the debtor (as in the second stage of the Latin American debt crisis when the IMF decided to help the debtors on the terms of the Baker Plan). Consider a liquidity crisis where the debtor is solvent (worth 130) but the current capacity to pay is insufficient to service debt (with face value of 100). The actions available to each of these players are as follows: the creditor may either roll over the debt or grab the assets – i.e., withdraw funds or seize collateral; while the IMF can either bail out the debtor or take no action.

These actions and the resulting payoffs are shown in table 11.1 and figure 11.2. As the arrows indicate, there are two Pareto-efficient Nash equilibria on the diagonal of this normal form game (which resembles the Battle of the Sexes). In the top left (Roll over, No action), the debtor is in good shape as the rollover involves some concessionality; the creditor's payoff is only 80, leaving 50 for the debtor. In the bottom right (Grab, Bail-out), the creditor's demand for accelerated payment of face value is met thanks to emergency funding by the IMF, with the remaining net worth of 30 going to the debtor – *minus* a cost of 5 needed to satisfy tough IMF conditionality! The off-diagonal payoffs for (Grab, No action) at bottom left highlight the losses that may occur when the IMF refuses a bail-out – the creditor gets the collateral, worth 40, but the debtor is 'punished' (gets nothing) as trade is strangled because of unilateral default. (As there is no need for bail-out when the creditor rolls over debt, the off-diagonal payoffs for (Roll over, Bail-out) are the same as for (Roll over, No action).

Table 11.1. *A liquidity crisis: outcomes and payoffs*

		IMF/debtor's actions	
		No action	Bail-out
Creditor's action	Roll over	(80, 50)	(80, 50)
	Grab	(40, 0)	(100, 25)

As far as the IMF and the debtor are concerned (Roll over, No action) is the preferred Nash equilibrium; and it might appear that the IMF can secure this outcome by simply refusing all bail-outs. Given that the creditor has first-mover advantage, however, this is not a credible threat and it is the other equilibrium which is selected. To show this we represent the game in extensive form in figure 11.2, letting 'nature' first determine either a good or a bad state.[11] In the good state, the debtor has sufficient resources to service the debt, and there will be no strategic interactions between the creditor and the IMF, so we ignore this branch. In the bad state, the country is in a liquidity crisis, and the creditor can choose either voluntarily to roll over the debt or to attack (accelerate repayment). Only then is it the IMF's turn to move. With roll overs, no action is called for; but asset-grabbing by the creditor is so disastrous for both the creditor and the debtor that the IMF will be forced to act (even though this involves a 100 per cent guarantee for the creditor).

When the equilibrium is 'refined' by specifying this realistic move order, there is only one (subgame-perfect) Nash equilibrium – constant bail-outs: using backward induction, the creditor will opt for attack rather than roll-over – knowing that the IMF will respond with a bail-out. This is the 'time-consistency trap' facing the IMF (and its partner institutions who supply

Figure 11.2   *The strategic case for a payments standstill*

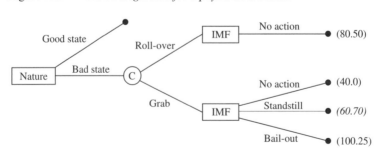

emergency funds). To escape, the IMF must be able credibly to threaten not to bail-out. How is this achieved? Not, we believe, by further 'refinements of equilibrium', but rather by changing the game through institutional reform: specifically by enabling the IMF to act as a bankruptcy court as well as the lender of last resort.

How increasing the options available to the IMF changes the equilibrium is shown by including the standstill in the extensive game, see the thin line in figure 11.2. In the last stage of the game, it is obvious that the standstill dominates the bail-out as the appropriate IMF response to an attack. (As the creditor is forced to accept a debt-service reduction this leaves 70 for the debtor.) Consequently, the creditor, faced with burden-sharing under the standstill (i.e., 'having a haircut' or 'taking a hit'), will prefer to roll over rather than attack. More than that, creditors will now have the incentive to increase coordination to avoid the hit – changing debt contracts to allow for sharing and for majority voting as recommended in the Rey Report, for example. (Put differently, such 'voluntary' contractual changes – and the creation of a bondholders' committee proposed by Eichengreen and Portes, 1995 – are unlikely to be implemented without the credible threat of a payments standstill.)

In the above account (and in figure 11.2) it is 'nature' that initially determines whether there is a good or bad state: but this is a crude simplification. In reality, the probability of good or bad outcomes will depend on the nature of the global financial system. If, for example, there is no standstill mechanism and the IMF is gamed into guaranteeing bail-outs for investors, there will be no incentive for the latter to monitor their investments and the probability of failure will go up (unless domestic regulators take firm action to prevent this). A dramatic illustration of this argument is provided in Krugman (1998a), where deposit guarantees generate such inflated asset values ('Pangloss' values) that financial collapse will occur in all but the best of all possible worlds! It is to prevent this degradation of the global financial system that guarantees must be limited.

There is yet another reason for deliberate changes in the rules: the risk of something worse. If, for reasons just given, the current system is unsustainable, then change is inevitable, either by deliberate rule changes or in a less desirable fashion. If the system continues to promise bailouts (and encourage carefree lending and callous capital flight), emerging countries will be forced to take things into their own hands and impose outright capital controls (which could also be shown as a change in figure 11.2, replacing the thin line for standstills). This is what Malaysia has done.[12] The risk that more countries will follow the Malaysian example could give policy makers added incentive to make the changes suggested below.

5 Improving the financial architecture

5.1 Crisis prevention and management

When invited by Congress to comment on the Asian crisis, George Soros shocked his listeners by comparing global financial markets to 'a wrecking ball, knocking over one economy after another' (Soros, 1998, pp. xi–xvii, statement to a US Congressional Committee taking evidence on the origins and course of the East Asian crisis). To many other observers the elemental forces that have recently swept through emerging market economies seem more like sudden storms at sea, ready to engulf the unwary[13]. Fatalism may be fine for those the gods protect: for lesser mortals, prudence is preferable. This is the subject of this section, looking first at steps for preventing or avoiding a crisis and then at crisis management and resolution, in the light of the key ideas, the various diagnoses and the strategic considerations of previous sections. (We end with a nightmare of sailors caught in storms at sea: the risk that there are sharks in the water.) As an *aide memoire*, we first summarise the salient characteristics of the recent crisis.

5.2 Key features of the East Asian crisis

It may be useful to summarise four key features of the East Asian financial crisis:

- The first feature is *weak fundamentals*. In previous crises, attention focused on weak macro-fundamentals such as fiscal profligacy or an overvalued exchange rate: and IMF conditionality correspondingly involved fiscal stabilisation and devaluation. The Thai baht was doubtless overvalued in early 1997, so macro fundamentals were not sound. But it was microeconomic distortions that played a much greater role both in Thailand and elsewhere in East Asia, (in particular, incentives for risk-taking in the financial sector) where the combination of poor regulation and widespread deposit insurance led to over-lending, excessive investment and asset bubbles.

- The second feature is what we may call the *magnification effect* of global capital flows which amplify the impact of domestic distortions. Surging inflows into a poorly regulated banking system can soon generate massive exposure and push asset prices to unrealistic levels from which collapse is the only exit.

- The third feature is the presence of *contagion*, with creditor panic spreading from country to country, so a shift from good to bad equilibrium in Thailand, for example, is soon followed by financial crisis and recession in Korea. George Soros' alarming description of global capital flows (quoted above) captures how dramatically the ebbs and flows of finance can transform the fate of the open economies and leads him to conclude that these forces need to be controlled if crises are to be averted.

- The fourth feature is the existence of *multiple equilibria*. The presence of low-level equilibria in the domestic economy can dramatically increase the downside risk of macroeconomic shocks: in the 1930s, US prosperity came to an end as banks collapsed, dragging industry down with them, and the economy slid into the Great Depression. Paul Masson (1998 and chapter 8 in this volume) has argued that multiple equilibria may help to account for contagion. Rather than appealing to common shocks or to spillover effects to account for contagion, Masson suggests that crisis elsewhere can coordinate expectations and shift equilibrium. There are reasons why developing countries may be more exposed to such shifts than long-standing members of OECD. Their interest rates and exchange rates are more volatile, and the capacity of private sector balance sheets to cope is less and the facilities to deal with work-outs is weaker. Adverse shocks are likely to leave a greater overhang of debt for the banks and businesses and there is a correspondingly greater danger of a shift to a low-level equilibrium.

5.3 Crisis prevention

5.3.1 Strengthening fundamentals

First and most obvious is the need to deal with weak fundamentals that could trigger a crisis: this is common sense, not magic. Incentives may be distorted at the level of *macroeconomic policy*, with an unsustainable public sector deficit being financed by depleting official foreign currency reserves, for example. Excessive government deficits are what drive so-called 'first-generation' models of currency crisis (Krugman, 1979) and are what IMF conditionality is typically designed to check. But for East Asian economies the problem lay mainly elsewhere, with distorted incentives in *inadequately regulated banking systems*. As Stiglitz (1997) puts it, the problem was not that governments did too much but that they did too little! Further to the

'Washington consensus' (Williamson, 1994, pp. 26–8), there has now emerged a broad-based agenda to reduce distortions by greater transparency and disclosure (see section 2.1, p. 359), by better corporate governance and by closer prudential regulation of banks.

With crises originating in the private sector, the focus of disclosure needs must shift from the macroeconomic reporting covered by the SDSS to information on corporations, banks and International Financial Institutions (IFIs); and the terms of conditionality also need to change. Has IMF conditionality moved with the times? Not in the eyes of Radelet and Sachs (1998), who attribute the severity of the recessions in East Asia to inappropriate monetary and fiscal programmes. Cline (1998, p. 24), on the other hand, in his assessment of adjustment programmes in the region, concludes that

> IMF programs generally do not appear to be out-of-date recipes irrelevant to the East Asian circumstances. Instead, they correctly place great emphasis on structural reform, especially in the financial sector where serious weaknesses were a major reason for the break in confidence of foreign investors ... the fiscal content, especially of the revised packages, has not been extremely restrictive and thus has recognized that the principal origin of the problems in those economies was not fiscal irresponsibility.

It is self-evident that prudential regulation is important for the domestic allocation of financial resources. It is even more important in the context of liberalised capital markets, where capital inflows can greatly magnify the effect of domestic distortions. Poor regulation, together with guaranteed investor bail-outs, may put the viability of the global financial system at risk as the lack of incentives to monitor increases the probability of collapse and the cost of bail-outs. This is how the structure of the financial system can 'feed back' onto the probability of adverse outcomes in figure 11.2 (as discussed in section 4, p. 371 above).

5.3.2 Limiting vulnerability

Correcting distorted corporate and financial incentives will, of course, take time, so policy must be designed for a second-best world. Because short-term funds that flood into emerging markets when profits beckon are liable to rush out again when danger threatens, and because this can lead to substantial – even disastrous – devaluation, it is vital for the proper functioning of global capital markets that financial vulnerability be reduced.[14] This is surely the prime lesson to take from the East Asian crisis, and financial and legal regulations in both debtor and creditor countries can be designed accordingly.

Taking debtor countries first:

Banks can be limited in the magnitude of the foreign exchang
and maturity mismatches might also be subjected to discipline by the ᵥ
authority. On-lending by financial intermediaries in foreign currency could be pro-
hibited ... and the insertion of bullet repayment clauses subject to the discretion of
the lender (a widespread practice in Korea's borrowing) might be declared illegal
and thereby rendered unenforceable.   (Williamson, 1999, p. 9)

Rules on improved corporate governance and financial disclosure may
reduce vulnerability and avert panic. The enactment of appropriate bankruptcy laws should help, cf. chapter 11 of the US Bankruptcy Code, which
provides protection for debtors against liquidity crisis. (Under this chapter,
firms that are judged to be viable can obtain an automatic stay on debt payments; can borrow extra funds despite current arrears; and may arrange
debt equity swaps, possibly under new management.) Indeed, it might be
appropriate to extend extra protection against extreme, unanticipated
exchange rate shocks in a sort of 'super' chapter 11 for emerging market
economies (Miller and Stiglitz, 1999).

Important steps can also be taken in creditor countries: 'What better way
to ensure that bankruptcy rules are passed than making access to the
NewYork or London markets conditional on having such legislation in
place?' as *The Economist* (1999a, p.22) put it in its recent Survey of Global
Finance. Changes in the terms governing investment in emerging markets
might also help. Thus the BIS could change the capital adequacy rules
which require far greater provisioning for long-term lending than for short
– giving every incentive for creditors to lend short. Insurance and pension
funds are often restricted to investment-grade paper, so downgrades of
countries in trouble by credit-rating agencies precipitate an avalanche of
selling. These rules might be changed to avoid self-fulfilling creditor runs.

But the virulence of creditor panic in East Asia suggests that, in addition
to these improvements to the financial infrastructure, emerging market
countries may also need to use inflow controls to limit external vulnerability owing to short-term government or corporate foreign currency borrowing. Chile provides a precedent, with rules designed to tax short-term and
portfolio flows while exempting FDI, as discussed in section 2.6, p. 365
above: the negative externalities characteristic of financial collapse provide
a powerful economic case for such taxes.

5.3.3 Improved contracts

The proposal by Eichengreen and Portes (1995) for debt contracts that
permit a country to reschedule payments in the event of a crisis has been

supported by the reports of the G-10 deputies (after the Mexican crisis), and of the G-22 deputies (after the East Asian crisis); and more recently by Stanley Fischer in his address to the AEA, where he recommended that

clauses on collective representation and majority decisions by creditors could be included in bond and other contracts, to facilitate the reaching of agreements with creditors in times of crisis. (Fischer, 1999, p. 11)

If revising bond contracts is such a good idea, why has it not been adopted? One reason may be the lack of incentives already mentioned (section 2.4, p. 363): why volunteer for 'burden-sharing' when you don't have to? But the factor stressed by Eichengreen (1999, pp. 69, 70) is the negative signalling effect that emerging countries might transmit by inserting such clauses in their bonds. To counter this, he argues that, in addition to leadership by OECD countries,

the IMF [should] urge its members to add majority voting, sharing, non-acceleration, minimum-legal threshold, and collective-representation clauses . . . to international bonds as a condition for their being admitted to domestic markets. It should provide an incentive for countries to do so by indicating that it is prepared to lend at more attractive interest rates to countries that issue debt securities featuring these provisions.

There is no denying the attraction of the state-contingent bond contracts for avoiding creditor races by bond holders and for expediting debt write-downs; but it is not clear how much difference the presence of such bond contracts would have made to the East Asian crisis where the problems were centred in short-term lending to banks and not in bond markets.

5.3.4 Contingent finance and loan guarantees

What countries need in a time of creditor panic is liquidity – both in the form of own-reserves and in the form of prepositioned credit lines. Prearranged 'bail-in' procedures were given general endorsement when the G-7

adopted the principle of establishing precautionary and multilateral lines of credit to countries that are at risk and pursuing strong IMF-approved policies – to be drawn only in the event of a liquidity need. (World Bank, 1998, pp. 153–4)

A specific example is provided by the credit lines taken out by Argentina to limit the 'Tequila effect' on its domestic economy – being run with a strict currency board. In its Survey of Global Finance, *The Economist* (1999a, p. 22) concluded that

Argentina's contingency-finance arrangement seems to be working well, so the World Bank should be nudged to support similar arrangements elsewhere. If the World Bank or other multilateral organisations were to guarantee a portion of such emergency credit lines, more banks would be prepared to offer them to more countries. This would not solve the question of providing liquidity in a crisis, but it might help at the margin.

(Other steps could include setting up regional systems for emergency credit recycling.)

5.4 Crisis resolution

5.4.1 Lender of last resort

Is an agency to act as LOLR for countries facing a crisis also needed? In his speech at the AEA, which echoed the sentiments of Walter Bagehot in an earlier century, Fischer, (1999, pp. 8–9) gave an unequivocal answer:

> there is such a need: it arises both because international capital flows are not only extremely volatile but also contagious, exhibiting the classic signs of financial panics, and because an international lender of last resort can help mitigate the effects of this instability, and perhaps the instability itself. This applies particularly to emerging market countries, where the crises of the last five years have been concentrated.

He went on to argue

> not only that the international system needs a lender of last resort, but also that the IMF is increasingly playing that role, and that changes in the international system now under consideration will make it possible for it to exercise that function more effectively.

In the terminology we have used earlier, he could as well have said that there are multiple equilibria in financial systems and that well designed institutions can help to select the good ones. But two obvious problems need to be faced: the lack of resources available and the risk of moral hazard if bail-outs are guaranteed. Both were tackled with more optimism than realism. As regards the former, Fischer made a strong case for more resources for the IMF. As for the latter, he expressed the belief that moral hazard could be limited by appropriate international standards, domestic prudential controls and the threat of bankruptcy. But the strategic analysis in the previous section implies that the IMF may be gamed into repeated bail-outs unless either standstill procedures are implemented or the countries concerned take the law into their own hands (and impose outright capital controls).

5.4.2 Standstills and work-outs

As an alternative to Malaysian-style capital controls – and as a supplement to domestic bankruptcy law – official standstill provisions are an essential strategic threat needed to limit investors' moral hazard. When creditors realise that the authorities may protect borrowers – instead of simply bailing out lenders – they will have the incentive to lend with more caution (see section 4, p. 371 above, and the Round Table comments by Richard Portes in chapter 13).

While the IMF has not endorsed official standstills it has, as in the Latin American debt crisis,

> agreed that the Fund may lend to countries in arrears to private creditors, provided they are pursuing appropriate policies and making good faith efforts to cooperate with the creditors.   (Fischer, 1999, pp. 11-12)

Official lending into arrears is a strong signal that non-payment is being condoned, and that – at least for large international banks – rollovers are in order. (Such rollovers may well be in the best interest of creditors, as in Korea in December 1997: the problem is that of securing creditor coordination.)

Even for countries needing a debt work-out, payment standstills play a crucial role, as noted by the World Bank in its assessment of the East Asia crisis; it commented that:

> The most critical aspect of a debt workout, however, is the temporary suspension of debt payments, which helps stop the decline in the currency and buys time to put in place a credible adjustment program and to organize creditor–debtor negotiations. By allowing an orderly debt restructuring, it could result in better outcomes for both the debtor country and the creditors.   (World Bank, 1998, p.156)

The G-7 Statement of October 1998 supported an active role for the World Bank and other Multilateral Development Banks in responding to the crisis, including the use of loan guarantees and other innovative means to leverage private sector lending for investment projects in emerging markets (G-7, 1998, p. 3). Soon after that, in November 1998, President Clinton and Prime Minister Obuchi announced the Asian Growth and Recovery Plan to finance bank recapitalisation and accelerate bank and corporate restructuring, with the support of the World Bank, the ADB and bilateral contributors. Among other things the $5 bn programme aims to promote mechanisms for dispute settlement and burden-sharing between creditors and debtors in the region, and safety nets to mitigate the social effects on the poor and unemployed.

The most appropriate forum for international negotiations on debt restructuring and debt work-outs is still a matter of debate: Edwards

(1998), for example, proposes a new agency. How the write-down of Indonesian debt is be handled is an important case in point, discussed by Corbett and Vines in chapter 2 in this volume.

5.4.3 Suspending convertibility – and catching sharks?

Chilean-style 'capital taxes' to limit short-term inflows have already been discussed as appropriate prudential measures that might be taken to avert crisis. But in a crisis, *faute de mieux*, countries can resort to further capital controls. Bearing in mind the strictures laid at the door of global financial markets by George Soros, for example, other devices worth considering in a crisis include: (1) more public disclosure of the position taken by hedge funds, as proposed by Malaysia; (2) banning borrowing in local currency by hedge funds and other foreign banks, see the actions of the Hong Kong monetary authorities against speculators (Dieter, 1998); (3) including hedge funds and merchant banks in a target group of creditors whose exit will attract regulatory censure – by increasing the withholding penalties in Chilean capital controls, or by regulatory action in their G-7 host countries ('exit taxes'), for example; (4) two-tier exchange rates – with a floating rate on capital account.

The outright suspension of convertibility on capital account, as in Malaysia, is a radical alternative not to be taken lightly; it delivers protection against speculative attacks and allows for the lower domestic interest rates but it disrupts the immediate financing of international trade and, as an arbitrary interference with property rights, reduces future access to international finance. But Malaysia has served notice that the costs of going along with unregulated liberalism may, on occasion, exceed the benefits.

6 Conclusions

Views on the reform of the international system are bound to be influenced by interpretations of recent financial crises. Inasmuch as the reasons lay in domestic mismanagement, it is incumbent on the economies concerned to 'put their house in order'. But the G-7 statement of October 1998 acknowledged that many of the outflows were not in fact driven by country-specific fundamentals;[15] and Fischer was quite explicit about the role of creditor panic in spreading contagion. If the crisis in East Asia involved a regionwide 'bank run' (where shifts of international confidence transformed a temporary liquidity crisis into a serious crisis of solvency), then systemic reform is surely necessary, with a focus on institutions and regulations which help to coordinate on 'good equilibria' (see Paul Masson's chapter 8 in this volume and (1999, p. 19).

In the absence of distortions, full capital account convertibility is a condition for the efficient allocation of resources; but asymmetric information generates distortions. The bank runs in the model of Diamond and Dybvig (1983), for example, arise because individuals' liquidity preference is not observable. The fact that borrowers typically know more about their projects than do lenders is a well known source of (borrowers') moral hazard (Stiglitz and Weiss, 1981); and unmonitored deposit insurance engenders lenders' moral hazard (Krugman, 1998a). Given such asymmetries, to insist on unconditional capital account liberalisation is inappropriate: financial integration becomes an exercise in second best with the pace of liberalisation determined by the strength of the regulatory framework and the financial institutions.

In this context, there is no 'silver bullet' to do the trick: what is needed is a strategy for crisis prevention and resolution. Thus a LOLR may well avoid bank runs but only at the risk of increasing moral hazard. To limit borrowers' moral hazard, *prudential regulation* in borrowing countries is needed, for example; together with *domestic bankruptcy* and the threat of an *international payments standstill* to check lenders' moral hazard. Of course, borrowing countries must do their best to ensure sound fundamentals including, in particular, prudential regulations of banks. But this will take time and in any case is not sufficient, so we have discussed above the various other steps that should, in our view, be taken. In the short run, for example, debtor countries must strive to reduce vulnerability owing to short-term dollar exposure, which may involve the use of Chilean-style taxation on inflows. Creditors must also play their part – by incorporating collective action clauses in loan contracts, for example and by offering contingent emergency finance. When crises nevertheless occur, damage limitation involves the provision of LOLR facilities, enforced debt rollovers, exit taxes and debt write-downs. (How far this will require changes in the role of current institutions is not considered here.)

Because of capital market imperfections, emerging market economies emboldened – or bullied – into premature liberalisation may face financial disaster. As a last resort, therefore, they may be tempted unilaterally to suspend convertibility. This is what Malaysia has done. If creditor countries can make the system safe enough for their emerging partners, there should be no need for them to 'get radical' in this way. One objective of reforming global institutions and sequencing liberalisation is to achieve this: to make outright capital controls the path not taken.

Postscript

Meeting in Bonn in February 1999, the Finance Ministers from G-7 approved a new forum proposed by Hans Tietmeyer, President of Germany's Bundesbank, whose task is 'to assess the issues and vulnerability affecting the global financial system and to identify and oversee the actions needed to address them'. It will meet twice a year and will be chaired for the first three years by Andrew Crockett, head of the BIS. This new forum, intended to replace the G-22, will include G-7 central bankers, Finance Ministry officials and regulators and representatives from the World Bank and the IMF; but it does not yet include emerging market economies and 'its only sanction will be peer pressure' (*Economist*, 1999b).

NOTES

We are grateful for discussions with Christian Brachet, Paul Masson, Joseph Stiglitz and John Williamson, for helpful comments from David Vines and for the technical assistance of Pongsak Luangaram, courtesy of the ESRC Centre for the Study of Regionalisation and Globalisation, University of Warwick. The views expressed are those of the authors and do not necessarily reflect those of the World Bank or its Directors.

1. This section draws on chapter 6, 'What won't work', in Eichengreen (1999), as we are happy to acknowledge.
2. As proposed by the Canadian Department of Finance (1998). Radelet and Sachs (1998) also discuss the idea that the IMF could officially approve such a moratorium.
3. As in Miller and Luangaram (1998).
4. See also Sachs (1998).
5. The simplest illustration is that of a currency attack (Obstfeld, 1996). There are three players – a government selling reserves to defend its exchange rate peg and two holders of domestic currency who can trade it in for reserves if they expect devaluation. In this strategic game of speculative attack, fundamentals – in the form of the reserves – do play a role. If there were no reserves the currency would surely collapse, and vice versa for massive reserves. But the interesting case is when it takes two to tango – i.e. when neither trader alone can 'run' the government's reserves but together they can. Then there are two equilibria: survival – if neither believes the other will attack; collapse of the peg, if each believes the other will attack. With intermediate levels of reserves the way is open for expectations to play a critical role. Or is it? The same game, played with many small traders, still has two equilibria – in that coordinated attacks can succeed in dislodging a peg which is otherwise viable. But if it takes two hundred rather than two to overwhelm the official defences, a coordinated attack seems a lot less plausible. Indeed, it can – and has – been argued that a little uncertainty about the behaviour of other traders (technically, 'lack of common knowledge') leads

to a unique equilibrium (Morris and Shin,1998a, 1998b). The idea is that individual traders, unsure of what other traders are thinking, will use the level of reserves as a guide: and the role reserves then play in coordinating expectations leads to a unique equilibrium: an attack will take place when reserves fall to a critical level, but not before. (See also chapter 7 in this volume.)

6. See Obstfeld (1996), for example.

7. In the second, 'signalling', case, it is the large traders, not the fundamentals, that coordinate expectations and, as the authors note, there are several theoretical reasons why this might be true, including asymmetric information in financial firms. If this leads firms to evaluate traders by trading outturns, then 'money managers prefer to follow the same strategies as their competitors (or "hide in the herd") in order not to be easily evaluated' (Eichengreen and Mathieson, 1998, p. 25).

8. Speculators attacking the Hong Kong dollar used a 'double play' where they shorted the stock market before attacking the currency. This way they would make money even when the attack failed! (The reason is that, when speculators moved out of Hong Kong dollars, the currency board mechanism meant money became tight, interest rates went up and the stock market fell.) This colourful episode revealed three things. First speculators knew they were big enough for their actions to change interest rates. Second they knew that the market did not know they were going to attack – otherwise how could they make money on the forward sales? Thirdly, they chose to use their power not to push an over-valued currency towards equilibrium, but to try to destroy the fulcrum of currency stability in East Asia. The situation was so alarming that, to bust the double play, the central bank took the highly unusual step of making massive purchases of shares in the Hang Seng index – so prices went up not down and the bets went wrong. They had to use their market power to counter that of the big private sector players.

9. Based on Miller and Zhang (1998).

10. In the language of Kydland and Prescott (1977), such a policy is not 'time-consistent': the 'time-consistent' outcome is that the Fund will intervene.

11. In fact, the probability of either state is endogenous, as discussed below.

12. The fact that countries like mainland China have – so far – escaped contagion from the East Asian crisis is commonly attributed to the inconvertibility of their currency on capital account (Miller and Zhang, 1998), something other emerging market countries cannot fail to notice.

13. See, for example, Stiglitz (1998a): 'Small open economies are like rowing boats on an open sea ...'

14. Corbett and Vines (chapter 2 in this volume) show how financial crisis together with foreign currency exposure can lead to collapse.

15. Specifically it expressed

concern about the extent of the general withdrawal of funds from emerging markets that had occurred without respect to the diversity of prospects facing those economies or to the significant progress that has been made in many economies in carrying out strong macroeconomic policies and structural reforms that enhance long-term growth prospects.   (G-7, 1998, p. 3)

REFERENCES

Agosin, M. and R. Ffrench-Davis (1996). 'Managing Capital Flows in Latin America', in M. ul Haque, I. Kaul and I. Grunberg (eds.), *The Tobin Tax: Coping with Financial Volatility,* Oxford: Oxford University Press: 161–91

Bagehot, W. (1873). *Lombard Street: A Description of the Money Market,* London: William Clowers & Sons

Calomiris, C. (1998). 'Blueprints for a New Global Financial Architecture', Columbia University, unpublished manuscript

Canadian Government (1998). 'Finance Minister Announces Six-point Canadian Plan to Deal with Financial Turmoil', Press Release, **98–094**, Ottawa: Department of Finance

Chang, R. and A. Velasco (1998). 'Financial Crises in Emerging Markets: A Canonical Model', *NBER Working Paper,* **6606**

Cline, W. R. (1995). *International Debt Re-examined,* Washington, DC: Institute for International Economics

(1998). 'IMF-supported Adjustment Programs in the East Asian Financial Crisis', *IIF Research Paper,* **98–1,** Washington, DC: Institute for International Finance

Corbett, J. and D. Vines (1998) 'The Asian Crisis: Lessons from the Collapse of Financial Systems, Exchange Rates and Macroeconomic Policy', chapter 2 in this volume.

Cornelli, F. and L. Felli (1995). 'The Theory of Bankruptcy and Mechanism Design', in B. Eichengreen and R. Portes (eds.), *Crisis? What Crisis? Orderly Workouts for Sovereign Debtors,* London: CEPR: 69–85

Diamond, D. W. and P. H. Dybvig (1983). 'Bank Runs, Deposit Insurance, and Liquidity', *Journal of Political Economy,* **91**: 401–19

Dieter, H. (1998). 'Crisis in Asia or Crisis of Globalisation?', *CSGR Working Paper,* **15,** Centre for the Study of Regionalisation and Globalisation, University of Warwick; Available at csgr.org

Dooley, M. (1998). 'A Model of Crises in Emerging Markets', *NBER Working Paper,* **6300**

Economist, The (1999a). *Survey of Global Finance,* Supplement (January)

(1999b). '*World Financial Regulation: Plumb Lines*' (27 February): 90–1

Edwards, S. (1998). 'Abolish the IMF', *Financial Times,* (13 December)

Eichengreen, B. (1999). *Toward A New International Financial Architecture: A Practical Post-Asia Agenda,* Washington, DC: Institute for International Economics

Eichengreen, B. and D. Mathieson (1998). 'Hedge Funds and Financial Market Dynamics', *IMF Occasional Paper,* **66,** Washington, DC: International Monetary Fund

Eichengreen, B. and R. Portes (eds.) (1995). *Crisis? What Crisis? Orderly Workouts for Sovereign Debtors,* London: CEPR

Fischer, S. (1999). 'On the Need for an International Lender of Last Resort', Washington, DC: International Monetary Fund (January), mimeo

Flemming, J. (1999). 'Bubbles, Exchange Rates, Capital Flows', in R. Skidelsky, N. Lawson, J. Flemming, M. Desai and P. Davidson (eds.), *Capital Regulation: For and Against,* London: Social Market Foundation: 30–42

Frankel, J. (1996). 'How Well do Markets Work? Might a Tobin Tax Help?', in M. ul Haque, I. Kaul and I. Grunberg (eds.), *The Tobin Tax: Coping with Financial Volatility*, Oxford: Oxford University Press: 41–81

G-7 (1998). *Statement of G–7 Finance Ministers and Central Bank Governors*, Washington, DC: International Monetary Fund (October)

G-10 (1996). *The Resolution of Sovereign Liquidity Crises*, Washington, DC: International Monetary Fund

G-22 (1998). *Report of the Working Group on International Financial Crises*, Washington, DC: World Bank (October)

Goldstein, M. (1998). *The Asian Financial Crisis: Causes, Cures, and Systemic Implications, Policy Analyses in International Economics*, **55**, Washington, DC: Institute for International Economics

Guardian, The (1999). 'US Sinks Brown's IMF Plans' (7 January): 21

Jardine, L. (1996). *Worldly Goods: A New History of the Renaissance*, London: W. W. Norton

Krugman, P. (1979). 'A Model of Balance-of-Payments Crises', *Journal of Money, Credit, and Banking*, **11**: 311–25

(1998a). 'What Happened to Asia', MIT, mimeo

(1998b). 'Saving Asia: It's Time to get Radical'. *Fortune Investor* (7 September): 33–8: available at http://www.pathfinder.com/fortune/investor/1998/980907/sol.html

Kydland, F. and E. Prescott (1977). 'Rules Rather than Discretion: The Inconsistency of Optimal Plans', *Journal of Political Economy*, **85**: 619–37

Masson, P. (1998). 'Contagion: Monsoonal Effects, Spillovers, and Jumps Between Multiple Equilibria', *IMF Working Paper*, **WP/98/142**: see also chapter 8 in this volume

(1999). 'Multiple Equilibria, Contagion and the East Asian Crisis', Washington, DC: International Monetary Fund, mimeo

Miller, M. and J. Stiglitz (1999). 'Bankruptcy Protection against Macroeconomic Shocks: The Case for a 'Super' Chapter 11', presented at conference on 'Capital Flows, Financial Crises and Policies', Washington, DC: World Bank (April), mimeo

Miller, M. and L. Zhang (1998). 'Sovereign Liquidity Crises: The Strategic Case for a Payments Standstill', *CEPR Discussion Paper*, **1820**; forthcoming in *Economic Journal*

Miller, M. and P. Luangaram (1998). 'Financial Crisis in East Asia: Bank Runs, Asset Bubbles and Antidotes', *National Institute Economic Review*, **165**: 66–82

Morris, Stephen and H. S. Shin (1998a). 'Unique Equilibrium in a Model of Self-fulfilling Currency Attacks', *American Economic Review*, **88**: 587–97

(1998b). 'A Theory of the Onset of Currency Attacks', paper presented at CEPR/ESRC/GEI conference on 'World Capital Markets and Financial Crises', University of Warwick; reprinted as chapter 7 in this volume

Obstfeld, M. (1996). 'Models of Currency Crisis with Self-fulfilling Features', *European Economic Review*, **40**: 1037–48

Radelet, S. and J. Sachs (1998). 'The East Asian Financial Crisis: Diagnosis, Remedies, Prospects', *Brooking Papers on Economic Activity*, **1**: 1–90.

Sachs, J. (1993). 'Life in the Economic Emergency Room', chapter 11 in J. Williamson (ed.), *The Political Economy of Policy Reform*, Washington, DC: Institute for International Economics

(1998). 'Creditor Panics: Causes and Remedies', Harvard University, mimeo; available at www:hiid.harvard.edu.

Soros, G. (1997). 'Avoiding a Breakdown: Asia's Crisis Demands a Rethink of International Regulation', *Financial Times* (31 December): 12

(1998). *The Crisis of Global Capitalism*, New York: BBS

(1999). 'To Avert the Next Crisis', *Financial Times* (4 January)

Stiglitz, J. (1997). 'Statement to the Meeting of Finance Ministers of Asean plus Six, with the IMF and World Bank', Washington, DC: World Bank (December), mimeo

(1998a). 'Boats, Planes and Capital Flows', *Financial Times* (25 March)

(1998b). 'Must Financial Crises be so Frequent and so Painful?', Washington, DC: World Bank; reprinted as chapter 12 in this volume

Stiglitz, J. and A. Weiss (1981). 'Credit Rationing in Markets with Imperfect Competition', *American Economic Review*, **71**: 393–410

Tobin, J. (1974). 'The New Economics One Decade Older', *The Eliot Janeway Lecture on Historical Economics in Honor of Joseph Schumpeter, 1972*, Princeton: Princeton University Press

(1996). 'Prologue', in M. ul Haque, I. Kaul and I. Grunberg (eds.), *The Tobin Tax: Coping with Financial Volatility*, Oxford: Oxford University Press: ix–xviii

Williamson, J. (1985). 'On the Question of Debt Relief', in Statement of the North-South Round Table on Money and Finance, New York: Society for International Development (13–14 December)

(ed.) (1994). *The Political Economy of Policy Reform*, Washington, DC: Institute for International Economics

(1999). 'Implications of the East Asian Crisis for Debt Management', Washington, DC: World Bank mimeo; available at www.warwick.ac.uk/fac/soc/CSGR/glob-fin.html

World Bank (1998). 'Beyond Financial Crisis', *Global Economic Prospects*, Washington, DC: World Bank

12　Must financial crises be this frequent and this painful?

JOSEPH STIGLITZ

1　The evidence that crises are frequent and painful

Must financial crises be this frequent and this painful? Before discussing some of the considerations that go into answering this question, I first want to document my claim that they *are* frequent and painful. Clearly anyone watching the world from mid-1997 to late 1998 would be left with little doubt that financial crises *can* be very severe. But the East Asian crisis is only the latest in a series of spectacular economic catastrophes in developing countries. In the last 20 years there have been at least 10 countries that have suffered from the *simultaneous* onset of a currency crisis and a banking crisis. The result has been full-blown economic crises causing, in many cases, GDP contractions of 5–12 per cent in the first year of the crisis, and negative or only slightly positive growth for several years after. Many other countries have witnessed contractions of similar magnitude following currency or banking crises.

Financial crises are not strictly exogenous and in many cases the slowdown itself, or the same factors that led to it, also helped cause the financial crisis. But there is no doubt that the over-shooting of exchange rates, the withdrawal of foreign capital, the non-rollover of short-term debts, the internal credit crunches, the process of disintermediation and many of the other characteristics of external and internal crises played a large role in these collapses.

Crises are also becoming increasingly frequent, at least relative to the post-Second World War period. We have had, in Caprio's memorable phrase, 'a boom in bust[s]' (Caprio, 1997, p. 80). Caprio and Klingebiel (1996) identify banking crises, defined as episodes when the entire banking system has zero or negative net worth, in 69 countries since the late 1970s. The US Savings and Loan (S & L) débâcle, whose resolution cost, in real terms, was several times larger than the cost of resolving the US banking crisis of the 1930s, does not even make their list of the top 25 international

Figure 12.1   *Incidence of financial crises worldwide, 1970–1997*

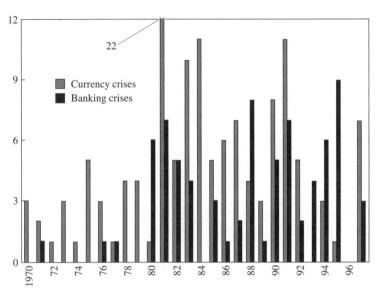

Sources: Caprio and Klingbiel (1996); Frankel and Rose (1996); Kaminsky and
Reinhart (1997).

banking crises since the early 1980s. With a less stringent definition,
Lindgren, Garcia and Saul (1996) estimate that three-quarters of IMF
member countries experienced 'significant bank sector problems' at some
time between 1980 and 1995. Currency crises have also been similarly per-
vasive, affecting at least 87 countries since 1975. A time series of crisis episodes is shown in figure 12.1.

The banking-cum-currency crises in East Asia have clearly exacted a
large toll. The East Asian economies continued to deteriorate following the
agreement of the initial and revised policy packages. Every month since the
initial devaluations has brought new downward revisions of the consensus
forecasts for growth (see figure 12.2). Many observers expected GDP in
Korea, Malaysia and Thailand to contract by 5–10 per cent in 1998. The
depth of the collapse in Indonesia, a 17 per cent GDP contraction in 1998
according to the latest consensus forecast, if not unparalleled, is among the
largest peacetime contractions since at least 1960 (excluding the experience
of the CEE transition economies).

Although more severe than average, the experience of East Asia is not a
historical aberration. The most systematic evidence, compiled by the IMF
(1998), demonstrates that banking and currency crises can exact a large toll,

Figure 12.2 *1998 GDP consensus forecast, June 1997–September 1998*

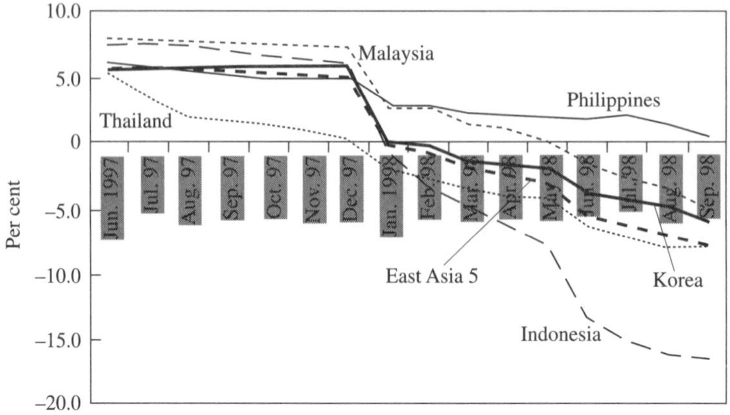

Source: Consensus Forecast.

especially when they occur simultaneously. Figure 12.3 shows the cumulative output loss relative to trend in the years following a currency crash, a banking crisis and their simultaneous onset. It shows that not only are currency crashes and banking crises on average very costly, but that they are especially costly for developing countries.

2 Should we do something about economic crises?

This relatively brief presentation of the evidence establishes that the current system is far from desirable. Similarly, when John Maynard Keynes wrote the *General Theory* (1936) he was motivated by the very far from desirable conditions of the leading industrial economies. The fact that US GDP contracted by more than 25 per cent in just three years and that unemployment rate rose to 25 per cent was, by itself, *prima facie* evidence that government action might be necessary to remedy the undesirable outcomes of the economy. 50 years after Keynes, however, a school of thought emerged – real business-cycle theory – which argued that all fluctuations in output are efficient movements to new equilibria given by the ever-changing technology and tastes of the economy. In this view, the Great Depression was the optimal outcome of a collective desire to take vacations pending the higher wages expected in the future. Furthermore, together with new classical macroeconomics, it endeavoured to convince us that even if we did not like

Figure 12.3   *Cumulative lost output relative to trend, 1998*

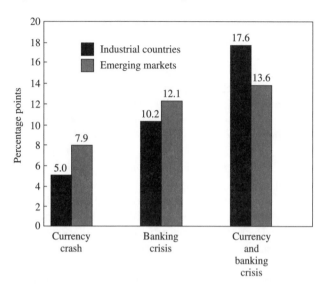

Source: IMF, *World Economic Outlook* (May 1998).

the current state of the economy, there was virtually nothing, at least nothing systematic, that policy makers could do about it.

In general the theorems under which the decentralised economic outcome is optimal are highly restrictive and include perfect information and complete markets, including markets for every period and every contingency, and are not even remotely satisfied in practice. It is worthwhile, however, to go through some of the economic motivation for public action, at the national and international level, in preventing and responding to economic crises. The point of this discussion is not just to put the motivation for government action on more solid footing, but also to help guide those actions. I will discuss the rationale for government actions in two areas – the financial system and the response to capital flows.

2.1 Government and the financial system

In introductory economics courses we teach our students to use demand and supply diagrams to analyse markets for apples and bananas. We also teach that, provided there are no externalities, the competitive price is efficient.

Some go on to apply this theory to financial markets, looking at the supply of funds, the demand for funds, and the market-clearing interest rate. This simplistic theory is the basis for the belief that financial markets need to be fully liberalised from the 'interference' of governments. Unfortunately, this framework makes little sense in approaching finance, which is concerned with the exchange of money today for the *promise* of repayment. Given the existence of uncertainty and the lack of complete futures markets, this inter-temporal transaction entails risks, especially the risk of bankruptcy. Information about these risks – both about the type of borrower and the actions she undertakes after borrowing the money – is essential.

The fundamental theorems of welfare economics, which assert that every competitive equilibrium is Pareto-efficient, provide no guidance with respect to the question of whether financial markets, which are essentially concerned with the production, processing, dissemination and utilisation of information, are efficient (Greenwald and Stiglitz, 1986). On the contrary, economies with imperfect information or incomplete markets are, in general, not Pareto-efficient: there are feasible government interventions that can make all individuals better off.

These are not just academic details. Governments play a large role in all of the most successful financial markets. Wall Street, the international emblem of free markets, is one of the most highly regulated markets in the US. But let me also be clear: this observation should not be the basis for the government to take over the financial system. History does not offer many examples of highly successful economies that did not accord the market a central role in the allocation and monitoring of capital. Theoretically, the case for a government-run economy rests on the same highly restrictive assumptions as the case for a purely free-market economy, notably the assumption that there is perfect information (see Stiglitz, 1994).

2.2 Public action and international capital flows

Next I would like to turn to issues in the regulation of international capital flows. Capital flows are at the heart of modern international crises. The withdrawal of capital or the refusal to roll over short-term loans are at the centre of most severe developing country (DC) balance of payments crises. It is not just foreign money that matters, both the 1994–5 Mexican crisis and the 1997–8 Indonesian crisis involved substantial capital outflows. Overall, in East Asia, there was a $109 bn reversal of net private capital flows (more than 10 per cent of GDP) to the region between 1996 and 1997 – with most of the adjustment taking place during the last half of the year

(Institute of International Finance, 1998). It is also noteworthy that foreign direct investment (FDI) to the five East Asian economies is estimated to have been essentially unchanged.

Some have made the case that the free movement of capital ensures that it finds its most productive use, maximising global welfare. For DCs in particular, it allows them to invest more than they save and diversify away some of the very large risks they face. If that were all there was to the story, then any government 'interference' in the global capital market would be distortionary and would reduce welfare. Too many people continue to argue this point quite literally, ruling out any public action on *a priori* grounds. At best, this is a highly consistent but totally misleading point of view. In practice, however, some of these same people also support IMF-led bail-outs, which are themselves very large interventions in the free workings of the market. One cannot simultaneously hold that these bail-outs are legitimate and that there should always be completely unfettered flows of capital.

There are two possible economic justifications for rescue packages, which will also motivate my discussion of other interventions. The first is that the social risk is not equal to the private risk so that, left to themselves, markets will accumulate more risk than is socially efficient. This is analogous to pollution, which imposes greater costs on society than are borne by the polluter alone. In this case, we typically tax or regulate the pollution. The same logic would suggest some type of tax or regulation on international capital flows. We should recognise that most countries have various forms of taxes or regulation on the domestic financial system, including measures such as reserve requirements or deposit insurance. These are justified by the contagion and systemic risk to which financial decisions give rise and by the interventions (e.g. bail-outs) which so frequently arise. Although these may or may not be feasible or desirable at the international level, I do not think it would be consistent with our other policies to rule these steps out on *a priori* grounds.

Another possible economic justification for intervening in the market with the rescue package is that the market is not even pricing private risk efficiently – that is, that the market is irrational. One form of irrationality that is sometimes discussed is the claim that market participants can be overly focused on the immediate term, particularly in figuring out what other market participants are going to do. This is what Keynes referred to as a 'beauty contest' in which contestants are trying to guess who the other judges think is most beautiful, not who actually is the most beautiful. As a result, markets can diverge from long-run fundamentals which, according to this view, are more stable than the actual market outcomes.

There is an extensive economics literature documenting what is called the market's 'excess volatility'. If it is correct, then some measure like a Tobin tax (a tax on certain transactions) could increase the cost of short-term speculation by raising the cost of round-tripping, while still allowing markets to respond to changes in the long-run fundamentals. I am raising the Tobin tax just as an illustration; in practice, there are serious questions about its feasibility, especially in a world of rapid financial innovation, where it could be easy to circumvent.

(The argument sometimes put forward that the bail-outs do not cost anybody anything can, similarly, be looked at in two different ways. If markets are 'rational' then the fact that the interest rate charged is below the market interest rate for these loans is evidence that there is, in an *ex ante* sense, a real subsidy to the borrower, even if *ex post* we have been repaid for the loans made in previous bail-outs. Alternatively, markets may be 'irrational', charging an excessively high risk premium – one that cannot be justified by the real risk. Then the intervention in the market may be costless; but this argument certainly undermines confidence that markets by themselves are likely to yield efficient outcomes.)

3 Are there feasible interventions to prevent crises?

I have argued that we are facing a very serious problem. I have also argued that there is an economic rationale for addressing this problem. I would now like to consider if there are feasible government interventions that can help prevent crises, and discuss the issue of responding to crises when they do occur.

We cannot expect to eliminate all fluctuations or all crises. Even if we could eliminate all of the 'problems' and 'mistakes' in economic policy, it is unlikely that we could fully insulate economies against shocks, including events such as the OPEC oil price increases in the 1970s or changes in market sentiment, such as occurred in the East Asian crisis. Furthermore, although there is much more scope for policy reforms in developing countries, we should not delude ourselves into thinking that this can take place overnight. Building robust financial systems is a long and difficult process. In the meantime, we need to be realistic and recognise that DCs have less capacity for financial regulation and greater vulnerability to shocks. We need to take this into account in policy recommendations in all areas, especially in the timing and sequencing of opening up capital markets to the outside world and in the liberalisation of the financial sector.

We must bear in mind, too, in designing policy regimes (such as opening up capital markets) that we cannot assume that other aspects of economic policy, such as macroeconomic policy or exchange rates, will be flawlessly carried out. The policy regimes we adopt must be robust against at least a modicum of human fallibility. Airplanes are not designed to be flown just by ace pilots, and nuclear power plants have built into them a huge margin of safety for human error.

3.1 The importance and limitations of better information

One of the international reforms to have come out of the Mexican crisis was the almost universal call for better information, in terms of accuracy, scope and timeliness. The East Asian crisis has reinvigorated the calls for better information, as foreign investors have blamed the East Asian governments for not giving them enough information. Much of this has just been blame-shifting. Just as Mahatirs blame Soroses for their problems, so too do international investors blame the countries they invest in for not providing them with full information: if only they had been told the truth, they would not have got into the problems they did. But most of the supposed problems in East Asia, including the 'lack of transparency,' were not news, they were widely known prior to the crisis. Indeed, there is a serious question about whether or not all of the available information was even being used. There is no systematic evidence linking lack of transparency to economic crises – the last major banking-cum-currency crises were in Scandinavia – models of transparency. And even if there were, there is no evidence that corruption or transparency were significant problems in *all* of the East Asian countries affected by the crisis. According to a number of ratings of transparency and corruption, Indonesia was one of the worst middle-income countries. But Thailand and the Philippines were about average (and substantially above average compared to DCs as a whole). And Korea and Malaysia were consistently rated among the least corrupt and most transparent of any developing country.

There is no doubt, however, that more information is usually better. In the case of East Asia, it is likely that the general lack of information made it difficult for investors to distinguish between firms and financial institutions that are healthy and those that are not. In response, investors shied away from all. With more credible information systems, firms that remain healthy would be able to retain access to credit.

The standard macroeconomic data would not have been very helpful in predicting the East Asian crisis, which had to do with the composition and allocation of private/private capital flows. Unfortunately, getting information about private sector spending and borrowing is much more difficult than obtaining comparable information about public finances. This is especially the case when transparency is limited. In a world where private/private capital flows are increasingly important, we will need to recognise that monitoring and surveillance are going to be especially challenging. The growing use of derivatives is increasingly making the full disclosure of relevant information, or at least the full interpretation of the disclosed information, even more difficult. We should remember, too, that the great merit of a market economy is that dispersed information is aggregated through prices and the incentives they create for behaviour, without the need for any centralised collection of information or planning. There is a certain irony about praising a market economy for this decentralisation of information, and at the same time complaining about the lack of aggregate data necessary to assess systemic risks.

Moreover, we should not be under the illusion that having improved data is sufficient for financial markets to function well. In East Asia much of the important information was available, but it had not been integrated into the assessment of the market. Furthermore, it is impossible to eliminate all uncertainty and asymmetries of information. Entrepreneurs will always know more about their investments than will the banks that lend to them, and managers will always know more about their actions than shareholders will. Without the correct incentives, even perfect aggregate information would not be sufficient for the efficient, or stable, functioning of markets.

Although our information about private capital flows is imperfect, and although even with vastly improved information I am not sanguine that we – or the market – would be able to predict or forestall all crises, I do think that the returns from improving our statistical bases are significant. My caution is only that we should not be misled into thinking that this will solve our problems. Better information – seemingly the most important improvement in the international financial architecture to come out of the last crisis – should not lull us into complacency.

3.2 Financial regulation and financial restraint

The second set of widely endorsed policies is better financial regulation. Again, there is no doubt that better financial regulation would be a good thing: after all, how could anyone object to 'better'? The more important question is, how much do we expect better financial regulation to accomplish, and what form should this regulation take? This is a huge topic that I have addressed elsewhere (Stiglitz and Greenwald, 1993). In this context, however, I would like to focus on the role of financial regulation in crisis-prevention and contrast Basle-style financial regulation with mild financial restraints.

We can examine the effects of financial regulation on crisis-prevention by conducting a thought experiment about whether better financial regulation, along the lines of the Basle accord, would have prevented East Asia's crisis. Although better financial regulation is clearly desirable – for both growth and stability – we should not over-estimate the ability of financial regulation to overcome the macroeconomic incentives.

What would have happened if the government had maintained the same misguided foreign exchange policy, but had had a better regulated financial sector? In this case, regulators would have limited banks' ability to borrow short in foreign currency and lend long to buy non-tradeable assets. But the expected constancy of the exchange rate and the differential between foreign and domestic interest rates, which was increased by the attempts to sterilise the capital inflows, driving up the domestic rate, would still have created the same incentives to borrow short-term money from abroad. The result could have been that instead of banks, corporations or non-bank financial institutions would have accessed international markets directly. This is, of course, what happened in Indonesia where roughly two-thirds of the external debt was incurred by the non-bank private sector, among the highest fraction of any country in the world. No country can, does, or probably should regulate individual corporations at the level of detail that would be required to prevent the foreign exchange and maturity mismatches that arose.

Furthermore, in contrast to its neighbours, Malaysia's central bank adopted much more prudent policies *vis-à-vis* short-term borrowing, and as a result its ratio of short-term debt to reserves in end-December 1996 was 0.54 compared to 1.74 for Thailand. (Other aspects of Malaysia's situation were comparable to that elsewhere in East Asia – for instance, their level of non-performing loans. But even this may be misleading, since Malaysia required larger reserves against losses, so that their banks were in better financial positions.) As a result, Malaysia did not suffer as much from the failure of foreign creditors to roll over short-term loans, and thus it did not face the imminent threat of a default that brought Korea and Indonesia to the brink. Despite this fact, Malaysia's crisis, measured by the depreciation of its exchange rate or its expected growth in 1998, has been just as severe as that of Korea or Thailand. Taiwan (China) had strong financial institutions, sound macroeconomic policies and an exchange rate that was widely believed to be reasonable. As a result, it saw its exchange rate gradually depreciate by *only* 20 per cent, which represented an almost equally substantial depreciation of its real exchange rate.

Well designed bank regulations – such as risk-adjusted capital adequacy standards and risk-adjusted deposit premia – might have gone some way toward reducing financial market vulnerabilities. For instance, when lending to borrowers who have large uncovered foreign exchange exposures and very high debt equity ratios, banks would have charged higher interest rates to reflect this greater risk; and the threat of higher interest rates would have provided a disincentive for firms to have risky financial positions.

To the degree that better financial regulation would have been helpful, three observations are in order:

- First, countries with more advanced institutions have found it difficult to develop a regulatory framework that *insulates them from financial crises*. Even banks in the supposedly well regulated advanced countries made loans not just to Korean banks, but also directly to its *chaebol*, with their high debt/equity ratios. As a practical matter, however, no government has imposed good systems of capital adequacy. One important lacuna is that although credit risk is typically recognised (though gauged imperfectly), market value risk associated with changes in interest rates or risk premia is not. Furthermore, regulations do not examine total portfolio risk, including the correlations among market risks and between market risk and credit risk. Even countries such as the US have deliberately shied away from fully transparent risk-adequacy standards based on modern risk analysis. Accordingly, it is unreasonable to expect such indirect control devices to work effectively in DCs.

- Second, given these limitations there are arguments for a whole variety of lending restrictions – not only sectoral limits, but also speed limits, as well as restrictions on the liability structures of the firms to which the banks lend. Greater financial sector restraints, rather than the weaker restraints that were adopted in practice, might have gone some way toward changing the composition of capital inflows (by raising the cost of short-term borrowing) and their use (by restricting investment in non-tradeables). Further restraints on international capital flows, justified by the externality imposed by international capital flows, could potentially have complemented these policies, further lengthening the duration, and reducing the risk, of capital inflows.

- Third, the problems of designing an appropriate regulatory structure are becoming more difficult with derivatives and off-balance sheet items, and are more difficult for DCs, both because they are likely to face a shortage of good regulators and because they face greater risks. These problems are highlighted by the fact that both in Indonesia and Korea, some firms and banks thought they had covered positions, but bankruptcy of the party providing the hedge left them in an exposed position (Dooley, 1998). For a regulator to ferret out these problems would require it to assess the credit risk of innumerable firms. That is why regulators in more developed countries are switching to an evaluation of the risk-management systems, rather than monitoring individual transactions or even portfolio positions. It is likely to be some time before DC financial institutions can put in place risk-management systems that evaluate accurately portfolio risks taking into account both credit and market risks and the correlations within and between these risk categories. There is some concern that the Basle standards, by setting up a regulatory framework that does not deal adequately with these broader (and more relevant) aspects of risk may give banks (and their depositors and investors) comfort when they should not, and may actually lead to excessive risk in the relevant sense.

The thrust of the Basle standards – setting up a 'level playing field' so that banks throughout the world face similar standards – has itself come into question, as the differences in circumstances may in fact necessitate different standards for countries in different positions. Even when adopting the Basle standards is understood as a minimal recommendation, the more prudent policies are measured by, for instance, higher capital-adequacy requirements, not changes in the regulatory objectives or structure. Similarly, the thrust of financial market liberalisation has been to replace quantitative and other ad hoc constraints (for example, on lending to real estate) with broad-based capital adequacy and risk management standards. But given the deficiencies in those, which may have particularly severe consequences for DCs, this strategy clearly has its problems. Indeed, I have argued that this misguided strategy shares a considerable part of the blame for the problems in Thailand, which prior to financial market liberalisation actually had a relatively sound financial system.

3.3 Controlling capital flows

A consensus is beginning to form that governments, and possibly the international system, need to do more to restrain the movements of capital, especially of short-term 'hot money'. Although better information and better regulation are important first steps they are, as I have argued, far from sufficient. Instead, I have argued that there is a theoretical rationale for policies that bring private risks into line with the social risks.

Specifically, these policies aim to influence both the *pattern* and *timing* of capital flows. Currently, 75 per cent of private capital flows to only a dozen countries, and most low-income countries have little access to private capital relative to the size of their economies. Procyclicality is another undesirable feature of international capital flows. Countries seem to get the most private capital when they are growing strongly and need it least, and they have a relatively difficult time accessing capital in hard times when they need it most; as a result capital flows do relatively little to smooth the business cycle and may even amplify it. Accomplishing this objective, however, may be very difficult.

Another objective concerns the *composition* of capital flows. There is now broad agreement about the value of FDI, which brings not just capital but also technology and training. Preliminary evidence from East Asia also shows that consistent with past experience, FDI is relatively stable, and certainly far more stable than other forms of capital flows. Unlike FDI, short-term capital does not bring with it ancillary benefits. In the form of trade credits it provides an important, and relatively inexpensive, source of international liquidity without which no economy, especially an export-oriented economy, can run. In addition to providing liquidity, short-term capital, along with other forms of flows, allows a country to invest more than it saves. When this money is invested productively, the benefits to the economy are large. But when the saving rate is already high, and when the money is misallocated, the additional capital flows just increase the vulnerability of the economy. Moreover, given their volatility, what well managed economy would risk basing long-term investments on short-term flows? More generally, it is not considered prudent to hold international reserves equal to or greater than short-term foreign debt, a policy that amounts to DCs borrowing from industrial-country banks at high interest rates only to relend the money to industrial country treasuries at low interest rates. Perhaps for these reasons, several systematic empirical studies have failed to find any relationship between capital account liberalisation and growth or investment (see Rodrik, 1998).

The large benefits of FDI, and the costs and benefits of short-term capital flows, have led many people to investigate ways to encourage long-term investments while discouraging rapid round trips of short-term money. There are many components of such a strategy:

- First, we need to eliminate the *tax, regulatory* and *policy distortions* that may, in the past, have stimulated short-term capital flows. Examples of such distortions are evident in the case of Thailand where the tax advantages for the Bangkok International Banking Facility (BIBF) encouraged short-term external borrowing, but subtle examples exist almost everywhere. Without risk-based capital requirements for banks, for instance, incentives for holding certain assets and liabilities will be distorted.

- Second, several countries have imposed *prudential bank regulations* to limit the currency exposure of their institutions.

- Third, these measures may not go far enough, especially once it is recalled that corporate exposure may itself give rise to vulnerabilities. And the systemic risks to which such exposure can give rise provide ample justification for taking further measures. Among the ideas currently under discussion are *inhibitions on capital inflows*. In thinking about how to accomplish this, we should look to the lessons of the Chilean experience. Chile has imposed a reserve requirement on all short-term capital inflows – essentially a tax on short-maturity loans (see chapter 11 in this volume). The overall efficacy of these controls is the subject of much discussion, but even most critics of the Chilean system acknowledge that the reserve requirement has significantly lengthened the maturity composition of capital inflows to Chile without having adverse effects on valuable long-term capital.

- Still other measures employ *tax policies* – for example, limiting the extent of tax deductibility for interest in debt denominated or linked to foreign currencies. The problems of implementing these policies may in fact be less than those associated with the Chilean system.

In evaluating these proposals, we must be clear what the objectives of the interventions are. Two seem uncontroversial: reducing (though not eliminating) the volatility of flows and reducing (though not eliminating) the discrepancy between private and social returns.

3.4 Summary

The prevention of crises has important domestic and international dimensions. I have argued that we should not over-estimate the ability of purely domestic policies, such as greater transparency and better financial regulation, in averting crises. Although these are important, they must be supplemented by additional policies to restrain overly volatile short-term capital flows.

This raises another question: who will implement these policies? The most important and feasible (especially in the near term) actions toward international capital flows are all at the national level – carried out either by developed countries or DCs. But there is also a currently very active dialogue at the international level. At a minimum, international groups and institutions can play an important role in encouraging the adoption of sound policies, and especially by persuading investors that the adoption of some restraints on capital flows is not necessarily a sign that a country is unfriendly to investment, but simply that it wants to insulate itself against some risk.

4 Are there feasible interventions to improve responses to crises?

Some crises are inevitable. The most important policy responses to economic crises are all at the domestic level, including the proper stance of macroeconomic policy, structural responses and the establishment and strengthening of social safety net programmes. I have discussed these policy responses elsewhere; here, I would like to continue to focus on the international dimension of responding to crises. When crises occur, they unleash a wave of capital outflows and increased uncertainty in international transactions. Mitigating these reversals – or, at least, dealing with them in an orderly way – would greatly speed up the resolution of crises and the resumption of economic growth.

A keystone in the development of modern capitalism has been limited liability and bankruptcy laws. Modern bankruptcy laws attempt to balance two sometimes conflicting considerations: promoting orderly work-outs so that business values can be retained and production losses kept to a minimum, and providing appropriate incentives so that those engaged in risky behaviour bear the consequences of their actions. In the international context, the flight of capital or withdrawal of short-term debt does not remove any of the actual factories; the goal is to ensure that they continue to produce and that the assets are not stripped. In the absence of orderly work-out procedures, countries may worry that unless they issue guarantees or assume private debts, the disruption to the economy will be unbearable.

Similarly, the international community has long complained about the problem of moral hazard – the fact that lenders have been at least partially bailed out. To be sure, in many cases the bail-out has been far from complete and lenders have lost money. Still, to the extent that there is any bail-out, they have not been forced to bear the full risks associated with their investment, and the belief that in the future this pattern will continue can give rise to the moral hazard. Again, the international community faces a dilemma: it often sees no alternative to a bail-out – the risks of not undertaking an action seem unacceptable. After each crisis, we bemoan the extent of the bail-out and make strong speeches saying that never again will lenders be let off the hook to the same extent. But, if anything, the 'moral hazard problem' has increased, not decreased, with each successive crisis.

While the experience of the last 20 years suggests that lenders can be forced to bear more of the costs than they have in at least some of the more recent crises, the middle of the crisis may not be the right time to deal with these issues. We can, however, prepare for the next one. There is more that we can do to facilitate orderly work-outs, to reduce moral hazard, to make those investors who are most likely to reap the benefits of a bailout pay part of the costs and, more broadly, to reduce the discrepancy between social and private returns to certain forms of risky international lending. One aspect of this may be a greater willingness to accept standstills that temporarily stop the outflow of money and create the time necessary to negotiate orderly work-outs. Another may be recognising that proper burden-sharing, including possibly 'haircuts' for international creditors, is necessary both for equity and efficiency. Ultimately the goal of these policies is to create space for the very difficult job of a work-out in the context of private/private capital flows with many lenders and borrowers. Imposing standstills and worrying about appropriate burden-sharing prior to bail-outs, rather than the recent practice of waiting until after the fact, may be a key.

5 Conclusions

I have presented three overarching points here:

- The first is that the frequency and severe consequences of economic crises is intolerable. Crises appear to be getting ever more frequent and ever more severe. The search for something to remedy this situation is one of the biggest challenges facing much of the developing world.

- Second, the economic theory of imperfect information provides an economic rationale for public action, at the national and international level, to mitigate some of the major international economic problems.

- Third, this economic rationale can be used as the basis for designing feasible policies to help prevent crises and respond to them better when they do occur.

Several threads have run through this chapter. One is that we cannot understand crises, or the policies to address them, without integrating macroeconomics on a sound microeconomic footing, with especial attention to the financial system. Another is that we should design policies that are robust against a modicum of human failure. We have been approaching global integration piecemeal, with the integration of the private sector far outpacing the development of complementary international economic institutions to monitor, regulate and adjudicate international economic relations. Today, we stand on the edge of a new world economy. But we do not have international institutions to play the role that the nation-states did in promoting and regulating trade and finance, competition and bankruptcy, corporate governance and accounting practices, taxation and standards, within their borders. Navigating these uncharted shoals will be a great challenge. But just as much of the prosperity of the past 150 years can be related to the expansion of markets that those transformations afforded, so too the prosperity of the next century will depend in no small measure on our seizing the opportunities afforded by globalisation.

In approaching the challenges of globalisation, we must eschew ideology and over-simplified models. With the continuing decline in economic activity in East Asia, with the new crisis in Russia and with the contagion threatening economies elsewhere, faith in the market economy is eroding in many parts of the world. It is now clear that the emphasis on privatisation, liberalisation and macroeconomic stability that dominated thinking about developing economies neither fully captured the essentials of a market economy nor provided a recipe for growth and stability, let alone for the broader goals of democratic, sustainable and equitable development.

Our challenge today is to prevent the pendulum from swinging too far to the other side. A sound market economy integrated into the global system is the key to economic success. But this requires a sound institutional infrastructure, which in turn requires an effective and efficient government focusing on the essential functions of the public sector. We have a huge task in redesigning the international architecture. But if we set our sights high, if we keep our objectives broad, if we keep our instruments wide, if we eschew ideology but use all of the limited knowledge that we have effectively, we can make progress.

We must not let the perfect be the enemy of the good. In a downpour, it is better to have a leaky umbrella than no umbrella at all. There are reforms to the international economic architecture that can bring the advantages of globalisation, including global capital markets, while mitigating their risks. We are beginning to see a new consensus forming around ways to restrain the risk of 'hot money' and the goal of developing procedures for orderly work-outs. Hopefully the continuing international dialogue on these and other issues will continue to make progress in these and other areas.

NOTES

This chapter contains the slightly amended text of the McKay Lecture given by Joseph Stiglitz in Pittsburgh, Pennsylvania on 23 September 1998.

REFERENCES

Caprio, G. (1997). 'Safe and Sound Banking in Developing Countries: We're not in Kansas Anymore', *Research in Financial Services: Private and Public Policy* **9**: 79–97

Caprio, G. and D. Klingebiel (1996). 'Bank Insolvencies: Cross-country Experience', *Policy Research Working Paper,* **1620**, Washington, DC: World Bank

Dooley, M. (1998). 'Indonesia: Is the Light at the End of the Tunnel Oncoming Traffic?', Deutsche Bank Research, Emerging Markets Research (June)

Greenwald, B. and J. E. Stiglitz (1986). 'Externalities in Markets with Imperfect Information and Incomplete Markets', *Quarterly Journal of Economics*, **101**: 229–64

Frankel, J. and A. K. Rose (1996). 'Currency Crashes in Emerging Markets', *Journal of Internation Economics*, **41**: 351–66

IMF (1998). *World Economic Outlook: May 1998*, Washington, DC: International Monetary Fund

Institute of International Finance (1998). 'Capital Flows to Emerging Markets Economies', 30 April

Kaminsky, G. and C. Reinhart (1996). 'The Twin Crises: The Causes of Banking and Balance-of-payments Problems', *International Finance Discussion Paper*, **544**, Board of Governers of the Federal Reserve System

Lindgren, C.-J., G. Garcia and M. Saul (1996). *Banking Soundness and Macroeconomic Policy,* Washington: International Monetary Fund

Rodrik, D. (1998). 'Who Needs Capital-account Convertibility?', *Essays in International Finance*, **207**, International Finance Section, Department of Economics, Princeton University (May): 55–65

Stiglitz, J. E. (1994). *Whither Socialism?*, Cambridge, Mass.: MIT Press

Stiglitz, J. E. and B. Greenwald (1993). 'Financial Market Imperfections and Business Cycles', *Quarterly Journal of Economics*, **108(1)**: 77–114

13 Round Table discussion

RICHARD PORTES, PHILLIP TURNER AND
CHARLES A. GOODHART

The final section of the book is an updated report on a Round Table discussion which was held at the conclusion of the conference on 'World Capital Markets and Financial Crises', University of Warwick (24–25 July 1998). The discussion produced a comprehensive review of thinking about the crisis, which is why we report it in full here. Richard Portes talked about early-warning indicators and LOLR facilities. Phillip Turner spoke about risk in financial markets and the role of the public sector in the context of such risk. Finally, Charles Goodhart talked about the impact of external events on the exchange rate and also on the treatment of foreign currency debt, both of which have implications for the IMF programmes.

1 Richard Portes

Robert Rubin says that 'The purpose of IMF packages is to help Korea, a by-product is that we help investors and creditors.' Do we really agree with this? Or do we think that IMF packages do this? Or do they mainly create moral hazard? Start with Mexico. Of course it is impossible to demonstrate from the data that the Mexican bail-out, through creating moral hazard, contributed to what we have observed in Asia. But I believe passionately that it did. I would be delighted if anybody here could suggest ways in which we could observe in the data the effects of the moral hazard that such rescues create. But what we have observed in the Asian sequence is the creation of *further* moral hazard.

Take the Korean bail-out. What happened? During three weeks in December 1997 the IMF package of 10 bn dollars went directly into reducing the short-term exposure of the banks. That is demonstrable, and the Fund itself at the highest level will concede precisely that. It was not until the orchestrated rescheduling that the banks stopped taking out their short-term funds. In general these mega-packages just keep on growing, and it is very hard to figure out where they are going to stop.

The last time around, after Mexico, there was discussion on trying to make the creditors take a bigger hit. There was the work I did with Barry Eichengreen, followed by the G-10 report in May 1996. But market participants reacted so strongly to what we had said that the G-10 report pulled its punches. Indeed they surveyed market participants, who said 'If you do what Eichengreen and Portes say, the debtors will just take that as an invitation to default.' So the G-10 said that markets had to do it themselves, had to come up with orderly work-out arrangements, contractual changes in debt contracts, and so forth. Of course, nothing has happened.

Now, it is said that this time around the creditors have taken some hits. This is not obvious to me. Of course equity investors took a hit, but they did so in Mexico as well. No news. Bond owners? Yes, bond prices have fallen, but people are holding. You can hold bonds to redemption after all, and meanwhile get paid. There have been no defaults as far as I know on bond interest.[1] In Indonesia we may see the banks finally taking some loss on loans to the private sector. They are not, of course, taking losses on loans to private sector banks in Korea, because the Korean government guaranteed all those. So all this, as I say, is evidence of considerable moral hazard, part of that created by intervention by the Fund and by the international community.

To move to the international LOLR issue. Can the Fund be an international LOLR? It cannot create money, it does not have a sustained supervisory presence in any of the countries that it deals with, and that is a very important element in exacerbating the moral hazard dangers arising from Fund bail-out intervention. In addition, the Fund does not have the fiscal redistributive authority that a LOLR has to be able to call on if there are actually solvency issues, rather than merely temporary liquidity questions. So the Fund cannot deal with the cross-country incidence, creditor/debtor incidence, of loss. The Fund has therefore played international LOLR without the key supporting structures that are necessary to do so. I conclude from that that we need more market-based solutions and more incentives for the markets to come up with the solutions, such as changes in debt contracts, such as *ex ante* tiered-debt instruments, credit insurance, that sort of thing. That will come only if the creditors have to take much more in the way of losses than they have done so far.

Finally I want to express scepticism about the 'early-warning' literature. David Vines and I dealt with that in our Commonwealth Secretariat Paper (1997), and we quoted Morris Goldstein, who at that point was rather sceptical himself. Now Morris is adding to the literature, which is extensive. It is a big literature dating back over 25 years to the efforts of Cline and Frank to predict debt rescheduling. It is no more successful today.

Goldstein (1998) argues that 'Real exchange rate misalignment is a good predictor, but further work should repeat the exercise, and actually from the perspective adopted in this paper exchange rate crises are largely unpredictable events.' In fact, further work shows that the real exchange rate is not much good.

Take Corsetti, Pesenti and Roubini's 'Paper Tigers' article (1998; see also chapter 4 in this volume). They find that the real exchange rate taken alone does not work so well. So what do they do? They interact it with the current account, and then we get a story. But that's exactly what all this literature does. We have some vague theoretical ideas that suggest what variables ought to go on the RHS. Theory tells us nothing about lag structures, nothing about functional form- and permits us to do as much data-mining as is necessary.

The results typically do not indicate vulnerability in advance, only as the crisis is about to occur. Of course some of the key variables are very slow-moving variables anyway, relatively speaking, in terms of crisis-prediction (current account, real exchange rate, non-performing loans – if you can get that kind of variable – etc.). I think the bottom line of this is that every crisis is different. This explains why we get a new generation of literature every time we have a crisis, a new set of theories about crises, and a new series of empirical papers. But I do not think that these empirical papers will be useful for policy.

2 Phillip Turner

I start with the observation that behind recent crises there is a paradox. In theory, we would have expected a big increase in capital flows to have made economies more stable, because risks would have been better spread across different countries. But in practice they have made economies more vulnerable. The answer to this paradox is not of course an autarchic solution. The case for sharing the risks involved in domestic investment with foreigners is clearly a strong one. Risks need to be diversified. The problem, of course, is that the market for risks is more difficult to manage than the market for goods. Unlike the market for goods, when you are dealing in international transactions of risks you don't really 'get what you see'. Outcomes depend on how well risks are managed, on how well information is processed, and so on. It is here that there are major shortcomings.

The response to recent crises has been an enormous increase in resources devoted to quantifying risk, including country risks, and also other research examining correlations between different sectors of the market, in order to design more efficient portfolios. A key element has been the development of sophisticated value-at-risk models (VaR). In theory, such models are fine but the problem in practice is that they may engender in banks and institutional investors a certain blasé attitude towards risk in the same way as ABS brakes make some drivers more reckless. One lesson of the crisis is just how difficult it is to quantify risk with any degree of precision. The scale of the adjustment of the key variables, of exchange rates and of interest rates is almost always under-estimated. This will be all the more likely if several market participants seek to simultaneously take or reverse very similar positions.

A second lesson is that the correlations between markets that can be established when markets are calm are quite different from what emerges when markets are under pressure. A common experience is that the correlations between markets tend to rise in a crisis, so that diversification possibilities (which market participants imagined were there on the basis of correlations computed over calm times) are actually not there precisely when markets most need them. Thirdly, the assumption in such models that banks and others can smoothly reverse their positions at well defined prices and narrow spreads may well be violated when market liquidity dries up. The experience of September and October 1998, when normally well functioning and deep markets in major financial centres suffered periods of illiquidity and extreme volatility, shocked almost everybody. (It should not have caused such surprise because the same thing happened in October 1987.) There is, of course, a much greater risk of illiquidity in the smaller and thinner markets seen in most of the developing world.

One implication of the fact that risks are difficult to quantify is that it is necessary to build into the financial system some kind of prudential buffers which protect the financial system against shocks that cannot be quantified with any degree of precision. In particular, it is necessary to take measures to limit leverage in the economy. This can be done in many ways. It can be done in a regulatory way through a higher capital ratio for banks and a lower loan/value ratio applied by banks to people who want to borrow. Or it can be done in a market-orientated way, making 'stress tests' more demanding: by allowing for shocks which go well beyond the normal experience.

Getting the benefits of capital flows, and making sure that risks are properly measured, means that a number of things need to be done. If information is to flow properly, and risks are to be properly internalised, the list of what needs to be done is actually quite long. I will mention only three elements that seem crucial:

- The first one is that it is very important to *avoid government policies that lead to risks being mispriced.* There has been a lot of discussion about implicit guarantees before the event, and I share Richard Portes' concerns about the effects of bail-outs on moral hazard. Moreover, there has been some tendency in recent bail-outs for short-term foreign currency-denominated debt to be protected while other forms of liabilities (e.g. equities, long-term bonds or local currency debt) are not. This apparent selectivity of bail-outs may serve to distort the pattern of capital flows – from equity to debt, from long- to short-term and from local to foreign currency – in exactly the wrong way. Borrowing countries thus become more, not less, vulnerable to sudden liquidity crises. Similarly, fixed exchange rates maintained for many years lead markets to systematically under-estimate the risks of the exchange rate.

- Secondly, something must be done to *prevent borrowers absorbing excessive risks* and to allow lenders to take more of the risks. In particular, governments who borrow short-term are exposing themselves to very large liquidity risks. If short-term government borrowing had been limited, in the case of both Mexico and several Asian countries, short-term capital inflows would have been less. Likewise banks should price exchange rate and interest rate risks properly. They did not prior to the Asian crisis, and once again if banks had been pricing the risks they were running correctly, they would have been much less active in international interbank markets and short-term capital inflows would have been lower. The destabilising features of capital inflows would thus have been greatly reduced by putting simple prudential measures in place.

- The final observation is that a proper market for risk *requires full and accurate disclosure.* Three aspects of this are important. First, there needs to be much fuller disclosure of foreign exchange liabilities, public and private, contingent and actual. This data should include information on the maturity of claims. It should also include information on central bank forward obligations. Secondly, there needs to be much better information on aggregate exposures. For instance an important function of the BIS banking statistics is to compute each country's aggregate borrowing from banks in the major financial centres so that everybody can see when a particular country is becoming over-indebted. However, these statistics cover only balance sheet positions; the enormous growth of derivative instruments has enabled banks and others to change their underlying exposure without altering the assets or liabilities held on their balance sheet. Ways of satisfactorily aggregating such exposures have yet to be developed. The use of exchange-traded instruments tends to further disclosure and facilitate the computation of aggregate positions while over-the-counter

(OTC) instruments tend to frustrate these ends. Counterparty risks are also less with exchange-traded instruments. How far these advantages outweigh the flexibility and cheapness of OTC products needs to be carefully explored. Thirdly there should be fuller information on public debt – in particular, how much of it is short-term and how much is foreign currency-denominated. We do not have good information about public debt in several emerging markets.

This is quite an ambitious agenda that will not be achieved overnight. It is important to sustain the sense of urgency that the Russian default and the events that followed have produced.

3 Charles A. Goodhart

In my current work, I am trying to compare the Asian crises with nineteenth-century financial crises. In some ways what is surprising is how amazed everyone is about the Asian crises, because they have an enormous amount of common ground with the nineteenth-century crises. Almost all the kind of preconditions, both empirical and theoretical – as set out in Philippe Aghion's chapter 5 in this volume – occurred in the nineteenth-century crises as much as in 1997–8. Just to emphasise that this is not something specifically, necessarily, to do with Asia or Asian characteristics, you will recall that, during the nineteenth century, crises were more common and frequent in the USA than in any other single country in the world. Consider, for example, the crises in 1873, 1890, 1893 and 1907. In every single case the USA was at the heart of the crisis. So that, if we regard Asian virtue as not being so great in the twentieth century, we must also remember that American virtues were not so great in the nineteenth century. Not only were the preconditions really similar, but the actual context and arrangement of the collapse (with a downturn in housing prices, land prices and equity prices, impinging on a fragile banking system, with weaknesses – and, on occasions, fraud – leading to banking failures in the banking system) being similar in both cases.

The key difference between the nineteenth-century crises and the 1997–8 crisis so far has actually been on the external side. What happened in the nineteenth-century crises was that in most cases the countries were pretty firmly on the gold standard – or, in the case of Australia in 1893, effectively on a sterling standard. This case was expected to remain stable although in several cases – again in Australia or in the USA, for example in, 1907 – there was a temporary gold premium, which was expected to be short-term. Now the combination of a belief that the exchange rate would revert to the underlying anchor, combined with the temporary premium and a decline in asset prices, led to a situation of capital inflows for bottom-fishing. Capital inflows on a short-term basis took advantage of what was seen as a temporary opportunity, with the result that in these countries there was a very large gold inflow, more or less immediately after the crisis. The monetary base thus expanded again really quite rapidly, and nominal interest rates that had spiked upwards briefly, quickly reverted to levels that were actually lower than they had been previously.

That was not always the case. It was not the case, for example, in Argentina because of credibility problems of a well known form: investors did not actually expect, when the Peso went further away from gold, that it would come back. What happened in the Argentinean case in the 1890s was that the Argentines repudiated. As a result they neither fully paid interest nor repaid principal. That meant that the underlying strong shift in the current account surplus (exactly the same as is now happening in East Asia) lead to very large gold inflows, rebuilding the financial base and lowering the interest rates in those countries. Not of course, that you did not have very strong effects. Many banks went bust, and imports fell sharply. Nevertheless, in the nineteenth century there was either a nominal anchor and expected reversion, or repudiation.

Neither has occurred in the Asian crisis. You have had neither a nominal anchor (people were worried that the won and the rupiah would go on going down) nor effectively a repudiation – and therefore a removal of the outstanding foreign currency debts. The combination of devaluation and the failure to write down the outstanding debt has imposed a stronger burden on the Asian countries than that which was present in the nineteenth century, and this has made the whole situation very much worse.

How do we get away from this continuously worsening spiral? One of the suggestions is that you make the creditors lose money on interbank debt. I think that there is a problem with that. If you start telling banks that they are going to lose money on interbank debt then that drives contagion even faster from one country to another, and it could lead to collapse of the interbank market which is generally highly undesirable. I would, however, strongly support the argument that there ought to be a supervisory and capital adequacy requirement, which depends on the perceived and publicly known standards of regulation in the DCs.

Dealing with private sector debt is a difficult matter. The only time when it looked, temporarily, as if the Indonesian crisis was going to be resolved was when it appeared that there was going to be an orderly work-out of the private sector debt, that this would impose very considerable losses on creditors and that it would reduce the outpayments of capital from Indonesia.

There is a problem there for the IMF, because if the purpose of the exercise is to reduce the outstanding weight of the debt of the private sector debtors, what can the Fund do to help? It finds itself in a very difficult position. I think that 'how do you deal with the Fund or, rather, how should the Fund, if at all, deal with an overwhelming problem of private sector foreign currency debt?' is the particular policy problem that we have at the moment. Maybe the answer is that the Fund cannot deal with it, and when the problem is essentially private sector foreign currency debt the Fund ought to say, 'Please sir, not me sir' and allow the country to get on with whatever moratorium, perhaps at the limit repudiation and work-out, is actually necessary.

As a final comment, when you are dealing with private sector net indebtedness do not expect information improvements to get you out of the problem. It just is never going to be possible to calculate the net private sector indebtedness of a country. For example, if the USA, the UK, or Germany was asked 'what is your net private sector indebtedness, say of under one-year maturity?', the answer would be, for all three countries: 'We have not got the slightest idea!'

NOTES

A transcript of the Round Table was prepared by Eric le Borgne, University of Warwick, to whom the editors extend their thanks, and which initially appeared in the *Newsletter* of the Global Economic Institutions Research Programme (Global Economic Institutions, 1998). Phillip Turner and Charles Goodhart have revised their contributions. At the initial Round Table there was also a contribution by David Vines (which has been subsumed in his chapter 2 with Jenny Corbett in this volume) and by Vinod Aggarwal who discussed the USA as a political actor in the Asia crisis and the implications of its hegemony. Sadly we have not been able to include Vinod Aggarwal's contribution here.

1. Portes' comments were prepared before the Russian crisis.

REFERENCES

Corsetti, P., P. Pesenti and N. Roubini (1998). 'Paper Tigers'. A model of the Asian Crisis', *NBER Working Paper*, **6783** (November)

Global Economic Institutions (1998). *Newsletter*, **8**: 8–14

Goldstein, M. (1998). 'The Asian Financial Crisis: Causes, Cures, and Systemic Implications', *Policy Analysis in International Economics*, **55**, Washington, DC: Institute for International Economics

Portes, R. and D. Vines (1997). *Coping with International Capital Flows*, London: Commonwealth Secretariat

Index